THE IN-BETWEEN WORLD OF KENYA'S MEDIA

South Asian Journalism, 1900-1992

To Fuoze
a Comrade
Zarina Patel
19.04.2016

ABOUT THE AUTHOR

Zarina Patel is a Kenyan activist and author who is involved in the struggle for social justice, equity and women's rights. She is best known for her virtually single-handed campaign to save Jeevanjee Gardens from land grabbers – a park donated by her maternal grandfather to the residents of Nairobi. She hails from the South Asian community and has focused much of her attention on the issue of minority rights, researching and writing about the South Asian leaders who played a part in Kenya's anti-colonial struggle. *The In-Between World of Kenya's Media* explores and documents the contribution of South Asian journalists and media practitioners in the twentieth century. She is the Managing Editor of *AwaaZ* magazine which covers minority and diversity issues and is now in its eleventh year of publication.

She has been honoured with the Jaramogi Oginga Odinga Foundation and the Asian Foundation Awards for her life-long commitment to the struggle for peace, justice and democracy. A biography authored by Dr George Gona of the University of Nairobi, *Zarina Patel – An Indomitable Spirit,* was published in 2014.

BY THE SAME AUTHOR:

Challenge to Colonialism – The Struggle of Alibhai Mulla Jeevanjee for Equal Rights in Kenya.
Unquiet – The Life and Times of Makhan Singh.
The Stormy Petrel – Manilal Ambalal Desai.

Edited: Doings, Non-Doings and Mis-Doings by Kenyan Chief Justices
    1963-1998 by Justice Abdul Majid Cockar, EGH.

THE IN-BETWEEN WORLD OF KENYA'S MEDIA

South Asian Journalism, 1900-1992

Published by Zand Graphics Ltd.
PO Box 32843 – 00600, Nairobi
Email: zand.graphics@gmail.com

First published in 2016

Printed and bound in Kenya by
Colourprint Ltd., Nairobi

Design and layout by Pixelskenya Ltd.

ISBN   978-9966-094-64-3

To all those
JOURNALISTS
who keep the
TORCH
of Press FREEDOM
ALIGHT

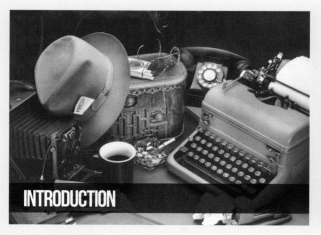

INTRODUCTION

THE NEWSPAPER

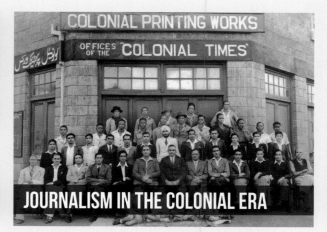

JOURNALISM IN THE COLONIAL ERA

CONTENTS

THE PRINT JOURNALISTS

THE RADIO JOURNALISTS

THE PHOTO JOURNALISTS

FOREWORD

Time present and time past
Are both perhaps present in time future
And time future contained in time past
(T S Eliot: The Four Quartets)

We may think of the past as history (or vice versa) but in the continuum of time history is not past, because it can live on in our memories, in our folklore, in our literature and art and architecture and monuments, in our personal archives and so on. In the pages of this book, history is certainly not dead or gone but rather brought alive as a vivid reminder of Kenya's past, both pre- and postcolonial, spanning practically the whole of the last century. To people of my generation it has a special appeal and meaning, because not only did we live through a large chunk of that period ourselves but we were also the beneficiaries of our parents and elders' tales about earlier years.

What the book does is to fill a vital gap in the documented history of the South Asian contribution to the development of Kenya from a British colonial territory to a full-fledged independent nation and beyond. Most of us are familiar with the established works of Robert Gregory, J S Mangat, Cynthia Salvadori, Dana Seidenberg, and the brothers Dharam and Yash Ghai, all of which dealt with the phenomenon of Asian migration and settlement in East Africa largely in terms of its political and economic significance. Zarina is an accomplished biographer of certain leading players in that field, and therefore also a historian of record. She has followed in the same tradition here, to focus on the specific subject of the sub-title of the book across its whole spectrum, with a follow-up to the present.

But why write about journalism? As Zarina explains in the opening chapter (`The Newspaper`), journalists are essential because in a democracy `they inform its citizens, give voice to the voiceless and hold the powerful accountable`, and `Newspapers make events public that would otherwise remain private and act as watchdogs on the

workings of the government`. And why about South Asian journalism in particular? Again, in her own words (in the `Introduction`), for her it was `one more realisation on the journey to research and record the presence of a minority in Kenya's multi-cultured society – a journey that more and more travellers are embarking upon and in so doing helping to shed light on hitherto unknown (hi)stories`.

Not only `unknown` but, she might have added, actually ignored rather than just overlooked, even denied and distorted, to suit different agendas at different times. That became clear to her when she found a book celebrating the 50th anniversary of the *Nation* group of newspapers lacking in `substantial information on the South Asian journalistic output`, with only cursory references to its most outstanding editor Joe Rodrigues and such stalwart reporters as Kul Bhushan and Cyprian Fernandes. But of course the story of South Asian (or Indian) journalists and their publications went back well before independence, to the very first decade of the 20th century, and this too had not figured much in the wider public's imagination. There was clearly much ground that needed to be covered, if a factual history was to be written about them.

For Zarina this was a logical continuation of a journey that had begun when, *circa* 1991, she successfully mounted a campaign to save Nairobi's Jeevanjee Gardens, bearing her maternal grandfather's name, from a land grab by the Moi administration, a process that prompted people to ask who Jeevanjee was. This resulted in publication of her first book, *Challenge to Colonialism – The Struggle of Alibhai Mulla Jeevanjee for Equal Rights in Kenya,* in 1997. As it happened, it was Jeevanjee who had started the *African Standard, Mombasa Times & Uganda Argus* in 1901 at a time when Kenya as a colonial entity was just beginning to take shape. *The African Standard,* for short, was later to become the *East African Standard*, the principal English language daily newspaper in Kenya for several decades. In that sense, Zarina carried a vicarious journalist's gene in her blood (!), which eventually bore fruit in the *AwaaZ* magazine she launched together with her partner Zahid Rajan five years later in 2002 (`becoming journalists ourselves`). There was a consistency and a symmetry in her biographical bent, for she continued to research and write about other forgotten Asian heroes. One can only hope that others will follow her example to explore and highlight the Asian contribution to other professions such as the law and medicine in Kenya`s history.

So what we now have is a work of immense historical importance: you only have to look at the list of contents to measure its scale and depth.

We are treated to a journey of discovery and wonder, starting with the role and place of South Asian journalism and its noteworthy organs and practitioners during the colonial era. We read about A M Jeevanjee, already mentioned, and other legendary figures such as A C L de Sousa, Manilal A Desai, Sitaram Achariar, Girdhari Lal Vidyarthi, Makhan Singh, Haroon Ahmed, D K Sharda, Pranlal Sheth, and Pio Gama Pinto, and about their struggles to be published at all. Hardly any of the papers or periodicals (including, among the longer lasting ones, *The Democrat, Colonial Times,* and *Daily Chronicle,* though the *Kenya Daily Mail* may have been an exception) could be said to have been a profitable enterprise. Most were funded by proprietors and through generous donations with no returns. There was neither a thriving commercial market nor a wide readership to sustain them for long, but their promoters, editors and writers persisted out of a sense of mission to air Asian and also African grievances and seek proper representation for them. In that they did succeed, for they were regarded as a thorn in the flesh of the colonial authorities, who were quick to resort to harsh measures to silence or punish them.

This was the broad profile of South Asian journalism during the first four decades of the 20th century, against a background of continuing agitation for greater Asian and African rights. Then came WWII, and it was to be the real game-changer. A new breed of young Asian writers, which included Chanan Singh in addition to those already mentioned, born and/or bred in Kenya, appeared and began to flex their muscles. They were more concerned about local politics than the fight for Indian independence, which by then was on the horizon. As Zarina informs us, Girdhari Lal Vidyarthi, together with his team of these young men, spearheaded a revolutionary brand of political journalism in the colony, under the `Frank, Free and Fearless` motto of his *Colonial Times,* that `provided a pivotal channel of expression for emerging freedom fighters like Tom Mboya and Jomo Kenyatta`, and in the process landed himself in prison on three occasions on politically related offences. Indeed, as we are repeatedly told, Girdhari Lal Vidyarthi was the first person in colonial Kenya to be charged with

and convicted of sedition early in 1946, for publishing an article highly critical of the government for its unequal treatment of returning African soldiers at the end of the war vis-a-vis their white counterparts. Ironically, as we learn later, his second-born son Anil Vidyarthi was the last person to be also charged with sedition, 50 years later in independent Kenya, only to be acquitted after a two year trial and a change in the law. The parallel also extended to their respective lawyers, Achhroo Kapila, who had defended the older Vidyarthi, while his son Ishan Kapila defended the younger!

The 1950s was a period of turbulence, with the Mau Mau emergency in full swing. All journalists had to contend with press censorship and other draconian controls. As the decade progressed however there were developments elsewhere in the continent towards decolonisation, culminating in the 'wind of change' speech of the British Prime Minister Harold Macmillan early in 1960, signalling that independence was just around the corner. 1960 was also a crucial moment in the broader history of Kenyan journalism with the arrival of the *Nation.* At this point, the book becomes really exciting, a sort of non-fiction thriller that keeps the reader glued, eager to know what to expect next.

Until the *Nation* appeared, the *East African Standard* was the sole national English language daily newspaper – a conservative, white settler-oriented mouthpiece of the colonial establishment. It had no Asian or African journalists on its staff, even though it must have derived a significant part of both its advertising and sales revenue from non-Europeans. The *Nation* was to change all that, and indeed it overtook the *Standard* in 1969 on both fronts. The book provides a fascinating insight into the relative merits and working practices of the two papers.

A unique feature of the book is the personal narratives of a whole parade, an A to Z, of South Asian journalists – print, photo and broadcasting, with separate sections devoted to each category. It is a very long list, but suffice it to name a few of them here at random: Abdul Karim Hudani, `Billy` Chibber, Chander Mehra, Cyprian Fernandes, Kul Bhushan, Gaytri (Syal) Sagar, Jasmer Singh, Norman Da Costa, Salim Lone and Shamlal Puri amongst the print journalists alone. The varied collection of radio/tv and photo-journalists is equally extensive. This is where Zarina`s dogged pursuit of all this massive biographical material for the book has paid off. She has managed to trace the individuals concerned or their families or friends and obtain their stories stretching back over half a century of their working lives. And how revealing and instructive they are!

We learn that unlike their first-generation predecessors, what budding South Asian journalists post-1960 had to battle through was a narrow leeway into the mainstream of the trade, against a whole array of odds stacked against them by the very nature of colonial society. The *East African Standard* had a European-only closed shop employment policy and later, in the `60s and `70s, those recruited to its staff still faced discriminatory pay and other conditions (which latter was also true of the *Nation* as well). Its editor, Kenneth Bolton, comes across as a formidable establishment figure but more about that later.

The *Nation*, owned by the Aga Khan, was a breath of fresh air. True, it gave Asian journalists a pull-up into the profession but it also flourished under them. That is why Kul Bhushan, in a far-reaching review of its in-house commemorative publication *The Golden Years,* laments that it contained hardly any references to Asian-related events (the Kenyan Asian Exodus of 1968 or anything in the Indian sub-continent apart from the assassination of Z A Bhutto) and that Professor Yash Pal Ghai was mentioned as ` (t)he sole Asian news maker in Kenya during this half century .... as "the lawyer hired as convenor of the Bomas talks"`! Nor, moreover, was any past Asian journalist invited to contribute, whereas some half a dozen Europeans were. As for *Birth of a Nation* by Gerry Loughran, a work commissioned by the Nation, he adds, `no Asian journalist, except Joe Rodrigues, has been mentioned except for a passing reference to [himself] Kul Bhushan`, despite the fact that the bylines of some `20-odd full time Asian journalists who worked for the Nation during its first 25 years` would easily have been discoverable and could have been given `their due credit in the success story`.

Nevertheless, the accounts of the various journalists appearing in the book (not just those associated with the *Nation*) are a veritable cornucopia of their professionalism, daring, hair-raising escapades and sheer determination to get the story out, to publish and be damned! They were subject to violence, intimidation, imprisonment, deportation, harassment, death threats, and worse. Their life-stories are truly inspiring. Most of them, especially sports and photo journalists, came from humble backgrounds and worked their way up, overcoming all manner of obstacles. Cyprian Fernandes is a shining example. He grew up in Nairobi`s Mathare Valley ghetto. His account of being caught up in the round up of Kikuyus by British soldiers during the Emergency is actually more harrowing than can be seen from these few disjointed extracts:

`We were marched up the valley and made to sit with our hands on our heads on Eastleigh Road stretching several kilometres four deep. I tried to explain to a soldier in English that I was not an African .... (a)ll I got was a huge kick that doubled me up .... a Kikuyu elder who knew me spoke to an African policeman and explained that I was an Indian .... [my] head was hurting from the kick and a couple of hands were soothing my head and drying my tears. Don't worry, I was told, we will defend you as much as we can.`

He left school at 12 years of age but in early 1960, when he was barely 16, he conned his way `to an interview with *Daily Nation* founding Editor John Bierman, and got a job as a junior sports reporter`. He was promoted to a senior position after just 24 hours, from which moment he rose to great heights until his departure in 1974 when he was Chief Reporter and Editor writer, `with presidents and ministers from around Africa` on his contact list.

This is typical of that crop of journalists. Once the doors of opportunity were thrown open, they were soon able to prove their mettle. The most outstanding of them, by common consent, was undoubtedly Joe Rodrigues, the *Nation*`s Editor in Chief – a man of impeccable integrity, professional brilliance and technical perfection. Cyprian`s account of his ignominious sacking on July 31, 1981, is a damning indictment of the culture of political interference, unwritten codes of self-restraint and other repressive limitations on press freedom under which all journalists had to operate in those days, and indeed later. Cyprian himself had to flee the country when his wife was informed that there was a bullet out with his name on it. As he tells us:

`Death threats to journalists and other prominent people were fairly common place in … Kenya during the late 1960s until my departure in 1974. It was also pretty common to be picked up by the dreaded Special Branch for interrogation and/or deportation. As a political journalist in Kenya, you had to walk the political tightrope with the precision of a brain surgeon. You lived with fear of deportation every day …`

Elsewhere in the book we find many stories of journalists and editors being hauled before ministers, officials and others in high authority (to account for what may have appeared in their papers) whose words of displeasure or condemnation often sealed their fate. `Was that the effect of people in power? Oh yes! Njonjo's word was IT!` – Sudhir Vidyarthi. But then this was not much different from the colonial days in general and, as Richard Nunes observed, the Emergency `was also the time when the Special Branch took an interest in anyone who was connected with a newspaper. It was definitely not a healthy career choice`.

Mid-60s onwards Kenya became a focal point for international news coverage in East and Central Africa. This brought South Asian print and in particular photo journalists into the limelight, to score many scoops with headline-grabbing pictures and stories. Apart from the most iconic of them all - Mo Amin, Mohinder Dhillon and Priya Ramrakha – the bios of the others listed in that category too are a testament of their extraordinary courage and achievements. And of course they had to face many occupational hazards too. Here are some typical examples:

'Like many international photojournalists, I too have been subjected to personal violence, notably once in Uganda. As I entered Mulago Hospital where President Obote was hospitalised after the failed attempt to assassinate him, five plain clothed security bodyguards beat me with rifle butts and kicks. I too was hospitalised at the same hospital and the camera equipment was trashed to pieces' – Satwant Matharoo.

And Mohinder Dhillon: 'But there were risks ... in 1964 I was almost executed at Stanleyville airport in the Congo'! And Krishan Sharma puts it in more explicit language: 'But all wasn't rosy. These were dangerous times for photojournalists. I lost two friends in the Congo around 1964. The new independent countries in Africa were all of a sudden governed by politicians who had no idea of the rules of engagement with the press and could react in a most undesirable and unpredictable manner, with impunity if I might add. I almost never made it out of Zanzibar after the revolution.'

Some of the accounts Zarina has so diligently collated do however suffer from a lack of clarity or detail, but then these were written by people now in their retirement or old age, and from a retrospective perspective, removed in time and space. Editing to sanitise them, apart from being a logistical nightmare, would have affected their authenticity and immediacy. Even so together they constitute a body of credible anecdotal evidence of the state of journalism and of behind the scenes dynamics during the period in question.

The frank and endearing story of Gaytri (Syal) Sagar is also interesting for other reasons. The International Press Institute (IPI) were running a pioneering course in journalism based at the Royal Technical College, soon to be turned into Nairobi University, but exclusively for men. She nevertheless applied and so impressed them that they created a special programme for her and five other (African) women, from which she graduated with distinction. She then joined the *Daily Nation* in 1966 to become the first Asian woman journalist in Kenya and worked there until 1970. What she has to say about her interactions with colleagues of other races confirms that those were still early days for inter-racial social mixing across the board. She remembers being chided by no less than the wife of the then Indian High Commissioner (who at the time was Prem Bhatia, not a career diplomat but an ex-journalist himself) for 'frolicking with the natives'!

Kul Bhushan also had finished the IPI course with distinction, and a prize: 'Now I wanted to contribute to a daily newspaper and in March 1967, I approached the *East African Standard* for reviewing Asian films. The Features Editor wanted me on board and arranged an interview with its editor, Kenneth Bolton. Despite my top performance at the IPI Advanced Journalism Course, I was rejected. Although I did not need a job, I struck back by getting one at the *Nation* within a week as a Senior Journalist and Education Editor.' From there on, as we now know, he amassed an impressive cv, and still continues to write from another part of the world.

Kenneth Bolton's name is mentioned by others too, as a somewhat dour man who and whose paper had little time for Asians as journalists. Many of them also say that what drew them into journalism was their passion for writing while still at school. Their first step and only outlet into publishing was via the letters page of the newspapers, and this was also my own experience. Later, as a practising lawyer from the mid-60s to the mid-70s, I was a regular contributor to the *Standard,* the *Nation* and other papers, and my name also appeared frequently in reports of court cases in the news columns.

I often used to write critically about matters relating to administration of justice but never once did I receive any threat or attempt to muzzle me, even when I represented opposition politicians in criminal proceedings arising from public meetings or assisted in election petition cases after the formation of KPU. Until the end of the '60s, the government left the lawyers more or less alone, though things were to change adversely soon afterwards. But it was in relation to British immigration controls that I became very vocal and had some nasty exchanges with one or two diehard British expats in both the *Nation* and *E A Standard*. Bolton however did not suppress any of my views, even though they were highly condemnatory of British policy on the Asian exodus and other issues, except once. That was in 1967 (just a month before the six-day Arab-Israeli war), when the *Standard* carried a report that I thought was unfair and unduly biased against Nasser. I wrote to the Editor complaining about it and was surprised to get, by return of post, a two-page letter from Kenneth Bolton himself explaining the rationale behind the piece and why he could not publish my criticism.

What else? The candid reminiscences of Hilary Ng`weno and Joe Kadhi remind us of the press and power politics that they (have) had to navigate all through their distinguished careers. Ng`weno is an artful survivor, while Kadhi, who was the *Nation*`s first African Managing Editor at the time Joe Rodrigues was unceremoniously despatched from the paper and whose reflections throw more light on that disreputable episode, was himself to become a victim of high level shenanigans ten years later! And to bring us up to date, in the closing chapters of the book we have learned critiques and commentaries on the contemporary media scene in Kenya, including an overview of the continuing threats to press freedom (`Gagging the Messenger`) which neatly encapsulates the 'In Between World' of the main title, itself an echo of M G Vassanji`s take on the Asian dilemma!

Dear reader, this is just a flavour of what the book has to offer. A great deal more is packed into it. Zarina has excelled herself in presenting a most comprehensive picture of South Asian journalism in Kenya during the last century – of the various papers and periodicals and their proprietors, editors, managers and writers - their fortunes, ups and downs, battles with authorities and financial and personal hardships – the lot. Above all, it is the collective trajectories and portrayals of all the past and present and better or lesser known people featured in the book that will make it a definitive and encyclopaedic work of reference on the subject - a valuable addition to the growing literature about East African Asians in general. We needed this, to learn for ourselves and for the world at large to know. For that Zarina deserves singular plaudits, and our gratitude.

Ramnik Shah
03/03/2015

PREFACE

South Asian Journalism in Kenya is concurrent with the country's political evolution in the 20th century and has addressed both the colonial period as well as the early decades of Independence. It had its roots in the Independence struggle in India but developed its own Kenyan identity as it became a major player in the anti-colonial movement. The post-independence period, however, saw a gradual decline in its scope as South Asian journalists either emigrated or in certain cases, were deported or silenced.

The earliest newspaper, founded by a South Asian in Kenya, was Alibhai Mulla Jeevanjee's *African Standard, Mombasa Times* & *Uganda Argus*. Jeevanjee, himself an entrepreneur, had brought in W H Tiller from England to edit and publish the paper. Although it was primarily established to put a stop to the racist anti-Asian propaganda being vented by its contemporary, the *Uganda Mail*; it was printed in English and catered to the British colonial and settler community. When the *Mail* folded up in 1904, the *African Standard* was sold and renamed the *East African Standard*.

Seven years later, D K Bhutt started the *Indian Voice* – a bi-lingual paper in Gujarati and English which strove to represent the Indian community. The editor was a white settler, H C Smith, who had a cosmopolitan and multi-racial outlook and this was reflected in the paper; it set white settler interests apart from the policies of the Colonial Office and identified the Home Government as having 'no axes to grind'. While it defended the interests of the 'native' population it nevertheless considered them 'inferior'. The *Indian Voice*, lacking funds, ceased publication in 1913.

The *East African Chronicle* and the *Democrat* were established in the late 1910s. Manilal Desai, editor of the *Chronicle* and Secretary of the East Africa Indian National Congress was a political leader and a close friend of Harry Thuku, the African nationalist. By this time Indian leaders had not only become fully engaged in the anti-colonial struggle but some of them were actively allying with the Africans. The 1917 October Revolution had raised awareness of Imperialism; the presence and influence of the Ghadarites (revolutionaries of India's Ghadar Party) in Kenya and knowledge of Mahatma Gandhi's mass movement in India added to the inspiration for an open defiance of the colonial structure. The writings in the *East African Chronicle* began to threaten the colonial power and in 1921, it forced the closure of the paper by imposing a hefty fine on flimsy grounds.

In 1928, Jeevanjee recruited, ostensibly as his secretary, Isher Dass - a Marxist. Dass, among his many activities, accompanied Jomo Kenyatta to Moscow, was elected to the Legislative Council and helped to organise the Kamba sit-in of Muindu Mbingu. Left ideology had taken a firm foothold in Kenya.

By 1933 Makhan Singh was setting up a trade union to fight for labour rights; it was the year G L Vidyarthi launched his *Colonial Times*, printed in English and Gujarati. 'Free, Frank and Fearless' was the motto of the *Colonial Times* and it was exactly that. Vidyarthi became the first Kenyan journalist to be jailed for sedition, others associated with the *Times* were also charged.

Earlier the *Democrat* outfit had printed Kenyatta's *Muigwithania*; the Colonial Times Printing Works published Oneko's *Ramogi*; Ruhinda's *Habari za Dunia* and other African publications. Makhan Singh had brought Indian and African workers together in the trade union movement and his newsletter, *Kirti* (Worker), focused on issues of colonial exploitation. The demands for equality and justice were fast transforming into notions of freedom and even class struggle. Vidyarthi was invited to a session of the Natal Indian Congress but did not attend. Naicker and Dadoo of the South African Communist Party visited Nairobi and met with Indian comrades.

In 1947, the group of radical, young journalists who had joined the *Colonial Times,* broke away and started their own newspaper, the *Daily Chronicle.* Some of them belonged to a Marxist study group and the paper took an anti-colonialist as well as anti-imperialist stand, a humanist and pro-people focus was its baseline. After constant harassment from the authorities, the paper had to be sold and its editor was forced into exile. The colonial government instituted a brutal repression – The Kenya African Union and the East African Trade Union Congress were banned; Makhan Singh, Fred Kubai and others were detained; the Kenya Land and Freedom Army (Mau Mau) took up arms; an Emergency was declared and the Kapenguria Six were imprisoned. The *Colonial Times* and the *Daily Chronicle* limped on and closed down at independence.

Asian photo, radio and print journalists entered the new Kenya with great enthusiasm but the directions on the political signboard were not encouraging. Progressive and Left-leaning Kenyans were being side-lined, the ideals they had fought for in the anti-colonial struggle were no longer welcome. The dismissal of upper echelon Asian staff in the Civil Service had begun even prior to independence. Africanisation in various sectors including the press validated the Asian journalists' retention of their British citizenship; and the British Government's down-grading of this status resulted in a mass exodus which included the departure of many of the Asian journalists.

Idi Amin's 1972 expulsion of the Ugandan Asians, and the corresponding approval voiced in Kenya, further exacerbated the apprehension; the August 1982 attempted coup in Kenya, during which South Asians became one of the targets, drew the line for those journalists employed in the newspaper outfits.

Noteworthy is the sudden and unexplained dismissal of Joe Rodrigues, Editor-in-Chief of the *Daily Nation* reputed to be one of the finest journalists Kenya's media has ever had. Salim Lone was hounded out of Kenya more than once; Pranlal Sheth was too close to Jaramogi Odinga; Cyprian Fernandes, a brilliant investigator, apparently knew too much; Karim Hudani criticised the Africanisation programme; Billy Chibber was declared a prohibited immigrant in Uganda, Chander Mehra wrote the obvious – all were forced into exile. Pio Gama Pinto who challenged the Jomo Kenyatta regime was assassinated. The disappearance of Mohinder Singh Marjara and his driver in the Congo was deliberately ignored by the Government.

Chandu Vasani refused to sensationalise the Asian Exodus and walked off the job and Anil Vidyarthi was imprisoned for printing information critical of the Moi Government.

The people's vision of building a democratic and just Kenya was not to be. The South Asian community was an economically strong minority but had no political influence - racism and the manipulation of ethnic divides threatened the journalists' survival, a few persevered but the majority left the country. In 1992, after a bitter struggle, Kenyans won back a multi-party system and the democratic space opened up.

After a period of nascent democracy and relative press freedom, sadly as I write Kenya is once again in the grip of a creeping dictatorship. A court battle is being waged, the protagonists are the local mainstream Kenyan Media Television stations which are being forced into a position subservient to two foreign media organisations; both these have only recently entered the market and are set to monopolise the digital platform in Kenya. And the Communications Authority of Kenya appears to be rooting for the foreigners. The Media Council of Kenya has threatened at least one newspaper with closure. The Security Laws Amendment Bill 2014 which was introduced in Parliament last December is an ominous foreboding for the media and for civil society in Kenya.

This book documents the stories of the pre-1992 South Asian journalists and presents some related perspectives. Kul Bhushan, veteran journalist of the *Nation,* gives an insider's view of the newspaper's formative years; Warris Viani's review of Gerry Loughran's *Birth of a Nation* underscores some of the gaps in the story and Ali Zaidi, former Senior Editor of *The East African*, gives a captivating account of journalist practices in days gone by in India and then Kenya. Sudhir Vidyarthi, scion of a patriotic printing family, speaks of some of their challenges; Neera Kapur-Dromson traces the story of the Voice of Kenya's Hindustani Service of which she was a keen listener in her youth; Tom Maliti, former journalist in the *Associated Press* gives his perspective on media policy while George Nyabuga brings the reader up-to-date with his overview of the media in independent Kenya.

Zarina Patel
Author
April 2015

INTRODUCTION

The compilation and writing of this book on South Asian Journalism in Kenya is one more realisation on the journey to research and record the presence of a minority in Kenya's multi-cultured society – a journey that more and more travellers are embarking upon and in so doing helping to shed light on hitherto unknown (hi)stories.

I myself had begun to delve into my community's past in Kenya soon after its independence. Having lived through the tail end of colonialism and experienced some of its injustices, I had eagerly embraced the onset of *uhuru*. Yet as the initial euphoria morphed into a betrayal of dreams I was increasingly driven to learn more of my history as a member of a minority 'tribe' in Kenya.

In 1991, in former President Moi's single party dictatorship, an event was to launch me unexpectedly into the world of biographical writing. An attempt was made to 'grab' Jeevanjee Gardens in Nairobi – a park that my maternal grandfather, Alibhai Mulla Jeevanjee, had donated to the town way back in 1906. Together with *wananchi* and other environmentalists we resisted, and Nairobians today continue to relax in the Gardens.

'But who was Jeevanjee?' and 'Why did he give us this Garden?' they asked. I knew I had to put my physiotherapy career aside and find the answers. The search led to *Challenge to Colonialism – The Struggle for Equal Rights by Alibhai Mulla Jeevanjee.* I learnt so much about my grandfather, myself, my family, my community – about Kenya, about India and about British colonialism. I learnt too about the South Asian inroad into journalism. The *African Standard* which Jeevanjee established in the period 1901-1904 is the forerunner of our present day *Standard* newspaper.

In 2002, my partner Zahid Rajan and I launched *AwaaZ* magazine; becoming journalists ourselves. I continued

my biographical interest and wrote *Unquiet* and *The Stormy Petrel,* the first was the story of Makhan Singh – the founder of Kenya's Trade Union Movement. Manilal Ambalal Desai was the Stormy Petrel, one of Kenya's most dedicated freedom fighters. In both histories the importance given to journalism was significant. As Zahid and I struggle to keep *AwaaZ* afloat, we have become acutely aware of the challenges which Makhan Singh, Desai and so many other journalists must have faced in pursuing their vision and fulfilling their objectives.

These stories needed to be told and there was much to learn from them. I was able to publish my findings in *AwaaZ* and thus share them with a wider audience, but the expose on the whole remained confined to the colonial period. Apart from the much publicised woes of the Colourprint Press and of exiled Salim Lone of *Viva* magazine, the legendary fame of Joe Rodrigues and the well-known name of Kul Bhushan; I was largely unaware of the existence of South Asian journalists post-independence.

And then in 2010, the Nation Media Group celebrated its 50th Anniversary with well-deserved pomp and publicity. There were a sumptuous gathering, photographic exhibition and newspaper supplement topped by the publication of Gerard Loughran's *Birth of a Nation – The Story of a Newspaper in Kenya.* It was the first time in Kenya's history that a media was documenting its own story - journalists are usually more concerned about writing other peoples' stories.

As we Kenyans celebrate 50 years of our country's independence from British rule, we are privileged to get the insider view that *Birth* gives us of this era. Loughran must be congratulated for laying bare many sacred cows and guiding us gently through the maze of cloak and

dagger politics that the owner of the Nation Media Group and its journalists had to manoeuvre through. Of course there is much more of interest therein to both scholars as well as the lay public.

What I searched for and did not find in *Birth*, however, was any substantive information on the South Asian journalistic input. There were cursory references to Joe Rodrigues and Anil Vidyarthi, and passing mentions of Kul Bhushan and Cyprian Fernandes. It was as if the dynamic South Asian journalism I had encountered in the colonial era had just died with the advent of *uhuru*. I knew that the major national newspaper in the early 1960s, the *East African Standard,* that 'house-journal of the settler society in Kenya' as Warris Vianni so aptly describes it; and which carried Britain's coat of arms on its front page until the day before Kenya achieved independence, would have little or no South Asian component. I was well aware that in 1992, no South Asian journalists had been invited to the opening of the new Nation Centre on Kimathi Street.

When the *Nation* was launched in 1960, the *East African Standard* was the only national daily and the *Nation* was considered an upstart, a 'cheap' paper by the Europeans, and even the educated South Asians. It took nine years, in June 1969 precisely, for the *Nation* to overtake the *Standard* in circulation. Kul Bhushan maintains that the extensive coverage given to the Asian Exodus from February 1968 onwards was partly responsible. These were events that the *Standard* could not cover with much depth because they had no South Asian journalist. In 1968, inside the *Nation* newsroom, a poster urged all journalists to 'Close the Gap' between the circulations of the *Nation* and the *Standard*.

So were there no South Asian journalists in practice when the *Nation* newspaper was launched? My perplexity was clarified when I received an email from Kul Bhushan from Delhi, India. 'Have you read the *Birth of a Nation* …….. where are all the Asian journalists who helped to build the *Nation* in its early years? What is *AwaaZ* going to do about this omission?' Kul was clearly agitated and I knew then there was work to be done on the concern he was expressing, and which I had already felt.

I decided first and foremost to get in touch with the *ex-Nation* South Asian journalists who were scattered across the globe. As responses poured in and the network grew so did my curiosity about South Asian journalism and writing generally. I took stock of the actors in this field and sought to understand their worldview.

I found that in the colonial era, our interaction with British colonialism had been the focal point of our discourse. As is said, 'History is written by the victors'; and sure enough there is a plethora of books authored by the devotees of the colonial system. But even then there were a few writers who turned their attention to the colonised and their stories and left us invaluable gems of their findings.

In the arena of South Asian literature we had J S Mangat's seminal book, *A History of the Asians in East Africa* (1969) and Prof. Robert G Gregory's invaluable *India and East Africa* (1971). With the onset of independence, Kenyan writers moved from recording the colonial experience to examining the new dispensation and the accommodation of the different communities which made up the mosaic of the population.

To understand the present and plan for the future, it is essential to know the past. Dharam Ghai's and Yash Ghai's *Portrait of a Minority*, Dana Seidenberg's *Uhuru and the Kenya Indians* and J M Nazareth's *Black Man Brown Skin* were major landmarks in this quest.

As the euphoria of Independence began to morph into a betrayal of dreams, the South Asian community was side-lined and became an easy scapegoat for the burgeoning economic inequalities and creeping dictatorship. Africanisation, ethnicism, the assassination of Pio Gama Pinto, the British creation of a second class citizenship and Idi Amin's expulsion of the Ugandan Asians further served to drive the already fearful community either out of the country, or into a tightly guarded isolation. All creative activity, literary or cultural, seemed to cease and it was not until multi-partyism with its promise of democracy was achieved that South Asian writers began to put pen to paper once again.

In the early years of the *Nation's* existence, colonial and racist attitudes were still in force. Not only were all the editorial and managerial staff all white but as the late Jerry Okungu has written: 'Up till 1965, Nation had separate loos for whites and non-whites.' This was replaced by Africanisation which soon deteriorated into ethnic chauvinism. According to Jerry Okungu, at one time the MD, Group Managing Editor, Assistant Group Managing Editor, Managing Editor *Daily Nation,* Managing Editor *Sunday Nation,* Managing Editor *Taifa,* Chief Sub Editor, News Editor, Production Manager, Circulation Manager, two Assistant Circulation Managers, Advertising Manager, Agency Advertising Manager, Data Manager and Personnel Manager were all from the GEMA alliance.

On the commercial front, even though the *Daily Nation* sold four times the *Standard's* circulation, the *Standard* was beating the *Daily Nation* in advertising revenue. And it must be noted that then the bulk of the advertising revenue for the *Nation* accrued from the South Asian business persons, especially from the Aga Khan's Ismaili community. All these developments were causing jitters in Aeglemont where the principal shareholder, the Aga

Khan, resided. The Nation Media Group had to put its house in order by shedding off the ethnic image, improve its relations with the government and by extension the business community who were getting apprehensive with the confrontational editorial angle the paper was taking.

The *In-Between World of Kenya's Media* covers the period 1900-1992. With the advent of multi-partyism in 1992 the air waves were freed; and later the digitisation of the media brought a whole new dimension to journalism. Besides by then, almost all of the South Asian journalists of the early independence period had emigrated.

The colonial policy of down-playing and down-grading the roles and contributions of South Asians in Kenya dates back to the early 1920s when 'African Paramountcy' was made the stated objective in the 1923 Devonshire Declaration. Stark evidence of this is the elimination of the names of Indian doctors from the medical register after 1923. The side-lining and removal of South Asians from the national stage had commenced even prior to independence – according to Professor Godfrey Muriuki, the veteran historian, 'Jomo Kenyatta had already decided to remove Asians from the upper echelons of Kenya's civil service'.

Soon after, the policy of 'Africanisation' caused a mass exodus of Asians from Kenya and the August 1982 coup attempt, when Asians became a target for the rampaging vandals, expedited the process. Also at the advent of independence KBC's Hindustani Service had been moved to the Vernacular Service and its time allocation and financing severely curtailed; Narain Singh of the *Sunday Post* had died in 1978; Joe Rodrigues had been ignominiously 'fired', Salim Lone had been forced into exile – it was the end of an era for South Asian journalism with its roots in colonial Kenya. The few African journalists at *Uhuru* time, like Boaz Omori, Hilary Ng'weno and Joe Kadhi had been joined by a new crop of young African media specialists trained and eager to step into the shoes of the departing South Asians.

A few journalists did soldier on, Zoeb Tayabjee; Sayyid Azim; the late photo journalists Priya Ramrakha and Mohammed Amin; Mohinder Dhillon and others. Since 1992 young Kenyan South Asians, men and women, have once again begun to write, broadcast or click their cameras. The faces of Zain Verjee, Smirti Vidyarthi, Julie Gichuru and Anjlee Alifya Noorani are, or have been, on our National TV screens; the dynamic teams that run the South Asian FM radio stations including the late Ruhila Adatia so tragically gunned down in the 2013 Westgate massacre; and the scions of Mohammed Amin, (Salim) and Mohinder Dhillon, (Sam) are reaching out to Kenyans and beyond – to the region, to Africa and the world. These journalists no longer carry the baggage of colonialism as they forge ahead to new horizons and in the process usher in a new age of South Asian journalism in Kenya.

In spite of the internet and the mobile phone, newspaper sales worldwide remain buoyant and in Kenya several South Asian writers continue to operate in, and contribute to, the world of Kenya's print media. Among these are Ali Zaidi, Zihan Kassam, Rasna Warah, Prof Yash Pal Ghai and Zarina Patel, to name a few.

This book seeks to capture the stories and happenings of Kenya's South Asian journalists; and in so doing add a vital component to the history of the country's media as it continues to be researched and recorded. A few journalists failed to respond to the invitation to submit their bios. They are: Dr Piyo Rattansi, Amin Kassam Alfred de Araujo, Polly Fernandes, Gina Din, Aziz Islamshah and Chaman Lal Chaman. Philip Ochieng could not be reached.

THE NEWSPAPER

Were it left to me to decide whether we should have a government without newspapers, or newspapers without a government, I should not hesitate a moment to prefer the latter.
Thomas Jefferson 1787

Freedom of expression is a fundamental human right. *Article 19 of the Universal Declaration of Human Rights.*

Journalists are essential in a democratic society because they inform its citizens, give voice to the voiceless and hold the powerful accountable. Newspapers make events public that would otherwise remain private and act as watchdogs on the workings of the government.

Information is power and control for it is only on the basis of information that one can take purposeful and determined action. With the advent of colonialism, information expanded from the oral tradition to the printed word, later to sound, then visual and now digital. In the modern world, governance and socio-economic parameters are dependent on a free flow of information. Information can change the way we see the world around us, know our place in it, and learn how to adjust our lives in order to maximize the benefits available through our local resources. Fact driven decision-making can significantly alter our political, social and economic perspectives.

Media freedom and access to information feed into the wider development objective of empowering people. Empowerment is a multi-dimensional social and political process that helps people gain control over their own lives. This can only be achieved through access to accurate, fair and unbiased information, representing a plurality of opinions that is freely communicated vertically and horizontally, thereby facilitating participation in the active life of the community.

A newspaper's role is to find out fresh information on matters of public interest and to relay it as quickly, and as accurately as possible, to readers in an honest and balanced way. However, behind this seemingly simple statement lies a web of complex issues which involves, amongst others, the content of newspapers; how that content is selected; the economics; who owns the newspaper and determines its policies; editorial and commercial concerns; threats from the government or competing media and the age-old question of how free should freedom of the press be. The role of the journalist to find out and expose is unlikely to be fulfilled by any other technology – somebody still has to go out there and find things out.

Issues of objectivity, balance, neutrality and fairness are universally debated. Marianne Thamm, of the *Daily Maverick,* states: 'The myth of the objective journalist has long been shattered. It never existed. Journalists are human and by nature gravitate towards specific ideologies and ways of thinking shaped by a myriad of influences and factors. We are not blank slates. Ultimately, however, our job is to monitor and to hold power to account — whatever its colours.' Bill Kovach and Tom Rosenstiel, in their book *The Elements of Journalism,* claim that, 'the first principle of journalism – its disinterested pursuit of the truth – is ultimately what sets it apart from all other forms of communication'.

Kipkurui Tonui writing in the *Star* urged the press to 'rise above the evils it condemns'. 'Will the Fourth Estate engage in extortion, political partisanship, conspiracy, lies and perversion of family values, tribal chauvinism, greed, corruption, theft and adultery?' he asked. Writing on the same page Dickens Olewe stated, 'the media should jealously guard its role as "sense-makers" and not risk irrelevance by amplifying rumours'.

With the availability of news via 24-hour television channels, the advent of the internet and the widespread use of social networking accessories such as Facebook, Twitter, Instagram and Whats App; the future of journalism may seem bleak. However the reality is that no new technology, no new medium, has ever replaced an old one. The first book was published in 1475 and books are still with us and are selling in vast quantities. Similarly with the first magazine dated 1663, the birth of new magazines is on the rise. In 1922 we heard the first radio broadcast, and just after WWII television which was invented in 1926 became widely available. In 1975 we had the first personal computer. And all are still around. More information is available, and being consumed, in more ways than ever.

The development of newspapers

In ancient Rome in 59BC, government announcements and bulletins were carved in metal or stone and posted in public spaces. In China in the second and third centuries AD the government produced news sheets which were hand-written on silk and read by government officials. Newspapers, privately published, first appeared in 1582. In early modern Europe, concise hand-written news sheets were introduced and in 1556, the Government of Venice published a monthly which cost one gazetta – a coin in circulation at that time.

The newspaper as we know it today appeared in the 17th century and was closely connected to the spread of the printing press. In 1440, Johannes Gutenberg in Germany completed his wooden press which used moveable metal type; and news pamphlets and broadsides were printed. Earlier in 1423, the Europeans had used xylography – engraving on wood and block printing – to produce books. In 1041 China had invented the moveable clay type. The *Diamond Sutra,* a Buddhist scripture, is the first dated (888AD) example we have of block printing. Advances in printing technology related to the Industrial Revolution enabled newspapers to become even more widely circulated as a means of communication.

In 1631 the French printed the *Gazette* and this was followed by the *London Gazette.* The world's oldest newspaper still in circulation, *Post-och Inrikes Tidningar,* was published in Sweden in 1645. Britain's oldest surviving newspaper is the *Worcester Journal* founded in 1690; it began regular weekly publication in 1709. To subsidise the cost of printing, advertising was first introduced in 1833 and in 1873, the first illustrated daily newspaper was published in New York. In India, the first printing apparatus was established in Bombay in 1674 followed by Madras in 1772. India's first newspaper, *Calcutta General Advertiser,* also known as *Hicky's Bengal Gazette* was established in January 1780, and the first Hindi daily, *Samachar Sudha Varshan,* began in 1854. So the printing press preceded the advent of printed news in India by about 100 years. The oldest existing newspaper in India is the *Bombay Samachar,* started in 1822. The *Times of India* was founded in 1838. The first newspaper to be published in Africa was the *Cape Town Gazette* and *African Advertiser* in 1800. It was started by two slave dealers, Alexander Walker and John Robertson. In its early stages, the newspaper was simply used by the government as a mouth-piece and was published in both English and Dutch.

The first printing press in East Africa was established by a Christian missionary, Dr Steere, in Zanzibar in 1875. In Kenya, then British East Africa, the Christian Missionary Society installed a printing press in 1887 at Freretown on the mainland near Mombasa Island. These presses were used largely to print Kiswahili vocabularies and translations of hymns and scriptures.

The *Gazette for Zanzibar* and *East Africa* was published in Zanzibar in February 1892, and was followed by the *Taveta Chronicle,* a quarterly periodical of the Taveta Mission Press. It was printed on a No.2 'model' press costing £6 in London - 25 issues were published between Easter 1895 and November 1901. The price started at one rupee (2 shillings) and later dropped to one shilling.

By the end of the 19th century the population of Europeans and Indians had increased considerably and in August 1899, the *East Africa and Uganda Mail* was launched by Charles Palmer, the owner and publisher, and edited by Olive Grey, an Australian married to an Anglo-Indian. This weekly contained overseas and local news, despatches from up-country, social events and sports coverage, stories and poetry. Its standard of English was considered 'wanting'.

Soon after establishing itself, the *Mail* became bitterly and unrelentingly critical of Mr A M Jeevanjee, a South Asian entrepreneur. The latter retaliated to the racist diatribe by founding a newspaper which he called the *African Standard, Mombasa Times and Uganda Argus,* and appointed Mr W H Tiller as its editor. The printing works were based in Mombasa and the first issue appeared on 18 November, 1901. In August 1904 the *Mail* was adjudged bankrupt and ceased publication. Jeevanjee, having silenced the *Mail,* then sold the *African Standard* to Messrs A G W Anderson and F Mayer in August 1905. They renamed it the *East African Standard* and moved it to Nairobi in May 1910 where it continues to be published to date.

Source: Ndegwa's Printing & Publishing in EA
Patel Zarina, 1997
The Star, Friday, May 3, 2013, p24
https://goo.gl/4mj6Sz

JOURNALISM IN THE COLONIAL ERA

In this period new intermediary groups of African and Indian entrepreneurs, activists and publicists, collaborating around newspaper production, captured fairly large and significant non-European audiences (some papers had print runs of around ten thousand) and engaged them in new ways, incorporating their aspirations, writings and points of view in newspapers. They depended on voluntary and political associations and anti-colonial struggles in Kenya and on links to nationalists in India and the passive resistance movement in South Africa. They sidestepped the European-dominated print culture and created an anti-colonial counter-voice. Editors insisted on the right to write freely and be heard, and traditions of freedom of speech put a brake on censorship. Furthermore, the shifting networks of financial, editorial and journalistic collaboration, and the newspapers' language choice – African vernaculars, Gujarati, Swahili and English – made intervention difficult for the authorities.

Bodil Folke Frederiksen

The early migrants from the Indian sub-continent in East Africa maintained regular contact with their country of origin and it is self-evident that they would be imbued with India's vibrant anti-colonial journalism. India is the world's largest democracy and its mass media culture is a system that has evolved over centuries, its newspaper evolution is nearly unmatched in world press history.

Newspaper history in India is inextricably tangled with political history. In 1780, James Augustus Hicky was the founder of India's first newspaper, the *Calcutta General Advertiser* also known as *Hicky's Bengal Gazette*; it earned the rulers' wrath due to its criticism of the government. In November 1780 its circulation was halted by government decree. Hicky protested against this arbitrary harassment without avail, and was imprisoned.

Patriotic movements grew in proportion to the colonial ruthlessness, and a vehicle of information dissemination became a tool for the freedom struggle. In the struggle for freedom, journalists in the twentieth century performed a dual role as professionals and nationalists. Indeed many national leaders, from Gandhi to Vajpayee, were journalists as well.

Freedom of speech and expression is a constitutionally guaranteed fundamental right of the Indian people, as well as peoples of the world. While constitutional guarantees ensure freedom of the press and expression, press and media are obligated by a self-regulatory system of ethics that protects individuals and organizations from libellous behaviour. The Press Council of India was established in 1966 to uphold editorial autonomy. Resurrected in 1979, it has no legal standing to impose penalties. The Indian press, generally believed as 'managed,' is a self-restrained institution generally reluctant to take on governmental policies. The first diploma in journalism was offered at Aligarh Muslim University in 1938 but journalists, and other mass communicators, can perform without specialized training and skills, and can succeed without advanced degrees.

In British East Africa, publishing was officially recognised in 1906 when the Books and Newspapers Registration Ordinance was passed. The East African Protectorate Blue Book 1915-16 has the following as the principal publications during the year 1913: The Official Gazette; *East African Standard; The Leader; Mombasa Samachar* (Gujarati newspaper); The Red Book; The Handbook of East Africa. The English Press Law of 1662 continued to inform the practice of colonial Kenya's courts up until the 1940s.

Until well after the start of WWII, publishing emanated from the printing industry largely operated, and owned, by Indian master and artisan printers who maintained regular contact with India and collaborated with, and trained, the newly literate sectors of the African population.

Bodil Folke Frederiksen states that: 'the collective character of newspaper production made authorship uncertain . . . editors, journalists and printers of Asian and African papers migrated from one enterprise to the other, keeping up a steady flow of newspapers in very unstable economic and political situations, sometimes assisted by family members and other close associates. The instability and fluidity resulting from these and other factors, like the use of several languages, assisted the survival of an African–Indian print culture from the point of view of contributors, while representing for the authorities a problem that was much resented and problematic to handle'.

By the 1930s, readership of all races had grown tremendously, and awareness, both political and social, had increased. It was consequently inevitable that newspapers would increase in number, be they national, factional or regional. The Christian Missionary Bookshop established the first publishing house, the Ndia Kuu Press, in Mombasa.

The colonial government regarded the African newspapers as scurrilous and extreme, and the Indian press as being under the influence of communists. To the contrary, several of the African editors were moderate in their political demands, asking for self-government and not complete independence, as seen in the writings of Henry Moria, Francis Khamisi and others. Increasingly the Indian press was divided, first along communal or religious lines in the build-up to India's independence and anticipated partition, and then between moderates and radicals. Editors and journalists disagreed over questions of constitutionalism – whether to accept the representation of different communities in the municipality and central government, whether to keep up Indian representation in the Legislative Council and other official bodies despite the lack of elected African representation – and, more broadly, over how to react to persistent racial discrimination, known in Kenya as the colour bar.

The objective of Jeevanjee's *African Standard,* the earliest Indian newspaper in Kenya and printed entirely in English, was to counter the virulent racism of its contemporary, the *East Africa and Uganda Mail.* It was the *Indian Voice* which promoted self-representation of the East African Indians and set the trend for later Indian newspapers such as Desai's *East African Chronicle* and Achariar's *Democrat* in the anti-colonial struggle. The variations now became more ideological. The *Kenya Daily Mail* was the voice of the moderates while the *Colonial Times* was more radical, but both publications focused more on the anti-colonial movements in India. The *Daily Chronicle* which had broken away from the *Colonial Times,* took a Left line and had avowed socialists amongst its editorial staff and contributors.

Shiraz Durrani in his book, *Never Be Silent* states: 'The editorial policies of *Colonial Times* and *Daily Chronicle* consistently favoured African constitutional advance and the improvement of economic and social conditions of African people. Both gave much publicity to Kenya African Union (K.A.U.) before its suppression in 1953 and afterwards D. K. Sharda campaigned for its continued existence as a national party. Their pages were available to African writers.' Their achievements included, 'pointing

to the inevitability of African majority rule [and] contributing to the growth of the nationalist movement'.

Desai's Chronicle press was the first, around 1920, to print an African paper, Harry Thuku's *Tangazo.* Later this became a common practice – the *Democrat* accommodated Jomo Kenyatta's *Muigwithania.* Vidyarthi's Colonial Printing Works printed *Jicho, Ramogi, Mumengerere, Sauti ya Mwafrika, Mwalimu and others.* In the early 1950s, Bildad Kaggia's *Afrika Mpya,* Isaac Gathangu's *Wihuge* and Mbugua Book Writers' *Njokia-Gwitu* were printed by D K Sharda's Tribune press. These last three publications were 'outlawed' under the Emergency laws.

Frederiksen writes that 'there was in fact significant collaboration and mutual awareness between politically active Africans and Indians in Kenya's late colonial period, and that the authorities tried to deal with the effects of this political consciousness in ways that were not very effective'. The Book and Newspaper Ordinance of 1906 did not give the government much control of the press. Control was exercised by the 1950 Penal Code, which allowed confiscation of printing presses which published materials considered seditious. In practice control could be affected only after the fact, after publication and circulation of material. This is why the government resorted to financial blackmail to effect closure or sale of a newspaper.

Foreign publications were banned routinely. By 1948, workers' struggles for political and economic rights had begun to worry the colonial administration so they banned *Labour Monthly* (London), *New Africa* (New York), *The Guardian* (Cape Town), and *People's Age* and *Blitz.* The last two were left-wing papers published in Mumbai, India. Blitz had a wide circulation in Kenya and

its banning was condemned by the *Daily Chronicle.* In 1951, all publications of the World Federation of Trade Unions (WFTU) were proscribed in Kenya.

What had been impossible for the state in its long negotiation with the African and Indian press, the suppression of allegedly subversive papers, became a reality in October 1952 with the declaration of Emergency powers in order to suppress the Mau Mau freedom fighters. Just prior to this, the Printing Press Rules of 1952 were issued giving the government broad powers to refuse or cancel a printing license in order to prevent publication of material seemingly prejudicial to public order. The nationalist African publications were closed down; the South Asian ones which survived did so by adopting a conservative line and changing their tactics. The committed journalists, writers, press workers and printers moved from paper to paper, finding a home in the most progressive publications. D K Sharda's attempt to continue the *Daily Chronicle's* radical stance by launching cyclostyled copies of the *Tribune* ended just after a few months, and he was forced into exile in India.

In 1960, when *uhuru* became unstoppable, new legislation was introduced placing prohibitive restrictions on local publishers. This required a surety bond of £500 for registration of a new newspaper. This greatly hampered the establishment of a free, national press, especially in nationality languages, after independence.

It will suffice to sum up this survey on the development of the newspaper in the colonial period by quoting Prof. Robert G Gregory's statement in his book, *Quest for Equality:* 'In their efforts towards reform the Asian journalists on the whole contributed substantially to the furtherance of African interests including the development of a strong nationalist movement and the establishment of an African press. Most of the founders and editors of the Asian newspapers – notably M. A. Desai, Achariar, G. L. Vidyarthi, F. R. S. de Souza, Pinto, Ahmed, Sharda, J. M. Desai,Oza, Boal and Randir Thaker [the last two were journalists in Tanganyika] – and the reporters and contributors like Nazareth, Pranlal Sheth and Chanan Singh added African grievances to those of the Asians and vigorously supported African aspirations. Some of them, especially M. A. Desai, Achariar, Oza, Vidyarthi and Pinto, took on the publication of African newspapers, and, in many instances, not only subsidized the African press but also provided the essential training for the African staff. In 1948 Asian printing personnel in Kenya outnumbered Europeans by 55 to 10, and in 1962 by 383 to 98. Nearly all the Asian printers employed Africans. The Vidyarthi firm alone is estimated to have hired and trained more than two hundred Africans including at least seventy-five in Uganda. Of course, African initiative in this way as in others has been an essential determinant, but African journalism, as well as African nationalism, clearly owes much to the Asians.'

In the colonial era almost all the printing presses were founded and owned by Asian businessmen, and even today the majority of the large printing firms continue to be Asian-owned.

Sources: Gregory, Robert G, 1993
          Durrani, Shiraz, 2006
          Frederiksen, Bodil Folke,2011
          Patel, Zarina, 1997
          India Office: Intelligence Reports in File on 'Kenya Colony Intelligence and Security Summaries', 1947-48.
          Ndegwa's Printing & Publishing in EA

THE AFRICAN STANDARD (1901-1904)

The *African Standard* was launched on 15 November, 1901. Until then there had been three publications in Kenya (then the EAP), all established in Mombasa: the *Gazette of British East Africa* in 1895 and the *Taveta Chronicle,* a missionary paper which ran from 1895 to 1901. The third was the *East Africa and Uganda Mail* started in 1899 by the owner and publisher, Charles Palmer, who had been dismissed from Government Service. He took on as editor Olive Grey, an Australian woman married to an Anglo-Indian – her 'tainted' racial identity in this white-ruled British colony became for her a major source of frustration and anger.

Alibhai Mulla Jeevanjee, a highly successful business man originally from Karachi (then India), was enjoined with Palmer in the fuel-supply business. Hence the *Mail* often printed laudatory articles about Jeevanjee. However, at some point the two partners fell out and the articles then started becoming acrimonious; especially as Palmer's new ventures could not succeed against Jeevanjee's extremely shrewd business acumen.

At first Jeevanjee checked his urge to take action but when the personal vendetta developed into racist diatribe, he opted for a simple remedy: a tit for tat. Never one to do things by halves, he launched the *African Standard, Mombasa Times & Uganda Argus.* He imported Kenya's first high speed press and recruited as editor, William Henry Tiller, at that time the night editor of the London News Agency. Previous to this, Tiller had editorial experience in Ceylon and South Africa. His professional ability together with Jeevanjee's financial resources quickly made the *African Standard* a formidable competitor to the *Mail.*

Thirty-six year old Tiller settled down to his task with great gusto. He was editor, sub-editor, reporter, proof-

reader, advertising manager and saw to dispatch and sales. He was able to compose, type, lock up and print his frames. News consisted of a much attenuated Reuter service; shipping arrivals and departures with passenger lists and destinations; and the doings and movements of

Mombasa residents. Published too were stories received from correspondents in Mombasa and Nairobi, news items from senior government officials and the police.

The very first editorial stated that the paper would do its utmost to prevent the perpetuation of racial differences. The *African Standard* was 'the first national newspaper to oppose racial differentiation'. Every issue of the *Mail* printed verbal attacks on what it termed 'Our Native Contemporary', Tiller retaliated by naming his adversary 'the Old Grey Mare'! But the *Mail's* sarcasm turned increasingly vitriolic as it compared 'hardy Britons' to 'effete Asians,' and printed articles headed 'The Asiatic Curse in South Africa' which claimed that 'the Indian destroys legitimate trade and eats like a cancer into the inheritance of the European'. It irked the *Mail* management no end when the *Manchester Evening Chronicle* described the *African Standard* as 'a small but very credible journal'; when Lord Delamere, leader of the Settlers, corresponded with Tiller and when VIP Government guests and officials attended functions and parties in Jeevanjee Villa.

Attentive to the possibility that his wealth could attract libel suits, Jeevanjee named Tiller as the 'Responsible Editor'. Jeevanjee was away most of the time doing business in India - Tiller hardly ever met him, just sent him copies of the paper. When the *Mail* described the *Standard* as 'unclean, filthy literature and vile journalism polluting the atmosphere of Mombasa …..' Tiller had had enough. He brought criminal and civil libel charges against the publisher and editor. The case dragged on for six months and the *Mail* was fined. The journalistic fencing went on for another six months with the *Mail* advocating that, 'colonists should as far as possible be married men, so as to keep a pure race'.

The important government and commercial news was always first published in the *African Standard* while the

pages of the *Mail* became more and more filled with gossip. By 1903 the *Standard* had outstripped its rival in circulation and advertising. Even the Settlers turned against the *Mail* when it stridently supported the British Foreign Office's proposal to settle Jews from Poland and Russia in East Africa. The *Standard* had called the immigration plan 'wicked'.

In August 1904, the *Mail* was declared bankrupt and ceased publication. Exactly a year later Jeevanjee sold his paper and the printing works to A G Anderson and F Mayer. The paper was then free of all liabilities and had a circulation five times as large as that of any East African journal and was sold at four outlets in Mombasa, Nairobi, Entebbe and London. Tiller's three-year contract was ending and with the demise of the *Mail*, Jeevanjee had scored a bull's eye.

With the influx of Boers from South Africa in 1904, racism against Asians and Africans mounted. The renamed *East African Standard* under Anderson tried to steer a moderate line but soon had to succumb to the dictates of Delamere and his cronies. Aware of this eventuality, Jeevanjee inserted a clause in the sale agreement that nothing derogatory could ever be published about him or his firm. It explains why in the ensuing years when Jeevanjee became a fiery antagonist of the Settlers, the *East African Standard* carried no articles critical of him. The worst it could do was to deny him coverage. Jeevanjee's foray into journalism was brief but he left for us a newspaper that endures to this day.

Sources: Marika Sherwood, Senior Research Fellow, Institute of Commonwealth Studies, University of London; Editor Black & Asian Studies Patel, Association Newsletter Patel Zarina, 1997.

ALIBHAI MULLA JEEVANJEE (1859–1936)

Alibhai Mulla Jeevanjee was born in Karachi, then part of the British colony of India. His family belonged to the Bohra Shia Islamic sect. At the age of thirty he left home to wander throughout India and learnt modern ways and the intricacies of doing business. His next stop was eastern Australia, where as a hawker of spices, he became fluent in English. He set up a trading company specializing in Eastern produce, participated in the 1887 Jubilee Exhibition celebrating the fiftieth anniversary of Queen Victoria's enthronement, and met British officials familiar with trade opportunities in far-off East Africa.

Back in Karachi he established A M Jeevanjee & Co. to provide stevedoring and translation services to ships visiting Karachi. Always looking for more challenges, in 1890 he sailed on a dhow to Mombasa, East Africa; made contact with officials of the Imperial British East Africa Company and set up his own company. In 1895, British officials building the Uganda Railway contracted Jeevanjee to recruit workers and skilled artisans from India, offload wagons and other equipment at the port, and supply rations, blankets, and other goods. He amassed a fortune and at the government's request and under specified contracts, he built a range of government facilities in the major towns. He donated the land and design for Jeevanjee Gardens, today the only green space in Nairobi's city centre; as well as to other philanthropic causes.

At the turn of the century, an influx of settlers from Britain and South Africa gave rise to increasing racial discrimination and segregation. Jeevanjee founded the Mombasa Indian Association in response to the Settlers' Convention of Associations, and mobilized the Indian community in a struggle for equal rights. He recruited an editor from England and established a newspaper, the

ALIBHAI MULLA JEEVANJEE

African Standard, to counter the *Mail's* anti-Asian racism – it was later sold and renamed the *East African Standard*. In 1910, he was nominated to the Legislative Council. Being the only non-white member, he found his position quite untenable and resigned after a few sessions. He published *An Appeal on behalf of the Indians in East Africa* in 1912 and plunged headlong into the political fray, fully aware of the consequences this would have on his financial empire and family affairs. Jeevanjee made

several trips to the Colonial Office in London to meet with the secretaries of state, and took the opportunity to brief the British media on the injustices being meted out to Kenya Indians. In 1914, he founded the East Africa Indian National Congress. He was instrumental therefore in projecting Kenya's colonial injustices onto a national and international stage.

At the end of World War I, he recruited Manilal Desai to invigorate the Congress. Many more Indian Associations were formed and in 1920, as president-elect of its third session, Jeevanjee gave a fiery address in which he castigated the colonial policy that denied Indians access to the franchise and the White Highlands, and discriminated against them in matters of taxation, education, municipal services, and residential areas. Desai had a close friendship with the African nationalist leader Harry Thuku, and the Congress began to include the African and Arab causes in its deliberations and to petition on their behalf.

In 1923, Jeevanjee participated in a delegation led by Desai that met with the Duke of Devonshire at the Colonial Office. Another delegation of Settlers led by Lord Delamere was also in attendance. The outcome was a White Paper that emphasized 'African Paramountcy'. Though the Indians' demands were ignored, it did arrest the Settlers' plan for dominion status.

Approaching the age of seventy, Jeevanjee, though still active, became more of a mentor and guide to the younger Indian political leaders. However, in 1926, in an attempt to heal the emerging rift between radicals and moderates, Jeevanjee was called upon to preside over the sixth session of the East Africa Indian National Congress.

When Desai passed away in 1926, Jeevanjee brought in, ostensibly as his private secretary, Isher Dass, a Marxist

he had met working as a waiter in London. Dass quickly took over Desai's work, got into the legislature, and advanced the campaign for basic human rights for the Indians as well as the Africans.

A combination of family feuds, colonial defaults, threats of excommunication by the Bohra priesthood and failed business deals had begun to take their toll. Soon Jeevanjee's financial empire was in disarray and his properties were auctioned, leaving him in strained circumstances.

Jeevanjee died of a heart attack on 2 May 1936, in Nairobi, at the age of eighty. The colonial government made no official acknowledgement of his passing, but people from all communities attended his funeral. Shops were closed, memorial meetings were held, newspapers lauded him and streets were named after him. One newspaper, the *Kenya Daily Mail,* described him as 'The Grand Old Man of Kenya' who, though not a man of much education or fine words, had indomitable courage and foresight. The *Coast Guardian* stated that, 'He was the first man to demand equality. He laid the foundations of an organized political movement [in Kenya].'

Source: Patel, Zarina, 1997.

THE INDIAN VOICE (1911-1913)

The *Indian Voice* has hitherto been considered an insignificant publication. It is Samia Nasar who, in her PhD thesis, has highlighted the important role it played in the militant South Asian press in colonial times and I am deeply grateful to her for allowing me to summarise her findings in this book. Her paper, The Indian Voice: Connecting Self-Representation and Identity Formulation in Diaspora, first appeared in *History in Africa,* Volume 40 (2013), pp99-124.

The *Indian Voice* of British East Africa, Uganda and Zanzibar was printed in Nairobi between 1911 and 1913. Its proprietor was D K Bhutt. Published by the Oriental Press based in Victoria Street, Nairobi, it was one of the earliest non-European newspapers to appear in Kenya. The *Indian Voice* only started printing in both English and Gujarati on 5 July, 1911 two weeks after the Oriental Press obtained a typewriter which had a Gujarati typeface. Circulated every Wednesday, the *Indian Voice* was priced at 25 cents, registered at the General Post Office, and was relatively easy to gain access to. This publication was propped up by support from an active audience of local Indian businessmen. Advertisements from successful Indian merchants included the likes of Allidina Visram, Suleman Virji and A M Jeevanjee.

In terms of print organization, the *Indian Voice* was very much a collaborative project amongst print elites: its headquarters were housed by the Goan Union, it employed Indian journalists who spoke and wrote in English, and at its helm was its editor, H C Smith, a white settler. Smith, an experienced editor, had a liberal, cosmopolitan outlook which helped to validate the newspaper as a serious news organ. In so doing the *Indian Voice* deviated from the European norm by espousing a message of cosmopolitism and multi-racialism within colonial society.

While it is impossible to provide an accurate number, there appears to be three volumes and 155 issues in total – 113 of which have survived. Copies of the newspaper can be found in the Colindale Library, London. Printed in both English and Gujarati, the bilingual publication – the first of its kind in Kenya – emerged when 'the need for a community oriented press carrying news of events in South Asia and East Africa' arose. At a time when Indian immigration intensified within the Indian Ocean

realm, the newspaper aspired to, 'promote, protect and give voice to the interests of Indians overseas'. Lasting for a total of three years, its editors strived to carefully collate trustworthy local intelligence within an 'up-to-date (…) efficient and truthful journal'. (*Indian Voice,* 8 February 1911, p8). By providing a platform for its Indian writers to articulate a mosaic of social and political currents, the publication was one of the very first sites for Indian self-representation.

Though largely dismissed as 'insignificant' in the wider context of Kenya's militant press, Saima Nasar demonstrates how the *Indian Voice* offered an invaluable means of generating new insights into the complexities of self-representation and diasporic identity formulation. Her thesis contributes to remapping the historical perspective of East African Indians within the early colonial period.

She notes that in the early twentieth century, as opposed to the dispersed coastal settlements, Indian workers were actively encouraged to settle inland and that the migrant families included a whole range of occupations. This shift gave rise to more established Indian communities and hence, post-1910, generated the 'Indian Question'. The *Indian Voice* shed light on a number of issues that affected settler communities during this period. (See *Indian Voice:* 8 February 1911, p6; 22 January 1913, p3; 20 August 1913, p3; 3 December 1913, p5.)

Each issue of the *Indian Voice* clearly stated its maxim: 'The hope of all who suffer, the dread of all who wrong'. Taken from John Greenleaf Whittier's *The Mantle of St. John de Matha,* these two lines, which appeared on the editorial page, summarized the paper's policy and revealed its purpose as a communicative medium that expounded social justice. Marketed as a journal

representing the interests of Indians resident in British East Africa, Uganda and Zanzibar, the paper vowed that: 'it will conscientiously fill its mission for which it was really founded, viz. the treatment of all alike, without prejudice'. (*Indian Voice,* 8 February 1911, p10). A 'cosmopolitan organ in a cosmopolitan country,' the *Indian Voice* was subsequently described by its contemporaries as 'quite a moderate evangelistic warrior that had the potential to help others consider the Asiatic as a broad–gauged and fair minded individual.'

The subscribers to the weekly consisted of those, 'In Nairobi. Outside Nairobi. And Overseas'. It catered for a diverse range of reading publics helping to connect British Indian, Goan, African and European audiences. This was reflected in its layout which usually began with advertisements for local businesses; an editorial page detailing local and 'national' concerns; a section on the Goan community; updates from around the world; and news from India.

While the *Indian Voice* regularly provided a critical commentary on what was deemed imperialist propaganda in 'its local contemporary' the *East African Standard;* it was engaged in wider transnational networks and frequently reprinted articles from the *London Times,* the *Times of India,* the *Indian Review* and others. South Africa's *Indian Opinion* commented and reprinted news items in the *Indian Voice.* In this way, the *Indian Voice* was demonstrably embedded within a 'mature alternative print media network that enabled cross-regional dialogue between diasporic settler communities'.

However, it is important to note that the newspaper was not free from reproducing negative stereotypes. This was particularly the case in writings concerning 'the African native, the European other, and women more generally'.

The *Indian Voice* ceased publication in 1913 but its legacy endured. In 1920 Manilal Desai's *East African Chronicle* started publication and its structure and news layout were strikingly familiar. It is quite likely that it employed some staff of the defunct *Indian Voice*. In 1931, the *Daily Advertiser,* a Gujarati Indian newspaper printed in Mombasa, included the *Indian Voice* as an English print counterpart.

The *Indian Voice* printed articles outlining land rights; the availability of plots for British Indians; imperial restrictions; the Highlands; and neighbourhood concerns which served to not only inform audiences of current affairs, but also provoke conversation and critical commentary. This meant, for example when plague broke out in 1911, the newspaper offered hygiene advice, as well as regular updates on the severity of the disease and the impact it had on the Indian population. It criticized the European press for 'reducing the causes of the plague to the conditions of the Indian bazaar', and protested against its closure, however temporary. The newspaper therefore functioned as an important channel for collective governance and gave a distinctive collective voice to the many communities which formed the Indian minority population.

One of its editorials boldly challenged the claim of the Colonists Convention that Kenya was a 'white man's country', and its anti-Indian rhetoric. It pointed out the benefits of Indian labour, which during this period helped to maintain the Uganda Railway; establish retail enterprise along the coast and in remote villages; and included a class of artisans and 'professional gentlemen'. This challenged the hierarchies of difference that were so deeply embedded in the racial politics of empire, and empire-builders. Interestingly, it set white settler interests apart from the policies of the Colonial Office and identified the Home Government as having 'no axes to grind'.

The editor made particular reference to the distinct lack of representation on the Legislative Council, Municipal Council and the Chamber of Commerce. At the time there was only one Indian member, A M Jeevanjee, in the Legislative Council. The editor quoted the last census figures which showed 3,175 Europeans against 11,886 Asians to prove his point.

At a local level, the *Indian Voice* served to unite the various Indian communities and to maintain a cultural and ethnic identity in diaspora. This ethnic consciousness perhaps explains why the publication referred to an Indian voice, and not to a collection of Indian voices. This demonstrated a desire for inter-faith, inter-cultural and inter-ethnic dialogue and exchange. Indians in East Africa constituted their identities within the boundaries of Empire. So while the *Indian Voice* championed equality it did so on a certain set of terms. It defended African interests yet strategically positioned the Indian population within a 'colonial sandwich' with Europeans occupying the top tier and Africans the bottom. The *Indian Voice* did not therefore completely abandon or dispute negative stereotypes of the 'native', whom it described as 'naturally thoughtless and thinks not of the future'. (*Indian Voice,* 11 February 1911, p3).

The *African Standard,* published entirely in English, had failed to focus on Indian interests – representation of the Indian community in the press was made possible seven years later by the *Indian Voice* which then became a regular critic of the *East African Standard,* among others.

Sources: Nasar, Saima, History in Africa, Volume 40 (2013), pp99-124
Gregory, Robert G., 1993
East African Standard, 14 January 1911, p15.

A C L de SOUSA (1883-1958)

Dr A C L de Sousa, born in Goa, India in 1883, arrived in Kenya in 1915 and was appointed Government Medical Officer in Mombasa. He served in Giriama country during the revolt by Me Katilili and her community against British colonization.

In 1919 he set up a private practice in Nairobi together with his bride who was also a medical doctor. Dr A C L de Sousa was an outstanding physician, a pioneer journalist, a great politician and an active social worker as evidenced by his sterling work in establishing the Lady Grigg Indian Maternity Hospital, the Goans Overseas Association, the Desai Memorial Hall & Library and the East African Goan Conference. He was the greatest protagonist of Goan education, and in fact the architect of Goan history, in East Africa.

He was a member of the E A Indian National Congress and a close compatriot of M A Desai, Shams ud Deen and others. He was elected to the Legislative Council, 1934-1938, and joined five other Asian members - it was the first time that the Asian MLCs were elected, not nominated, and this was on a country-wide platform. In those days there was not a single African Member on the Council, a padre represented African interests. Dr de Sousa, however, was not returned as a great deal of propaganda against him was done by the other candidates, implying that he was a Goan and was not likely to look after the Indian cause in the Council. His own Goan community largely holding Portuguese passports was not eligible to vote.

In the East Africa Indian National Congress he was assigned a secondary position and generally elbowed out from other institutions to make room for narrow-minded communalists. It must be said though that Dr de

A C L de SOUSA

Sousa did take an extreme anti-Indian pro-Portuguese line which surprised the colleagues who worked with him in Indian politics.

Dr A C L de Sousa had a great flare for journalism and could write forcibly and with great vigour attacking his opponent without mercy. This also made him some enemies, but he never took the slightest notice of anyone. The bar to further promotion in the colonial medical service fuelled his anti-colonial sentiments.

In the 1920s, he used to write in the local Indian paper, the *Democrat,* which was then owned and edited by Sitaram Achariar. In fact very often when Achariar was out of town or was touring to collect money to keep the paper alive, he handed over the editing of the paper to Dr de Sousa. Being a weekly paper Dr de Sousa could do this in addition to his own work, though often he actually neglected his work in order to get the paper out in time.

When the pungent pen of Sitaram Achariar fearlessly attacked the jingoism of British Settlers and defended the Indian community from their vile, libellous accusations; Dr de Sousa always supported Achariar and his popular weekly, the *Democrat.* He wrote freely in that paper and his forceful weekly notes were masterly political writings full of sound facts, fearless arguments and logical criticism. The subjects he covered were not confined to politics alone. He ventured into matters educational, professional and social on which he wrote with authority and erudition.

After the closing down of the *Democrat,* in 1930, the doctor floated a company and started *Fairplay,* and ably edited it for a number of years. The paper ultimately folded up during the recession of the early thirties. Soon after, when the daily *Pioneer* appeared in Nairobi, the doctor was again connected with it. This venture soon came to grief, creating a sort of a vacuum in South Asian journalism in Nairobi, and that fact really disturbed this medico-journalist.

In mid-1933, Girdhari Lal Vidyarthi launched his *Colonial Times* and A C L de Sousa volunteered to take charge of the editorial policy. He maintained this voluntary work for 15 years and Girdhari Lal Vidyarthi said that even after he left, the relations between him and the *Colonial Times* always remained friendly.

The side-lining of A C L de Sousa in the East Africa Indian National Congress and the general antipathy drove him to focus more on his own Goan community. He decided to establish a Goan weekly in Nairobi. He spoke to the community and championed their cause through the *Goan Voice,* which was an organ devoted to the welfare of Goans where-ever they may be. He founded the weekly and edited it until his death. He had the tenacity of a lion, working away at his typewriter though physically crippled by hemiplegia.

A C L de Sousa was a tall dark brown figure who drove an equally big Pontiac car. Hot tempered, he could brook no opposition from anybody, but was very kind and caring to those who were straight forward with him, and wanted his help. He passed away on the morning of Thursday 17 July, 1958 and was survived by a daughter and two sons. His beloved wife, Mary, had passed away earlier.

Source:1959 Memorial Booklet to celebrate the first anniversary of Dr A C L de Sousa's death.

THE DEMOCRAT (?1920-1930)

The *Democrat* was a weekly newspaper published in Mombasa and edited by Sitaram Achariar. The 16 February, 1923 issue was the only copy of the newspaper the author was able to find and it is not known when exactly it was started – the earliest reference to it so far is May 1920. Almost ninety per cent of the articles were written by Sitaram Achariar who called himself editor, proprietor and publisher. Clearly the paper was his mouth piece and his irascible personality dominated the writing, including the News and Notes.

Dr A C L de Sousa, a leading Goan personality, was a supporter of, and a regular contributor to, the *Democrat.* He wrote the editorials whenever Achariar was away on fund-raising trips for the newspaper.

The *Democrat* ceased to appear in 1930 when publication costs could not be met. The manager and assistant editor was Narayan Shrinivas Thakur. Apart from highlighting news about the struggle of the Indian community against Kenya's colonial government and relevant events in India; Achariar and Thakur devoted many pages to the tribulations of the African community.

In 1923, Sitaram Achariar, at the special request of the congress, agreed to run his *Democrat* newspaper for propaganda purposes weekly at Nairobi instead of Mombasa. It was felt that a daily Indian paper was an indispensable necessity but the question of funds stood in the way. The enterprise was not an ordinary one especially in view of the fact that Achariar personally had no funds to run the paper. But he possessed admirable plunk and determination and unhesitatingly consented to start the weekly paper with the small support he received from the community. The *Democrat* was housed in a humble structure opposite where the Desai Memorial Hall was later built.

In a letter addressed to M H Malik of The Kenya Printing Works, Nairobi; Manilal Desai, president of the East Africa Indian National Congress (EAINC), instructed:

.... Funds should be collected – aim for approximately Shs 20,000. The Kenya Times Ltd. should be put into operation and Democrat be made a daily paper under its auspices; and Mr Achariar to be employed as editor on a salary basis.

Malik's quote for printing 500 copies per week of a 16-page weekly newspaper in English, same size as the *Chronicle*, was Shs 1250/- per month. A list of donations towards starting a new paper was started but by January 1924, Achariar was to inform the EAINC that,

The local Indian community has not acquired a taste for newspaper reading to any appreciable degree which I believe is at the bottom of our various newspaper failures. Difficult to get advertisements. Therefore daily Democrat is not feasible. Better to make Democrat bigger and more attractive.

The Annual Report of the 1923 Session of the EAINC stated that:

It is high time for the Indian community to wake up from their lethargic slumber and have a daily paper which can be the only effective weapon of success in the political struggle under present circumstances.

In July 1924, at a meeting of the Standing Committee of the EAINC held in Jeevanjee Villa in Mombasa; Shrimati Sarojini Naidu was in the chair and it was resolved to give 100 pounds to Achariar and his *Democrat*.

Principal journal of the EAINC

The *Democrat* took over from the terminated *East African Chronicle* and served as the principal journal of the EAINC until the paper's closure in 1930. Its mast head declared it to be 'The People's Paper' and it was published every Tuesday. It was outstanding in its stand and fight for the rights of the South Asian community, and supported the rights of all.

Throughout its 10-year history, the *Democrat* rankled the colonial authorities. Coryndon described it to J H Thomas, Secretary of State for the Colonies, as:
a scurrilous and sometimes lewd publication entirely for political purposes, it has a small circulation, it is

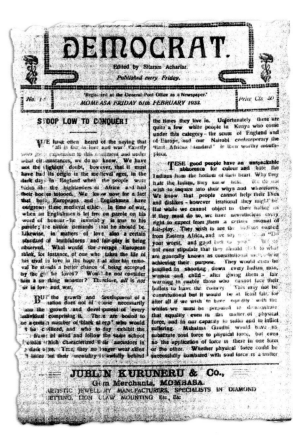

always bitter and often very untruthful with allegations of racial discrimination against Indians by government departments. First published on 22nd December, 1923. It concerns mail delivery; arrival of passengers, ship and train; taxation; use of tax monies; land allocation; possession of firearms; promotions in civil service salaries; police harassment; immigration; invitations to Government House; court trials; recognition of Indian degrees; education; and import duties.

Source: *Gregory, Robert G, 1971*
CO533/310, National Archives, London.

SITARAM ACHARIAR (?-1939)

Sitaram Achariar was a highly excitable journalist who was vehemently opposed to colonial injustice. A slow moving, sitar playing stoic; he was fearless too and did not hesitate to speak his mind. As a result he was often arrested and was constantly out of favour with the authorities. Manilal Desai, a leader of the Indian community, would be inundated with telegrams from Indian Associations and the East Africa Indian National Congress (EAINC) to 'rescue' him. Clearly the court was a 'second home' to Achariar!

Achariar, who had arrived in Kenya in 1912, was the editor of the *Democrat* newspaper established in Mombasa around 1920. Desai may have decided, in 1922, to keep a closer watch on his friend, and so mooted the proposition to bring the *Democrat* to Nairobi.

Achariar faces deportation

In early 1923, Achariar was once again a cause for concern. A Rev. Shaw of Nyeri, compared the prophet Mohammed to Belial and provoked cabled protests from Muslims 'from all over the world.' Partly as a rebuttal of Shaw's remarks, Achariar published in the *Democrat* a disparaging editorial on the morals of Kenya's white women. He was promptly arrested, found guilty of breach of the peace and of blasphemy, remanded by the Mombasa court and recommended to the Governor for deportation. The Indians all over Kenya were incensed and observed a one-day *hartal* (strike)and in Mombasa over 10,000 African and Indian Muslims threatened to take legal action against Rev. Shaw.

Desai then made 'herculean' efforts to get Achariar released. Interestingly, Governor Coryndon did not deport Achariar, but released him after a short imprisonment. The latter took his imprisonment philosophically. His ten page letter to Desai had the following paragraph, 'I believe good comes out of evil. No drink or smoke which I do too much. Cannot understand what all the fuss is about. You are doubtless doing all you can to secure my immediate release. Be a good boy and buck up'. It was handwritten in pencil and sent *salaams* to *lalas* (comrades) Varma, Shams-ud-Deen, Mangal Dass, Akbar, Omar, and others.

Sitaram Achariar had several libel cases brought not only by whites but also by Indians. His take on this was: 'I am not seditious but I am not a sycophant – I call a spade a spade and that is what the authorities do not like.' He desired that, 'cases should be undertaken by big wigs such as Verjee, Waljee Hirjee, Nanji Kalidas, Karimji Jivanjee and Jaffer Dewji. Not by paupers like Desai, Achariar and Shams-ud-Deen.'

Muigwithania

In 1928, Achariar and Thakur began to print, in addition to the *Democrat, Muigwithania* (The Reconciler) for the Kikuyu Central Association. It was in Gikuyu and was initially edited by Jomo Kenyatta. A graduate of Bombay University, U K Oza, who had been sent by Gandhi to East Africa in 1924 to assist the Indians in their struggle against discrimination, had befriended the late Desai. Though based in Tanganyika as editor of *Tanganyika Opinion*, he had assisted in editing the *Democrat,* helped Kenyatta to found *Muigwithania* and served for a while as secretary of the EAINC. The paper was banned after the outbreak of WWII and 'Indian agitators' were blamed for creating unrest among the Kikuyu.

Owing to financial constraints, the *Democrat* closed down in 1930. The following year Sitaram Achariar was employed as a secretary by Sir Ali bin Salim but the call of the editorial desk was too great to resist and he returned to India to edit the *Sun*. He visited Kenya in 1938 and passed away in Bombay the next year. One writer compared his demise to a 'dog's death' as he died unknown in some *dharamsala* (guest house) in South India.

Sources: *Patel, Ambu, Sitaram Achariar, Unpublished MS*
Patel, Zarina, 2010
Aiyar, Sana, 2015.

THE EAST AFRICAN CHRONICLE (?1920-1922)

Manilal A Desai, one of Kenya's most dynamic anti-colonial leaders, realised early in his public career that the press was an essential weapon for political warfare. He made full use of the correspondence columns of the *East African Standard* and the *Leader* to publicise his political views but these were, of course, often rejected by the colonial editors. He fully realised the necessity of a newspaper not only for propaganda, but also to rally the community to rise above class and communal differences and to become politically involved. Thus it was that he set about starting his own paper, the *East African Chronicle* (EAC). The earliest copy of the EAC that the author could trace was the issue of Saturday 7August, 1920.

The East African Chronicle (EAC)

Thirty Indian leaders, including a Goan gentleman, met in Nairobi on 1 March, 1918, to start a weekly newspaper in English, Gujarati and Urdu. The initial capital required was estimated at Rs 20,000. It was decided to issue shares of Rs1.00 each so that, as Desai affirmed, 'the humblest of the community may have a chance of participating in this work'. A limited company was formed called the 'The

East African Chronicle Co. Ltd.' with a board of twelve directors. The latter did not take any remuneration and the managing director (Desai) was given a nominal fee of Rs 100 per month. Govind Bhimrao Tadwalker was appointed as the secretary to the board; Sitaram Achariar was appointed to the editorial post; Desai became the managing director while a European called G Mellor, was the general manager.

In May, 1919, Achariar from Mombasa informed Desai that the Chief Justice had confirmed that the Indian Press Act was not in operation in Kenya and hence he was not authorised to interfere with the affairs of the *Chronicle*. 'The days of determining seditious people by smelling their faces are gone . . .' rejoiced Achariar. This explains the inability of the colonial authorities to shut down newspapers on the basis of 'sedition' and the expediency to fines and jail terms.

The *East African Chronicle* was published as a mouthpiece of the EAINC which in turn supported it both financially and organisationally. In it, Desai published the many

grievances of the Indians, and of Africans, over land, labour and wages. He printed articles and pamphlets in Kiswahili for Harry Thuku at a time when no other publisher or printer was ready to do so. Desai's newspaper offices were raided by the police many times for such activities.

Just how effective Indian agitation was is captured in this plea made by Governor Edward Northey. The *East African Chronicle* dated October 15, 1921 ran an article headed 'Governor Edward Northey asks for a truce'. It read: 'We want peace from political strife, for the good of the country which they [Indians] have made their home and which they love. I beg the people of Kenya to pause and take breath while I do my best to arrive at a satisfactory settlement of this most difficult problem

without which we cannot hope for that prosperity which peace should bring us.'

Appeal for funds

The appeal for funds was constant. At one time the *EAC* printed: 'The times are we know very hard and most of

us find ourselves hard put to make both ends meet . . . Mr Desai does not ask for fabulous contributions. He would rather receive a thousand small sums of 5 or 10 florins than that of 500 florins.'

Some of the regular advertisers in the *East African Chronicle* were Suleman Verjee & Sons, C J Khambhatta & Sons, S Imtiazali & Son, and Alibhai Ahamen & Co. These were usually displayed on the front page. Other regulars on the inside pages were A Allidina Visram, Meghji Ahmed & Co, Eastern Bazaar, Abdulla Suleman Damji, The Sharif Agency and Munshiram Kalasingh & Co.

The last issue

The 24 December, 1921 issue had an article on the meeting of Indian and European municipal councillors; and the report a week later of Desai's telegram to the Governor regarding the franchise. This appears to have been the last issue published of the *East African Chronicle*. In the same month, the paper came under threat of closure by the government and ceased publication in April 1922 because it could not meet a court decree for damages awarded against it for libel.

The libel in question was trivial: in the report of a criminal case, the name of Hon. Mr Berkley Cole had been printed instead of that of Hon. Galbraith Cole and this provided the government with the opportunity to remove this thorn in the flesh! The sum needed to save the paper was Rs 50,000, well beyond the finances available to the *Chronicle*. Desai's offer to publish an apology was not accepted as the Government was clearly looking for an excuse to close down the *Chronicle*, and in doing so, silence the voice of the South Asian community.

Harry Thuku who was arrested on 14 March, 1922 wrote: 'It was a difficult time for my Indian friends . . . the police raided the offices of Mr. Desai, and also of his paper, East African Chronicle. You see they wanted to arrest people like Desai, Shams-ud-Deen, and Mangal Dass, but they could not find any proof against them unless they used me. That is why the first night in prison in Nairobi, I got word that if I said those three men had really engineered my whole protest and my Association, then they would let me off. I saw that this was a bluff to put them in along with me. I told them, 'If you want to arrest my "guilty" friends, then start earlier with the Europeans – especially the dangerous ones who taught me English!'

The way forward

Desai then got busy trying to raise funds to start a new publication. On 5 September, 1922, the *Kenya Chronicle* appeared with Sitaram Achariar as the editor but it had a short lifespan. The *Democrat* newspaper then continued as the voice of the Indian community.

Sources: CO533/212, National Archives, London
Rosberg and Nottingham, 1966
Patel, Zarina, 1997.

MANILAL AMBALAL DESAI (1879-1926)

Manilal Desai was born in 1879 in a small village near Surat, India. Trained as a law clerk, he came to Kenya in 1915 and was employed by the Harrison, Salmon and Creswell law firm in Nairobi. He, however, quit in 1917 – one of the reasons being that he was told 'No cigars' yet his white bosses smoked them in the office!

Desai then joined politics and never looked back. He was elected president of the Nairobi Indian Association and later, Secretary of the East Africa Indian National Congress (EAINC). The latter had been set up in 1914 by A M Jeevanjee but had remained largely dormant. Desai

MANILAL AMBALAL DESAI

lifted the community and the Congress from lethargy and political inertia.

Having experienced while in India the power of media to mobilise the masses; Desai made full use of the correspondence columns of newspapers. In 1920, he started his own paper, the *East African Chronicle,* to give publicity to causes nearest to his heart. A European contemporary once declared: 'Its native policy is a danger to this European settlement'. Desai as editor of the *East African Chronicle,* and an outspoken critic of colonial

rule, publicized African grievances over land, labour and wages.

Desai helped Harry Thuku to print leaflets and pamphlets in Kiswahili including later the broadsheet *Tangazo* (TheAnnouncement). The offices of the *Chronicle* became a meeting place of Indian and African political activists for their political work and were in effect the headquarters of the East African Association and its ancillary, the Young Kikuyu Association.

The *Leader*, a Settler contemporary of the *Chronicle*, was constantly and vehemently at loggerheads with Desai's paper. The *East African Standard,* a mouthpiece of the colonial government and the Settlers, were antipathetic to its avowedly anti-colonial stance. In 1920, the *Chronicle* of 16 July printed a letter by Desai which the *East African Standard* had refused to publish. In it he had predicted that 'the coming problem of the colony was the native problem'.

In July, 1921 the *Chronicle* published a letter which the *Standard* had again refused to print. Desai had written: 'The issue is not British or Indian. The real issue, as I put it to the Round Table Conference, is "The Empire for British subjects of the world or for the White?"'

The running antagonism between the *Chronicle* and the *Leader* broke into print from time to time and Desai gave lengthy interviews to the *Chronicle* reporter to counter the accusations made by Davis, the managing editor of the *Leader*. He wrote informative and protest features about the Government policy of segregation, its Indian policy, the Municipal Council debate on land allocation, the franchise, et al.

In 1922, the paper was beset with an expensive libel suit engineered by the government and was forced to close.

Desai himself lived a life of subsistence. In July 1924, at a meeting of the Standing Committee of the EAINC held in Jeevanjee Villa in Mombasa; Shrimati Sarojini Naidu was in the chair and it was resolved to give 35 pounds monthly to Desai for his maintenance.

Subsequently Desai used the *Democrat* and the paper he set up briefly, the *Kenya Chronicle*, to air his views. However in 1924, Desai became one of the five members 'nominated to the Legislative Council to represent the Indian electoral area. He took the requisite oath on November 12, the others nominated were Shams-ud-Deen, Pandya, Kassim and Nehra.

This new responsibility and the closure of his newspapers appear to have moved Desai away from his journalistic activity. But not for long as, soon after the May meeting of the Legislative Council, Desai set off with his friend, Sitaram Achariar on a tour of East Africa to collect subscriptions and donations for their paper, the *Democrat*. But on 15 July, 1926, during this tour he suddenly fell ill in Bukoba and died. The death left the Indian community stunned.

As a token of gratitude to him, all sections of the Indian Community combined to collect funds to erect a lasting memorial to him. In time the Desai Memorial Hall was erected; the funds were contributed by all members of the South Asian community regardless of religious or organizational affiliation. It was situated on Tom Mboya Street (then Victoria Street) next to the Fire Brigade Station. Behind it was an open ground called Azad Maidan (Freedom Ground). Desai Memorial Hall became a meeting place for African and Indian politicians and housed the offices of the East African Trade Union Congress and a well-stocked and much used library. In 1993, a group of 'trustees' sold this historic building

to a private developer who immediately proceeded to demolish it.

Source: Patel, Zarina, 2010.

KENYA DAILY MAIL (1926-1963)

The 1923 Annual Report of the East Africa Indian National Congress (EAINC) stated that:

It is high time for the Indian community to wake up from their lethargic slumber and have a daily paper which can be the only effective weapon of success in the political struggle under present circumstances.

In January 1924, the EAINC held its fifth session in Mombasa and Sarojini Naidu, a member of the Working Committee of India's National Congress, was the president elect. During her stay in Jeevanjee Villa she met with Jaganath Bhavanishankar Pandya who was the secretary of the EAINC.

She stressed on him the pressing need to have a newspaper that could serve as a voice of the Indian community in Kenya and East Africa. Manilal Desai's *East Africa Chronicle* had had to close in 1922 after being slapped with heavy libel charges by the colonial authorities. The *Democrat*, which had in 1923 taken over as the voice of the EAINC, was actually the mouthpiece of Sitaram Achariar - a somewhat cantankerous editor prone to sensational reporting.

Pandya had come to East Africa in 1907 and had engaged in commercial activities from printing to ironmongery. Like several other immigrants from India, he had come to Kenya as a businessman but had been driven into politics by the colonial circumstances. Resident in Mombasa, he founded the *Kenya Daily Mail (KDM)* which was launched

on 17 June, 1927 at a public meeting of Indians in the Kenya Cinema. Unlike Desai and Achariar, he believed the drive to end racial discrimination and introduce the common roll could be achieved, not by confrontation, but by petition, resolution and cooperation.

The meeting was presided over by Alibhai Mulla Jeevanjee and had Srinivasa Sastri, India's first Agent to the Republic of South Africa, as the chief guest. The paper had English and Gujarati sections - Ambalal Z Patel, Poet Jeevanlal Bhrambatt and Ishwarlal Vasa were the editors of the Gujarati Section. In 1945, Mr Manubhai Lalji Bhatia became *KDM's* editor of the English section, before him there was an Englishman, Mr Dolton. Another editor was Mohanlal Rupani. The *KDM* was popular among the business community as it reported news from India and brought readers local news as well as news from Uganda and Tanganyika.

Its 13 November, 1938, issue demanded a 'definite promise of equality in the status of our community in all three territories'. The paper basically reported events, published correspondence and articles by contributors and interviews of African leaders overseas. Its coverage was wide-ranging but essentially anti-imperialist and anti-colonialist. It published a Gujarati translation of a speech by Stalin addressing issues of imperialism, fascism, capitalist wars and the contest for business and markets abroad, the China-Japan war and the Spanish Civil war. Makhan Singh often used the platform to further his trade union activities.

A correspondent, Mr Batlivala, discussed the ideological merits of a 'true Congressman'. 'Even right wingers are anti-imperialist ...,' he insisted. The 22 December, 1937 issue had an open letter written by the League Against Communalism to M D Gautama, the acting president of the Nairobi Hindu Union. In the campaign for nominations to the Legco, the *KDM* supported C B Madan whom it described as 'a young but intelligent politician and diplomat ... popular among the younger generation ... the candidate most likely to promote and preserve the solidarity of the Indian community'.

In July 1926, the *KDM* ran a special edition on the death of Manilal Desai – this highly revered leader was in Bukoba with Sitaram Achariar on a fund-raising mission to start a newspaper when he suffered a heart attack.

Ten years later in May 1936, the *KDM* recorded the death of Alibhai Mulla Jeevanjee with an obituary titled 'The Grand Old Man of Kenya'. It described Jeevanjee as 'not a man of much education or fine words, but having indomitable courage and will power which gave him confidence and strength to express opinions freely and without fear of anybody ... it was this courage and frankness which had made him a respected and honoured leader of the Indian community'.

J B Pandya died in 1942 of a heart attack and the responsibility of his business and the paper then fell upon his younger brother, Ravishankar B Pandya. The paper now supported the policies of the more liberal A B Patel, J B's political successor. Unlike the more militant *East African Chronicle*, and later the *Colonial Times* and *Daily Chronicle*; the *Kenya Daily Mail* represented those who wished to see developments along constitutional lines and this more conservative approach probably ensured its survival. Patel and Pandya campaigned around the country to discredit the *Daily Chronicle* and in the Legislative Council declared, apparently without foundation, that the newspaper was receiving 'financial assistance from abroad'. 'Being an old establishment, we had very sound financial support of our local and

overseas advertisers, as well as subscribers,' said Mahesh C Kavi, a journalist in *KDM*.

During the fifties the *KDM* became increasingly more supportive of Africans and declared that none of the immigrant races had any right to flout the unanimous wishes of the sons of the soil. 'This land belongs to the African and in all affairs, political and economic, it is their word which must count,' it said.

The *KDM* was distributed all over East Africa - Kenya, Uganda, Tanganyika and Zanzibar. A few copies went to Congo, Burundi, Mozambique and South Africa as well. These were *KDM's* weekly edition, the daily edition was mainly for Mombasa, a few hundred copies were sent to Nairobi. The average circulation was five thousand of the weekly, and two thousand of the daily. The newspaper lasted 37 years, closing in 1964, a year after Kenya's independence.

Sources: Gregory, Robert G, 1971
*   Ibid, 1993*
*   Patel, Zarina, 1997*
*   Ibid, 2006*
*   Opinion, 26 November, 2004*
*   Durrani, Shiraz, 2006*

COLONIAL TIMES (1933-1962)

On Saturday 1st July, 1933, a little 16-page journal called The *Colonial Times*, a politico-social weekly, saw the light of day. This was six years after the appearance of the *Kenya Daily Mail* and shortly after the closure of the *Democrat*. The Colonial Times Printing Works was a family undertaking, exploiting 'free' labour and conforming to the business model of most Asian and

African printing firms in colonial Kenya. It was owned and run by the brothers, Girdhari Lal Vidyarthi (GL) and Vanshi Dhar, their father, Sham Dass, and their nephew, Sarya Vrat; and was situated along Reata Road (then Grogan) Road in Nairobi.

GL was the publisher and he had already enlisted the support of Dr A C L de Sousa, a well-known Goan medical practitioner who had a flare for journalism having run his own newspaper, *Fairplay,* and been associated with the *Democrat* and the *Pioneer.* Dr de Sousa being a committed anti-colonialist, was enthusiastic but warned GL of the hazards of the journalistic field in Kenya, both as regards the financial success of the venture, as well as its legal implications. He offered to take charge of the editorial policy of the paper, provided GL could shoulder the rest of the responsibilities of a weekly press.

The *Colonial Times* which started as a 'small, modest weekly in Nairobi', became a daily and was a strident voice for freedom from British colonialism. Its motto was 'Frank, Free and Fearless'. Dr de Sousa wrote the editorials

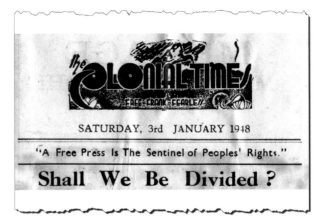

unfailingly for almost fifteen years; week in and week out, the doctor pleaded the cause of the Asian community with zeal, sincerity and steadfastness. Eminent journalist as he was, with a vast store of facts and figures at his finger-tips, his forthright and convincing writings in the *Colonial Times* won him praise and approbation from all 'reasonable' persons. As the paper established a name for itself for searching analyses of contemporary problems and guidance in their solution, the people developed respect for its views.

A quotation from the first Editorial Note in its issue of 1st July, 1933, headed 'About Ourselves,' shows the scope of the editorial. 'It is customary for the first issue of a journal to express itself on its policy. Our policy… is a very modest one … Our policy is service in its simplest meaning. We must make it very clear to our supporters and to the Indian public generally, that we do not profess to belong to any party and that the common good is the only ideal we have set before us. Primarily, we stand for the great body of Indians who have settled in this Colony, but we are not so conservative and exclusive as to exclude from our scope of work, Indians in the Colonies generally and the various non-Indians who naturally share with us the privileges and disabilities common to all of us. In this sense, we hope to make the Journal a cosmopolitan organ, always ready to render every possible assistance to every deserving cause.' The goal, in short, was to champion the cause of the under-dog.

It was able to stay afloat largely due to 'Indian large- and small-scale commercial activities in the whole of East Africa. It included several pages devoted exclusively to advertisements for shipping and insurance companies, car sellers, mechanics, accountants and lawyers' firms, as well as glowing notices for medical products, hotels, restaurants and – not least – Indian films performed in privately owned cinemas.'

Circulation of the *Colonial Times* reached over ten thousand and its pages consistently aired the grievances of both Asians and Africans, thus reviving the militant journalism of Desai and Achariar. The newspaper attacked the colonial government on the inequalities of Kenyan society and focused on issues ranging from the White Highlands' reservation to communal electoral rolls and racial discrimination.

Dr de Sousa was joined in time by a group of zealous young South Asians which included Haroon Ahmed, DK Sharda, Chanan Singh, Nathoo Amlani, and Pranlal Sheth who served as sub-editor. The *Colonial Times* now made vigorous attacks on the white highlands reservation, communal electoral rolls and all manifestations of racial discrimination; its circulation reached 10,000.

The paper lived up fully to its motto of 'Frank, Free and Fearless'. Its 5 January, 1946 issue carried a letter to the editor penned by one of the Indian political activists, W H Sohan, which read: 'Anybody outside a Lunatic Asylum can safely perceive the very basis of the Administration in Kenya, namely Colour Bar. We need not bother our heads whether this is practised under the guise of statutory legislation or convenient administrative practices. One wonders if Britain is carrying two faces under one hood. There appear to be two distinct sets of British ideals, one for home consumption and another for export abroad.'

This public denunciation of colonial injustice was a real threat to the authorities who then charged GL with sedition and jailed him twice. While he was in prison, Chanan Singh took over as part-time editor of the *Colonial Times*, and was marked as 'anti-British' by the Intelligence. GL's brother, Vanshi Dar, was conservative and started placing restrictions on the team of journalists. DK Sharda was told he could not write for Karanja's *Blitz*

in India while employed by the Vidyarthis. There was also a growing divergence of interests – the *Colonial Times* largely focussed on the freedom movement in India; the younger journalists were more concerned with the anti-colonial struggle in East Africa. In 1947, Ahmed, Sheth, Sharda, Amlani and Chanan Singh left to found the *Daily Chronicle*. In 1948, Dr de Sousa handed over editorship to N Thakur and others.

During the Emergency and the Mau Mau insurrection, the *Colonial Times* came under constant surveillance by the CID and by 1958; European firms had virtually withdrawn their advertisements. GL now handed over financial and editorial control of the paper to Bachulal T Gathani, the Nairobi commercial and political leader and his son, Batuk, a journalist. They continued GL's policy of combating European privilege and all forms of repression and discrimination as well as welcoming articles from Africans. Tom Mboya wrote exclusively in the *Colonial Times*. Catherine Hoskyns, who worked briefly in the editorial section in 1957, told the author that she worked closely with Thakur and Ahmed, and Priya Ramrakha who provided most of the photographs. She would also meet Tom Mboya and Dennis Akumu and all of them would visit 'whites only' cafes, much to the annoyance of the settler community. She particularly mentions the 'Whites Only' toilet in the press.

During 1959-60, the paper became a forum for debate on the constitutional issues of the Lancaster House conferences. Over the years, they were thrice raided by police, GL and Haroon Ahmed were jailed for sedition and VG Patel, the major shareholder together with Amar Singh, Temal Singh and Besant, were heavily fined. In 1962, after struggling for 29 years, the *Colonial Times* ceased publication.

Sources: *Frederiksen, Bodil Folke, 2011*
Rattansi, Piyo – email 2014
Vidyarthi, Girdhari Lal, obituary in 1959
memorial brochure of Dr ACL de Sousa
Gregory, Robert G, 1993
Patel, Zarina, 2006
Catherine Hoskyns, interviewed by Zarina Patel,
December 2014

GIRDHARI LAL VIDYARTHI (1907-1985)

GL Vidyarthi was born Girdhari Lal Horra, the son of Shamdass Bootamal Horra, in 1907 in Mombasa. Shamdass arrived in Kenya in 1889 and began employment as a stationmaster on the Uganda railway. Girdhari Lal Horra began his education at the Indian Primary School, at the time a makeshift *banda* where today's Kencom building stands on Moi Avenue. This was followed by a stint in India during which he spent time at one of the Gurukul schools, noted for its emphasis on intense study, physical activity, and spiritual reflection.

Returning to Nairobi, GL enrolled at the Duke of Gloucester Secondary School, later to be called Jamhuri High School, where he completed his final Standard Eight examinations. A special class was created at the School for GL and two other exceptional students to sit for the London Matriculation Exam, which GL passed with distinction. A plaque bearing G LVidyarthi's name in recognition of his academic achievements at the former Duke of Gloucester Secondary School has since been torn down.

Girdhari Lal Vidyarthi began employment in the Ministry of Transport. It was during his spare time, however, that his passion for journalism began to manifest itself and he adopted the penname '*Vidyarthi,*' a Hindi word meaning 'student'. He began producing a hand written,

GIRDHARI LAL VIDYARTHI

trilingual (English, Hindi, Urdu) newspaper called *Mitrom* (Friendship). Aged just twenty two, GL was already displaying an effervescent nationalism against the injustices of the colonial regime and developing a philosophy of liberation fostered by his experiences in India and the day to day oppression of colonial rule in Kenya.

GL was a radical. He, Haroon Ahmed, Chanan Singh and others joined the Young Atheists Society of Nairobi. Still in his early twenties, with a close friend, he built a bomb-like contraption and planned to detonate it at the

Colonial Government Headquarters at State House. But the plan was aborted and instead GL channelled his anti-colonial anger into militant journalism; it was this that gave birth to the Colonial Times Printing Works and the *Colonial Times* newspaper in 1933.

Under the motto 'Frank, Free and Fearless,' Vidyarthi in cooperation with the Goan physician, ACL de Sousa, and his team of young writers which included Pranlal Seth, DK Sharda, Haroon Ahmed, Chanan Singh and Nathoo Amlani, spearheaded the politics of journalism in Kenya and provided a pivotal channel of expression for emerging freedom fighters like Tom Mboya and Jomo Kenyatta. Vidyarthi's radical and unwavering fight saw him convicted and sentenced to prison on three separate occasions. Indeed, it signified a campaign for press freedom and unrestricted national expression that was to last not only throughout the independence struggle but also well into the contemporary period.

In 1945, GL established two newspapers in African languages. *Habari Za Dunia* edited by FM Ruhinda, was the very first Swahili newspaper in East Africa to be printed by a private press. The Luo weekly paper *Ramogi*, edited by Achieng Oneko, soon followed it. Oneko shared Vidyarthi's journalistic vision. 'I am very happy with you Bwana Vidyarthi,' he said. 'You have answered the *Nakuru Weekly News . . .* which writes very bad things about young African leaders'.

In April of 1945 Vidyarthi was convicted for sedition on two separate occasions. His first sentence earned him a one hundred pound fine. The second sedition charge was earned after Vidyarthi published an article criticizing the conscription of African soldiers to fight British wars around the Empire. GL exposed the injustice where wounded African soldiers returned penniless to Kenya whereas their white counterparts were rewarded with land and property throughout the country. The story resulted in him being sentenced to four months of hard labour in a Nairobi prison. After one of his releases from jail, he was invited to open the annual session of the Natal Indian Congress, but declined.

Undaunted, in September of 1946, GL invited Johnstone Kamau wa Ngengi, who was to become Kenya's first President as Jomo Kenyatta, to his home in Westlands. Over tea, Vidyarthi offered to reserve a section of the *Colonial Times* as a special forum for the Kenya African Union. This association with one of Kenya's most prominent African anti-colonial agitators made his second arrest practically inevitable. In May, 1947 he was sentenced to eighteen months in prison after an allegedly seditious letter was printed in *Habari Za Dunia*, which was then banned.

Frederiksen describes this in great detail: 'Of the three charges of sedition against the editor and owner, two concerned material in English and one the publication of an editorial in Gujarati. The *Colonial Times* of 1 June, 1946, covered the trial fully, including the subsequent appeals in April and a correspondence between the Indian Association and the government that led to reduction of the sentences from "hard labour" to "ordinary prison"'.

'An earlier case against the *Colonial Times* had been brought under the Defence Regulations in September 1945. Here the editor, G. L. Vidyarthi, was convicted of having published seditious material, an editorial headed "Burma Week", and was sentenced to a fine of "100 pounds or three months of imprisonment with hard labour" (*Colonial Times*, 19 January 1946). In the present case, as well as in the earlier one, in order to get a conviction of sedition the state had to prove that the

material in question was intended to create divisions between various communities or races in Kenya, and this is where the question of language and attribution of responsibility become central.

'The editorial now under accusation concerned British rule in India and East Africa under the heading, "The Old Deceitful Scheme of Creating Division". It was written by the editor of the Gujarati section of the newspaper, Haroon Ahmed. After an introduction accusing the British race of "blossoming" on the "blood, sweat and tears of the people of foreign countries", and of being unrivalled in the art of separating people by splitting up and thus creating "disunion" and a "rule of terror" in India, the article went on to describe the "longing of the Whites to appropriate the land of the Black men in East Africa and to enjoy exuberantly its green and fertile soil". However, the presence of Indians in Kenya made this project difficult; they "pricked like thorns", and the British wanted to draw out the thorns "when the time comes" (*Colonial Times*, 9 February 1946).

'Under questioning it became clear that as Vidyarthi, the editor of the English section, did not know Gujarati, Ahmed had assumed responsibility for its publication. It further emerged that this was the normal procedure of dividing labour and responsibility. Seeking to refute the allegation of the publications creating "ill will" between the different communities, the counsel for the defence questioned Mr Motichand, a "Nairobi merchant", to gauge the possible effect of the article. The latter responded that "he had not experienced any ill will towards any community after reading it". Another witness, an inspector of the Criminal Investigation Department, Mr Singh, told the Court that he "had never come across a Gujarati-knowing European or African". Therefore, argued the counsel, "no Britisher or African could have been excited by its contents".

'Haroon Ahmed himself argued that articles making similarly critical comments were widely available in Kenya, both in Gujarati and English. In support, he read out several passages from The *East African Standard*, publications from the South African Information Office, and a work called *Strangers in India* by one Penderas Moonas. In doing so, he also demonstrated that the measures the government took were pitifully inadequate as against the growing tide of publications available in a modern printing culture. The brothers Vidyarthi and Dhar were found guilty and sentenced to either substantial fines or some months of "hard labour".

'The second charge concerned a letter to the editor by a political activist, the ex-secretary of the Nairobi Indian Association, W. L. Sohan, which had first appeared in December 1945, comparing the condition of Indians under British rule in India to that of Jews in the Belsen concentration camp during the Second World War: "Belsen has never impressed me. For us, the Indians, whole of India has been virtually a big Belsen camp" (*Colonial Times*, 9 February 1946).

'Sohan was not represented and used the courtroom as a political platform. Like Vidyarthi, he was convicted of sedition and sentenced to four months of "rigorous" imprisonment. In his statement after the sentence Sohan delivered a vigorous address to the public: "I am a British slave myself. That arises from the status of my country at the present moment . . . .My idea is to spread the spirit of revolt for I believe that there lies the salvation of the suffering and enslaved humanity, brown or black, Asiatic or Occidental" (*Colonial Times*, 9 February 1946).

'. . . The convicted journalists were applauded inside the court room, hailed by a crowd outside it, and accompanied to the jail by hundreds of supporters. The subsequent days saw protests and demonstrations in the streets and community halls of Nairobi, organized by a newly established Civil Liberties Union of Kenya, the Indian Printers Union and other groups. They were fired by the perceived racial and anti-Indian sentiment expressed in the sentence, and by the government offensive against freedom of the press. The conviction was noted in India, particularly in Communist-affiliated circles – the *Blitz* newspaper sent a telegram, "We salute you Martyred Crusader" – and among individuals and the numerous Indian political organizations in East Africa, whose protests were made public in the *Colonial Times* (16 February,1946). The organizations included Indian Youth (in Tanga), the Indian Youth League (in Kisumu) and the Youth League (in Jinja). The reaction demonstrated the effectiveness of political and information links across the ocean from India to connected regions of East Africa.'

On his release, GL continued with the *Colonial Times* despite the fact that his brother's conservative management during GL's prison sentence had brought about the exodus of the paper's original staff of writers. Between 1953 and 1958 GL concentrated on publishing the new vernacular newspapers which were printed by militant Africans and, in many instances, subsidized by South Asians. *Jicho*, a Kiswahili newspaper edited by NS Thakur, had a top circulation of 18,000 which showed that it was widely read by Africans. After 4 years, Henry Gathigira took over from Thakur. Other papers were Fred Kubai's *Sauti ya Mwafrika*, Francis Khamisi's *Mwalimu* and Henry Mwaniki Moria's *Mumengerere* (The Knife). Vidyarthi's publications always remained under close scrutiny during this period and any subversive materials were met with heavy fines for the paper's shareholders and prison sentences for the offending writers.

Vidyarthi and his press in Reata Road were always closely associated with the young politicians of the pre-independence era. His newspapers became synonymous with names like Mboya, Odinga, Moi, Kenyatta, Oneko and Koinange. They discovered in GL a publisher who was willing to disseminate their views and nationalistic appeals despite the ever-present threat of official reprisal at the hands of a reactionary colonial regime.

The integrity GL displayed towards his journalistic vocation can never be faulted. Any politician living in Kenya who wanted to speak their mind and share their opinion with an audience knew that GL would be willing to publish it for them. And never mind if it meant that colonial officers would come knocking on the doors of his printing press to investigate the 'seditious' statements a few days later. His spirit lives on in the Colourprint Press run by his sons, Bhushan, Anil and Sudhir.

GL passed away in 1985 in Nairobi. He is best remembered as a journalist of humble courage; and the integrity he displayed in a pioneering fight for all Kenyans and their future generations to be able to speak for themselves and their freedom in a 'frank, free and fearless' manner.

Sources: Seidenberg, Dana, 1983
Patel, Zarina, 2006
AwaaZ, Issue 2, 2002.

BALDEV MOOLRAJ

Moolraj Mediratta, Baldev's father, sailed from Punjab, India, to East Africa in 1914. World War I was declared while he was on the high seas and the ship was torpedoed but managed to limp into the Tanga harbour under German protection. He then made his way to Mombasa where he joined the post office and served as postmaster general, later being posted to Kisumu. He ultimately settled in Elementaita where he bought a general goods shop from a Nayar family. Business was good as the shop catered to the surrounding prominent white settlers such as Delamere.

Baldev Moolraj was born in 1925 in Elementaita. After studying up to Standard 6 in Nakuru, in 1941 he moved to Nairobi to attend Jamhuri High School (then Government Indian Boys School). There he stayed with his brother-in-law, Gidhari Lal Vidyarthi who was publishing the English/Gujerati *Colonial Times* newpaper; so Baldev started a weekly column under the heading 'Student Affairs'.

In 1942 he participated in a student strike – an art student had drawn a pencil portrait of Jawaharlal Nehru who was then one of the many brave anti-colonial leaders in India and a close ally of Mahatma Gandhi. The art teacher, A Verma, framed it and hung it up. But the head master, an Englishman by the name of D Somen, ordered it taken down. When Verma refused saying, 'this is art not politics', Somen took it down himself and smashed it.

Word spread through the entire school and the students decided to go on strike. They decided to assemble in the school compound and refused to go to class. The strike lasted over a week and was led by a Form IV boy named Mohamed Alam. Baldev and others mobilised the Arya Girls' School across the road, the Government Indian Girls' School opposite Jeevanjee Gardens and the Muslim Girls School in Park Road – all of which joined in the strike. The art teacher was dismissed together with 52 other students. Baldev escaped the dragnet.

After completing his matriculation exam, Baldev moved back to Elementaita to help his father. From there he reported for the *Colonial Times* on happenings around

BALDEV MOOLRAJ

Nakuru and Indian Association matters. His older brother, Harnam Das, worked for the *Colonial Times* together with D K Sharda, Haroon Ahmed and Pranlal Sheth.

In 1947 the three journalists left to set up the *Daily Chronicle* and Baldev joined them in Nairobi. It was an amicable separation as the *Chronicle* was to be more Kenya-centered than the India-centered *Colonial Times*. Both papers were unabashedly anti-colonial in their overall policy and the journalists were often in trouble

with the colonial authorities. Baldev reported mainly on matters of the Legislative Council, Indian Associations, Indian Women's Association and the Congress.

The government made several attempts to muzzle the press – the East African Indian National Congress at its 20th session held in Eldoret in August, 1950 and presided over by J M Nazareth, had two resolutions on this topic. One entitled 'Freedom of the Press' expressed 'grave alarm [at] the recent legislation providing for drastic penalties by way of confiscation of printing machinery, etc. of newspapers ....'. This was moved by M V Dave and seconded by Baldev Moolraj. The other resolution referred to the ban imposed on the *Daily Chronicle* and stated that the ban should be removed. It was moved by K P Shah and seconded by Chanan Singh.

Baldev had been appointed to the Executive and Standing committees of the East African Indian National Congress having been proposed by Chanan Singh who was then the General Secretary. He also served as the president of the Nakuru Indian Association. Baldev remembered one particular incident when the *East African Standard* reported that a visiting VIP had been told that Indian women were available for his pleasure. The *Chronicle* took up the matter and asked the Mayor, Norman Harris, to comment. His Worship stated that he had consulted his Indian council members and they had no objections. Baldev was a close friend of Cllr B S Sehmi's younger brother and was given the facts emphatically by the Cllr: 'At no time were we consulted, we were "informed".'

When Baldev conveyed the story to D K Sharda, the *Chronicle* editor, he was asked to write it up. It appeared in two consecutive issues as an editorial with the title, 'The Mayor's Lie'. This was one of the many statements in the *Daily Chronicle* which drove the colonial government

to manoeuvre the closing down of the newspaper in 1951; and its subsequent sale to more conservative forces.

Meanwhile Baldev's older brother had died so he then moved back to Elementaita to help in the family business, and expanded it to Mau Narok and Nakuru. He joined the East Africa Indian National Congress and later became president of the Nakuru Indian National Congress. In 1954, he could converse in Gikuyu and was anointed as a Kikuyu elder and given the name Kamau. In 2005 he retired and emigrated to the U K with his wife to be with his daughter who had settled there. His son and family continue to reside in Nairobi and Baldev and his wife are regular visitors to their home country.

Source: Baldev Moolraj, interviewed by Zarina Patel, 2013.

EAST AFRICAN KIRTI (1936-1939)

The *East African Kirti* and its earlier versions, *Kenya Worker* and *Kirti*, published between 1936 and 1939 were organs of the workers' unions led by Makhan Singh. The word 'kirti' means 'worker' in the Punjabi language and it was the alternate name for the Ghadar Party, a revolutionary organisation with its roots in the Punjab in India and its international front based in San Francisco, USA. Formed in 1913, its goal was the overthrow of British rule in India through armed struggle.

The Ghadar Party was active globally in 22 countries including Kenya where its members received and circulated the party newspaper, Ghadar. In 1916 it was estimated that one million copies of Ghadar were printed each week by the Party. Just before the outbreak of World War II, a group of Indians in Kenya were arrested and charged with 'Ghadrite' activities. The charges against them included 'possessing seditious publications, assisting the enemy, and spreading false intelligence and alarmist reports'. Some were deported, others imprisoned and a few hanged.

This crackdown was replicated in other colonies and on a very wide scale in India. The Party reorganised itself between the two World Wars and Kenya became an underground conduit for revolutionaries en route to Moscow. One of its chief protagonists was Gopal Singh who stood in for Makhan Singh as Acting Secretary General of the Labour Trade Union of East Africa during the latter's detention in India, 1940-1945.

British Intelligence kept a close eye on the activities of Kenya's Ghadarites. A report dated 1934 noted that [the group] had 'raised subscription for Kirti; corresponded with the editor and with Teja Singh alias Lal Singh of Sansarpur on Communist organisation among Indians and Africans of Kenya . . . asked Lal Singh for Rules of the Punjabi Kirti Kisan Party and Communist literature'. A 1938 entry states: 'Contributed to the *Kirtikehar* of Meerut and asked the AITUC to ventilate grievances East African workers, Invited by the "Friends of Africa" organisation to go to London to study industrial organization . . .'.

Gopal Singh with his 'progressive ideas and association with the freedom struggle' was active in Sikh institutions in Kenya. The Singh Saba situated in the downtown area of Nairobi was a front organisation for the Ghadar/Kirti party. The Ghadar activists in Kenya learnt valuable lessons on the appropriate forms and contents of publications as tools in their struggle. These lessons became part of the growing experience in the communication field in the country.

Sources: Patel, Zarina, 2006
Durrani, Shiraz, 2006
Chandan, Amarjit, 2004
India Office: Intelligence Reports in File on 'Kenya Colony Intelligence and Security Summaries', 1947-48.

MAKHAN SINGH (1913-1973)

Makhan Singh was born in 1913 in a village called Gharjak now in Pakistan. He grew up at a time when India was still the 'jewel in the British crown' and so experienced both colonial oppression and the struggle for freedom. His father was an itinerant carpenter who arrived in Kenya in 1920, Makhan Singh followed in 1927.

After graduating from the then Duke of Gloucester School he joined his father's Khalsa Printing Press which functioned as a disseminator of Punjabi and Gujarati texts and business stationery. Here his interaction with his fellow workers became the basis of his life-long struggle against both colonial and class oppression. Drawing on his knowledge of trade union activities in India, Makhan Singh set about organising at first the Indian, and soon after, the African workers. Starting from his work place in his father's printing press, he organised a press workers' union. The Labour Trade Union of Kenya was formed in 1935 and Makhan Singh started publishing a hand-written monthly pamphlet called *Kenyan Worker*. After three issues, two in Punjabi and one in Urdu, it was replaced by a weekly Punjabi newspaper called *Kirti* (Worker), later re-issued as the *East African Kirti*.

The pamphlets contained articles about the Union's policies and news about workers' struggles and national and international news of general interest. Clearly the authorities kept a close watch on these publications and

MAKHAN SINGH

Makhan Singh was secretly monitored by the British Government; notes found in the India Office Intelligence Reports vouch for this:
Note 1: A letter entitled a 'United Non-European Front', in the *Chronicle* of 30/10/48, signed by Benjamin Mangu, Executive Officers of the Kenya National Union; the letter was in fact drafted by Makhan Singh.'

Note 2: '1936: Visited India; worked for Ghadr and Communist causes; attended conferences, 'associated with revolutionaries'; 'requested despatch to Moscow';

Achieng Oneko (far left), Jomo Kenyatta, Makhan Singh, Jaramogi Oginga Odinga

'Full extent of the grave threat Makhan Singh's activities pose to imperial rule in Kenya now becoming fully evident: The civil service is next on Makhan Singh's list of employees which he wishes to unionise and thereby subvert.'

While on a trip to India Makhan Singh was detained there by the British authorities from 1940-1945. Under restriction he acted as sub-editor of a newspaper called *Jang-i-Azadi* which was published in Lahore by the Punjab Committee of the Indian Communist Party. Mota

Singh, an ally of Makhan Singh, was also detained 1939-1945; he was a member of the Communist Party of India.

In Kenya, the fledgling unions coalesced and in 1949 an umbrella body was formed: The East African Trade Union Congress. It was banned soon after by the colonial authorities and Kenya's workers lost a forum they are yet to regain. Makhan Singh was detained for eleven years (1950-1961) in the Northern Frontier District of Kenya.

He was released on 22 October, 1961 and returned home in Park Road to a tumultuous welcome. Visitors included

dignitaries no less than Jomo Kenyatta, Jaramogi Oginga Odinga and Achieng Oneko. And yet in the years ahead Makhan Singh was totally side-lined from the political life of the newly independent nation and the workers' movement.

Unbending and seemingly unperturbed, Makhan Singh soldiered on. He wrote two books which remain to date, the only recorded history of the struggles and achievements of Kenya's workers in the colonial era. He passed away on 15 May, 1973.

Sources: Patel, Zarina, 2006
India Office: Intelligence Reports in File on 'Kenya Colony Intelligence and Security Summaries', 1947-48.

DAILY CHRONICLE (1947-1964)

The *Daily Chronicle* was set up by a group of young radical journalists, press workers and financiers. Most of the journalists worked part time on the *Colonial Times* newspaper owned by the G L Vidyarthi family. When GL was imprisoned for sedition in 1947, his brother, Vanshi Dar, stepped into his shoes but his conservative and authoritarian style soon came into conflict with this group of journalists. Another factor was that the main focus of the *Colonial Times* was on India's independence struggle, victory and Partition in India whereas the younger writers were much more concerned about the anti-colonial struggle taking place in Kenya. The *East African Tribune* was launched for a brief period to act as a spoiler.

Early 1947, the group attended a public rally addressed by Jomo Kenyatta - it was then that they decided to establish their own newspaper. D K Sharda, Haroon

Ahmed, and Pranlal Sheth committed their full time services to publishers Govind Rawal and Natwarlal Amlani. A press was established in Nairobi's Njugu Lane in the then Bazaar area. Financial contributions came from Amlani's brother; from Prabudas, Pranlal's brother and from Ibrahim, brother of Salim Yakub who was related to Haroon and was a supporter of the *Chronicle*. After a trial run with a non-entity as editor, Sharda took up the post and Abu Alarakhia did the type setting on the monotype machine. 'He was very fast in his work,' says Salim.

Salim and his brother owned a car garage and so provided transport when necessary. It was the garage to which Kenyatta brought his car for servicing. The Chronicle press became a meeting place for the nationalists; Makhan Singh, Pio Gama Pinto, Achhroo Kapila, Hassan Rattansi, A S Rao as well as John Keen, Njoroge Mungai, Achieng Oneko, Tom Mboya, Fred Kubai and Charles Njonjo were frequent visitors. 'Many were the conversations in which bitterness about the colour bar, racism and exploitation would be expressed and lamented about; but the invariable conclusion would be a hopeless 'yes, but what can we do?" I know what we can do,' Makhan Singh would assert, and captivate the others. 'Class struggle hey *bhai* (brother),' he would declare.

The above was narrated to me by Prof. Piyo Rattansi, Hassan Rattansi's younger brother, who was then a cub reporter who joined the team in the early years. Unfortunately he was not able to write his experiences for this book. He also stated that the *Chronicle* journos worked for long hours without pay. 'The government prosecuted us so many times. There were frequent police raids which disrupted our work and cost us money. In addition to providing the copy, we had to get up at five in the morning to print and publish the paper ourselves on an antiquated press. After collating we delivered the paper ourselves on bicycles.'

The *Daily Chronicle* pursued anti-colonial and pro-African policies which were singled out for special criticism by the Colonial Office. It charged the paper with 'blatant bias against both Government and the European, never missing an opportunity of supporting African claims, however fantastic or subversive'. The *Daily Chronicle* was tarred with a 'Leftist' label immediately after it began publication, particularly by pointing to its usage of cartoons by Gabriel who had first supplied them to the *Daily Worker*, a British Communist newspaper. A later bone of contention was Makhan Singh's close ties to the *Chronicle*. In 1947 two newspapers from India, the *People's Age* and *Blitz* were prohibited; the *Chronicle* protested vigorously at the banning.

Jaramogi Odinga writes that, 'The *Daily Chronicle* was the first and only English language newspaper in Kenya to advocate a militant nationalist policy, and to issue a call for the total independence of the colony under majority African rule. There were continuous police raids on the offices of the newspaper and a succession of prosecutions for sedition against the paper, its editors and publishers. It was the *Daily Chronicle* group which had sold us the flatbed printing machine on which the Luo Thrift and Trading Corporation ran off the first African language newspapers in Nairobi and later in Kisumu.'

By establishing relationships with international news agencies other than Reuters, which the staff considered reactionary, the paper was able to inform its readers about freedom movements in other parts of the world. Apart from confronting the colonial machinery, the *Daily Chronicle* journalists had to contend with adverse reactions from the East Africa Indian National Congress in which they were active members, and for which the paper was a publicity organ. The radical young men exerted pressure directed at reversing the timid trend of the more conservative elements in the leadership of the Congress and in getting the community to cooperate with KAU in a working front against the settlers.

On one occasion the Congress decided to boycott the Legislative Council. However not every member agreed with the resolution, especially so Hon. A B Patel who was one of the three Asian parliamentarians. Piyo then wrote an article entitled, 'The Man who could not Resist'. Earlier Patel had declared in the Legislative Council, apparently without foundation, that the newspaper was receiving 'financial assistance from communists abroad'. Piyo's father, a close friend of Patel, prevailed upon him to retract the story but Piyo stood by what he had written. This led the Congress to cancel its subscription to the paper and Rattansi Senior withdrew Piyo's allowance. The Congress action against the paper did not last long as it needed the publicity but for some time Piyo went around in worn-out clothes!

In May, 1950, the Government of Uganda banned the importation of the *Daily Chronicle* from Nairobi. That same month the paper had addressed a Mr Robinson thus: 'Purely in a spirit of cooperation you should agitate with all the saw-dust in your brain to try and have the definition of "sedition" altered in the Penal Code. Define sedition as the unforgivable sin of demanding freedom for anyone the colour of whose skin is not colourless. THEN you can put the handcuffs on the chaps who seek to dislodge you from your cosy positions of exploitation.'

On 30 March, 1950 Nairobi was raised to the status of 'city'. The East African Trade Union Congress led by Makhan Singh boycotted the celebrations and was refused permission by the police to hold a march of its own. The *Chronicle* team was incensed and suggested setting fire to the main VIP stage but Makhan Singh would not hear of it. 'We communists don't believe in individual terrorism,' he stated. Sharda in his usual jovial and impish manner, teasingly rejoined, 'You believe in collective terrorism!'

It was financial difficulty caused by government repression which brought the enterprise to an end. There were fifty cases of libel registered against the staff, and no European firms would buy advertising space. Constant police surveillance was maintained on the office of the *Daily Chronicle,* the secretary of a Civil Liberties Union was a frequent visitor.

In 1947, soon after its inception, the *Daily Chronicle* was charged with 'making a false statement ' for reporting that 'a party consisting of Police chiefs, the A-G, the Labour Commissioner, and 12 African Police flew to Mombasa, where there was a strike of African labourers at the port, *with definite instructions to fire on the strikers'.* Both editor, Haroon Ahmed, and publisher, Govind Rawal, were charged with sedition. The barrister, Achhroo Kapila, assessed the charge as 'not serious, meriting at the most a small fine' and advised his two friends to plead guilty. All concerned were shocked when the court handed down a conviction of six months' simple imprisonment for Haroon and a fine of Sh. 4,000 or three months' simple imprisonment for Govind. The latter chose to go to prison. The fact is that the Mombasa General Strike was on and the information had been leaked to them by Gurwand Sheth, a civil servant. Haroon refused to reveal his source in court.

In 1952 the *Daily Chronicle* was sold after the Colonial Government had charged it with about 50 cases of libel

and European firms had withdrawn their advertisements in the paper. The last straw was when a Mr Alexander sued the paper for defamation of character. Alexander was a very anti-Asian racist and Sharda being rather hot-headed had written a derogatory article about his daughter. Sharda as editor was charged and fined 50,000/-. Of course the paper had no money. 'We had to beg and borrow money from S M Bhatt, we were now completely broke, so Bhatt took the machines,' says Salim.

The *Daily Chronicle* was bought initially by the A B Patel group and later by M M Bhatt & Sons. Under the new ownership it 'adopted a more moderate policy far removed from the fiery stance of the young radicals'. They set up the Express Printers Ltd and employed Michael Fernandes as editor. In the Government's view, however, the paper was still too extreme. Fernandes was declared *persona non grata* and had to leave the country.

In 1950 Pio Gama Pinto had made his first foray into journalism when he was still employed as a civil servant and wrote reports on hockey matches for the *Daily Chronicle.* After it was sold he briefly became its editor but was detained by the colonial government. The paper then took an even more conservative stand and employed an editor from India, Jawaharlal F Rodrigues, former assistant editor of the *Times of India.* In 1963 Rodrigues joined the *Daily Nation*; the *Chronicle* was sold again and closed down a year later.

Sources: Patel, Zarina, 2006
           India Office: Intelligence Reports in File on 'Kenya Colony Intelligence and Security Summaries', 1947-48
           Gregory, Robert G., 1993
           Seidenberg, Dana, 1983
           Oginga, Odinga, 1967.

HAROON AHMED (1912-2002)

Haroon Ahmed was born in 1912 in a tin shack opposite the then Supreme Hotel in Nairobi. His father, Ahmed Ebrahim, came to Kenya in 1890 and was soon criss-crossing all over Maasai land as a trader. The family was among the founders of Narok town and also established a shop in Kijabe.

Haroon had a strong aversion to injustice and quit school because of the 'unreasonableness' of the teacher. Virtually self-taught, he joined G L Vidyarthi's *Colonial Times* as a proof-reader, clerk, salesman and accountant but was soon writing the editorials thus replacing A B Patel who had gone on leave. His mastery of the Gujarati language combined with his incisive anti-colonial analyses shot him into the limelight. 'Haroon's editorials in the *Colonial Times* were quite sensational. Several calls were made and letters written to the publisher commenting on the new editor. In three years the newspaper's circulation shot up to 7000 in paid subscribers and there were queues outside the office on Friday evenings when the paper came off the press', so wrote Ambu Patel.

Haroon worked closely with African and Indian freedom fighters like Bildad Kaggia, Pio Gama Pinto, Fred Kubai and Makhan Singh but distanced himself from any left-wing ideology. When a group of journalists from the *Colonial Times* set up the more Kenya-centred *Daily Chronicle,* Haroon became the editor of the Gujarati section.

In 1947, there was a general strike in Mombasa and the *Daily Chronicle* published a government document leaked to it by Gurwand Sheth, a civil servant. Haroon refused to divulge his source in court. He was arrested, charged with making an alarmist statement and sentenced to six

HAROON AHMED

months imprisonment with hard labour. Even in prison he continued to fight for his rights.

In the early 1950s, when the *Daily Chronicle* was taken over by more conservative forces, Haroon re-joined the *Colonial Times* where the owner soon asked him to tone down his politics. Together with Hirabhai Patel he then started the *Africa Samachar*. In 1959 Mwalimu Nyerere invited him to help with press publicity for TANU. 'For the first time in my life I actually had some money in a bank account', Haroon was to say. There he started

the *National Weekly, Wananchi* and *Nootan Africa* – a Gujarati paper.

In late 1960 as Kenya edged towards independence, the government appointed Haroon as director of the Hindustani channel of the Kenya Broadcasting Service. With programmes in Hindustani, Gujarati, Urdu and Konkani, the channel in those days shared equal air time with English and Kiswahili. With this appointment Haroon became the highest paid non-white civil servant in the colony.

At independence the Hindustani Service was closed down and Haroon moved to the *Nation* as a proof reader. He dabbled in some small business ventures and tried his hand at parliamentary politics but was defeated by Samuel Kivuitu. Following a series of personal tragedies and the constant insecurity in his career, he then took a spiritual path. Haroon passed away in Nairobi in 2002.

Sources: Patel, Zarina, 2006
Patel, Ambu, Haroon Ahmed, Unpublished MS
AwaaZ Issue 2 2002.

DHARAM KUMAR SHARDA (1921-1961)

Dharam Kumar Sharda, or DK as he was generally known, was a very capable and committed journalist who put his heart and soul in the anti-colonial struggle in Kenya and paid the price for doing so. Together with other South Asian and African journalists he gave voice to the injustices of colonialism and the nationalists' demand for freedom. Dr Visho Sharma has this to say about him: 'Including GL Vidyarthi, who happened to be our tenant at Park Road, there was no journalist of our breed who had a greater impact on East African affairs than Dharam Kumar Sharda. DK (as he was fondly called) started out as a school teacher in the Government Indian Primary School, Nairobi -- in fact, he was my

class teacher, in 1943, and an early influence (though I can't blame him entirely for the way I turned out, Marxist and all).

During his brief stint at the school, he was recruited into reading news on a regular basis for the Hindustani Service of 7LO. Possessed of a beautiful voice, he was a true artist -- played the sitar with considerable skill. Soon he found his true vocation. An inordinately well-read man, committed to the Left in political philosophy, DK was recruited by 'Chacha' Girdhari Lal to edit his *Colonial Times*, joining Haroon Ahmed, Mussa Ayub's uncle, who took care of its Gujarati section and advised on Kiswahili matters.

Later, much later, with the AB Patel imbroglio, they were joined by two other journalists that made considerable if not equal impact; but this part of the story moves the action to the *Daily Chronicle*. The journalists, Pranlal Sheth and initially cub reporter Piyo Rattansi (later known as Dr PM Rattansi of international history of science fame) formed a tranche that included vital links with Kenya's political broil of the time, through Makhan Singh and Pio Pinto.'

Nikhil Sharda, DK Sharda's grandson, in November 2012 posted this profile of DK online under the heading 'Kenya's Unsung Heroes':

'WHAT attracted D K Sharda to this paper was that he too had started, audaciously, a weekly in Nairobi which he had called *Tribune* and which he had run, by himself, until the colonial authorities pounced on the press in which it was being printed and later stopped it by executive order when they found that the intrepid young editor continued to bring it out after the closure of the press by cyclostyling it on a small multigraph machine.

That was the end of the *Tribune*, the bound volumes of which Sharda treasured as his most loved possession, but

DHARAM KUMAR SHARDA

it was by no means the end of his career as a journalist. It was rather a prelude to venturing into wider fields — correspondent-ship of the *New Statesman, the Times of India; and the Hindu* — and subsequently his return or rather his migrating to India. For, Sharda had been born and brought up in East Africa and had also married there.

The *Tribune* was a different type of paper and by no means, or even primarily, a fighting political organ of this or that group. It was a publication of great distinction, lurid, urbane and courageous, but not heavy, doctrinaire or propagandist. Modelled on the *New Statesman,* it attempted a wide coverage in a small compass and published, besides book reviews, well-written, adult reviews of films, music and whatever other cultural activities came into the lives of the people in that part of the world.

Beginning life as a school teacher, Sharda had been impelled into journalism by his urge to write and his keen and wide interest in men and affairs as also in life and literature. The going had never been very good. Though basically not political, he could not keep away — did not feel it decent and proper to keep away — from the struggle for freedom, living under a colonial administration.

He found it rather surprising that other Indians, successful in business and well-placed, who apparently felt the same way he did, turned the other way and held aloof when it came to doing something practical to support his venture when he started a paper of his own. Of course, the disillusionment had started earlier when he first joined a daily paper, started or backed by leading Indian settlers, but this left no bitterness, and I never heard him complain.

His friendship with PG Woodehouse and Mul[k] Raj Anand were well known and the letters exchanged are in itself a pleasure to read. Never have I in my career found wit, sarcasm, politics and philosophy intertwined so seamlessly. And the friendship continued till the end. On the professional front, the *Tribune* had attracted the attention of Kingsley Martin and it was he who had been instrumental in getting Sharda over to the *Times of India* from where he moved out a few months ago to take up the editorship of the Searchlight [now the *Hindustan Times*]. This he did with his characteristic spirit of adventure and also in pursuit of his conception of good life. What he would have loved best was to seek a quiet spot, build himself a home with a large plot of ground around, live closer to nature and write. But his sense of humour, springing from a clear perception of reality, would not let him brood or hanker after what was for him at the moment unattainable — he had to earn a living and support a family.

The next best thing he could think of was to take over the editorship of a paper and build it up. So he jumped at the offer of *Searchlight* when it came to him. In India he was virtually a stranger and had not lived here long enough to know the country well. He had lived only in Bombay and hardly knew anything of life in the provincial capital, its local politics, its lack of amenities and comforts. These things did not weigh with him at all. This would be a new kind of life for him, a new world of experience; it interested him, and he took it up.

For one who had run a weekly with such loving care and attention, Sharda threw himself into his new job with his whole heart, with the dedication of a craftsman and the daemonic compulsion of a perfectionist. He would not send out a copy of *Searchlight* until it had come up to what he regarded as a possible standard. Till then, as he wrote only two days before his sudden death: 'It was not fit for your august eyes.'

What had attracted Sharda to this paper became a common bond. Since circumstances prevented him from working for it whole time, he did the next best thing — write for it regularly in spite of his very heavy schedule of work and other commitments and give it his best, for, writing for this paper was a labour of love for him. And in it he found a freedom which he rarely enjoyed when writing to suit a dictated policy. Handsome, bright and always smiling, he had a light kind of humour which never hurt, a rare zest for living and capacity for enjoying a good book, Indian classical music, or even a good dinner and fondness for the open places of travel. This tight and heavy programme, frilled with music lessons, French classes, physical exercise, the allotted quota of reading and regular writing was, of course, exhausting even for one of a stronger constitution and a dour, determined spirit.

And he was by no means dour, nor did he ever look grimly determined. But he managed to keep up with this packed programme with an ease and agility and apparent absence of fatigue, which was a wonder for all those who knew the load he had to bear with a dilated heart. The fell disease struck him down just when he thought that he had got rid of it. All that the public would ever know is that in Sharda we have lost perhaps our best expert on Africa. Few beyond those who had the privilege of knowing him intimately will realise how much more the country has lost in his premature death.'

DK was a man of immense humour, two anecdotes were related to the author by Dr Piyo Rattansi who served briefly under DK on the *Daily Chronicle:* 'DK would warn Makhan Singh, one of the contributors to the *Daily Chronicle,* not to venture out in the sunshine. 'Makhan' in Punjabi means 'butter' which of course melts when heated! MI Fernandes was another regular contributor and DK would insist that he had an identity problem – am I or am I not? – which became an oft repeated pun.

Sources: Dr Visho Sharma by email, 24 May 2013
     http://www.epw.in/system/files/pdf/1961_13/48/
     d_k_sharda.pdf

PRANLAL SHETH (1924-2003)

Pranlal Sheth was born in Nairobi, Kenya, on 20 December, 1924. He was educated at the Duke of Gloucester School and was an avid reader. One of the books which made a great impact on him was *My Experiments with Truth,* the autobiography of Mahatma Gandhi. He learnt never to put up with injustice or discrimination without protest or resistance; but also that such resistance must be peaceful and non-violent.

In the 1940s there was one bilingual Indian daily paper, the *Kenya Daily Mail* published in Mombasa, and the *Colonial Times,* published in Nairobi. They closely followed the Indian independence struggle, which had assumed a militant if non-violent Quit India phase under the Indian Congress leadership. In 1943, G L Vidyarthi, the editor of the *Colonial Times,* decided to transform his weekly into an expanded and more ambitious bilingual (English and Gujarati) venture and recruited a team of gifted and committed young men. Pranlal was one of them.

Pranlal also worked on *Habari za Dunia* - a Kiswahili paper published weekly, edited by Henry Gathigira and published by Vidyarthi.

This group of journalists had a socialist orientation and later broke away to found a more Kenya-centric newspaper - the *Daily Chronicle,* the first issue appeared in January 1947. The same year saw the return to Kenya both of Jomo Kenyatta, and of the trade union organiser Makhan Singh. These were heady times!

Pranlal, who wrote both English and Gujarati with equal facility, contributed to each section. The paper, with its lively style of writing and presentation, quickly became a great success. It took a vigorous stand on local issues

and the fight for equal rights for Asians and Africans against the government and the settlers. Some Asians of the older generation and the business classes were made uneasy by the newspaper's forthright policy but the paper developed a large and wide readership in the three East African territories.

Piyo Rattansi who accompanied Pranlal on his reporting rounds, noticed his 'quickness in penetrating to the heart of the essentials on every issue of the moment and identifying the principles which were at stake. Combined with his unwavering persistence when he detected confusion or deliberate obfuscation and stonewalling, it made him a formidable interviewer and questioner at press conferences and public meetings for officials and leaders'.

Piyo adds: 'But I also saw the humanity which underlay his inquisitorial style: he aimed at exposing inequity, not at outing an enemy of the people. He exposed hypocrisy and self- seeking when it compromised public interest, but also sought out the potential for good that he believed resided in everyone. Criticism was not sufficient in itself, and must be supplemented by the search for alternatives, through study and analysis. He sought realistic solutions, but that did not mean settling for the second best, since that would be to grossly under-estimate the potential for change and a capacity for striving for disinterested justice, far greater among the most ordinary human beings. Pranlal perceived clearly that with India's achievement of independence, the same principle of self-determination must be applied to East Africa to free it from colonial rule as rapidly as possible.

'Harry Thuku, was released, and a new organisation to embrace all Africans (the Kenya African Union) was founded and began to organise rallies and mass meetings in Nairobi and the countryside. I accompanied Pranlal to those meetings [KAU], travelling on African buses, and discovered in him a total absence of the prejudices which complicated relations between the racial groups in Kenya. His brilliant pieces were attacked in the European press as conferring respectability on misguided and demagogic agitators through vivid and dramatic reportage.'

The *Chronicle* led a concerted campaign advocating a common front with the Africans to obtain equal rights for all Kenyans, and opposition to the highly divisive communal roll pitting Hindus against Muslims. The association with Makhan Singh drew Pranlal into taking a much more active role in trade union activities, which developed a new spirit of militancy by late 1948 and into 1949. In so doing Pranlal angered many Asian employers.

Police raids to seize originals of material printed in the *Chronicle* were followed by another sedition trial in 1950, this time of Pranlal whose name appeared as editor, and the magistrate imposed a heavy fine. A more effective way of silencing the paper was through what seemed to be an organised advertisement boycott by European and Asian businesses, which placed it in a financially precarious position. The paper was sold off and most of the original editorial team then left the newspaper.

Pranlal saw no immediate prospect of continuing in journalism and moved to Kisumu in December 1952 to join a family run business of building contractors. In July 1962 he completed his final law examinations and was called to the Bar at Lincoln's Inn in London and on his return opened his own legal practice in Kisumu. He worked on Achieng Oneko's *Ramogi* – a weekly in Dholuo. Through it Pranlal became acquainted with Jaramogi Oginga Odinga, Kenya's first vice-president who found in Pranlal, a mentor and a close ally. But Pranlal's life was to change abruptly within three years.

He was to be the victim of a deep rift which began to develop between the president and his vice-president and Pranlal's life was now felt to be in danger.

When urged to stay away from Kenya for some time he said: 'What would my African friends think of me if I deserted them at the first whiff of danger?' The Government moved against Pranlal on Friday 14 August, 1966. It cancelled his citizenship, put him on a plane and deported him to India. After a brief sojourn there, with the help of the Government of India, he was allowed into the UK where he finally settled. There, after initial setbacks and struggles, he embarked on a very successful high level quasi-legal career and in public life.

In 1994 he was conferred with a CBE for his selfless services to over fifty organisations. From being charged for sedition by the British colonialists in Kenya, 46 years later he was honoured by the British Queen. He died on June 30, 2003. The vagaries of history have unpredictable consequences!

Source: AwaaZ, Issue 1 2004.

CITIZEN NEWSPAPER (1951-1956)

The *Citizen* newspaper was the brain-child of the Patwa family which was in the book business. Residents of Mombasa, in 1944 they had started a bookshop in the Kadherbhoy building, on what is now Nkrumah Road. The shop specialised in stocking newspapers and literature and was, at that time, Kenya's largest importer of foreign publications. In subsequent years the family established the East African Printing Press in Sadler Street (present Koinange Street), Nairobi and they were joined in this venture by two other Bohra entrepreneurs, the Sachak and Diamond families.

Saifuddin Patwa, Nurdin's older brother, was a proponent of freedom and democracy and in 1951, based in Nairobi; he founded the *Citizen* newspaper to give voice to the colonised. The militant *Daily Chronicle* under its left-leaning editor, D K Sharda, had just been forced to hand over to a more conservative owner and the *Citizen* stepped into the breach. Bobby Naidoo, a South African exiled in the UK, was hired to be the editor. He worked on the *Citizen* for two years before he was hounded out by fellow journalists in the settler press. Saifuddin and Shabbir Patwa and their sister, Ameena, then took over as editors as well as having to oversee a staff of 32 and a correspondent (Richard Nunes) in Zanzibar.

Citizen was a weekly newspaper published in English; when it closed in 1956 its circulation had reached 5000. Its readership comprised mainly the South Asian and African elite, but it was also read by the European population who, though opposed to its persuasion, nevertheless valued the well-grounded foreign and local news. The paper syndicated with papers such as the *Sunday Dispatch* in the UK and ran a regular cartoon strip by Garth. During the Emergency, Cyril Dunn of the Observer stayed with the Patwas in their Limuru home and filed stories sympathetic to the Mau Mau forest fighters. In 1952, when George VI died, *Citizen* was the first to publish his photograph which came by radio transmission. *Game Animals of Eastern Africa,* written by a Swedish naturalist, C A W Guggisberg, and printed and published by the Patwas in 1963; was a major boost to the fledgling tourist industry.

The *Citizen* printed news and stories for and about the independence struggle and was the first, and perhaps only, newspaper to receive and publish Dedan Kimathi's letter written to President Tito of Yugoslavia detailing the hardships being suffered under colonialism. In October

1953, the national liberation movement published in the *Citizen* the charter issued by Field Marshall Dedan Kimathi on behalf of the Kenya Defence Council. Needless to say the colonial authorities were not pleased and they set about crippling the paper financially. The favourite ploy of the government was to either inflict a heavy fine on some flimsy excuse as it did on the *Daily Chronicle* or withdraw advertisements. The latter tactic was applied to the *Citizen* leaving the Patwas no option but to close it down in 1956.

In the late forties the family had also established three branches of the Patwa News Agencies in Sadler and Victoria Streets and Government Road. When the Jomo Kenyatta International Airport (formerly Embakasi Airport) was opened in May 1958 by Sir Evelyn Baring (who officiated instead of the Queen Mother who was not able to come); the Patwas were given a concession to run a bookshop, a curio shop and a transit shop at the airport. This was a 24-hour job, immensely profitable as well as intellectually satisfying. African leaders like Tom Mboya, Awori and others were regular customers searching for political books. Helped by British suppliers a bookshop was also opened in Nakuru.

Unfortunately in the late 1990s this concession like many others in the airport, were abruptly ended and the owners had to vacate their premises overnight, unable even to salvage their stock. The family then ran a coffee shop in Yaya Centre and a small bookshop in Karen before they finally called it a day.

Source: Nurdin Patwa interviewed by Zarina Patel, 17 May 2013.

MICHAEL I FERNANDES

Michael Fernandes was a lively 'clerk' who worked as a paid secretary to Shanti Pandit, the Hon. Secretary of the E A Indian National Congress. Piyo Rattansi remembers the name, M I Fernandes, because D K Sharda, the *Daily Chronicle* editor, used to pun that he had a permanent identity problem, Am I or Am I not! He wrote an interesting column for the *Chronicle* under a nom-de-plume.

Later when the *Chronicle* came under a more conservative management, Michael was employed as an editor. In the Government's view, however, the paper was still too extreme. Fernandes was declared *persona non grata* and had to leave the country. Piyo remembers that in the 1950s Michael moved to Tanganyika and had to keep his border crossing into Kenya secret from the Kenyan authorities.

RICHARD NELSON NUNES
Writer

I was born in 1933 in Dar es Salaam, then Tanganyika. My parents were already in Zanzibar where my father worked for Cable & Wireless. I believe my paternal grandfather also worked in Zanzibar. I studied in Zanzibar and Dar es Salaam, in Convent Schools, before moving to Bombay (Mumbai) for two years and then to Goa for a further stint of two years of secondary schooling. In 1949 I returned to Dar es Salaam and after two years proceeded to Zanzibar. When in school in Bombay I edited the class journal, took part in debates and was considered quite proficient in the English language.

My introduction to journalism started off in Zanzibar where I was appointed a freelance reporter for what was then the only weekly newspaper on the island, the *Zanzibar Voice* founded in 1920. To place this publication in some perspective, it was run by the owner, B N Antani who was the editor, the typesetter and the printer, all

RICHARD NELSON NUNES

rolled into one. The paper was printed on an old letter-press machine which had an enormous flywheel.

After several jobs, I met Michael Fernandes who was recruiting for the new venture in Nairobi, the *Daily Chronicle*. I started off as a proof-reader, moving on to reporting and subsequently writing features. I was also involved in interviewing and writing on up-coming politicians. I was fortunate to be working under D K Sharda who was the editor. He would invariably greet me in the morning with 'And how is our budding journalist today?' And Michael would be pacing up and down because he did not have a lead story. 'Why don't we have a plane crash or a train derailment,' he would ask aloud. Then there was the typesetter, a Mr Paracha, who I spent a great deal of time with. I was also quite friendly with Priya Ramrakha, who was called upon whenever we needed a photographer.

These were exciting times as one never knew when the authorities could decide that 'enough was enough'. I think there was a sense of common purpose driving us – it certainly was not for monetary gain. Friends did not come to visit because most people considered it risky. We had a strong African readership as the *Chronicle* was considered to be in line with the aspirations of the people and independence movement. I can remember interviewing F R S De Souza, Arwings-Khodek, and Tom Mboya, among others.

As there was very little revenue coming in to sustain the paper it was forced to close down. Here it should be mentioned that all the advertising agencies were owned by the 'white' establishment. I was sent on a futile mission to try and secure some advertisements. The replies were invariably the same: Tone down your paper's anti-colonial policy and editorials and we might reconsider our policy.

Subsequently, I was appointed Zanzibar correspondent for the *Citizen* which was a weekly established by Patwa News Agency in Nairobi in 1951/52. The publishers had promised me a position when I returned to Nairobi. Sadly, my arrival in Nairobi in 1955 coincided with the closure of the newspaper. I have no idea why it closed down but I presume it was somewhat anti-colonialist.

I would like to mention here that not all Asians supported the freedom struggle. Quite a number of them felt that we journalists were jeopardizing the status quo as they were enjoying a good life under the colonialists.

This was also the time of the Emergency. It was the time when the Special Branch took an interest in anyone who was connected with a newspaper. It was definitely not a healthy career choice. Nonetheless these were exciting times and I feel proud to have played a role, however small, in the struggle for freedom for Kenya.

I subsequently worked for around ten years in the PR department of a major oil company. After leaving I joined up with my wife who had started the first Asian-owned secretarial bureau in Kenya, the Beezee Secretarial Bureau in 1965. All the existing bureaus at that time were 'white'. We then established Beeline Printing Ltd which printed mainly house journals and books, where my experience in journalism was put to good use. As a result of a burglary I lost all my records and hence I am not able to provide any articles or relevant material for this book. We left Kenya five years ago to retire in Goa, after spending five generations in East Africa. My wife, Betsy, and I have both turned 80 this year and are happily retired.

AMBU H PATEL

Ambu Patel was an earnest young man who arrived in Nairobi with his wife, Lila, from India in 1933 and started a book binding and publishing business, London Book Binders in Nairobi's Duke Street. In India he had participated in the movement for independence; and nationalist concerns continued to be the focus of his life in Kenya.

Ambu founded the New Kenya Publishers. He wrote many articles for underground papers, and also helped in printing and personally distributing these. As a South Asian he was able to evade the colonial police and moved freely in areas that others could not go. In spite of being an ardent follower of Mahatma Gandhi and therefore of non-violence; he organised printing facilities opposite Parklands Police Station and in Mathare valley for Mau Mau publications. Lila, his wife, was known to hide freedom fighters in her coal shed in Parklands and there are photographs of her, and other South Asian women, holding up placards in a demonstration. Many in the Asian community vilified them for portraying Mau Mau as a 'heroic' movement.

The colonial government did not release the judgement in the Kapenguria trials released to the public. It was Ambu who, with the help of Pio Gama Pinto, managed to 'borrow' a copy of the 100 page judgement, and arranged with a progressive typist, Shirin Meghji Ahmed, to type it on stencil. He reproduced 300 copies on a second-hand Gestetner duplicating machine and posted 250 copies to leaders all over the world as the government was not willing to let the world read it. Ambu was the organising

Ambu Patel and his wife Lila Patel

Ambu Patel (centre) with Jomo Kenyatta and Makhan Sigh

secretary for the 'Release Jomo Kenyatta and other Detainees Committee'.

Ambu looked after Jomo Kenyatta's daughter, Margaret, while the former was in detention and at great personal risk, sent him food, clothing and shoes when no-one else would, or did. However after Independence, as with so many of his colleagues, he was side-lined and even mistreated by the Kenyatta government.

Ambu was an avid photographer and had a priceless collection of images and press cuttings of the historical period he lived in. Unfortunately this was either stolen from him or wantonly destroyed. He died in Nairobi in 1977.

Sources: Patel, Ambu. Ed., Struggle for 'Release Jomo and
*   his Colleagues'*
*   Patel, Zarina, 2006*
*   Durrani, Shiraz, 2006.*

SOUTH ASIAN JOURNALISM IN THE 1950'S

The decade of the 1950s was, in Kenya, ushered in by the banning of the East Africa Trade Union Congress, the detention of its General Secretary, Makhan Singh, and the arrest of his colleagues in the Trade Union Movement. The colonial authorities' desperate attempt to stifle the heightened struggle for independence saw, amongst other policies, an onslaught on radical journalism.

When the *Daily Chronicle* was sold in 1952, its radical group of journalists sought other means of disseminating their views. Its editor, D K Sharda, founded a newspaper of his own, the **Tribune**, which is considered the true successor to the original *Daily Chronicle*. Apart from Sharda the main contributor was the independent Goan barrister and politician, J M Nazareth, who wrote weekly articles under the pseudonym 'Tribunus' which well illustrated the editorial policies. Sharda and Nazareth eloquently and persuasively opposed the move for an East African Federation – one article termed it 'a short cut to chaos,' another warned, 'clearly the whole of Central and East Africa is in the gravest danger'. It decried the new apartheid policy in South Africa and blamed the rise of Mau Mau on the long-standing inequalities in Kenya. The paper also included many articles written by Africans. Not surprisingly, in 1952, only sixteen months after its appearance the *Tribune* had its licence revoked. Sharda, disheartened, moved to India where he joined the Patna *Searchlight*, now the *Hindustan Times*.

When the *Tribune's* license was revoked, DK sold his press to WWW Awori who transferred it to Apa B Pant, the resident High Commissioner for the Government of India. In collaboration with Haroon Ahmed, FRS de Souza, Pio Gama Pinto and Nazareth, Pant arranged for the press to publish another radical newspaper. The **Africa Samachar** (Africa News) 1954-1974, a weekly printed entirely in Gujarati, had Ahmed as its editor and continued to advocate 'the struggle for equality, democracy and common franchise'. Like so many of its predecessors, however, *Africa Samachar* in its radical form was unable to attract sufficient capital and control was relinquished to T A Bhatt (no relation of M M Bhatt), a generous financier of the *Samachar*. Then the story of the *Daily Chronicle* was repeated as the new owner, to make the paper financially solvent, avoided all controversial issues. The original staff of *Africa Samachar* left to turn their attention more to politics than journalism and the paper continued its conservative course into the seventies; its circulation reached 16,000.

The *Globe* was published from 1955-58 in English and Konkni. Other newspapers directed to the Goan community were A C L de Sousa's **Fairplay** and **Goan Weekly** and Pio Gama Pinto's **Uzwod**.

In 1959, J M Desai founded the **National Guardian**, a Nairobi weekly in English and Gujarati. J M arrived from India in 1925, built a network of insurance agencies and after World War II had formed remarkably close associations with African nationalists such as Harry Thuku, Mbiyu Koinange, Jomo Kenyatta and Tom Mboya. The first few issues which were printed by Pinto carried a series of interviews with the African leaders – so informative were the articles that the newspaper was distributed by government at the Lancaster House Conferences. By then the 'winds of change' were sufficiently strong to prevent his prosecution. The paper was edited in the evenings by Indu Desai and Joe Rodrigues after finishing their work at the *Daily Chronicle*. However, due to lack of financial support, J M had to abandon his project after two years and Rodrigues went on to a full-time position at the *Nation*.

The **Nyanza Advertiser** of Kisumu was started in 1949 by a printer, V H Jobanputra, founder of the Nyanza Printing Works Ltd. A social organ more than a newspaper, it was distinct in its provincial orientation and long eighteen-year run. **Navyug** (Contemporary news) was a tabloid sized weekly published in Gujarati and English. The news carried by both sections concerned the South Asian community and their fight for equal rights and justice. Business news was an important element here. The Gujarati editorials were powerful and made an impression. The English section was usually not so extensive but the front page headlines attracted attention. Features in English were sourced from various agencies and missions as long as they were non-political. In the early 1960s, Kul Bhushan started to write as a contributor under the pen name 'Enterprise' and covered matters relating to business and economics. Like other Asian newspapers at the time, it had scant advertising from the community and so folded up in 1963 when its circulation was 3000.

Newspapers in Tanzania and Uganda

Tanzania's first Indian newspaper, the weekly *Samachar*, was established in Zanzibar in 1900 by Fazal Janmohammed Master, a Shi'a Ithna'asheri Khoja from Jamnagar, Kachchh. Zanzibar's *Samachar* began as a single-sheet Gujarati paper dealing only with communal affairs, and began to cover politics and print English-language items only in 1918. It was at this point after the First World War – as East Africa's Indian population underwent rapid politicization over the future of Indians in Kenya and ex-German East Africa – that key figures emerged to lead Dar es Salaam's Indian press expansion.

This coincided with and flowed directly from Gandhi's efforts to wed press activity with nationalist mobilization in India following the war.

Indian nationalism in East Africa blossomed during the First World War. The conflict between the British and German colonial states in East Africa forced Britain to dispatch Indian regiments to the theatre, intimating to India that, in return, Indians would receive settlement privileges in the territory or even be given the territory itself as a colony. Britain ultimately dropped the plan, and the ex-German colony became the British territory of Tanganyika mandated by the League of Nations.

Tanganyika Opinion was founded in 1923 by Mohanlal Devchand Patel who had arrived in Tanganyika in 1920 and had started the Kanti printing press. Publishing in English and Gujarati, *Opinion* was initially edited by a Gujarati Jain named Tribhowan Bechardas Sheth, who was succeeded in 1925–6 by U K Oza who took over its editorship and radicalised its content serving as editor from 1926–34 and 1938–40. Oza was an emissary of Gandhi sent to 'assist the Asian community in its struggle against discrimination and closer union'. He had close ties to M A Desai of the *East Africa Chronicle*, edited the *Democrat* for a time and helped Jomo Kenyatta to finance *Muigwithania*. Because of his pro-African views and hostility to Britain he was 'asked' by the Tanganyika government to return to India.

The *Opinion* gained the attention of intelligence officials by advertising George Padmore's banned book *Africa: Britain's Third Empire*, as well as by borrowing liberally from the *Daily Chronicle*, the 'Communist Indian paper published in Nairobi' that, in the words of intelligence officials, produced 'anti-white, anti-government bias'. In 1951 the *Opinion* made the first outright demand for

liberation made in registered print media in Tanganyika's history, as well as being the first to implicitly invoke violence as a means to that end. It must be noted that in Kenya, Makhan Singh had been detained for demanding independence at a public rally in 1950, and guerilla warfare was in the offing. Short of funds, the paper announced its cessation of publication in its final issue on 30 December, 1955.

V R Boal, a Gujarati Brahmin who had arrived in Zanzibar in 1911, in 1929 became the founder, proprietor, printer and editor of Tanganyika's second Indian newspaper, *Tanganyika Herald*, with its associated Herald Printing Works. In this venture, Boal was backed by the fabulously wealthy entrepreneur Mathuradas Kalidas Mehta. Both the *Opinion* and the *Herald* took an anti-colonial stance with an 'anti-white, anti-government bias'. Struggling against the massive expansion of both literacy and government censorship in World War II, Boal left Tanganyika in late 1939 and sold the Herald Printing Works in 1941. He re-purchased the press in 1942 but the paper closed down in 1950, ostensibly for 'economic problems'. Boal returned to Tanganyika in 1958 to restart the *Herald* which gradually became a forum for 'dyspeptic Indian opinion about the future of an African-ruled Tanganyika'. Boal retired to Bombay in 1962.

The end of the *Herald* and *Opinion* coincided roughly with the rise of the Tanganyika African National Union (TANU) in the late 1950s and Tanganyika's independence in December 1961. Though pioneering in their rhetorical confrontations with the colonial state at various junctures between 1923 and 1951, by the 1950s both *Opinion* and *Herald* had become hollow shells of their former selves.

Another short-lived Indian newspaper, the Ismaili Khoja-owned *Africa Sentinel*, had been launched in

1940. Kassum Sunderji Samji, the leading Ismaili figure in Tanganyika, explained that 'the patriotic and pro-British sentiment of the Khoja community found no proper representation in the local Indian Press, and that the community wished for this to be rectified'. *Africa Sentinel* was succeeded by another Ismaili-owned Anglo-Gujarati paper, *Young Africa*, which remained in print into the 1950s.

As in Kenya, South Asians in Tanganyika assisted Africans to publish their own newspapers. In 1937, M O Abbasi helped a talented Ugandan, Erica Fiah, to start *Kwetu* in Dar es Salaam. It was Tanganyika's first African newspaper. The second was *Habari za Dunia* established by M D Patel, proprietor of *Tanganyika Opinion*. Both newspapers became a forum for early African opinion. In 1952, M Machado Plantan, a Goan, founded a Kiswahili weekly called *Zuhra*. It was edited by the African poet, Mathias E Mnyampala but was short-lived. Following TANU's formation in 1954, Randhir Bhanushanker Thaker, a Dar es Salaam printer, began to issue the party's *Mwafrica* and *Sauti ya TANU* which thrived until the 1970s. He managed most of the editing and the distribution. In 1959 he launched the independent Swahili-language newspaper *Ngurumo* ('Thunder'), that same year Nyerere invited Haroon Ahmed, the Kenyan South Asian journalist, to establish and manage three newspapers: The *National Weekly* in English; *Wananchi* in Kiswahili and *Nootan Africa* (New Africa) in Gujarati. This venture collapsed after two years due to a dearth of advertising and promised capital.

In Uganda, South Asians never had their own newspaper nor did they have any major impact on the development of an African press. However, post-independence, President Obote established the Milton Obote Foundation (MOF) to establish a nationalist press, among other objectives. Gurdial Singh, an advocate, was appointed director of the Uganda Press Trust Ltd. In 1965, Obote invited the Kenya-based Vidyarthi family with the aim of establishing a newspaper. Details of this venture can be read in the interview of Sudhir Vidyarthi.

Sources: *Salvador, Cynthia, 2010*
Patel, Zarina, 2006
Durrani, Shiraz, 2006
Chandan, Amarjit, 2004, Gopal Singh Chandan, p17
Seidenberg, Dana, 1983
Gregory, Robert G., 1993
http://www.epw.in/system/files/pdf/1961_13/48/ d_k_sharda.pdf
Bhushan, Kul, email 2013.
https://husseindharsi.wordpress.com/tag/ zanzibar-samachar/
Brennan, James R, 2011.

LESSER KNOWN SOUTH ASIAN PUBLICATIONS IN PRE-INDEPENDENT EAST AFRICA

The Observer was a Nairobi weekly which carried articles in English, Urdu and Gujarati and was published between 1923 and 1928. The editor was I M Paracha. It welcomed constitutional change and emphasised the need for guarantees for minorities. The *Coast Guardian*, 1933-1937, was established by Rahemtulla Walji Hirji in partnership with Sir Ali bin Salim to give a voice to the Mombasa littoral. The editor was J J Robertson who published it in Gujarati and English until his death three years later.

The ***East African Kirti*** and its earlier versions, ***Kenya Worker*** and ***Kirti***, published between 1936 and 1939 were organs of the workers' unions led by Makhan Singh. The word 'kirti' means 'worker' in the Punjabi language and the pamphlets focused largely on workers' struggles both nationally and internationally. Its concerns were mainly around class issues and the need for unity.

All the publications were edited by Makhan Singh under a masthead of the Sikh emblem; but at one stage, for reasons of colonial scrutiny, Mota Singh was named as the editor. The Government, however, persecuted the editor for 'not having registered the paper' and it stopped appearing after three issues. Later Makhan Singh revived the *East African Kirti* and circulated cyclostyled copies, hand-written by him in Gurumukhi script. This time, Mota Singh was named as 'the proprietor'. The annual return made under the Newspaper Registration Ordinance in 1938 stated the *East African Kirti* was published weekly and that its average circulation was 1,000 copies per week.

EAST AFRICA KIRTI

Kirti was closely allied to the Ghadar Party, a revolutionary organisation with its roots in the Punjab in India and its international front based in San Francisco, USA. Formed in 1913, its goal was the overthrow of British rule in India through armed struggle. The Party was active globally in 22 countries including Kenya where its members received and circulated the party newspaper, *Ghadar*. Just before the outbreak of World War II, a group of Indians in Kenya were arrested and charged with 'Ghadrite' activities which included 'possessing seditious publications, assisting the enemy, and spreading false intelligence and alarmist reports'. Some were deported, others imprisoned and a few hanged. One of the chief protagonists was Gopal Singh who stood in for Makhan Singh as Acting Secretary General of the Labour Trade Union of East Africa during the latter's detention in India, 1940-1945.

Gopal Singh with his 'progressive ideas and association with the freedom struggle' was active in Sikh institutions in Kenya. The Sri Guru Singh Sabha situated in Nairobi's CBD was a front organisation for the Ghadar/Kirti party. The Ghadar activists in Kenya learnt valuable lessons on the appropriate forms and contents of publications as tools in their struggle. These lessons became part of the growing experience in the communication field in the country.

Muslim Newspapers

These newspapers were strongly slanted towards Pakistan. They were inspired by the Partition of India; they did not address the anti-colonial struggle and had a limited circulation and life span.

Allah Ditta Qureshi was born in 1902 in Jhelum, now Pakistan. His father, Khair Mohammed, was a timber merchant. Allah Ditta arrived in Kenya in 1925 and five years later he formed the Muslim League Party to cater for the Muslim community in Kenya. In 1946 he published the English language *Daily News*. In 1948 he started the *East African Star,* a weekly newspaper which covered the news and views of Muslims world-wide. In 1948, Mr Qureshi was elected as Alderman of the Nairobi Municipal Council, in 1950 he was nominated to the Legislative Council and was awarded an OBE by the British Government. He passed away on 4 May, 1952 and the *Star* then ceased publication. In 1946 Sami Ullah published the bi-lingual (English/Urdu) *Observer* and M A M Dar the *Muslim Opinion*, a trilingual (English/Urdu/Swahili).

THE NATION'S FIFTY GOLDEN YEARS

By Kul Bhushan

On 18 March 2010, our widely read and much admired newspaper, the Nation, published a supplement. Not the usual corporate advertising or some development project. No, this was a Souvenir Issue celebrating 50 Golden Years and for many of us old enough to remember those early beginnings, it was with great eagerness and expectation that we put everything aside to savour the memories from the distant and not-too-distant past.

And it did not disappoint. All kudos to the Nation Media Group for its success and achievement as 'journalistic *mzee* of East Africa'! And for reminding us of the historical highlights strewn along the path which our country has traversed since independence – many we can recall with pride, some we wish we did not have to record.

However, some readers of South Asian descent (and perhaps others too) searched in vain for the presence of some of the illustrious Asian leaders and journalists who have helped to shape Kenya's history as well as the *Nation's* success. When we read about the assassinations of Tom Mboya and J M Kariuki, we missed a reference to their contemporary, Pio Gama Pinto, surely one of our most revered patriots. In sports, was it not Seraphino Antao who in 1962 won two gold medals in the 100 and 220 yards' sprint at the Commonwealth Games in Christchurch, New Zealand; and sent many rushing to their world maps trying to pinpoint where Kenya was located in Africa? And it should not be forgotten that it is only cricket from all our sports which has to date made it

to a World Cup. Kenya's Flying Sikh Joginder Singh, who won the world's then toughest rally - the Safari - found no mention either. The list goes on with Kenyan hockey players who won many international tournaments and performed creditably at the Olympics.

The *Nation* also published a book to mark this milestone that has a chronology of major Kenyan and global events during these 50 years but no mention is made of a world event - the Asian Exodus in 1968. The only global event covered from the Indian subcontinent is the execution of Z A Bhutto of Pakistan and nothing from India for half a century! The sole Asian news maker in Kenya during this half century is Prof. Yash Pal Ghai, who is described as 'the lawyer hired as convenor of the Bomas talks'. In the commissioned book, *Birth of a Nation* by Gerry Loughran, no Asian journalist, except Joe Rodrigues, has been mentioned except for a passing reference to Kul Bhushan when he left the *Nation* after 14 years for the *Standard* for better terms of service. It is indeed surprising that Loughran did not come across the bylines of these 20-odd full time Asian journalists who worked for the *Nation* during its first 25 years when researching for his book so that they could get their due credit in the success story.

For the commemorative book, *The Golden Years* produced by a team from the media group, a number of European journalists who worked in the past for the *Nation* (Dick Dawson, Gavin Bennet, Paul Redfern, Gerry Loughran and John McHaffie) were invited to contribute but not a single Asian journalist was considered. Interestingly, an Asian columnist, Yusuf K Dawood, gets to talk about his contribution on a full page but not any of the Asian journalists who spent many - and their best - years on the paper get a chance to narrate their achievements and challenges.

The supplement did recognize editor Joe Roderigues, photo journalist Anil Vidyarthi, Akhtar Hussain, Noorbegum Kanani and Wilma de Souza. But missing in the supplement was that gallant band of South Asian journalists which helped to lay the foundations of the *Nation* and enable it to quickly emerge as Kenya's premier newspaper.

When the *Nation* was launched in 1960, the *Standard* had no full time Asian print journalist. In fact, it took another 20 years before one joined the *Standard* in 1980. The *Nation* employed Chottu Karadia and Cyprian Fernandes soon after it started. As years rolled by, more Asians joined the paper full time. This impressive list included Alfred De Araujo, Kul Bhushan, Sultan Jessa, Rashid Mughal, Karim Hudani, Billy Chibber, Monte Vianna, Lorraine Saldanha, Olinda Fernandes, Gayatri Sayal among others in the news and features departments; Cyprian Fernandes, Norman da Costa and Polly Fernandes in the sports department and Akhtar Hussain, Shashi Vasani, Chandu Vasani, Anil Vidyarthi, Azhar Chaudhry in the photographic department. Among the contributors were Shamlal Puri and Anwar Sidi. Joe Rodrigues joined as a Sub Editor, became the Chief Sub Editor, rose to the post of the Managing Editor and finally, the Editor in Chief from 1978 to 1981 when he suffered a heart attack and resigned.

The *East African Standard* reigned supreme when the *Nation* was launched. The new compact upstart declared its support for majority rule while the *Standard* was very much an establishment paper supporting the colonial government. Its upper crust readership of the Europeans and elite Asians considered the *Nation* as both a 'cheap' paper because it was tabloid sized with large headings and an 'Asian' paper because it was established and owned by the Aga Khan. At that time, even the *Sunday*

THE PAPER THAT MOST PEOPLE WANT

THE most recently audited newspaper circulation figures (July... of 57,972. This means the gap between the **NATION** and its long... of its sustained success. This most recent... Vigorous and youthful, the **DAILY NATION** cap-

Post was more conservative. To attract new readers, the *Nation* directed its appeal to those who rarely bought a newspaper, rather than those who would switch over or buy both. It was an uphill task.

A look at the chronology of Kenyan events that affected the South Asian community post-independence clearly shows that these events had a great impact on the Asians for their personal security, business decisions and, most importantly, their decision to stay or migrate from Kenya. This, in turn, affected the economy. While the *Standard* had only the interests of the Europeans in its reportage and editorial columns, the *Nation* reported Kenyan events without fear or favour. It also highlighted more human interest stories – be they for any race – while the *Standard* stuck to its style of mostly reporting events.

The sixties was a very turbulent time for South Asians. At the start of this decade, the Emergency had ended and Kenya was fast moving to independence. On the one hand the Asians were apprehensive of their future in the country, on the other the pro-colonial papers were not adequately reflecting the aspirations of the majority of Africans. In the *Nation*, the elected Asian leaders in the Legislative Council (Legco), and others who had joined the mainstream majority; had a new public media to present their views.

When Kenya became independent in December 1963, Asian journalists reported how the community joined the Africans in hailing the new era. Statements from the Kanu treasurer, K P Shah, always made good copy and the *Nation* featured him regularly. Interestingly, these stories were invariably written by African journalists. The fact that Joseph Murumbi who had a Goan mother was the Vice President; Dr F R S De Souza, another Goan, the Deputy Speaker of the Parliament; Jan Mohamed, an Assistant Minister for Tourism and Chanan Singh, a judge of the High Court – all served to boost Asian confidence showing that they had a future in independent Kenya.

In 1965, the imposition of exchange control hit Asians hard as they had sent their savings to Britain or were educating their children in Britain or the USA. Soon, they had to decide whether to take up Kenya citizenship or not as the two-year grace period was fast coming to an end by 1966. The *Nation* published some reports of Asians taking up citizenship but the majority remained unmoved. They thought that the 'life time' stamp to stay in Kenya on their British passports was enough security. In 1967, the government passed the Immigration Bill requiring all non-citizens to get work permits. British Asians now had no option but to emigrate to the UK.

In January 1968, the *Nation* was the first to report that an Asian Exodus was building up; the story hit international headlines a month later. The *Standard* had no inkling of this event except from their correspondent in London who reported news of a bill in the House of Commons to cover British Asians to stop their arrival. Britain announced a quota voucher system for the Asians. The Asian Exodus was in full swing and the *Nation* went to town with it. The British High Commission in Nairobi was flooded with voucher applications from Asians. This was the single most crucial event that boosted the *Nation* in its coverage both in words and pictures. Scenes of Asians at Nairobi Airport or at the British High Commission with interviews carried out in Gujarati or Punjabi, and written up in English, made good stories. Desperate stories of Asians fasting outside the British High Commission made heart-wrenching copy. The *Standard* could not come anywhere near this reporting as they had mostly Englishmen or Scotsmen working as journalists.

In June 1969, nine years after its inception, the *Nation* overtook the *Standard* in circulation. Is it a coincidence that the extensive coverage of the Asian Exodus from February 1968 onwards was partly responsible? In 1968, a poster inside the *Nation* newsroom urged all journalists to 'Close the Gap' between the circulations of the *Nation* and the *Standard*. That year the average daily net sale of the *Daily Nation* was 33,903; the equivalent for the *East*

Sales hit a new high!

MARCH 1968 was an all-time record for sales of the East African Newspapers (Nation Series) publishing group. For several years now, the circulation gap between the sixty-six-year-old E. A. *Standard* and the seven - year - old DAILY NATION has been steadily narrowing. Last month it was smaller still and, during the first quarter of this year, its tremendous growth rate accelerated still further.

"More and more people are joining the great family of East African *Standard* readers," announced our venerable contemporary last Friday. Amen!

The same is true of the NATION — young people, the growing numbers of high - income Africans, housewives of all races, men and women who seek a balanced and independent viewpoint and enjoy all the news that matters brightly and crisply presented. Hallelujah!

Our audited sales figure for the first half of 1968, officially confirmed by the Audit Bureau of Circulations in London, will be released as usual next July. Meanwhile, we are happy to announce that March recorded the highest-ever sales in the history of the

DAILY NATION, the SUNDAY NATION and of TAIFA WEEKLY (Swahili editions only).

A published claim by E. A. *Standard* (Newspapers) Ltd. that "Baraza" sold 20,756 copies more than its nearest Swahili competitor in March is totally untrue, and a correction will be called for.

TAIFA WEEKLIES' total sales in March (including the Uganda edition, published in the Luganda vernacular) exceeded 65,000 copies per issue. This is by far the largest-selling vernacular newspaper in East Africa.

African Standard was 36,912 (*Daily Nation, September 7, 1968*).

The seventies were dominated by Quit Notices for the Asian *dukawallas* or shopkeepers. The Exodus was followed by the big news on Quit Notices from 1969 to 1977. The *Nation*, again, had an edge in its reporting with its Business Editor interviewing the *dukawallas* who termed these notices as '*kankotris*' or invitations! The government policy then changed the terminology from 'Africanisation' to 'Kenyanisation' so that Kenyan Asians could continue as *dukawallas* if they took up Kenya citizenship. In 1971, Idi Amin took over Uganda and Kenyan MP Martin Shikuku declared that Kenya should follow Idi Amin and expel the Asians - sending shivers down Asian spines.

The Asian journalists brought new dimensions to reporting. Kul Bhushan started the Education Notebook that had a dedicated readership. Billy Chibber reported the court cases competently. Monte Vianna and Karim Hudani were incisive reporters. Sultan Jessa had a sharp nose for news when he spotted the King of Afghanistan at a Nairobi Conference when the monarch was overthrown in his country. His reports and interview made world headlines. Bhushan was later appointed the first Business Editor in Kenya. Rashid Mughal, who started off as a proofreader, rose to become the Features Editor. Alfred de Araujo who started as a sub editor rose to Chief Sub Editor and became the editor of the *Sunday Nation*.

Reporting of news from India and Pakistan was a sensitive issue for retaining Asian readership. The *Standard* was seen by the local Indians as pro Pakistani in line with the British 'divide and rule' policy. The *Nation* had to tread a delicate balance to remain neutral between the two countries because the Aga Khan had his community in both these countries. Thus, during the Indo-Pak Wars of 1965 and 1971, both the papers did not want to upset the local Indians who were the major advertisers and the Muslims who favoured Pakistan. When Kenneth Bolton, the editor of the *Standard,* flew to Pakistan and interviewed President Zia ul Haq and published this interview; the die was cast against his paper and many Kenyan Indians decided to stop advertising in the *Standard* and buying it, at least for some time.

The Safari was the biggest news happening around Easter every year. By 1960, it was still a local, Kenyan event with a lot of entrants coming from the 'tribe' of white settlers known as 'Kenya Cowboys'. These were joined by Asian mechanics who wanted to make a name for themselves and get publicity for their small time motor garages. During these 25 years, the Asian reporters for the *Nation* always had an edge with the Asian drivers and got many a scoop before, during and after the event. In the sports field, Asians dominated hockey, cricket and tennis during those years. The Asian reporters at the *Nation* reported their performances with a special understanding of their background.

In the cultural field, the *Nation* reviewed Bollywood films and interviewed Bollywood stars during their Kenya visits. Visiting Indian and Pakistani singers, musicians and performers and local cultural events were reported. The Asian gurus or spiritual leaders also got coverage. All this reportage helped to increase circulation and add revenue as well. Since the Asian journalists reported on Asian festivals like Diwali and Baishaki, gradually, the advertising department saw an opportunity to turn these events into lucrative supplements written by the Asian journalists. Thus in no small measure have Asian journalists contributed to build the *Nation* for its quality reporting, action photographs, competent sub-editing and attractive design.

A PEEK INTO THE NATION – PAST AND PRESENT
by Warris Vianni

This extract is taken from a Review of Birth of a NATION by Gerard Loughran, one time senior editor of the Nation newspaper. I am indebted to the reviewer, Warris Vianni, for allowing me to reproduce some of his important insights into the colonial dynamics and post-colonial impediments to journalism in Kenya, with a focus on the Nation newspapers.

The written word probably arrived in what is modern day Kenya by way of merchants' IOUs, religious tracts and letters bearing news from faraway places in Arabic, Farsi and Gujarati.

Perhaps it is fitting then that Kenya's oldest newspaper, the *East African Standard,* should have been founded in 1901 by a gentleman from Karachi and that its largest circulation daily today, the *Nation,* was founded in 1960 by a gentleman whose family hailed from Bombay. In between these two dates is a rich history of Asian engagement in the world of newspapers in Kenya. Asian printers and advertisers offered their presses and support for Johnstone Kenyatta's *Muigwithania* and Henry Muouria's *Mumenyereri;* men like Girdhari Lal Vidyarthi produced distinguished newspapers such as the mockingly titled *Colonial Times* and Pio Pinto edited the *Chronicle.* And all the while, the authorities looked on disapprovingly.

According to the *Corfield Report* on the origins and growth of Mau Mau, a meeting of Provincial Commissioners took place in October 1946 at which the question of 'pernicious propaganda and seditious articles' in vernacular newspapers was discussed. It resolved that a despatch be sent to the Secretary of State stressing among other matters:

"That certain vernacular newspapers were being financed and influenced by seditiously minded Indians and that their object was purely anti-Government and anti-European

That, as regards freedom of the Press, liberty was being mistaken for licence, and that in addition to deliberate distortion of facts, many of the articles in such newspapers contained a most dangerous and pernicious form of anti-European propaganda

That the effect of an unbridled Press amongst uneducated and politically immature Africans was infinitely more serious than that which could be achieved by inflammatory articles in newspapers in England."

It also recommended that the Criminal Investigations Department be expanded to increase scrutiny of vernacular newspapers, action in the courts to follow 'the slightest infringement of the law' and that editors to be so informed regularly. Vidyarthi and his editors made frequent appearances in the courts charged with sedition, suffering fines, imprisonment and cancellations of licences.

It would be easy to read the early history of the Nation Group of Newspapers in *Birth of a Nation* as a story about a bunch of Fleet Street boys having an adventure in the bush, on terrain inhabited only by a white settler press. The *Nation* consciously defined itself by reference only to its main rival, the *East African Standard,* then the house-journal of settler society Kenya. This reference point obscures the more complex narrative that is the heritage of the liberal press in Kenya today.

Commissioned by the Nation Group, Gerard Loughran's long gestating *Birth* is a highly readable history of the media group, fore grounded in the history of independent Kenya. This allows the author to record a richer, interwoven story about newspaper and country. Despite occasional frostbite, the Kibaki spring blooms and Kenyans continue to excavate their archives to record and analyse their sometimes troubling histories. *Birth* is a useful - if expensive - addition to this endeavour, with the author given access to company papers and records and the co-operation of a large number of interviewees.

Of the politicians approached for interviews, none responded; the student of Kenyan politics can draw his own conclusions about the value of scholarly enquiry to its practitioners. The author's acknowledgements suggest that he did not interview Karim Aga Khan, the man who founded the *Nation* (at the age of 23) or consult the papers of the late Eboo Pirbhai, the founder's principal representative in Kenya. Whilst we hear the founder's voice in communications with his management, it is at a remove. Of all the princes and presidents who have dealt with Kenya's rulers, none has had the continuity and regularity of engagement than the founder of the *Nation.* With his breadth of international experience and his perspective on the predicament of decolonised societies in Africa, the Middle East and Asia, the Aga Khan's insights into the states of mind of their Excellencies, their world-view as well as their concerns and demands could have been of great value to historians.

Newspapers, it is said, are the first drafts of history and so it is proper that the Nation Group engages in some measure of *mea culpa* for the occasions when it fell below its own standards and its newspapers failed to speak truth to power.

It cannot have been easy for proprietor and staff to navigate the darkest years, which make for chilling reading. The management could have chosen to settle for a quieter life by selling up to powerful interests or succumbing more often to casually made presidential demands. Sloppy sub-editing, a tendency to treat political issues in caricature fashion and lack of investigative zeal when there is much revealing information already in the public domain strike the reader of the *Nation* as some of its continuing problems today - and a detraction from a meaningfully free press.

A central problem confronting the press in Kenya is how to deal with a parallel shadow state that legislates secret laws through telephoned orders, decisions made by cabals meeting in obscure 2 star hotels, using brown envelopes and, occasionally, the assassin's bullet. Compounding the problem is the pretence, which the press - like the ordinary citizen, has to engage in when dealing with the shadow state. The press has to pretend that only the official state exists, and that it is acting according to the norms of constitutional order. This *Alice in Wonderland* predicament has been nourished by Kenya's obsession with formal legalism at the expense of common sense, basic decency and the truth. Sadly, our newspapers often abet this charade through their tortuously neutral, correct and boiler-plated editorials.

It was often said in the early years of Independence that a foreign owned press was a liability, making it vulnerable to politicians seeking an excuse to muzzle it. This charge is rarely heard today as Kenyans travel and learn the ways of the world for themselves. A locally owned press is no guarantee against factional interests, poor management

or susceptibility to pressure. In the case of the *Nation*, the founder's deep pockets, vision and, possibly, absence from local residence probably all helped in achieving one of its greatest successes: that it has survived, and survived as a national institution and not as a corporate football.

However, the question of ownership does not quite go away. Despite much corporate detail, we are unclear about a few basics: other than the principal shareholder (the founder no longer holds shares in a personal capacity), who are the Group's largest shareholders? Do these other shareholders nominate members to the Board? Who does sit on the main Board? How are these appointments managed? And how do the interests of Board members intersect with the incestuous Nairobi world of business and politics?

Birth confirms much that has circulated as gossip and speculation in Nairobi for many years, illuminating the tense relationship between press and government. A free press is often discomfiting to those in power. It was bound to be so for a defensive colonial authority, but it would have been interesting if the author had looked at historical continuities and teased out underlying differences. How were the anxieties of a colonial power different from the concerns of free Africa toward expressions of robust fact and opinion? What informed the differences?

Birth does not tackle interesting issues that touch on language and society and the production and flow of ideas in an oral culture. In a dangerous world, language can develop as a protective tool with a highly evolved capacity for subtlety, even downright slipperiness. But ambiguity breeds suspicion and distrust; misunderstanding is a daily hazard, circumspection good insurance.

Newspapermen, as loose purveyors of words and strange ideas - with print's distressing trail of evidence - inhabit a doubly dangerous territory. Tradition conferred little virtue on iconoclasm in the nations that were put together to construct modern Kenya. Men rarely had independent means such as would enable them to spurn society and live by their individuality. The ever-present threat of catastrophe from the risk of failed rains, inexplicable disease, a neighbour's jealous gaze or a raid from strangers enjoined co-operation, consensus and virtue in obedience. Failure to conform and to ask troubling questions was to invite censure, rejection or worse. Reverence for order - and authority - had powerful currency. Loyalty was not a dirty word. When a former president said that he used to sing like a parrot under his predecessor, having no ideas of his own, he spoke a profound truth about his society.

Before Independence, African newspapers operating as charge sheets against colonialism spoke a simpler message, and faced official disapproval. Then came the age of freedom; newspapers - this one owned by a stranger no less - introduced the people to new-fangled ideas, doubted the value of reverence and gave voice to those exiled from the council of elders. The press now conveyed a more difficult, dissonant message. And official disapproval followed. Colonialism was easier to slay, modernity a more monstrous beast.

In *Birth*, the *Nation* admits 'occasional descent to sycophancy', sometimes with hilarious results such as when it tried to airbrush a tall Aide de Camp out of a photograph to appease presidential vanity, only for the published image to show the hapless man half disembodied. Most remarkable is the disclosure that the newspaper once took a dispute between the Board and the Editor for presidential resolution, laying bare the sometimes troubling proximity between press and government. There are areas the reader wishes the author had ventured: the founder's insights being the most obvious, as well as the circumstances surrounding the disposition of Caledonia House, his former Nairobi home.

The dramatic resignation of George Githii, the *Nation's* most flamboyant editor remains perplexing. Githii had written an innocuous sounding editorial arising from a news story about the head of a sub-sect of the Mustaali Ismailis. Why did this so upset the proprietor, who is head of the Nizari Ismailis? Was Githii obliquely making a point? Ostensibly, Githii had breached a rule against commenting on religious matters that was 'carved in stone'. This raises interesting questions about how the rule has been applied subsequently given the involvement by Kenya's churches in its political controversies.

The book has a few errors, but they do not detract from its overall value. As examples, the *Colonial Times* is referred to as a Gujarati paper, we are told that Ronald Ngala died before Tom Mboya and that Mrs Charles Njonjo's maiden name was Nisbet (it was Bryson, and her first name is Margaret, not Elizabeth). More surprising is the reproduction of the Karimi & Ochieng account of the Ngoroko affair, a story now regarded with widespread doubt.

The Nation Group is to be commended for opening its archives for this significant publication of its history. Looking to its future, the big question must be how a purely locally owned and managed media group - which cannot be ruled out - will fare as it is drawn into the vortex of pressures engulfing Kenya's politics without the potential of a distant, restraining hand - or the excuse of it.

Birth of a Nation by Gerard Loughran, IB Tauris, London
© Warris Vianni.

RESURRECTING 19TH CENTURY VIRTUES
By Ali Zaidi

I began my career in publishing in the early 1980s in a dingy collection of sheds off a dingy side street in New Delhi's Paharganj, the industrial area that time forgot. Down that warren of mean streets a stone's throw from the colonial elegance of Connaught Circus, generations of underpaid workers had trudged since the mid 19th century to cramped, greasy, ill lit and ill ventilated workplaces to work with infernal machines from dawn to dusk. Not much had changed really. Our own premises boasted an actual hand-operated printing press worked by a scrawny, sweating, bare-chested old man but it was used only for fliers and posters.

There was a power operated press too, on which the prestigious little leftist weekly of current affairs on which I was a sub editor was printed. But don't run away with the wrong idea. Powered by electricity it may have been, but what it brought crashing down on to the paper was a wooden frame called a forme (which everyone pronounced farma). The forme enclosed a metal grid that could be loosened or tightened by butterfly screws on the side of the forme. The horizontal grid represented the lines on the page, the vertical grid was made to fit individual letters in the form of sorts (or fonts), inch-long ingots of steel surmounted by letters engraved proud of the steel and of course mirror images of the actual letter, so that when coated with ink and pressed on the paper they would come out the right way around (try to picture it or if you can't, carve a potato seal and try it out with an inkpad, the kind they use in Chief's offices).

A 20-strong army of compositors sat in a long narrow first floor shed (clear of the boundary wall and therefore enjoying a better light) each with his own bench and counter on which reposed the forme at a 45 degree angle and beside it a square partitioned wooden box containing piles of sorts from a to z and of course commas, full stops, hyphens, semi colons, ampersands and all that. The compositor would then compose the page, reading from a typescript on a stand in front of him, working from right to left, picking up the back to front sorts with tweezers and inserting them in place. The cricket commentary would be on the radio whenever there was a match on and the chatter would rise to a crescendo until the chief compositor sang out, 'I don't care if Gavaskar's about to get a century, get back to work or I'll dock your effing wages.' When the page was done, they would tighten the screws and run off a proof with an ink roller and a sheet of paper. The proof would descend to us subs in our shed across the inner compound from the print room, be butchered and go up again, where the screws would again be loosened, the corrections made and the formes finally despatched to the printing press.

The publication was strictly text, no pictures. On Mondays we would stroll into the place mid-morning, watch the tea boy and *askari* 'kill' the previous issue's pages, squatting on their heels under the stairway to the compositors' shed, using the inevitable tweezers to pluck the sorts out of the loosened forme and toss them into a large 'mother' box with separate compartments for a, b, c and so on. They'd be drinking tea, chatting about politics and cricket, barely looking at what they were doing. They were the same fellows who'd look over our shoulders while we were reading proofs and point out that we'd missed an upside down 's' or 'x' or a cracked font -- the point being, 'You may have been to university, sonny boy, but there's such a thing as experience...' We would loaf

around for a couple of hours, read books, correct a proof or two, then take off. I read the whole of the beautifully produced Bodley Head hardback edition of James Joyce's *Ulysses*, a gift from my mother, during my time there, learning a great deal about fonts, printing and publishing and their history -- for in between the adventures of Stephen Daedalus and Molly Bloom et al there's much abstruse discussion on these and other topics -- and quite a bit about syntax. I left after a lickspittle sub who had just joined us complained to the managing editor that I was butchering the great man's copy -- he had severe issues with the definite and indefinite articles. 'So will you leave my copy alone?' 'No, I won't.' 'You'd better leave, then.'

The years passed, I worked as a teacher and advertising copywriter and book editor and in 1989 found myself in Kenya working as a sub editor on *Executive magazine* ('Kenya's premier business journal,' no less) in its premises in Nairobi's Industrial Area. The technology had taken a leap forward (at least as far as I was concerned; the letterpress method described above had begun to be replaced at major newspapers by 'hot metal' typesetting as early as the late 19th century) and pages were created by phototypesetting -- the subs would mark up typed copy with a pencil, then send it to the typesetter, who would enter into her machine the typeface (Times New Roman) font size (10 pt), leading (12 pt), column width (5 cm) and justification (justified or, for pull quotes, ragged right) and then type it all in as on a typewriter. A long snake of glossy paper, called a galley proof, would emerge from the other end with a single column of text running down the middle -- text that, because this typesetter was the great unsung genius Annie Kyungu, was miraculously free of errors. The various editors who hung around the magazine those days had worked between them in the

UK, Ireland, the US, India and South Africa, and would gather around in wonderment as I held up a galley and announced, 'Look, 1,000 words without a single mistake.'

The galley would then go to the paste-up artists, who manned a hollow square of light tables in a large well-lit room. The galleys would be cut up and pasted with cow gum on the (A4) page in columns (4) leaving space for the pictures, which were in the form of bromides -- a special camera would take a picture of a black and white photograph that reduced the image to a collection of tiny dots, a bromide. At this stage, there was room for creativity, letting a picture jut into a column, or even having text wrap around a cut out (Paul Muite's gesturing hand sticking out into the text, for example), but it involved painstaking measurements and many trips back and forth to Annie's machine (for Muite's hand, make line 42 3.8 cm long -- forefinger; line 43, make 3.5 cm -- middle finger; line 44 say 3.6 cm -- ring finger; line 45 say 3.9 -- little finger; line 46 reverts to 5 cm). Fortunately, we were a monthly, and I spent many enjoyable, stress-free hours crouched over the light table with the patient, meticulous Josephat Kibiro. (He is dead, and I've lost track of Annie, alas; only now I realise you don't actually get to meet and work with very many true professionals in this world.)

In 1991 or thereabouts, Amstrads entered our lives -- little boxy computers with black screens across which crawled white sans-serif text. The only aspect of operations changed by their advent was the subs' job -- we edited on the Amstrad and printed out the copy to be sent to the typesetter. But they had two miraculous features: spell checkers and find-and-replace. One day a colleague walked in and said, 'Very sorry, Ali, so-and-so's name is spelled wrong throughout the copy we gave you; I know it's a tedious job, but please do the needful.' Before he could turn around and leave, I said, 'Done!' 'What did you do? Show me.' I showed him and he left muttering, 'Gimmicks, all gimmicks...'

The Amstrads turned out to be the first pebbles bouncing across the road. Soon the IT avalanche hit us. Proper computers with sophisticated word processors, the first desktop publishing programs (in which you laid out a page with miraculous swiftness, but had to leave boxes for the bromides to be pasted into), followed by scanners and the stunning image manipulation software Photoshop, magic made easy. You could do cut outs, text wraps, surrealistic graphics, everything. Soon we were creating the entire magazine on my desktop, and having a lot of fun; since everyone was on the same playing field, you would dream up a new stunt like dropping the shadow of a cut-out human figure positioned in the margin of the page behind a column of text -- and find the British or US papers doing the same thing a couple of months later (but did we say?). So a lot of fun, but some embarrassingly amateurish showing off too -- look, my headline has a drop shadow and a bevelled edge and I've sprayed the bottom half red!!!

Then in 1998 I joined *The East African*. Not only did it seem a rather prim looking paper, headlines no larger than 48 points, pictures all rectangular and not a cut out in sight; it was produced on something called the Atex system ('The Economist uses it, you know'), a precursor of the database-mounted systems newspapers use these days. And guess what, it was white letters crawling across a black screen! Talk about time machines... I used to watch with horror as deputy chief-sub Julius Maina 'laid out' a page -- manipulating a baffling array of dots, dashes, numbers and rules that through some mysterious alchemy emerged from the printer as text in neat columns, complete with pictures.

Fortunately, within a year or so, we got proper computers (if you can use such a description for the oh-so-cute first generation of iMacs with their round bloody mice). Then managing editor Joe Odindo, a complete newspaperman who thought always in both word and image, gave me my head to do fancy things in the Magazine pages, but I had by now got the 'clean, classy, elegant' bug and never went quite as hog wild as in the old days.

Unbeknownst to us, we had turned up a blind alley. Because the same person could edit and lay out pages on their machine, the distinction between designers and wordsmiths became blurred, and each sub-editor both edited copy and laid out their own pages. Not everybody has a visual sense alongside editing ability, the quality that subs are hired for in the first place. If the copy was short, pictures became menacingly big; if it was long, the pictures shrank until they appeared to crouch terrified in a corner of the page.

In late 2004 or thereabouts, Nation Newspapers purchased Pagespeed, a modern database-mounted system incorporating Adobe's Indesign and Incopy, and a complete redesign of *The East African* came as part of the package. Based on an 18-column grid that allowed you use combinations of four text columns of four grid columns each (i.e. 16 grid columns) with a strip of white space (two grid columns), it transformed *The East African* from a neat, clean and dowdy paper into a neat, clean, sharp and modern one.

I created templates for various sections and pages of the paper from the basic design, and for some months thereafter was able to police its implementation, with an explicit mandate from then managing editor Charles Kimathi, in the teeth of opposition from subs who muttered things like, 'Is the design supposed to serve

us or are we supposed to serve the design?' 'Yes, you're supposed to serve the design!' 'We're human beings, not slaves.' Slowly but surely, things began to slip...

Over the years, I began to bend the ears of editorial director Wangethi Mwangi and Joe Odindo, by now group ME, about returning to the old division of labour, especially as the new system made it practically possible, with the designers creating the page in Indesign and the subs editing copy in Incopy, where they could see the page and change text, captions, etc. without being able to resize pictures, for example. By this time, the appearance of the paper had become so text heavy that one loyal reader, responding to a questionnaire, said it looked like a physics 'textbook'.

Then, in 2009, having served under four managing editors -- Odindo, Mbatau wa Ngai, Charlie Kimathi and Jaindi Kisero -- I was appointed acting ME, as incoming editor Nick Wachira was still completing his studies abroad. As it turned, the major undertaking of my year-long tenure was to supervise the implementation of another redesign ordered from on high. The US-based designer who was brought in, Kelley Frankeny, was appalled at our system ('or lack thereof,') and straightaway brought in art director Anthony Sitti, assisted by a junior designer, to police her design and introduce the new concept of 'data visualisation'. And that, dear reader, is how the new all-singing, all-dancing publication you hold in your hands finally entered the 21st century -- by resurrecting 19th century virtues.

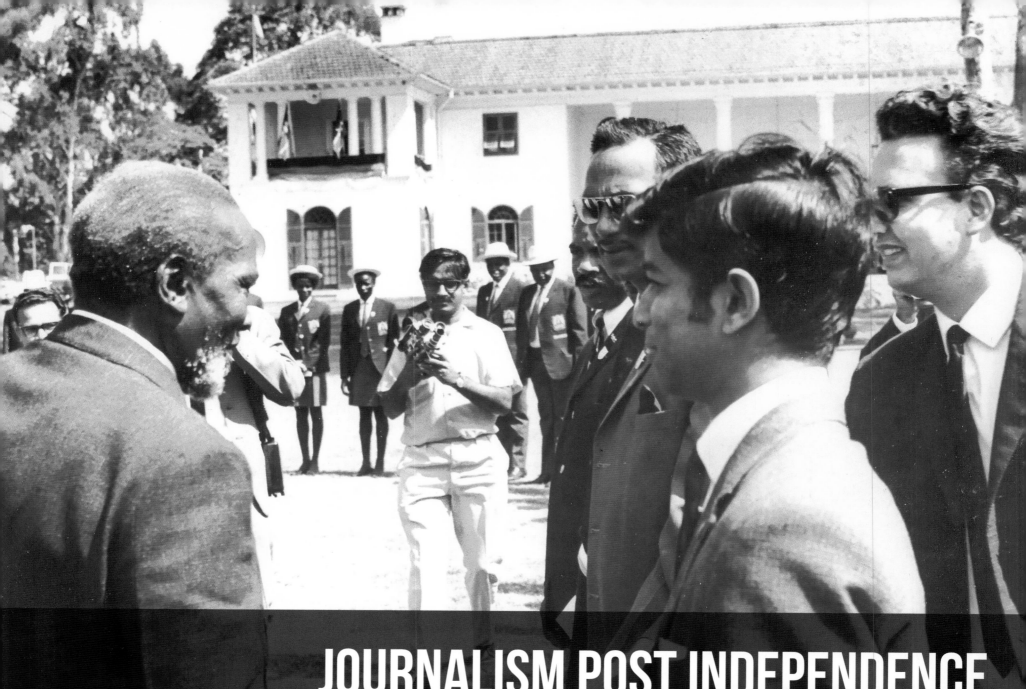

JOURNALISM POST INDEPENDENCE

THE PRINT JOURNALISTS

ABDUL-KARIM HUDANI

Writer

I was born in Kisumu in 1943 and started my career as a journalist around 1963 when I was still a student in High School. I wrote for Jaramogi Oginga Odinga's *Nyanza Times* which was bi-lingual in Dholuo and English, I was fluent in Dholuo. I also contributed to *Navyug*, *Africa Samaachar* and the *Colonial Times* as well as a Gujarati magazine called *Shobbha*.

ABDUL-KARIM HUDANI

I had no training in journalism - I consider myself a 'self-inspired man' and I guess I should thank my father for it all. He was very interested in reading many different newspapers and subscribed to Gujarati publications from India such as *Junam Bhumi,Chitra-Lekha* and *Ahand Anand*. These are some of my re-collections. My father was always reading in libraries and I followed his example. He was a role model that inspired me. I even remember that on numerous occasions my mother would ask me to go and fetch my father from the library for lunch/dinner.

My main interest was in Luo politics though I also wrote about general politics in Kenya. I was very very ambitious as a writer - I enjoyed writing and contributing to newspapers. My passion was I wanted to join the Aga Khan's newspaper, the *Nation* and succeeded in getting the job. To see one's name as a byline in the region's most widely read newspaper was a journalist's dream.

Just prior to the *Nation* I had worked for the French News Agency called AFP. I was one of the first Asian journalists to join the *Nation* and rose to be a 'Sub-Editor'. That promotion for an Asian journalist has greater import than normally acknowledged because the *Nation* at that time preferred blacks or whites to browns. I always faced resistance when interviewing ministers and other well-known personalities as they would be expecting an African or a *mzungu*.

The National Union of Journalists elected me as 'father' of the Nation chapel for a year. The Asian journalists were few and had a very minimal role and did not make much impact – they were the 'labourers' i.e. making stories out of news releases. It was very difficult under this 'colonial African management' as promotion was reserved for the blacks.

ALL the newspapers were pro-Israel and, generally speaking, I supported the Arab League. You can imagine the authorities were very hostile and they (Press Officers) even warned me personally to take it easy. To make matters worse I supported Jaramogi Odinga and criticised the Africanisation programme which, in my opinion, victimised the Asian *dukawalas*.

ALFRED DE ARAUJO

Following the constant harassment and threats I received; in 1968 I founded my own newspaper, the *Kenya Mirror* – the first locally owned public paper in independent Kenya. However, in 1978 I was arrested and charged with sedition - the latest incident was that I had demanded that an African student who had criticised the Aga Khan school, should be expelled. Little did I know that the student was related to an important politician! I closed down my newspaper, the *Kenya Mirror*, and the charge was dropped.

I then started another newspaper, *Mambo*, but could not continue with it. Much later I learnt that the printers had been threatened if they went ahead and produced my paper. In 1979 I applied to the UK Government for

political asylum and was granted it. I arrived in London in December 1979 as a refugee.

I started a newspaper in the UK which did not succeed. I am now 70 years old and retired and nearly blind. The FM Radio is my constant companion and I love my daily gym sessions.

ALFRED de ARAUJO
From a correspondent

Alfred de Araujo began his journalism career in 1964 just a few months after Kenya gained its independence. He was educated at Dr Ribeiro Goan School and was a

classmate of fellow *Nation* journalists Norman Da Costa and Polly Fernandes. Alfred trained with the *Nation* group and, during his 18-year career with the largest newspaper in East Africa; he also free-lanced for the Associated Press news agency, covering events in some dozen countries in Eastern Africa.

After a stint as a reporter at the *Nation*, Alfred quickly rose through the ranks and was a fixture on the sub-editor's desk, eventually taking over as chief copy editor. He was then promoted to managing editor of the *Sunday*

Nation. He immigrated to England with his wife and three daughters soon after the 1982 coup when censorship over news reporting became very stringent.

In the UK Alfred joined the Surrey Mirror Group of Newspapers and it wasn't long before this talented Kenyan was editor of the group. It is believed that at the time he was the only non-white editor of a provincial newspaper group in Britain.

He once described his years in Kenya as a delicate balancing act. 'It was very much like walking on eggshells most of the time. I opted not to become a Kenya citizen and yet was running the largest selling newspaper in Eastern Africa … It was an incongruous situation really, but in retrospect, those years were to be the most deeply satisfying and fulfilling moments of my life.'

Over the years Alfred met and interviewed a number of luminaries that included kings, presidents, astronauts and film stars. But the one assignment that Alfred calls the highlight of his reporting career was his coverage of the Entebbe Raid on July 3, 1976 when Israeli commandos swung into action to rescue hijacked Jewish passengers. He was one of the first newsmen to arrive at Nairobi's Embakasi Airport where the commandos refuelled after that lightning strike in Uganda and Alfred spent the next three days on the story, working virtually non-stop without sleep. 'For its sheer drama and international impact, few stories have given me a similar sense of thrill of enjoyment,' he was to say.

Alfred retired from journalism a couple of years ago, but has found a part-time gig with the British government and is enjoying every minute of it away from deadline pressures. (Author's note: Alfred de Araujo declined to send in his bio).

ANTO DE SOUZA
Writer

I was born in Nairobi, Kenya in 1952 of Goan parentage. By profession, I am a microbiologist and worked with Kenya Breweries Ltd till my departure in 1988 for Australia.

I got into sports reporting being a hockey player and athlete myself at club level. I can remember writing hockey reports from the nearby Railway hockey grounds from my high school days when Nairobi hockey league

ANTO DE SOUZA

matches were played; and sending reports to the clubs involved and to the school magazine. I was very fortunate to have a very good English teacher in the late Anthony D'Souza at Dr Ribeiro Goan School, now renamed Parklands School. Anthony was a former Kenya national hockey coach and one-time manager of Kenya's famous athlete, Kipchoge Keino.

This developed my interest in writing and I later published my own hockey scrapbook with newspaper hockey cuttings and pictures of Kenyan Olympians who had done well at Olympic Games from 1960-72 and thereafter.

My newspaper reporting commenced as a hockey reporter with the *Sunday Post* in 1972, just after the Munich Olympics. I had a long association with its Sports Editor, the late Saude George, who christened me into the sporting media and I learned from his accurate reporting and sometimes critical but positive views.

The *Post* was very competitive with the *Sunday Nation* in sports coverage, and perhaps had a better rating due to its live coverage at most matches and meetings; and detailed interviews with prominent sportsmen and women. The highlight was reporting the M R De Souza Gold Cup hockey tournament which took place every year during the Easter long weekend.

Teams from all over East Africa as well as overseas participated in this tournament. The most acclaimed were the Kampala Sikh Union, PIA from Pakistan and Real Club de Polo from Barcelona in Spain which won the Cup in 1977 beating the Nairobi Goan Institute in the final.

Another highlight was in the field of athletics where I had a column titled 'Stop Watch'. Prominent athletes

for a few years, I was the hockey correspondent for the *Standard* newspaper under Sports Editor, George Obiero.

At the *Daily* and the *Sunday Nation*, the Sports Editors were Philip Ndoo, a former Kenya marathon runner, and later Dick Agudah. The M R De Souza Gold Cup was again the highlight - in 1984, Kenya Breweries became the first African team to win this prestigious tournament at the City Park Stadium in Parklands, where later, in 1987, it got its first artificial hockey turf.

Interestingly, it was myself and former Kenya Olympic hockey captain, Avtar Singh Sohal, who had founded the Breweries hockey team, having both worked for this company. Several of its African players later went on to represent Kenya in hockey.

In 1986 I reported for the *Nation* newspaper at the World Hockey Cup in London where Kenya just missed selection. Australia, where I later migrated to, then won its first World Cup beating England 2-1 in the final.

Another memorable occasion was reporting in the hockey section at the All-Africa Games in Nairobi in 1987 where Kenya won that tournament and went on to represent Africa in the Olympic Games in Seoul in 1988, the year I emigrated to Australia.

In late 1987 the first ever Africa versus Asia hockey match was played in Nairobi just after the All-Africa Games where the top players from Africa and Asia were gathered. I actually put back my departure for Australia in order to witness, and report, this match which was a first in Kenya and Africa.

Emigrating to Australia in 1988, I took a short break from writing and later had a short stint in a regional

were featured such as John Ngugi, a multiple world cross country champion; as well as features on several of the Kenyan ethnic groupings which excelled in different running events, namely the Kalenjin, Kisii, Maasai and Kamba.

With the demise of the *Sunday Post*, I later became the hockey correspondent of the *Nairobi Times,* a daily evening newspaper which eventually also folded after some years.

After a short break, I joined the Nation Group in the late seventies and eighties as their hockey correspondent, and also wrote a few select stories on athletics. Simultaneously,

newspaper, the *Macarthur Advertiser,* writing a hockey column on the local hockey league on a weekly basis.

Then came the 1994 World Hockey Cup in Sydney - there I reported on the tournament and had a chance to catch up with Kenyan hockey officials and English and Indian hockey journalists whom I had met during the London World Cup.

At the 1994 World Cup I re-united with the Indian hockey captain Jude Felix, whom I had known as a young Indian player travelling with the Indian junior hockey team on a tour of Kenya in 1983. Felix was then a little known player but had gradually risen to the high echelons of Indian hockey.

With the coming of the Olympic Games in Sydney in 2000, I resumed full-time writing and started reporting for the *Wollongong Advertiser*, a regional weekly newspaper, not far from the Sydney metropolitan centre. *Wollongong*, my present residence on the coastal belt, has a setting similar to my home town, Mombasa, in Kenya.

I was the hockey and athletics journalist and covered all the hockey and track regional meetings including the

Sydney World Track Classic. Thus I met with Kenyan athletes David Rudisha and Asbel Kiprop, regulars to the Australian annual track meetings.

In hockey, the highlights were reporting on the traditional rivalries between clubs in the Wollongong area; comparable to the fierce rivalries I had reported on in Nairobi hockey circles between the Goan and Sikh clubs, and later the Kenya Breweries and Barclays Bank Club. In 2012, I reported on the Australian hockey teams in the London Olympics.

BAL RAJ (BILLY) CHIBBER (1923-1993)
By Shailja Chibber (daughter)

Billy Chibber was first a teacher and then studied for the Bar before embarking on his career as a newsman. He went on to a successful journalistic career that spanned three decades and as many continents.

A second generation Kenyan Indian, he was born to a family of Nairobi teachers in 1923. With his good looks and remarkable singing voice, he yearned to be an actor but instead, followed the family tradition to take up teaching at the tender age of 17. In the 1950s he was accepted to The Bar at Lincoln's Inn in London. Here, while scratching out his student allowance, he began writing articles for *Sport* magazine and hit on the career he most identified with - journalism.

In 1960 he returned to East Africa to join the *Uganda Argus* as a feature writer. In 1963, after his marriage to Prem Datta in India, he returned to Kenya where he wrote for the *Nation* series across several titles (*Drum, Trust, Daily Nation*) in key posts - including senior reporter and sub-editor. He was recognised among his

BILLY CHIBBER

peers as a journalist of 'considerable talent, impartiality and integrity', and gained a reputation for being a hard-nosed investigative journalist despite his persona as a mild-mannered intellectual.

Billy Chibber was one of the first journalists to be expelled from Uganda in 1966 in a high-profile case that led to the intervention of both the British Secretary of State for Commonwealth Relations and the then Kenyan President, Jomo Kenyatta.

He was posted in Kampala, working as a foreign correspondent for the Kenyan *Daily Nation* newspaper and the *Hindustan Times* when he was served with a deportation order which deemed him to be an 'undesirable immigrant' and was given 24 hours to leave the country. On account of holding a British passport, he was ordered to return to Britain despite being a permanent resident of Nairobi.

The British Secretary of State demanded to know the reasons behind the order. It was widely held that the actual reason was that Mr Chibber was simply a foreign journalist reporting on policy and events in post-independence Uganda. At the time there was an agreement between Uganda, Kenya and Tanzania which said that a deportee of any one country would not be allowed to enter either of the other two countries. This was overturned for Mr Chibber by the Kenyan President following an appeal by the Editor of the *Daily Nation*, so

EXCLUSIVE

WHILE I was working in Uganda for the *Nation* group of newspapers during Dr. Obote's rule, I was declared a prohibited immigrant and ordered to be deported within 24 hours from the country to Britain (because I held a British passport). But contrary to an understanding then existing between Kenya, Uganda and Tanzania, that a non-citizen deported from one state should be denied entry into either of the others, I was allowed to re-enter and remain in Kenya by a series of extraordinary incidents and the generosity of President Mzee Jomo Kenyatta.

The man who played a prominent part in this was Mr. George Githii, editor-in-chief of the *Nation* and a former private secretary to the President. I am the only non-citizen to whom this privilege was ever granted in East Africa.

Dr. Milton Obote (now in exile in Dar es Salaam) was Prime Minister of Uganda at the time that the late Edward Mutesa, Kabaka of Buganda, was the President. Dr. Obote and Sir Edward had been at loggerheads for some time because of the increasing interference by Dr. Obote in Presidential matters and affairs of the Buganda kingdom. This exploded into open conflict when the late Mr. Daudi Ocheng, one of the Edward supporters, introduced a motion in the National Assembly alleging corruption against Dr. Obote, the Minister for Planning and Community Development, Mr. A.

CHANDER MEHRA

Writer

I was born in Lahore, undivided India, in 1934 and was educated in Lahore and Delhi, with a degree in Humanities in 1953. I had a torrid introduction to journalism as a trainee in a yellow tabloid in the Indian capital. I soon discovered that the loud-mouthed Editor-Publisher of the weekly used the power of the pen to blackmail his targets, mostly important leaders in politics and business.

he praised the role of Indians in training Africans 'in manual occupations' and emphasized that African and Indian enterprise was mutually dependent and beneficial: 'Indians have trained more Africans than all the schools and workshops put together. This will be evident to anyone passing along River Road in Nairobi where a large number of Africans are at any time receiving training as tailors, carpenters, black-smiths, shoe-makers, masons, compositors and petty shop-keepers (*Colonial Times*, 9 February 1946)'. In a later series he accused the authorities of exaggerating the figures of Indians in Kenya, and made the case for unhindered Indian immigration (*Colonial Times*, 20 September 1947).

In 1946 he founded *Forward*. The paper's primary concern was with South Asians in Kenya and elsewhere, but also devoted a lot of space to international affairs, particularly the 'third world'. Its outlook was anti-colonial. It supported African opposition to the *kipande* and the demands for elected representatives and equality in employment.

In 1952, and again in 1961, he was elected to the Legco, joined KANU in 1962 and was appointed Assistant Minister in the Ministry for Constitutional Affairs. At

this time he broke from the Kenya Indian Congress (formerly EAINC) and formed the Kenya Freedom Party, wrote its constitution and served as its chairman. In 1963 when KANU swept into power he was elected by fellow MPs to the House of Representatives and was appointed Parliamentary Secretary in the Ministry of Constitutional Affairs and later to the Prime Minister, Jomo Kenyatta. In 1958 he had been elected president of the Law Society of Kenya and six years later, Chanan Singh resigned from Parliament and took up the office of Puisne judge of the High Court of Kenya – a post he retained until his death in 1977.

Chanan Singh was a prolific writer and a voracious reader, his home literally overflowed with books. Apart from the editorials and regular features for the newspapers, he contributed widely to legal, political and historical writing. He never sought publicity for himself; his sole concerns were for the country and the rejection of oppression.

Source: *Durrani, Shiraz, 2006*
             Frederiksen, Bodil Folke, 2011
             AwaaZ Issue No 1, 2002.

CHANDER MEHRA

I married my Kenyan Punjabi heartthrob, Sanyukata, in 1955 and moved to East Africa. There I tried to get a job as a greenhorn in the *East African Standard*, but British editor declined to meet me. Haroon Amador *Colonial Times* frankly admitted: 'We have no resources to hire anyone.' (Ironically during my second coming, I had a chance to interview an ailing Haroon towards the end of his own career in Kenya.)

So I had no choice but to take up a job in the colonial civil service. I worked in the Registrar General's Department. The Assistant Registrar General was Charles Njonjo - his first job on his return to Kenya after being called to the bar. Visho Sharma and I were his colleagues. During that period, I started *Gaiety*, a monthly magazine on art and culture. G L Vidyarthi, owner of the Colonial Times Press in Reata Road, Nairobi, was the printer. I knew Girdhari Lal well as a printer, not as a journalist.

But I felt out of place in that colonial service and returned to New Delhi to join the United States Information Service (USIS) where I worked as a program analyst for

ten years before being retrenched. I then joined the India News and Features Agency before becoming Executive Editor of the National Press Agency. I quit the position to return to Kenya and be with my family.

In 1979, Joe Rodrigues took me on as Revise Editor of *Nation* Newspapers and soon promoted me to Training Editor. However, Joe's successors made things difficult for me and my work permit was not renewed even though I continued to function as Africa Correspondent of The *Statesman*, India, and as Representative of the International Press Institute.

I was arrested thrice because my commentaries were inimical to the dictatorial regime. I exposed several aspects of mis-governance, corruption and foreign bank accounts, among other things. I was incarcerated in the Nyayo house basement twice and once somewhere around Naivasha. But never for more than 72 hours, the statutory limit of such arrests. The interrogators kept asking me to reveal the identity of my sources. I was repeatedly warned against telling anyone about my arrest, 'otherwise, your family will not be safe'. These arrests were harrowing for my family because they had to search for me at police stations, hospitals and even the City Mortuary.

Around 1985, Philip Ochieng, an ex-colleague at the *Nation*, took me in as Training Manager of the *Kenya Times*. My application for a work permit was, however, denied together with a note from Milton ole Ncharo of the Immigration Department that I should be told to leave the country within a week. I left the country promptly and proceeded to the Seychelles as a member of the Foreign Correspondents Association of East Africa.

I was able to 'manipulate' my return to Kenya on a visitor's pass and be with my family again. With no

possibility of getting a work permit, but with several renewals of my visitor's pass, I now moonlighted at odd jobs. In 2000 I was diagnosed with a cancer ailment and taken to the Apollo Hospital in New Delhi for treatment. I then decided to stay in India.

A cancer-survivor, I have been hospitalised for the last seven years but have continued to write on my ramshackle desktop and have completed the manuscripts of three books: *Soldiers of Allah* and *Anatomy of Diabolism*, political thrillers; as well as *CORRUPTION: The Tragedy of Africa*, a sequel to my earlier book on corruption. My published books include: *Corruption: Dealing with the Devil*, and a novel *Jihad Rediscovered*, banned by some Islamic states.

Having been detained without trial thrice because of my writing, even today, I am a 'Prohibited Immigrant' in the Kenya Immigration Department's voluminous file on myself. The manuscript of my book, *Good Governance: The Great Debate*, was seized by the special branch, and is lost forever.

CHHOTU KARADIA (1936-1990)

By Jasu Kishan (sister)

Chhotubhai Karadia, my older brother, was born at Karadi in Gujarat, India in 1936. That same year, our father, Bhananbhai Jasmat Karadia, travelled to Kenya in an Arab dhow. Nine years later, Chhotubhai and our mother, Dahiben, joined him. He was the third of six children; I am the youngest in the family, born in 1950 in Nairobi.

CHHOTU KARADIA

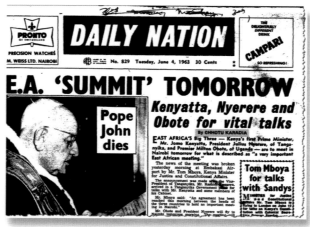

Chhotubhai attended the Duke of Gloucester School in Nairobi. His strongest subject was English and my mother says, 'he had his head stuck in books from the moment he arrived home from school'. He was a brilliant student and because of this was able to secure a scholarship to study further. To this end, in 1954-56 he went to India to study English at St Xavier's College in Mumbai.

Our father, Bhananbhai, was a carpenter by trade and worked as a foreman on building sites. But he had an interest in writing and used to write for newspapers and magazines when he was in India. Later in Nairobi he wrote for Haroon Ahmed's *Africa Samachar*. I believe Chhotubhai got his inspiration from my father.

He began his journalistic career in Nairobi as a news reader in Gujarati on the Hindustani Service of the VOK (Voice of Kenya). Among his colleagues were Shakoor Ahmed and Chaman lal Chaman. In 1960 he was one of Michael Curtis's team which launched the Aga Khan's *Daily Nation*. His oral and written skills in the English

language, his experience as a radio journalist and his liberal thinking could have been the deciding factors in choosing him.

He was very charismatic, a very down to earth person who had this ability to capture people's attention. For example, he used to do lot of canvassing for local elections. He was very people orientated and friendly and would help anyone, irrespective of their culture, race or status. He treated everyone with equal respect whether young or old and believed in equal opportunity for all.

In 1964 he moved to the UK to join the rest of his family who had immigrated there in early 1961. He worked at first as a freelance in Fleet Street specializing in race relations. Then he joined the *Birmingham Post* in 1967. Three years later he interrupted his career to continue his education. He read economics, politics and sociology as a mature student at Ruskin College, Oxford. From there he proceeded to Sussex University where he graduated in International Relations.

Chhotubhai returned to journalism and joined the *Western Mail* in Cardiff and later moved to the *Guardian*, London. In 1977 he was invited to India to become managing editor of *India Today*. He was a member of the Indian press council. In 1980 he left India and went to Vienna, where he worked as one of the founding editors of OPEC News Agency. He returned to England a year later to start a magazine of his own. In 1982 he founded *Asian Post* and edited it until April 1984.

Chhotu Karadia died on 11 February, 1990 at the age of 54, peacefully in his sleep, in London. My brother was born before his time. I miss him terribly especially on Raksha Bandhan Day...

CYPRIAN FERNANDES

Writer

During the 14 years (1960-1974) I was with the Nation, I tried to push every boundary I encountered, asked Why? at every opportunity, fearlessly and without a care for danger or deportation. I was forced to finally call it a day when a mystery person told my wife that 'they are going to put a bullet in his head.' I left school at a little over 12 years of age, worked as bank clerk, as a stock clerk, was the Colony Statistical Officer at the Probation and Remand Service and at the age of 16 was an instant journalist.

In early 1960, I came in off the street and conned, no almost barged (with the cheekiest smile ever), my way (I did not have an appointment) to an interview with *Daily Nation* founding Editor John Bierman, and got a job as a junior sports reporter which I held for just a day. Sports Editor Tom Clarke promoted me to a senior after 24 hours. From that moment on, my star shone and continued to shine until my departure in 1974.

The previous day I had come into the press room and Works Supervisor Stan Denman (later to become Managing Director of Nation Newspapers) had shown me the 'paste up' room where computer generated columns of print were composited into pages. I told him that was not what I was looking for and he virtually kicked my butt out of the door.

I had never seen the inside of a newspaper office before. Journalism was not my first choice for a career. My heart was set on criminal law but domestic issues meant university or even a secondary school education was out of the question. I learnt everything I know from the thousands of books I read. I got the yearning for criminal law from all the detective and courtroom drama books, especially the Perry Mason and Agatha Christie series. As a young boy, I was a book-aholic, reading an average of three to four books a day. I drove my friends raving mad behaving as in an investigation (interrogating friends) or in a courtroom drama (cross-examining friends). These make-believe skills were to hold me in brilliant stead as an interviewer later in life.

I went to St Teresa Boys' school in Eastleigh (a lower middle class western suburb designated originally for Asian settlement by the colonial government). Both the boys' and girls' schools were located on the northern ridge of Mathare Valley which was several kilometres long. Mathare Mental Hospital stood on the southern ridge.

By 1954 the whole valley was a wall-to-wall squatter camp of mud huts, corrugated iron sheet lean-tos - a complete shanty town home mainly to the Kikuyu. It was a hovel of the worst kind possible with no sanitation, no running water, no medical facilities or sewerage. At the bottom of the valley there was once a river of sorts and

CYPRIAN FERNANDES

in my earliest childhood I could remember seeing little fishes regularly.

I did not know it at the time but nationalist Pio Gama Pinto had set up and financed a Mau Mau war council in Mathare Valley. By 1954 it was mostly a cesspit. Somehow thousands of people called it home and lived generally peacefully. Illegally brewed local beer (*changaa*) was plentiful as were bicycle mechanics and a whole generation who were the pioneers of recycling motor car parts. There were barbers, charcoal makers, hut builders, thatched roof repairers, tailors, *karanis* (clerks who could read and write in English).

This was my university of the street and the playground of my childhood where I think I spent the happiest time of my life. It was here that I learnt of the unshakeable faith in Jomo Kenyatta and the other political leaders. The various tribes were always suspicious of each other. I sympathised with their many frustrations, especially the loss of their human dignity. I did not know it then but I supported the fight for freedom if only to remove the yoke of enslavement.

The Mau Mau rebellion during the Emergency (1952-1956), resulted in hundreds of deaths of Africans and a few white farmers and Asians. It was a peasant uprising with the rank and file recruited via powerful oathing ceremonies. Mathare Valley was the best classroom I ever knew and my teachers were the living proof of the history they were making. Nothing could have been more hands-on.

Unfortunately, as young as I was, I was caught in the round up of Kikuyus by British soldiers. Thousands of mothers screamed in terror. Everywhere a child was sobbing uncontrollably as shots rang out all around us. The loss of life of men, women and children was repeated throughout Kenya. Blood wetted the earth and death was everywhere. It was a supreme sacrifice for freedom and freedom equalled only one thing: land, give us back our earth and return to your own country.

We were marched up the valley and made to sit with our hands on our heads on Eastleigh Road stretching several kilometres four deep. I tried to explain to a soldier in English that I was not an African: Look at my straight hair and the chocolate brown colour of my skin.

All I got was a huge kick that doubled me up. Before the trucks arrived, a Kikuyu elder who knew me spoke to an African policeman and explained that I was an Indian. I was numbed and I just could not think. Except one thought, wish I was big enough and I would kick that bastard back. We boarded the trucks and headed for detention somewhere. I was a detainee, suspected of Mau Mau activities … rubbish I thought. My head was hurting from the kick and a couple of hands were soothing my head and drying my tears. Don't worry, I was told, we will defend you as much as we can. After travelling a few kilometres the truck stopped and I was dropped off at a police station. I sat alone in a cell until my father picked me up just after 6pm and we walked all the way back home.

Over the next few months, each day you would see several Africans hanging by the neck in the honeysuckle trees that line the northern boundary of our school. I never returned to my beloved valley again. Set against my own miserable life, it was easy to empathise, even be as one with their suffering. I had to move on, besides I was traumatised and scared shitless. That white soldier's size 15 military issue boot (pardon the exaggeration) haunted my nights for a long time.

On the other hand, I was full of grief and mourned the rape of Mathare Valley. I lost a complete world. I lost my teachers, my friends, smiles, the laughter, the tribal elders, the witchdoctors, tribal medicine men and the magic of seeing the shanty town survive against huge odds, the ingenuity of creating survival out of virtually nothing, even managing smiles and laughter even in the worst of times. The raids continued sporadically over the next few years but the valley never seemed to lose its numbers in population, 1000 detained, another 1000

28   DAILY NATION, Monday, June 14, 1971

TELLI URGES BIG SUPPORT FOR NAIROBI TRADE FAIR

IN HIS general report to the OAU Council of Ministers currently meeting here and the Heads of State meeting OAU Secretary - General Diallo Telli has warned that unless there is total participation by OAU members in the Pan-African Trade Fair, to be held in Nairobi next year, the current deficiencies in inter - African trade will remain.

From
CYPRIAN FERNANDES:
ADDIS ABABA, Sunday

M. Telli says in his report that the Trade Fair is one important tool of practical promotion of African trade and economy.

"The progress anticipated in the field of industrialisation as well as agriculture requires more effective organisation of inter-African trade as well as the access of African products to external markets.

"The fair is designed to offer OAU members an opportunity to familiarise economic production in Africa with variety, quality and prospects of economic production in Africa in order to stimulate intra-African trade."

M. Telli also explains that a feature of the trade fair will be a symposium which will discuss the role of development in Africa and this fair will be held jointly by the OAU and the ECA.

I understand that finance for this major symposium will be made available by UNCTAD and the OAU with some ECA contribution.

M. Telli has expressed the feeling that unless the success of the fair is established at this session, the desired results may not be forthcoming.

Proof of possible massive OAU support for the fair was given today when the plenary session — dealing with the budget — unanimously voted a further 30,000 dollars for fair expenditure.

With the Kenya Government spending some £98,000, the OAU had pledged 142,400 dollars and the new vote is to be used for filming the fair and for servicing OAU Organisation Committee meetings in Nairobi.

Pressing for the extra money in the plenary was Mr. Bernard Adundo, assistant to the director of the fair and a Senior Assistant Secretary in Kenya's Ministry of Foreign Affairs.

So far some 15 countries

successful fair in Nairobi."

While in Addis Ababa, Mr. Adundo is following up his meetings with respective governments on the fair.

QUEEN ELIZABETH re
Trooping the Colour cer

COMMITTEE OF SEVEN REPORT

FROM PAGE 1

attained such proportions that they might be extremely detrimental to the OAU united front by sowing seeds of discord, distrust and disunity."

His comments are apparently aimed at African countries which favour a dialogue with South Africa outside the framework of the Lusaka Manifesto, which does not give South Africa a certificate of respectability.

The committee's proposals include establishment of combat posts with military staff to channel aid to guerrilla groups fighting white minority Governments.

The proposed combat posts, to be established in countries bordering on areas where liberation groups are active, would form a direct link between guerrilla groups and the OAU.

In recent years there has been growing criticism of countries that do not more than seven countries contribute regularly to the Liberation Fund, mainly because of allegations of misappropriation and mismanagement.

Permanent

urges the summit to very close look at the affairs and make concre posals.

The major criticism ALC in the sector of libe movements came fror South-West Africa P Organisation, which c that organisations were fled by the ALC as "ge moderate and reactiona

It said the latter two es received meagre assi from the ALC and que its right to classify org tions. It claimed furthe liberation movements Eastern Socialist incli were favoured by the whose Executive Secret George Magombe of Tan

"We are carrying o armed struggle and not a gle for a triumph of any sophy. It is not necess read or recite Lenin, Ma tung or Abraham Linc retrieve our birthrigh unlock the chains of sla Swapo says.

Ruiru is best Kiambu choir

RUIRU Division in K District was declared th overall choir in the Divisional Music Festiv at the Secretarial Colleg

10 DAILY NATION, Monday, January 18, 1971

NATION Chief Reporter CYPRIAN FERNANDES continues his investigation of the Cabora Bassa dam project. The last article discussed the Rhodesian and Zambian views. Today he looks at the British involvement in Cabora Bassa.

British involvement in Cabora Bassa

BRITISH involvement in the Cabora Bassa dam project.

1. GEC-English Electric-AEI:
In autumn 1969, following the Swedish withdrawal from ZAMCO, it appeared that the British combine GEC-EE-AEI were ready to participate instead.

Shortly after, following some protests and public discussion, it was announced that GEC had not after all been invited to participate. The Labour Government said at the time: "It is not the Government's policy to dissuade or prevent companies from engaging in the legitimate trade or dealing in Mozambique". (Hansard 15-12-69).

They also said that if breach

3. Guest, Keen and Nettlefold: In April 1970 a Press release from South Africa House (London) announced that the British firm of GKN, major manufacturers of engineering equipment, was "expected to play an important part in supplying equipment" for the dam, through a new Mozambican subsidiary. After conflicting statements, GKN will neither confirm nor deny this.

4. United Transport Overseas Ltd: This is a wholly-owned subsidiary of United Transport Ltd., a British Company. Through one of its operating companies, Thornton's Transportation, it holds three of the major contracts for the carrying of equipment from South Africa and Rhodesia to Cabora

Company with British interests, it is supplying drilling equipment for the dam. (Material going to the dam was seen by an eye-witness on a train in Botswana).

Portland Cement: This British company has a Rhodesian subsidiary whose shares rocket-

ed as soon as the contract for the project was signed.

ICI: African Explosives and Imperial Chemical Industries (SA) has set up a subsidiary in Mozambique in connection with Cabora Bassa. ICI has a 42 per cent holding in the firm.

British Workers: A journalist

reporting from the site spoke of "British families" living in the technicians' village (Sunday Telegraph 10-10-70).

UN Sanctions: There is a strong case that participation in Cabora Bassa is in breach of the UN Sanctions Resolution on Southern Rhodesia.

International

CYPRIAN FERNANDES REPORTS FROM ZAIRE

LIFE PRESIDENCY NEXT FOR MOBUTU?

NATIONAL present The Mini Recorder

ARABS: Africa's new imperialists?

By CYPRIAN FERNANDES

THE BATTLE TO FREE AFRICA GOES ON

moved in. Mathare Valley continued to prosper even after independence in 1963. Many years later, the whole area would become a Somali kingdom.

Until the arrival of the *Nation*, sports reporting was a pretty mundane affair with the *East African Standard* concentrating mainly on the 'European' sports of rugby, golf, horse (and some motor) racing, cricket and a little soccer among the white settler clubs. Match reports were usually hum-drum. Fernandes changed all that. The *Nation* began intensive coverage of the national sport, soccer and its varied aspects: corruption, nepotism, favouritism or tribalism in team or national selection, and anything shady that Fernandes' investigative nose sniffed out. It was not long before the Kenya Football Association and the Kenya Hockey Association banned me, each backing down only a few days later. All the major clubs feared Fernandes: Gor Mahia, Luo United, Kenya Breweries, Maragoli, Abaluhya and the coastal clubs of Feisal and Liverpool. I spared no one. Suddenly soccer was hot reading.

Joe Rodrigues, the outstanding South Asian journalist, once told me jokingly: 'You are a destructive critic.' To which, I replied: 'If it is rotten, let us destroy it and build anew.' Hey, I was all for constructive criticism. I brought my campaigning zeal to athletics, cricket, hockey, golf, boxing, volleyball, rugby union and a myriad other sports. While my heart was in sport, my soul was elsewhere: in General News, especially politics; and it was not long before I was Head Court Reporter, Municipal Reporter, General News Reporter, Head Parliamentary Reporter, and, of course, Entertainment Reporter, Chief Reporter, Editor writer. I saw the paper to 'bed' (on the printing presses) each night and then went on to visit the night clubs in Nairobi.

I always felt that I was at my best interviewing people or asking the unthinkable at press conferences. I hope I was always respectful on Voice of Kenya TV's Meet the Press programme (I think it was called that), and even with the likes of President Jomo Kenyatta, President Julius Nyerere of Tanzania and President Milton Obote of Uganda. Ministers were always in my sights. It was not long before Africa and the world was in my sights, too. The Organisation of African Unity, based in Addis Ababa, was a regular part of my beat and the subject of many investigations. Here I built contact assets with presidents and ministers from around Africa. Soon I was travelling throughout Africa, mostly in the company of the then Foreign Minister, Njoroge Mungai or Vice President Daniel arap Moi, or as an embedded member of a Kenya delegation.

Some of my escapades:

- Went to Bradford, Leicester in England. Both cities had advertised asking Asians to stay away during the 1968 exodus.
- Smuggled myself into Mozambique to write an expose on the Caborra Bassa dam, exposing part of the South African and European conspiracy to build the dam.
- Exposed blatant racism in Gaberones, Botswana, after independence.
- Flew in a single engine Cessna within feet of the Mt Kenya peak to photograph and ascertain if an Austrian climber (stuck on a ledge without food or water for five days) was alive or dead.
- On October 25, 1969, I walked into the mortuary wearing a doctor's white coat at the newly built Russian Hospital and counted the 17 corpses and took notes on their wounds: Tom Mboya had been assassinated on July 5, 1969. Odinga had been sacked as Vice President and the prominent moderate Arwings Kodhek had been killed in a road accident. The Luo had polarised behind Odinga. Kenyatta went to Kisumu to show the Luo who was boss. At the opening of the Russian built hospital, all hell broke loose and Kenyatta's armed guards fired randomly. The Kenya News Agency was reporting only four or five dead.

- For nearly two years I worked with Njoroge Mungai to convince Britain and the rest of the British Commonwealth to ban the sale of arms to South Africa which, for all intents and purposes, wanted to use them on black South Africans. The campaign died in Singapore without a whimper as Britain's Alec Douglas Hume cleverly averted the showdown and there were many with wounded prides and dented reputations.
- Chased down Milton Obote who was in Singapore for the Commonwealth Heads of Government Summit. I flew back with the former president following the coupe d'etat by Idi Amin.
- Had many audacious exclusives from Addis Ababa including a rare audience with Emperor Haile Selassie.
- Broke curfew and illegally entered Uganda to write an exclusive situation report from the North and South of the country. I was also among the first to interview Idi Amin. I visited Uganda regularly at Amin's invitation until one day when I was a witness to the murder of Ugandans by Amin's soldiers at the Karuma River Falls Bridge. Crocodiles below made swift work of the corpses. An anonymous note at a hotel in Kampala simply said: Get out. Boaz Omori, the then Editor-in-Chief would not publish the story as Kenya was courting Amin at the time.
- Was the first journalist in the world to report and interview athletes from the Olympic track in Munich, 1972. I noticed that the only other people besides officials at the finish line were disabled spectators. I got a couple of painkilling injections in my butt, a Kenya team uniform, a couple crutches and two tape recorders for the Deutsche Welle network. I interviewed virtually every medal winner in track and field.
- I was respected by all sides of politics and worked as easily with the Kenya People's Union or the Kenya African Nation Union, and before that the Kenya African Democratic Union. I was equally at home with any of the main political players in Kenya. They found it easy to talk to me because they trusted me.

Having an excellent working relationship with all sides, I found it difficult to understand when the telephone threats started. They arrived on the office phone as I refused to have a phone at home. There was always someone telling me to be careful what I wrote, both friends and strangers, and I did not pay much attention to them. I was convinced the truth (fair and balanced) was sacrosanct and immune to partisan politics. I did not have a phone at home because I did not want to bring any work hassles home to my family. In extreme cases (such as Idi Amin or Njoroge Mungai) I used my mother-in-law's phone.

But the threats grew especially during and closer to an election:

> If you write good things about Mungai, you will be killed.
> Stop writing about Odinga, or you will be killed.
> Moi is not the president, don't write about him too much.
> If you write another story about J M Kariuki, you will be in a coffin.
> There is a hot necklace (burning tyre) waiting for you.
> You stupid *muhindi* get out of Kenya.
> You are anti Kikuyu/Luo/Gema/Luhya.

Police Commissioner Bernard Hinga looked into the threats three or four times but could not come up with any go-forwards. We left it at crank calls. I had not become a Kenya citizen because I needed my British passport to go where no Kenyan journalist had gone before, overseas and work in Britain where I would eventually emigrate. This was a black man's country and there was no place for a brown skin. However, everyone thought I was a Kenyan. KANU even embedded me in various delegations to countries in Africa. I was trusted. So why did I leave?

Two things happened. (1) An insurance salesman or someone posing as an insurance salesman went to my wife's office. She was personal secretary to the Director of Education. This man told her to get her husband out of the country as quickly as possible as 'there was a bullet with his name on it'. (2) Editor-in-Chief Boaz Omori had helped me take my investigative skills to the world. He had commissioned me to do an extensive piece on Asian migration to Canada keeping in mind that the *Nation's* owner had done a special deal to allow Ismailis to settle in Canada. Sadly, Omori died while I was away and was succeeded by George Githii by the time I returned.

When I got back, Githii told me he did not want me doing any foreign stories. I did not see anything wrong in finishing the Omori-requested Canada story and Features Editor Trevor Grundy went ahead and published it. On the morning of publication, at around 8 o'clock, Githii called Trevor and I to News Editor Henry Gathigira's desk and said: If you do this again, I will sack you both on the spot.

I made up my mind to leave in a few months or a couple of years or so, working in the Features Department. I did not reckon on the 'bullet with my name on it'. We left Kenya within a month because otherwise my wife would have left with our two children and that would have probably been the end of my marriage and I could

not have that. It was the hardest thing I had to do but I am a very determined man. My life has been one of knife through butter. I make a clean break and do not look back.

After a few years in England, we moved to Australia where journalism bloomed again. I was the founding Chief Sub-Editor of the *Fairfax's* colour magazine. I specialise in colour reproduction, newspaper design, edit a *Fairfax* paper and with friends produce Australia's longest running English language monthly *The Indian Down Under*. Life is good.

G S GREWAL (PAPPU)
Writer

I inherited the gene for journalism from my father, Jasmer Singh, and it is my real calling, but it has never been a full time profession for me as I worked in the hotel industry for six years before setting up my own restaurant. I called it Porterhouse which now, at 28 years, is one of the oldest restaurants in the city. It has been a watering hole for journalists over the years ranging from, in the early years, John McHaffie, Gerry Loughran, Joe Rodrigues, Brian Tetley, Peter Beard and Azhar Chaudry. Later it was Elias Makori, Onyunga Pala, Kathleen Kasavuli, Kathleen Openda and Clay Muganda.

I was born in May 1958 in Nairobi, and though my full name is Guminder Singh Grewal, I have always been known as G S Grewal in my journalistic career. My introduction to journalism came at a very early stage and in a strange manner.

One evening in 1974, at the Sikh Union bar, my father, Jasmer Singh, was having a chat with Norman Da Costa who was sports editor of the *Daily Nation*. It was

G S GREWAL

shortly before a Safari Rally and my father mentioned that I fancied myself as a rally journalist and liked to do 'pretend' articles on rallies. Norman turned round and asked me to do a short article on the entries the Safari Rally had received so far and he would 'edit' it for me to encourage my hobby.

I did this immediately the next day and sent it to Norman at his office and decided I would give him a week or so before asking him what he thought of it. You can imagine my utter amazement when I saw an article printed in the *Nation* the next day and with a byline, hence G S Grewal the journalist had been born at the age of 16 years!

From this early start, there was no turning back and I went on to cover the Safari Rally for a record consecutive 25 years; reporting for the *Nation, Standard, New African* magazine, *Drum* Publications as well as acting as a press officer for both the Nissan and Mercedes Rally teams. This allowed me to be involved with the Safari in its heyday and associate with the people who shaped rallying in Kenya such as Eric Cecil, Bharat Bhardwaj, Joginder Singh, Shekkar Mehta, the Prestons, Peter Shyukah and Patrick Njiru to mention a few.

I was also the cricket correspondent for the *Standard* for various years from the early seventies to 2003, covering the Champions Trophy held in Kenya in 2000 and the World Cup in 2003. Having played the game in the seventies and eighties I have had the privilege of playing alongside Kenya's great players such as Jawahir Shah, Zulfikar Ali, Charanjiv Sharma, Don Pringle, Derrick Pringle and Tom Tikolo as well as meeting stars Sunil Gavaskar, Dilip Vengsrkar and the Nawab of Pataudi. I am glad to have been part of the golden era of Kenya cricket. Other sports covered include hockey and squash. I also was the press officer in the first India/Kenya Trade Fair held in the Kenyatta International Conference Centre in 1982.

Business pressure now means very limited writing but I consider myself very fortunate to have seen the development of sports from the early sixties and to have been involved with some accomplished journalists and photographers of this country – it has certainly enhanced my life.

GAYTRI (SYAL) SAGAR

Writer
The first South Asian woman journalist in Kenya

I was born in Nairobi, Kenya in 1944 and passed my Senior Cambridge exams in 1960 from the Arya Girls Senior School. I did my BA in India and after returning the only profession open to me was teaching. However, I had no desire to be a teacher. I had always wanted to be a 'reporter'. When I was five or six, Princess Elizabeth had come to Nairobi with Prince Philip. My father's office was on Government Road and provided a real good view of the motorcade. He took us – my elder brother, sister and me to see the festivities. Before that day, I had never seen any white people so was really amazed to see the Royal couple. But more than that, I was surprised to see the photographers running alongside her motorcade. My father explained to me why they could be there while the rest of the people had to be behind the tape. Though I did not understand much about reporters and newspapers at that time, I knew 'that's the job I would want to do'.

I did not study journalism in India because journalism as a subject was introduced much later, not only in India, but all over the world. Journalists initially used to learn on the job. Also, getting a job as a reporter did not require any degrees. Some of the well-known reporters of the day had not even finished high school. What you needed was to be street smart and have writing skills. All a reporter had to do was report and not inject any of his ideas, beliefs or biases in that report. Things are a little different now and you need a diploma or a degree these days.

There being no Google or Internet access available in those days, I was trying to search for a job with some news organization; when one day there was a news item

GAYTRI (SYAL) SAGAR

in the *Daily Nation* about the graduation ceremony for twenty journalists from the International Press Institute (IPI). Though I knew nothing about this IPI, I wrote a letter to its Director, (whose name, I later found out, was Mr Tom Hopkinson) and asked him how I could apply to IPI. After a couple of weeks I got a letter asking me to see him. During the first meeting he informed me that the Institute only had three-month refresher courses for the already employed African journalists from different parts of the continent. They did not have any programme for women as there were no women that he knew of, working with any newspapers. Naturally, I was disappointed to hear this. However, before I left, he asked me to write an essay stating the reasons why I wanted to be a journalist and mail it to him.

After about six weeks I received a letter from him asking me to come for an interview. Later I learnt that he had discussed my essay with the people at the IPI headquarters in Zurich. It was agreed that six women would be trained to be journalists and if the programme proved to be successful, they would organize for a further batch. So besides five other African women, I was one of the six to be trained at the IPI in the class of 1965/66. Unfortunately, the programme did not prove to be successful and was discontinued.

One of my class mates was Charity Washiuma, sister-in-law of John Nottingham, the English book publisher. She was more interested in working with him in his publishing house. Charity Dahal got a job with the Dept. of News and Broadcasting and for some unknown reason committed suicide a few months later. Henriatta married one of our teachers from Zambia. Sylvia left a few months into the course and Jessica went back to whatever she was doing before joining IPI. I was the only one who took up journalism as a career. I believe Kul Bhushan went to the IPI after I had graduated. There were no other Asians that I know of, who were trained at IPI which in 1968 closed the African Branch of the school.

The school was affiliated to the Royal Technical College and we were housed in its dormitories and ate in its dining hall. We had no curfew and had our own key to come and go out of the hostel as we pleased. The classes were held on the road to the Delamere School for Girls and the Arboretum, near the Men's Halls - a small house had been converted into a school. The course was for three months for men, twenty in each session. For the women the course was for six months. When our course

started the men's group was in the last month of their course. The next group of men and our group graduated at the same time. I know that there were many well-known African journalists in the two groups, but over the years though I remember their faces, I have forgotten their names.

I passed with distinction and was hired by the *Daily Nation* becoming the first Asian Woman journalist in Kenya. I worked with the paper from 1966 to 1970. When I first started, I was asked to copy the horoscope page from the past horoscopes for the daily horoscope column. Later, I was asked to write Indian movie reviews. This was also from the pamphlets sent by the theatres. The first 'real' film review I wrote was for the film Waqt; I insisted on seeing the actual film and not just the film release pamphlets.

Next I wrote for the women's section of the newspaper. Articles like how to keep your hands soft, etc. Gradually, I was sent out to interview people, like Mrs Tom Mboya or the visiting astronauts from America and was asked to accompany the 'main' journalist to interview Robert Kennedy. Basically I did whatever I was asked to do and there was no special field that I was 'an expert' in. I was sent to cover from the mundane to the exotic and this variety kept the job interesting for me.

The copy editor was an Englishman and he was extremely kind to me and taught me a lot. He treated me like everyone else there and did not make me feel like I did not belong there. Sadly, I have forgotten his name. The African journalists were fine with me. They treated me with respect. Funny thing is that Indians used to think that Africans do not have any values and used to look down on them. Studying with them, and then working with them, I found that they were just like other men around the world. Not only did they have values but it

did matter to them that proper decorum be maintained at all times. The fact that I was an Indian worked to my advantage with them because that made them act really protective towards me. (Sadly, Indian journalists did not feel the same way).

There was one Indian man in the news room at the Nation. I believe his name was Mr Fernandes or Roderigues - I am not sure. He did not like me. He never talked to me, never responded to my greeting. Frankly, he really scared me and he made me feel guilty for being there. I don't know when Kul Bhushan started with the paper, but I would see him around. I don't think he thought much of me either and I don't remember ever talking to him. Shashi Vasani was a dear heart. He was like a big brother to me. If I ever was late in the evening finishing my assignment, he would take me home. If Shashi was not there, the copy editor made sure that the Nation car took me home. Shashi would always assign Anil Vidyarthi to go with me on my assignments. Anil, like me, was new there and was always very professional and friendly.

I didn't meet or see any other women journalists. The copy editor's wife used to do what I did when I started, like copying horoscopes etc. but she left when I joined. The greatest challenge for me was not at the newspaper. I did not have to fight for assignments or any such thing. I did my job to the best of my ability and did not think of my gender. The truth is that I did not feel that my being a journalist was something out of the norm. At work, except for a few people, I was treated like an equal. The only difference was that I did not join the others in the bar at the end of the day. The greatest challenge for me was my own community. I had made African friends and I had no problem in being seen with them. People would look at me askance whenever they saw me with my African friends or colleagues. The worst was the

Indian High Commissioner's wife. At one function that I was covering, she was outright rude to me and told me I was a disgrace to the Indian community for 'frolicking with the natives.' Coming from her it was ironic because her husband was a journalist before becoming a High Commissioner.

I took my African friends to the Arya Samaj 'Jalsa'. People were surprised and awed at the same time – I hope it convinced them that Africans were just people like us and should not be looked down upon just because of their colour. Meeting with different people was the best part of being a journalist. I was lucky enough to meet some amazing people whom I could never have met normally. My job entitled me to be at places where I would never have dreamt of going.

The British had started leaving before Independence. The Africans were not that experienced in running newspapers so the English were replaced by the Asians who kept the papers going and were loyal to the paper, as well as the country. I left because I got married, but I know that things had started changing when the Africans with no experience were promoted over the Asians. Also, the truth of the matter is (many won't agree with me) that Asians were used to work under the 'Whites' but could not agree to work under the 'Blacks'. The political situation too was becoming a little unhealthy for many people, forcing them to think of their future elsewhere.

The fact of the matter is that it was a very unsteady time for the Asians. The British had placed a quota on how many people would be allowed to migrate to England. People who didn't want to become citizens lost their jobs, so they were biding their time till they could go to England. It was a very difficult time for these unemployed people. Except for people who were directly involved with the newspaper business, I believe no one else paid any attention to me. Society was very different then and for me it was a job I enjoyed doing, but unlike the male journalists, I was never honoured at any function, nor given a plaque or a pat on the back. I only felt the society's snub at the community get-togethers like the Samaj Jalsa! My job would require me to interview visiting celebrities from Indian cinema. That I had an easy access to the 'actors and actresses' was not something that the Asian community could forgive me for easily. Many times my name would be linked with different actors I would be interviewing, complicating my life for the duration.

In December, 1970 I moved to Toronto, Canada. I was sure that in the Western world it would be easier for me to be accepted as a journalist but things were even more difficult here than in Kenya. There were very few women journalists working with newspapers and the ones who did, worked on women's issues only. Not only were they not very receptive of women journalists, but their knowledge of the outside world was really limited. Most people didn't know much of what was happening outside of America.

I started working with the Local Employment Development Programme of the Canadian Immigration Department as a Project Manager. However, I pursued my writing endeavours and eventually started getting work as a freelance writer. After staying in Toronto for ten years, we moved to California and have been here now for over thirty years.

I have worked here as a free-lance writer and have contributed to different magazines, periodicals and children's magazines. Besides working as a free-lance writer I also worked as a ghost writer. My first book, *Lost to Them*, was published in 2007. I am working on my second book now. These are novels about women in a multi-cultural context.

JASMER SINGH
Writer

I was born in 1930 in the Park Road area of Nairobi, my parents came from India in 1920. I received my pre-primary education in Sri Guru Singh Sabha Boys' School on Race Course Road – it is one of the oldest Sikh temples in Kenya and even now, every Sunday when I go to the temple, it brings nostalgic memories to see a picture of the 1936 class hanging in the office of the temple manager.

Sports came to me naturally from a very young age, specially cricket and hockey which we played on the pathways among the Railway quarters along Desai Road. My cricket career progressed and I went on to represent the Asians against the Europeans in the annual fixture at the age of nineteen and Kenya in 1956 at the age of twenty-six.

At one of these cricket matches I met the late Charles Disney, sports editor of the *Standard*, and I casually mentioned to him that I was keen to write for his newspaper - I could report on cricket and hockey and was good in English in school. He agreed to my suggestion and I became the *Standard's* cricket and hockey correspondent for the next 40 years, working also under sports editors Mick Jones, Don Beet and George Obiero.

I was also the correspondent for the international *Cricketer Magazine* and annually contributed a feature on Kenyan cricket in the *Wisden Almamnac*. The flair for writing led me to edit the Kenya Cricket Association Brochures for every major cricket tour for 20 years, the

JASMER SINGH

International Brochure for the Champions Trophy staged in Kenya in 2000 being a significant one.

In the late sixties and early seventies I joined the electronic media doing a 30-minute live programme on KBC radio sports on Sunday mornings and on television on Monday evenings. Though I was paid only Kshs 80.00 per session I thoroughly enjoyed it. I had the opportunity of meeting world class personalities such as Jackie Ickyx (racing driver), Sir Leonard Hutton (England cricketer), Everton Weekes (West Indian cricketer), Sir Lester Piggot (hockey player) and the Nawab of Pataudi

(India cricketer) and was able to socialise with them at the world famous Norfolk Hotel; far beyond the paltry Kshs80 I earned.

An encounter with Bailey, the South African billionaire and owner of *Drum* magazine and other daily newspapers led me to retire from government service and establish Drum Publication (EA) Ltd in Nairobi. This involved publishing *Drum* and later, *Trust, African Film* and *True Love.* I was able to increase the circulation of Drum from 12,000 copies to 120,000 copies over 24 years, until I retired in 1992.

During this period I had some challenging episodes. Our columnist, P G Okoth, wrote his humorous Malimoto piece, 'The Masai Spear and American Peace Corps Girl'. It caused an uproar at the USA embassy, but by the time they were able to contact me in the two or three days, we had sold every copy; and their insistence on withdrawing the copies was redundant. Another time our editor published a fictitious interview with Idi Amin, President of Uganda. Using personal contacts I managed to pacify the Ugandan authorities by publishing apologies in the magazine and the local newspapers and sacking the editor.

Jasmer Singh with Moody Awori.

I also received a summons from Kenya's Commissioner of Police – one regarding the Swazi King's Reed Dance photograph on the front cover; the other were the semi-nude cover pictures. This was satisfactorily explained: the first one was a national Swazi event and the second was a reprint from page 3 of the weekly UK papers which were openly sold in Kenya. These explanations were duly accepted.

Whilst being an MD at Drum Publications, I served a two year chairmanship of the E A Newspapers and Periodicals Association. Having no basic training in journalism but being a part time print and electronic media journalist for over 50 years, including 24 years as a publisher, has been a great and most satisfactory achievement.

JOE RODRIGUES (1931-1987)

By Cyprian Fernandes

ARGUABLY the finest South Asian journalist in Kenya, Jawaharlal Joel Joachim Rodrigues was nearly lost to medicine in Bombay where he grew up. His father, Francis, was an Indian nationalist and a senior executive on the *Times of India* and the *Indian Express*. He wanted his son to become a doctor rather than follow in his journalist footsteps.

For two years young Joe remained chained to science against his will. It took a considerable amount of courage for the young man to tell his mother that his heart was in the arts and journalism and not in science or medicine.

It was left to his mother to convince his autocratic father. Needless to say he did do his father proud.

Joe was one of seven children, five brothers and two sisters. His eldest brother Sunith was a general in the Indian army. He progressed to army Chief of Staff and later Governor of the Punjab. The family lived in Bombay but had their ancestral home in Cortalim, Salcette, Goa.

The oldest frontline newspaper in Kenya, the *East African Standard* was the exclusive domain of Her Britannic Majesty's colonial government and the white British settler community. It employed mostly only white journalists. Asians and Africans did not get a look in.

With the birth of the Aga Khan-owned Daily and Sunday newspapers, Africans and Asians finally found a medium for their stories, hopes and aspirations. These were real newspapers produced in the vein of Fleet Street journalism unlike their predecessor wannabes. Through its South Asian journalists, the *Nation* was able to attract a dormant Asian readership as well as tell their stories. The *Standard*, devoid of any Asian journalists, was not.

In 1960, the Aga Khan through his right hand man Michael Curtis (a former Fleet Street editor) aspired to a kind of freedom of the press in Kenya and pushed the boundaries as far as they would be allowed to by the colonial government. John Bierman, the fearless founding editor of the *Daily Nation*, gave Kenyans a taste of what real press freedom was about as the *Daily Nation* totally supported black Kenyans' push for independence. With Jack Beverley (Editor, *Sunday Nation*), they brought to Kenya the best of what Fleet Street could offer Kenyan journalism. This was a new experience for its readers. The *Nation* papers were no-one's mouthpiece, they were fair, balanced and sought the truth every time. For a little

JOE RODRIGUES

while, 1960-1963, Kenya enjoyed a freedom of the press in the *Nation* papers that came close to the Fleet Street ideal.

Without doubt, the South Asian journalist who excelled in most aspects of newspaper journalism was one Jawaharlal Joel Joachim Joe.

Joe was a journo's journo. He was an exquisite technician: excellent copy editor, layout specialist, editorial writer, and one of the tightest copy writers in the country. His

colleagues joked that Joe could rewrite the proverbial Bible on the back of a box of matches. They might have stretched that a bit but he certainly was a master surgeon in the word game. In effect, he was capable of putting together the whole paper on his own: he had all the skills and the capacity to do it too.

He seemed to spend almost every waking moment at his desk in Nation House. He was the first in and among the very last to leave. His wife Cyrilla (nee Amaral from Porvorim, Bardez, Goa), a Mombasa-born girl he married in 1953, often said he spent 16 hours a day at the Nation. He rested a bit on Saturdays and was back at work on Sunday. Cyrilla was a newspaper widow (as in golf widow) from the very start. Joe enjoyed a good laugh and regaled his close Goan friends with some real howlers but their soirees at the Nairobi Goan Gymkhana were rare, much to Cyrilla's chagrin. Some said newspaper production for Joe was an addiction he simply loved and thrived upon. In his life, Cyrilla often told him, the newspaper comes first ('your baby') and then your family. Above everything else, Joe was a very private person, even at home. Some wrongly interpreted this privacy for aloofness. He hid his emotions well at all times, even with Cyrilla. He was also miserly with his compliments.

He was blessed with ice-cool calm that not even a bomb could disturb. His quiet manner was both soothing and corrective when it needed to be. He was generous in more ways than one. He was 'St Vincent de Paul' to many of his colleagues and an easy touch for a short-term loan (until pay day). You could trust him impeccably. The bottom line was: If Joe said it, it must be true.

He did not have too many vices. He enjoyed his occasional du Maurier cigarette (which he gave up eventually), a

glass of imported beer or a scotch and soda. Other than that he was Mr Clean.

Yet, Joe was also something of an introvert, a very private person. He did not like and did not court the public limelight. Joe and Cyrilla had many Goan admirers but very few true friends, a special group of seven couples. Joe had an absolute ball with this group of people every time they met. Unlike most other Goans, they were not club-oholics and infrequently visited the Goan Gymkhana. Instead, their social life revolved around those infernal diplomatic cocktail parties Joe used to drag Cyrilla to. I suspect I was probably the only Goan who spent a lot of time with him away from work. I only went to his home for dinner once when he was down in the dumps. He was madly in love with Cyrilla but Cyrilla says he was not a romantic and did not tell her he loved her as was the want of autocratic men of that time. Cyrilla was the stronger of the two and she spoke her mind without hesitation, the very opposite of Joe. She voiced the things that the very private Joe would not. His only other care in the world was their two children, Joy and Allan John.

Gerard Loughran provides a glimpse of Joe away from work: 'He invited me to a Saturday curry lunch at his house. Out on the lawn was a table groaning with food. He took me round it saying, "This is so-and-so, it is very hot, this is something or other and it is quite mild, this is not hot at all", and so on and so on. I was flabbergasted and said something like, "Joe, what a spread!" He replied, "That's why we Goans are so poor, we spend all our money on food!"

Later there was a minor crisis when his children managed to lock themselves in the house. Cyrilla was frantic, Joe was as cool as a cucumber. The children were released after a while, I forget how, and normality returned.' Joe was not a coward nor did he go out of his way to seek out trouble or incur the wrath of the Kenya government or opposition politicians. He served the public interest. Everything Joe did or wrote was the end result of his own considered legal scrutiny. Was it true? Was it fact? Was it legal? Was it balanced? Was it in the public interest? Legal vetting is second skin to most good journalists. Joe was also probably born immune to bias, prejudice, partisanship and taking sides. He was super clean and no one, not even his family, the Aga Khan's Ismaili community, his own Goan community or other South Asians, were allowed to taint his integrity in any shape or form. He did not do anyone any favours. On the other hand, the *Nation* had iron-clad guidelines concerning religious/ethnic sensitivities and these were breached at an editor's peril.

John Bierman is also credited with a little sub-editing on his new sub-editor's name. The story goes that John told Joe no way was he going get his Queen's English Pommy tongue around 'Jawaharlal'.
Did he have another name?
Yes, Joel.
That will do, Joe.

By the time Joe reached Uganda in 1956 to join the *Uganda Mail*, he was already a pretty seasoned journalist. With a great command and love of the English language, he cut his journalistic teeth on the *Times of India* (based very much on the *London Times*), still one of India's greatest newspapers. He always had journalism in his DNA as he walked in his father's footsteps. He also spoke English without that lilting Bombay twang; it made him sound more East African or a London Asian, not quite that irritating upper class English nasal delivery.

It was Cyrilla's uncle, Louis Mascarenhas, who got Joe a job on the Patwa brothers' *Uganda Mail*. It was a short-lived association. The colonial government found the

Uganda Mail a tough customer and promptly shut it down on the grounds the premises were unsafe. Joe and Cyrilla moved to Nairobi and found an opportunity with the *Daily Chronicle* whose then editor, Pio Gama Pinto, was in detention. Pio was an extraordinary African socialist and freedom fighter. He would be assassinated on February 25, 1965. Joe and Pio became good friends and with the likes of Tom Mboya, Bildad Kaggia, Joe Murumbi (all outstanding politicians of the time) attended many political meetings. Joe, unlike his father, was not a political animal, he was, after all, a journalist. While in Nairobi, Joe also worked on a paper called the *Guardian* owned by J M Desai. Joe had applied to the *Standard* for any journalistic position but received a reply that there were no suitable positions vacant.

When, in 1960, Joe was snapped up by John Bierman as a sub-editor for the *Daily Nation,* he was first offered a three month probation on the 5pm to 11pm shift and continued working on the *Chronicle* and the *Guardian* during the day.

After the first night, he told Cyrilla: 'It is pretty simple work.'
After the second night: 'John Bierman stands over my shoulder all the time. That makes me a bit uncomfortable.'

What Joe did not know was that John was full of admiration. He was amazed at Joe's sub-editing skills, his speed and his accuracy.

After the third night: 'I have got the job full-time at 1900 shillings a month.'

He didn't bargain for his wages and this would remain one of his hallmarks. Some would say an unwelcome one since he never asked for a raise or a particular reimbursement. He never argued over money when he really should have.

The first four years: 1960-1964 were amongst the happiest for both Joe and me. Joe progressed from sub-editor, to night editor, to chief sub-editor. In 1966 he was editor of the *Daily Nation* and in 1968 became managing editor.

With the exception of Joe and Pio Gama Pinto (both became Kenya citizens) most South Asian journalists did not have a permanent stake in Kenya. I knew that one day I would have to move on. More importantly they were not aligned with any tribe, any party, or the dying embers of the colonial government.

When Joe and I joined the *Nation* in 1960, it was an era of great hope: surely independence would come sooner rather than later. From Day One, the *Nation* supported African independence which until then was unprecedented in frontline newspapers. The Mau Mau rebellion had ended and with it so did the state of emergency which had been declared in 1954. Now the likes of Oginga Odinga, Tom Mboya, James Gichuru, Mbiu Koinange, and the rest of Kenya (excepting most whites and a few Asians) were agitating for the release of Jomo Kenyatta from detention while also pushing for independence. For the time being there was a kind of peace among all those politicians scrambling for their piece of the independence pie.

Lurking in the political shadows was a huge struggle for power between Oginga Odinga's Luos and Kenyatta's Kikuyus. It would not be long before Odinga was on the outer periphery and Kenyatta's Kikuyus were dominant in government and were soon becoming the economic power force. Kenyatta and his cabinet colleagues also quickly grabbed all the available choice land instead of sharing it with their fellow Kenyans. Return of previously confiscated land was the chief reason for the Mau Mau rebellion and the ensuing push for independence.

We would meet regularly at the Lobster Pot restaurant (just off Victoria Street) for a beer after the first edition had been put to bed. This was the only time Joe allowed himself a moment or two of self-indulgence about his career. Naturally, there was a sliver of disappointment especially when Boaz Omori (Editor of the Kiswahili paper *Taifa* and a warm, gentle man with a beautiful smile) was made Editor in Chief. Joe accepted the Aga Khan's policy of having a black Kenyan as Editor in Chief. He was content with his lot as Managing Editor. He did not fancy all the political problems that the top job brought with it. When I suggested that he should be pushing harder for the top job, he asked: 'Why? I am happy with what I am doing. I don't need the headaches and threats the top job brings.'

At home, he shielded Cyrilla from all the goings-on at the *Nation*. He rarely talked about anything that was troubling him and he always kept a brave face about everything and did not allow anything to worry his wife. However, when Cyrilla did press him, he told her: 'So what if they want a black man as the Editor-in-chief. I have a good job (Managing Editor) and I am happy about it.' He only eventually got the top job because the management team could not find a suitable black skinned replacement after George Githii's acrimonious exit. Cyrilla tried hard to convince him to turn down the job. She had a strong sense of foreboding but Joe eventually took it on.

Joe understood the limitations of any journalist working in Kenya: President Jomo Kenyatta was a dictator, almost a demi-god and those closest to him ensured that nothing threatened the good name of the President, there was no public criticism of him in print, on radio or television. You could not be satirical (cartoons, in print or any other media) about Kenyatta as you would freely publish about prime ministers in the UK or Europe or presidents in the US. You could not take the micky about Kenyatta or any senior politician, if you valued your life. Even if you were right, you could not challenge a government policy which could be interpreted as challenging Kenyatta (and later President Daniel arap Moi) himself. Any normal criticism was taken personally. Kenyatta was ruthless and brutal. He harangued erring ministers at public rallies and he did not spare the language either.

At a private farewell party with no *Nation* management present, Joe said he neither resigned nor retired, he was fired. His long *Nation* career ended on July 31, 1981. He was succeeded by Peter Mwaura.

I have not been able to find any evidence that unerringly indicates why Joe was sacked. One source said that there was talk at high level in the company of incompetence by Joe, which seems highly unlikely after all those years and appears more a ploy to conceal the real reasons. These seem to boil down to: Either, Joe's independent stance angered the government and particularly Charles Njonjo (former Attorney-General, Minister for Constitutional Affairs and in Moi's case 'king maker'). Or, he fell victim to Ismaili/Islamic/Arab pressures, the theory favoured by Joe himself.

The following three elements sealed his fate: The first incident (early January or February) came in the aftermath of a terrorist bomb which destroyed the always magnificent Norfolk Hotel in Nairobi, killing 15 people and injuring 18 others. Gerard Loughran in the Birth of a Nation writes:

It is widely assumed that the attack was the work of Palestinian terrorists in reprisal for Kenya's assistance to Israel in Uganda hostage drama; also the Block family who owned the hotel were Jewish. Joe Kadhi wrote one of his 'Why?' columns, denouncing the Libyan-funded Nairobi newspaper Voice of Africa for claiming that the bomb was planted by Israel; he also attacked the Palestine Liberation Organisation for describing Kenya as a 'police station for US interventionism'. These comments were fair and in line with government policy, as Joe pointed out in a letter to the board, stating 'This country is moving closer to Israel in the intelligence and security fields and away from the Arab world. The promise of cheaper oil has not materialised and the machinations of Voice of Africa and its Libyan backers, particularly vis-à-vis the Norfolk bomb and its aftermath, have combined to harden the government's attitude.' The Kadhi column was felt in some circles to have a negative impression of Arabs generally and a barrage of complaints was directed to the Aga Khan. Since the editor-in-chief was responsible for all columns and commentaries, Joe came under fire for letting this one through.

In any western democracy, the column would not have raised a single eyebrow.

The second is Joe's famous Bondo editorial on April 18. The ruling Kenya African National Union (KANU) electoral machine barred Oginga Odinga (the Kikuyu's long-time Luo adversary) from standing in the seat of Bondo in the general elections. Joe defended Odinga's constitutional rights in an editorial headed 'A time for magnanimity.' The editorial said the decision to bar Odinga was 'unconstitutional, undemocratic and not conducive to the national compromise to which President Moi has been exhorting Kenyans' (from *Birth of a Nation*). Joe was arrested and interrogated and the Nation promptly published a back-down short of an official apology.

The third incident began with an angry President Moi calling Joe at home on the morning of Friday, May 22.(From *Birth of a Nation*):

Moi was angry about the use of the word 'anonymous' in a Nation story about a national strike by doctors. The relevant sentence said 'On Wednesday, the Kenya News Agency released an anonymous statement said to have been released by KANU, condemning the strike and calling on the government to deal with the strikers.' The wording seemed to throw doubt on whether this was a genuine KANU statement, but that was not what offended Moi. A Kenya News Agency (KNA) statement quoted him as saying, 'KANU is the ruling party. It is the government and therefore my voice. How can the publishers of Nation imagine the views of the party are anonymous? They also want to say Moi is anonymous.'

The word 'anonymous' had been inserted into the story by Chief Sub-editor Philip Ochieng, whose English is impeccable. The statement bore no indication which KANU official or officials had issued it, and this was what Ochieng was trying to point out. In the conspiratorial world of Kenya, his semantic intervention was given a sinister connotation. At about 4pm, Joe Kadhi the Daily Nation's Managing Editor, and the acting News Editor John Esibi were picked up. Soon after Joe, Ochieng and reporters Gideon Mulaki and Pius Nyamora were also arrested. Joe was released 24 hours later and the others after three days.

There was also Njonjo's outburst about 'sensationalist' reporting of a case involving his cousin. According to one observer, the 'internal' Kenyan issues (Bondo, the doctors' strike and Njonjo's outburst) were par for the course in the running battle at that time between Government and the media. Any support for Odinga, no matter how well argued and honourably based, was bound to infuriate the Kikuyu establishment; the 'anonymous' row seemed to be a mischievous dig by Ochieng whipped into a froth of dubious indignation; and as for 'sensationalism', in a Kenya context this seemed to mean reporting what a politician did not want reported.

The Why? column appeared to be different. The main objection was that it implied all Arabs were fanatics. The BBC correspondent Tim Llewellyn said there had been a concerted Arab and Muslim campaign pressuring the Aga Khan to get rid of Kadhi, and/or presumably Joe as his superior. It is difficult to establish whether this was true or not but it is notable that the Nation Newspaper Ltd board meeting which backed Joe referred to 'complaints directed to the principal shareholder.'

About Aiglemont (an estate at Gouvieux in the Picardie region of France, it functions as the secretariat and residence of His Highness Prince Karīm Aga Khan) sensitivities with regard to the Arab-Israel issue, Joe wrote to Michael Curtis on February 21, 1981 (*Birth of a Nation*, page 155) clearly implying the *Nation* should be nudging its policies towards the Israelis. Philip Ochieng said in an interview with Loughran: 'There was a perception Joe was siding too much with the Israelis, forgetting that his owner had certain affinities with the Palestinians. His argument was that to stay with the government, you had to favour the Israelis.'

Joe Kadhi told Loughran: 'People (Aiglemont) were angry about a trip I made to Israel but Joe gave permission provided I came back via Cairo to ensure my stories were balanced and I did that. Aiglemont hit the roof. I feared the *Nation* could never be impartial covering any Islamic issue, Pakistan or the Middle East, though I am a Muslim.' Kadhi recalled designing the foreign page, one time, with plans to use a story about Muslim terrorists in Afghanistan and Michael Curtis begged him to find a substitute.

Loughran adds: 'On July 22, in a (farewell) meeting with the Nation Newspapers Ltd Board, Joe said his departure from the company was not connected with government pressures as he was led to believe, but with the Why? affair

because the Editor-in-Chief approved all commentaries. He said the column was not a condemnation of Arabs but an expression of concern over the perpetuation of terrorism. The Board wished him well for the future. "One aspect of the Why? debacle remains unclear – whether Joe did or did not see Kadhi's column before publication". According to one source, Joe said he had not seen the column. He also did not discipline Kadhi as requested. The company assumed he did not discipline Kadhi because he had in fact seen the column. In a July 17 letter to Harry Evans (the brilliant editor of the *Sunday Times*), Joe said, "I now have good reason to believe that my departure has to do with the Arab League and local Muslim pressures."'

It is not clear exactly when the decision was taken to remove Joe but Njonjo hosted a dinner party for the Aga Khan when he came to Nairobi in March for the International Press Institute (IPI) assembly and it can be presumed Joe was discussed. Loughran again: 'Joe's letter to Evans claimed the company was negotiating with Mwaura during the IPI assembly in early March. Cyrilla said Sir Eboo Pirbhai (the leader of the Aga Khan's Ismaili community in Kenya and the highest ranking non-royal Ismaili after the Aga Khan) summoned Joe and told him the message from Paris was that he had to resign for his own security. I do not know when this meeting took place. Joe himself said he was told he had to go by Michael Curtis in Nairobi at the end of May because a decision had been taken to revert to a black Kenyan as Editor-in-Chief. Both times he was told he was "in personal danger." Presumably this was a reference to the Kenya security authorities since Joe had been detained after the Bondo editorial. It is unclear whether there was ever any serious threat to Joe or whether this was an attempt to frighten him into quitting. He himself did not seem to take it seriously.'

Did Joe err in:

1. Permitting Kadhi's mild criticism of the PLO and denunciation of the Libyan-funded paper in Nairobi (*Voice of Africa*) about the Norfolk bombing which must have seemed quite safe in view of the government's switch towards Israel. What he may have underestimated was the strength of the Muslim response and its demands on the Aga Khan.

2. The Bondo editorial was written within days of the IPI assembly at which Moi had stated, 'We in Kenya steadfastly uphold the freedom of the Press,' and Information Minister Aringo said the Press should be seen as an ally of government not an enemy. Of course, Joe was not so naïve as to take these statements at face value but like the courageous and canny political animal that he was, perhaps he decided now was a good time to test the sincerity of their claims and push the boundaries a bit -- just as the Western editors were still motoring out to Jomo Kenyatta International Airport. Some thought the headline, A Time for Magnanimity, was excellent.

3. The row over reporting the doctors' strike was nonsense. Joe did not know anything about it until he was called by Moi. Kadhi told Loughran, 'The Kanu statement came from KNA which said only that Kanu issued the statement without actually saying who issued it. Today such a statement would probably be signed and come by fax. The word anonymous was added by the Chief Sub-editor Philip Ochieng. He wanted to dramatise the story. I had the black (carbon copy) of the story but the word "anonymous" was not on the black. I would not have allowed it, I would not have doubted the story came from Kanu. I think Philip was being cheeky. At any rate, Joe seemed totally peripheral to this nonsense.'

The government, after having enjoyed almost complete control during George Githii's tenure as Editor-in-Chief, found it difficult to come to terms with the somewhat independent stance the *Nation* was taking under Joe. More importantly, the *Nation* dumped Joe with a pittance in severance pay. There was always colour bar at the *Nation* as far as remuneration was concerned. The expatriate whites were on huge salaries and benefits. When Stan Denman retired as Chairman he had a pension for life as he had been hired on expatriate terms. Joe, being an Indian, was not considered an expatriate and was only given a small lump sum, most of which was gobbled up by income tax. This was a brutal time for the Joe family.

Joe took over a magazine stable of three titles and increased this to twelve but this was no challenge, more a step backwards. Joe was never the same man but he never showed it and bottled everything up.

Within days, he had an offer of a job from the outstanding journalist of the modern era, Harold Evans, Editor of the *Sunday Times*. The *New Statesman* of India, was also quick to offer Joe a senior editorial position. Joe turned down both as he did the two other times he was head-hunted: once by the *Standard* for the job of Editor while he was still at the *Nation* and the other time by Moi, after Joe had been sacked by the *Nation*. Moi wanted him to edit a KANU newspaper.

I would like to think that Joe represented the South Asian community and he did it with such brilliance that his star still shines today and people speak of him with respect and sadness at his early passing.

With his IPI and UPI connections in the UK, US, and Australia, Joe could have migrated to a lucrative job overseas. On a visit to Australia, I tried to convince him of great opportunities for him Down Under. He would have none of it. He had always said 'Kenya will get my bones.' Prophetic but true.

Most journalists thought that the stress of the job eventually killed Joe of a massive heart attack at the age of 56 in 1987. The truth, however, is that the men in the Joe family were plagued with chronic heart disease. But it is still not drawing too long a bow that the *Nation* job somehow contributed to his death.

Note: I am indebted to Gerard Loughran (author of Birth of a Nation: The Story of a Newspaper in Kenya) for considerable research help and guidance. Birth of a Nation celebrated the paper's 50 years of publication. Loughran spent a dozen years at the Nation in senior editorial capacities. He has a high-level CV in international journalism. I am also indebted to Cyrilla, Joe Rodrigues' widow, for recalling some of the traumatic as well as the happy milestones of her husband's life and career.

KUL BHUSHAN

Writer

'People are thinking of leaving Kenya and you have come here,' said some Indians who invited my family to a welcoming meal in early 1955 in Nairobi which was then shaken by Mau Mau violence and uncertainty.

I was sixteen when I landed in Mombasa in December 1954 with my mother and sister to join my father, V P Sharma, who had arrived two years earlier. Realising that Nairobi did not offer any opportunities for higher education in those days, my father admitted me for a two-year course in teacher training after which a government job was assured as Kenya had an acute shortage of trained teachers.

This course was a boon – I got to know the history, geography and the culture of Kenya; I worked hard and enjoyed the learning. Having attended convent schools in India, I had a good command of the English language and had acquired a beautiful handwriting as my father taught me calligraphy in the six weeks before I joined the Teachers Training College (TTC). So my first essay, written in calligraphy, made quite an impact when the English lecturer displayed it for the class.

I worked as a teacher with the Kenya Ministry of Education for eight years and resigned in 1964 to join the New Era College established by my father a year earlier as the Vice Principal. Meanwhile I studied for a B. Sc. Economics from London University.

An Inner Urge to Write for Newspapers

While studying economics and politics, I developed a keen interest in international news and local politics and felt a strong urge to write for newspapers. Scouting for local outlets, I came across a weekly, *National Guardian*, published in English and Gujarati from Nairobi and contacted its editor, Indu Desai, if I could contribute on local topics and events. Under the pen name 'Enterprise', I launched my weekly column. Although I never got paid for my work nor was credited for it, the editor was very satisfied with it because the weekly published local material instead of promotional articles from embassies.

My first big break came with Kenya's Independence celebrations on 12 December, 1963. Gathering my press

KUL BHUSHAN

clippings, I went to the Kenya Information Department and got a Press Pass and the press kit for this historic event. I was thrilled to join the top local and international journalists for covering different events. But I wanted better exposure, especially as I had resigned from my job and established a business education institute and secondary school, New Era College, in Nairobi with my father as its principal. Now I could submit articles under my byline. So I purchased a copy of *The Artists and Writer's Yearbook* containing the names and addresses of British and American newspapers and magazines and

started submitting my articles to the provincial press. After receiving dozens of rejection slips, my articles started to be published in papers like the *Yorkshire Post, Birmingham Post, Scotsman* and *Boston Globe* among other media. Every payment I received was a great celebration!

'You make much noise as a journalist but do not have the skills of a journalist,' taunted my wife. The taunt provoked me. A local news item about the International Press Institute starting a course in advanced journalism at Nairobi University caught my eye. To gain admission, the candidates were required to be sponsored by a newspaper or a magazine. I came up with the idea of launching a magazine for young Kenyans which would sponsor me for this course. So I registered a publishing company, New Era Associates, and its magazine, New Era. I barely managed to print its first edition and enclosed it with the sponsorship for the IPI course. When accepted, I was ecstatic! From day one, I soaked up every little tip and technique I was taught. Tragedy struck mid-way as my father died after a heart attack. But I carried on, even contributing news items to the Nation and publishing my magazine - I finished the course in 1966 with distinction and a prize.

Education Editor

Now I wanted to contribute to a daily newspaper and in March 1967, I approached the *East African Standard* for reviewing Asian films. The Features Editor wanted me on board and arranged an interview with its editor, Kenneth Bolton. Despite my top performance at the IPI Advanced Journalism Course, I was rejected. Although I did not need a job, I struck back by getting one at the *Nation* within a week as a Senior Journalist and Education Editor. I joined during Easter as the 1967 Safari Rally was coming to a close. My first story touched

parents and administrators as education accounted for the biggest slice of the government budget. My articles on the lack of secondary school seats and mix-ups at Nairobi University and in the examination system attracted attention. With education as the top national priority, I sometimes wrote editorials. At times, the Ministry of Education took strong exception to my views resulting in irate phone calls and official statements.

In those days, the Royal Technical College, that later evolved into Nairobi University, celebrated a Rag Week every year when the students let down their hair, donned crazy costumes and paraded through Nairobi streets. Once, the procession was so listless and lifeless that when I wrote a scathing column terming it pathetic, the students decided to teach me a lesson. They invited me to cover an event at the Yagnik Fountain on the campus. When I got there, they dumped me into it! Next day, the photograph in the newspaper had a hilarious caption and a catchy headline – *Keeping Bhushan Kul.*

The Asian Exodus

In late 1967, as the Asian crisis was building up, I started to report on the uncertainty faced by the community. This situation soon blew up into a full-fledged crisis in early 1968 when thousands of Asians flew to Britain to beat the deadline for their entry, known as the Asian Exodus. The *Standard* did not have any Asian reporters to get the inside stories and covered the event from a British perspective, so I wrote scoops day after day. Later that year, I went to Britain at my own expense and reported with photographs and interviews on how the Asians were settling in Southall and Leicester. The *Nation's* circulation among the Asians shot up.

In 1968, the Kenya government started its Africanisation programme by sending Quit Notices to non-citizen Asian

on a controversy – a practice that became normal later on. In view of my background in education, the *Nation* decided to appoint me as the Education Editor and I was asked to write a weekly column, Education Notebook. The *Sunday Nation* agreed to the weekly review of Asian Films. Thus, I wrote two columns every week, in addition to full time reporting.

Since I had worked as a teacher and a principal for almost ten years, I regularly got scoops on education stories. My weekly column, Education Notebook, attracted teachers,

traders. This major setback for the trading community continued until 1977. My rapport with the *dukawallahs,* together with a good knowledge of spoken and written Gujarati, was the basis of the in-depth coverage. In 1969, the *Nation* overtook the *Standard* in circulation.

In 1972, when Idi Amin expelled the Uganda Asians, I went to Britain – again at my own expense – to report on how they were transiting in refugee camps and settling in other locations like Leicester. The articles I wrote created a lot of buzz and I got some nasty, anonymous letters from die-hard Britons in Kenya because I blasted the Tory leader Enoch Powell. For a short period, I was assigned work as a Sub Editor and honed my skills in production.

First Business Editor

The Editor in Chief of the *Nation*, George Githii, had the foresight to establish a Business Desk in June 1973, and I was put in charge to generate exclusive and incisive stories on the economy, finance, industry and business. This was the first time that a Business Desk was established in any Kenyan newspaper. The major change came with my reporting on the budget.

Up till then, the budget was mostly reported in abstract terms of public finance except for price increases for some goods like beer, cigarettes, petrol etc. and changes in income tax rates. The rest of the reporting was all about the government's total income and expenditure, deficit financing, development spending and similar issues.

I changed this format and interviewed taxpayers, housewives, homeowners, businessmen, industrialists, financiers, tour operators and other economic segments directly affected by the budget. This showed the impact of the budget in human terms. The *Standard* was to follow this style. From 1975-1977, I produced three issues of the annual *Nation Economic Review*. In 1977, I was confirmed as the Business Editor – the first in Kenyan journalism. I wrote two weekly columns: one on the Nairobi Stock Exchange and the other The Square Deal. After I wrote a series of articles exposing the unethical practices of the insurance companies after which the Kenya Government appointed a commission to look into the malpractices. The insurance industry put up a strong defence and I was grilled by their consul. The commission's report validated my reports and reforms were instituted to regulate this sector.

As the Business Editor, I was also in charge of producing Business Supplements on various industries and economic activities to generate more advertising revenue. One such supplement on 'Clothing the Nation' prompted the Marketing Director, Jerry Wilkinson, to send me a memo saying: 'Congratulations for a very fine supplement. If we can maintain this standard throughout, then selling of advertising becomes a self-generating

Leader of Safari Rally Reporting Team, Kul Bhushan, interviews Kenya's Flying Sikh, Joginder Singh, at the start of the Safari Rally, a world rally championship event, in Nairobi.

job.' After another supplement on Handyman, he sent a memo: 'If we can maintain this standard, we will win both ways – obtain readers and impress advertisers.'

By this time, Nairobi University had introduced a course in journalism and I was invited to lecture to the students on business reporting. My teacher training came in handy as I drew flow charts on the blackboard about news gathering and newspaper production and on how to create business news by talking to various key players.

During my term at the *Nation*, I reviewed Indian films, plays and cultural events regularly. I also reported on almost all Indian and Pakistani celebrities who visited Kenya. These ranged from industrialists and businessmen, Bollywood stars and singers; two Indian Miss World winners, famous dancers, musicians and singers, world famous gurus and godmen - in fact, any celebrity. This certainly helped to attract more Asian readers as the *Standard* did not provide this coverage.

When George Githii moved to the *Standard*, he made sure that I resigned and joined him after fourteen years at the *Nation*. The *Standard* made a very generous offer, one I could not refuse, and so I became the first Asian to join the *Standard* as a full time editor. With and without Githii, I had a tempestuous nine years at the *Standard*. In 1982, I was invited to the World Bank/IMF/IFC headquarters in Washington to interview its directors and its then President, Tom Clausen. In 1986, I was honoured with the Journalist of the Year Award by the then Kenyan President Moi.

Doyen of Safari Reporters

Reporting on the Safari has been my special love and I was appointed as the Team Leader for reporting this event. Knowing the drivers personally, mostly Asians, was an advantage. Fluency in Hindi, Punjabi and Gujarati also helped. Once rally winner and star Joginder Singh was on the route and so could not be interviewed but I spotted his wife at Safari headquarters and got a front page story by talking to her in Punjabi! In 1997, the Safari Rally committee celebrated its Silver Jubilee and honoured me with a silver medal for my reporting – the only journalist to get this award. Managing Director Wilkinson sent me a memo: 'Congratulations for excellent coverage. We have firmly established our strength as a newspaper and become extremely competitive.' I came to be known as the Doyen of Safari Reporters.

International Press Institute Representative

My interaction with the International Press Institute (IPI) lasted over many decades. After my initial training as a journalist at a course provided by IPI Africa Programme in 1966, I kept in touch with one of its star tutors and an eminent journalist, Frank Barton. I attended the IPI General Assemblies in Nairobi in 1968 and 1981. In

early eighties, IPI started a news resource for the African media to provide economic development news to counter the acute shortage of trained African journalists to report on this important aspect. After this project floundered, I was invited in 1983 to the IPI headquarters in London to take over their monthly publication, *African Economic Development News,* mailed to leading news media across the continent. As IPI Representative for Africa, I was invited in 1984 to address the IPI General Assembly in Stockholm on the challenges faced by African journalists and was introduced to the King of Sweden during a reception. In 1989, I co-authored with Frank Barton *Africa Factbook* a reference for the African media; and attended the IPI General Assembly in Berlin.

During my career with the two major newspapers, I worked for over 15 years as a correspondent for leading news agencies like the Press Trust of India (PTI), United News of India (UNI) and AFP of France; and All India Radio (AIR). I also contributed to *Daily Sketch*, London and *Wall Street Journal*, New York.

UNIDO Media Consultant

In 1988, I resigned from the *Standard* to manage my publishing company Newspread International and publishing *Kenya Factbook*. In 1997 I was invited by the United Nations Industrial Development Organization (UNIDO) to its headquarters in Vienna, Austria, for launching its publication for Africa. Soon after the launch of Industrial Africa, I was appointed as the Media Advisor for Africa to the Director General. In 2000, I moved to New Delhi and started my media consultancy to Dr George Assaf, the UNIDO Regional Director, editing and publishing a newsletter *UNIDO* in *Action in South East Asia* until 2006. In 2005, I started to write a weekly column on the overseas Indians for India's leading private news agency, IANS.

Globe Trotter

I have always had a great urge to travel and so have invested my time and money to visit different countries and experience them first-hand and learn about them. My first major trip happened in 1964 before I was trained as a journalist. Representing New Era College, I flew to London to attend the International Science Youth Fortnight, then moved to New York to address the Henry George International Conference and visited Washington and Toronto to address the UN Association for Students at Upper Canada College. This greatly widened my mental horizon and outlook. In all, I have visited 50 countries.

Author and Publisher

The author of 31 books up to 2013, I am known for my flagship publication *Kenya Factbook* that I wrote, compiled, designed and published for 16 editions from 1972 to 2000 by my company, Newspread International in Nairobi. Its unique feature was the charts presenting the major segments of the Kenyan economy and listing its main institutions and events since independence in chronological order. From less than a hundred in the first edition, these charts increased to 268 in the 16th edition. Initially, the charts were all hand drawn since computer generated charts only became the norm after1988. After the first three editions, the *Factbook* established itself as the standard reference on Kenya's economy and finance and was dubbed 'the diplomat's bible' and 'the senior executive's lifeline'. Advance copies were purchased by diplomatic missions, leading companies, financial institutions and multi-lateral organisations such as United Nations agencies, World Bank and IMF and IFC. Leading libraries in Kenya and abroad purchased copies and the US Library of Congress allocated a reference number for it. Its third edition was presented to President Jomo Kenyatta in 1975; and among the others heads of state who were presented with the *Kenya Factbook* were Indian Prime Minister Indira Gandhi in 1976, Kenyan President Daniel arap Moi in 1980 and German Chancellor Helmut Kohl in 1987.

From 2003 up to 2013, I have been editing a monthly *Osho World News* that developed into a 100-page magazine. With my trademark handlebar moustache, I have six books in progress at various stages, and continue to edit and write articles as nothing excites me more than seeing my work in print and on the web. I firmly believe that journalists never retire and even after celebrating my 75th birthday, my love affair with journalism goes on …

LORRAINE ALVARES
Writer

I was born in Nairobi, Kenya. My byline was Lorraine Saldanha. My married name is Alvares. I worked in the *Nation* briefly in 1968-9 writing for the Women's features pages. I emigrated to London, UK.

LORRAINE ALVARES

MONTE VIANNA (1946-1971)
By Ernest Vianna (brother)

Monte was born in Mombasa, Kenya in 1946. My father, Manuel and mother, Anne, were simple modest, yet hardworking, devout Catholics; generous and very established in all communities at the Coast. Monte completed his early education at the Star of the Sea Convent. His secondary education was at the Sacred Heart High School - both in Mombasa.

Academically, Monte was a top student and also very accomplished in extracurricular activities. He loved reading, had a retentive memory and became an unusually fast reader, able to assimilate the core of a book in a short period. Early in his youth, Monte had exhibited traits of inquisitiveness, intelligence and a commitment to progress with his studies. He had the desire and conviction to do the right thing and be part of everything positive.

Monte's life achievements were demonstrated not only in his perseverance to produce interesting and documented information for his employer - the *Nation*, but also in his dedication to numerous community projects. He initially reported for the *Nation's* Sports page at the Coast. He was constantly kept on his toes attending the numerous sports events, especially the local soccer, hockey, tennis and school sports. Monte's philosophy for sport was that 'the human side seemed more interesting'. This subsequently led him to a permanent reporting position at the Mombasa *Nation* Office. It was here that Monte learned the ins-and-outs of journalism - from grass roots reporting on the social scene to more arduous assignments on Court proceedings - reporting and interpretive analysis, local politics and economic reviews of Tourism and Wildlife along the Coast.

His favorite subject was space exploration and science, a topic that he wrote on with a passion for the *Nation* newspapers. Having developed a level of mutual trust and relationship with the Space Station personnel, he was allowed to witness and report the successful launching of the Space Rocket from Ngwana Bay, North of Malindi.

In 1969 Monte was invited to join the Nairobi office of the *Nation*. Here he became a confidante to numerous government and business policy makers - a role which

MONTE VIANNA

gradually ended due to his re-assignment and promotion to the *Nation's* Mombasa Office. His last article which was to be published in the *Nation* was a Mombasa Show Supplement.

During the search for Monte's missing aircraft; our family was accorded all the resources as directed by HE President Kenyatta. The Air Force and many individuals spent endless hours scouring the land and ocean prior to his crashed plane being spotted, by a Kenya Airways - Fokker, in the McKinnon Road Area.

Yes we lost a dear brother, a precious son and a wonderful *rafiki* to many.

NARAIN SINGH (1910-1978)
By Davinder Bhatyani (son)

Sardar Narain Singh was born in Nairobi in 1910. His father, Mangal Das, was an activist working with the Africans in the early independence movement in Kenya and earned a place in the history of this country.

He was educated at the Duke of Gloucester School and obtained his London Matriculation in 1927, coming first in the whole of the whole of the Commonwealth. Reading and writing were his two passions. Having contracted asthma at a very young age he could not participate in strenuous games and hence took to reading - his personal library contained some very rare books and his knowledge of world religions and politics was admirable.

After leaving school he joined the then Power and Lighting Company. In his spare time he wrote for the *Sunday Post*, and for the *Sunday Nation* under the pen name N S Toofan. ('Toofan' in Punjabi means 'storm'.) Eventually he ventured into full time journalism. Mr S M Shah bought over the *Kenya Weekly*, a settler paper, and invited him to take up the post of managing editor. Later he was to become the editor of both the *Sunday Post* and the *Evening Times*. Narain Singh took in Salim Lone as the chief editor whose critical political editorials soon made the *Post* 'one of the most analytical and independent media newspapers in Kenya at the time'.

In the run up to the 1974 General Election, the political environment was highly charged and the Government cracked down on any criticism of its policies. The *Post*

NARAIN SINGH

was first made to pay for its printing in advance and then to hire Brian Tetley as chief sub-editor who was to ensure that the maximum word count of any article was 600 words. That meant the end of the *Post's* popular analytical pieces. At no time did Narain Singh interfere in Lone's writing but Felix Pinto, who had bought the *Post* in 1972 and held pro-Israeli sentiments and status quo politics, urged for de-politicisation. Lone resigned and this led to a decline in the newspaper's readership.

Narain Singh was a loyal Kenyan and a dedicated member of the Sikh community. The *Sunday Post*, under

:Should the Asians keep out of politics?

A FREQUENT talking point among knowledgeable Asians in Kenya today — but one rarely aired in public—is the question: Should we keep out of politics now that African majority rule is so near, for fear of further exacerbating the racial tensions that exist between us? Would it

By

N. S. TOOFAN

his stewardship, gave a voice to many renowned South Asian journalists: Salim Lone was one of them; well-known sports writers Saude George and Anto de Souza were others. Narain Singh passed away in 1978.

Sir Mohinder Dhillon relates an incident which describes Narain Singh's religious fervour and his forthright speech. 'He [Sardar Narain Singh] was sitting in the VIP stand at an ASK show in Jamhuri Park so I went up to him to pay my respects, and he crucified me. My crime was: Why had I discarded my turban? Later, I was sitting underneath a camera platform and when I stood up, a large nail sticking out of the base of the platform went into the middle of my head. While I was being carried out on a stretcher, I heard him remarking that the injury was in the exact spot where a turban and the knotted bun of hair would have been; and I would have been protected! He really drove the point home'.

NORMAN DA COSTA

Writer

Few are fortunate enough to have their childhood dreams come true. Mine did. And in retirement today

this Kenyan journalist can reflect on a job that brought satisfaction and rewards. How many have sat metres away from the Olympic track finish line and scored prime time seats at boxing, World Cup soccer and cricket matches at the greatest stadiums in the world?

Since my high school days at Nairobi's Dr Ribeiro Goan School, I had one goal in mind and that was to become a journalist - and not just any journalist - but a sports journalist even though I had no journalism training. But I had a stellar career as captain of the school's field hockey and cricket teams and was a member of the 4x100 yards team that in 1963 won the Nairobi schools relay championships. In 1964 my dream of getting into the print media was realized after sports reporter Cyprian Fernandes introduced me to *Nation* sports editor Brian Marsden. Marsden was so impressed with my first match story that he assigned me to cover the M R de Souza Gold Cup as Cyprian was away. As Marsden couldn't offer me a full-time position - he did the next best thing - got me hired at the *Sunday Post*. *A year later came that call from Marsden that changed my life when he offered me a job with the Daily and Sunday Nation.*

I was fortunate to get into journalism when Kenya was fast becoming the focus of world attention for producing world-class athletes. A young policeman named Kipchoge Keino was busy blazing a trail of track supremacy.

My greatest thrill came in 1972 when I was on hand in Munich to record the country's nine-medal haul. One frightening and unforgettable moment for me came hours after our 4x400 metres relay won the gold ahead of Britain and France. In a city already reeling from the massacre of the Israeli athletes, I tried to scale a gate separating the athletes' village and the press village to file my copy in a hurry. This was a mere 10-minute route

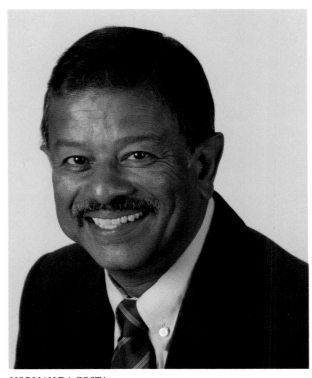

NORMAN DA COSTA

as opposed to taking the hour-long bus ride. Halfway up that dreaded fenced gate a German guard cocked his gun barked at me to get down or be shot. The army was put on high alert after the French started popping champagne bottles to celebrate their unexpected bronze and the gate was closed as they feared another massacre. That's the only time I can remember wetting my pants while on assignment.

In 1974 I became the first South Asian sports editor of a daily newspaper in East Africa, and later that same

In terms of staff relations, the Brits were very diplomatic. As long as you produced they were your buddies. One exception was my sports editor, Brian Marsden. I as sports editor was paid the usual local rates, but had I been an expatriate it would have been a whole lot different - they lived a life of luxury. That's something that rankles me till today.

Apart from covering every major event in East Africa I met President Jomo Kenyatta on two occasions; President Idi Amin and President Kenneth Kaunda; British Prime Minister Ted Heath and Princess Anne at Lancaster House in 1974 and of course the Aga Khan at Nation House. I was actively involved as a field hockey player – representing Kenya B on three occasions; was appointed Kenya Hockey Union national selector and managed Kenya's national team to India's Gold Cup tournament in 1975. In between I formed the Kenya Sports Writers Association and became first chairman of the Nairobi Hockey Association.

I do believe I raised the standard of sports reporting in Kenya because I spent a lot of time scouring British newspapers and a first-class magazine called *World Sports* to get an idea of how they reported on various matches, and many of the feature stories they carried. In fact every one of the South Asian journalists was a hard worker and they all did their part in helping the *Nation* to overtake the *Standard* in circulation and in the quality of reporting.

Not being a citizen of the country - although I was born in Nairobi in 1945 - my wife Delphine and three young children, Meryl, Nigel and Elaine, and I emigrated to Canada just prior to the 1976 Olympics. That was a tough decision to make with a young family but there

were rumblings in the office that the department should be run by an African. A couple of years earlier I had a confrontation with Member of Parliament Martin Shikuku whilst covering the Gossage Cup in Zanzibar. He threatened to deport me for what he termed my negative coverage of his club Abaluhya United. I reported this threat to my editor in chief George Githii and he laughed, adding I had nothing to worry about as long as he was in charge. Not only was he a first-class journalist, he was one man I trusted.

After arriving in Toronto I had a two-year stint with sporting giant Adidas and then joined the *Toronto Sun* as its chief soccer reporter. In 1981 I jumped ship to the *Toronto Star*, Canada's largest newspaper, and retired

year was presented with a gold medal at a ceremony in Barcelona for my contribution to sports journalism by AIPS, the International Sports Writers' Association. In the *Nation* I took over from Peter Moll who had succeeded Marsden a couple of years earlier. Former Kenya marathon runner Philip Ndoo, a person I had highly recommended, succeeded me in March of 1976.

in 2009 having covered the Barcelona Olympics, three World Cups, two women's World Cups, the 1991 Pan Am Games and the 1999 cricket World Cup in England. As chief soccer correspondent I travelled extensively reporting on Canada's men's and women's national teams that included Canada's Gold Cup triumph in 2000 in Los Angeles, the most by any Canadian journalist.

The highlight of my journalistic career came in 1989 when I broke the story that had the previous year captivated the entire world - Ben Johnson being stripped of his 100 metres gold for taking anabolic steroids. His physician Dr Jamie Astaphan admitted to me that he had administered drugs to the sprinter and the bombshell story made front pages of most newspapers and television stations around the world. Prior to that, in another exclusive, I revealed a couple of Canadian soccer players who were bribed $1,000 each to throw a game in an international tournament in Malaysia.

I enjoyed a great innings before retiring in 2009. The enjoyment now comes from spending time with my five grandchildren and taking vacations around the world. There is still work involved as I am a member of the Brampton Sports Hall of Fame, write a weekly cricket column for the *Sun* newspaper chain and am president of the 55 plus Goan Association that has 650 members. Did I say I was retired?

OLINDA FATIMA FERNANDES

Olinda Fatima Fernandes worked at the *Nation* from 1971 to 1974. She was a regular columnist under the byline 'Olinda' and wrote for the Features, Women's Page and Film Reviews. She emigrated to Canada in 1974 where she is a Producer/Project coordinator/Researcher for on-line educational videos.

OLINDA FATIMA FERNANDES

PIO GAMA PINTO (1927-1965)

Pio Gama Pinto is Kenya's patriot, socialist, freedom fighter and journalist. Born of Goan parents in 1927 in Nairobi, he was sent to India for further studies and there, at the age of seventeen, he started agitating against British rule in India and took part in a general strike – his first foray into mass action and organization.

Back in Kenya in 1951, he joined the East Africa Indian National Congress and the trade union movement. He obtained most of the secret information for the Kenya African Union (KAU), drafted press statements, organised secret fund-raising meetings with progressive Asians for the cost of the Kapenguria Six trials, and revitalized KAU after the arrest of its leaders. He also acquired arms, ammunition and food for the forest fighters, and with the help of his friend DK Sharda who had a small lino-press, printed various vernacular newspapers including Bildad Kaggia's *Inoro ria Gikuyu* and J D Kali's posters and pamphlets. He took the Mau Mau oath and became a conduit for the supply of intelligence information and firearms to the forest fighters, as well as for funds contributed by the Government of India. He worked closely with India's first high commissioner to Kenya, Appa Pant, who had also taken the oath.

Pinto's formal journalistic career started with his association with the *Colonial Times* and *Daily Chronicle* and with scribes such as D K Sharda, Haroon Ahmed and Pranlal Sheth. In 1953 he briefly became editor of the *Daily Chronicle;* he realised only too well the importance of the media in building a movement and mobilising the masses.

Pio Gama Pinto helped too with the preparation of the KAU memoranda, leading up to KAU's representations to the East Africa Royal Commission in 1951, but by then the period of petitioning to commissions was being overtaken by a far more inflammable method of struggle in which Pinto was to play an invaluable role, working closely together with the leaders of KAU, the KCA and the trade union movement, men like Jomo Kenyatta, James Beauttah, Mbiyu Koinange, Bildad Kaggia, Fred Kubai, Jesse Kariuki and others.

Pinto was detained from 1954 to 1959. After his release he worked tirelessly to bring KANU to victory in the

PIO GAMA PINTO

1961 elections and was one of the founders of the Kenya Freedom Party. He was elected as a member of the Central Legislative Assembly and became a Specially Elected member of the House of Representatives.

After his release from restriction, in 1960, with Jaramogi Odinga and James Gichuru, he founded the KANU newspaper, *Sauti ya Kanu*. The same year, he founded the Pan African Press with 700,000 Kenya shillings obtained from Jawaharlal Nehru, the first prime minister of India, and subsequently became director

and secretary. The other directors were Jomo Kenyatta, Achieng Oneko, Jaramogi Odinga and J D Kali. Pinto started the publication of three newspapers, namely *Sauti ya Mwafrika, Pan Africa* and *Nyanza Times*. *Sauti ya Mwafrika* had first been published as a weekly by KAU when it was formed in 1945. Its first editor then was Francis Khamisi. On 12 December, 1963 *Pan Africa* published a Kenya Uhuru Souvenir entitled 'Glimpses of Kenya's Nationalist Struggle'. In it Pinto gave a concise history of the colonial period from a peoples' perspective.

He established the Lumumba Institute in 1964 to train party officials, campaigned vigorously for an East African Federation and worked with the liberation movements of Angola, Mozambique and South Africa. It was at the Lumumba Institute, in a secret enclave chaired by Jaramogi Oginga Odinga that plans were laid to address in parliament the ideological rift that had developed between his group and the Kenyatta regime. Pinto was relentless in his exposure of neo-colonialism; he was assassinated on 24 February, 1965 in Nairobi, a few days after Kenyatta had sought legal counsel about how to deal with 'this bloody Goan'. He became thus Kenya's first post-independence political martyr.

Posthumously in September 1965, Pinto's widow, Emma, was invited to Santiago Chile to receive the prize awarded to her husband by the International Organisation of Journalists for his contribution in journalism to the liberation of African countries from foreign domination and exploitation. The editors of its organ, the *Democratic Journalist,* organ of International Organisation of Journalists, Prague wrote thus:

'On February 24 we received a report which upset us very profoundly and left us extremely dismayed. P. G. Pinto, the national deputy, member of the leadership of

the periodical *Panafrica*, the great African revolutionary and nationalist, a great man, had been murdered by hired assassins. A man had been killed who meant much to the international movement of progressive, democratic people, both to the trade union or journalist movement, and to the movement for the international co-operation of members of parliaments.

In P. G. Pinto we lose a man of great qualities, of great revolutionary enthusiasm, of great personal courage. His name is linked with the struggle against British colonialism. Pinto was several times held in colonial concentration camps together with thousands of other Kenyan patriots, together with those who today stand at the head of a free country. Since the winning of freedom Pinto has played an important role in the trade union and journalist movement, the periodical in which he had a leading position has become the spokes-man of democratic, freedom-loving ideas, an energetic fighter against colonialism, neo-colonialism and imperialism. His name will always be linked with the Lumumba Institute in Nairobi, which he helped to create, to which he gave much of his energies and part of his heart. The Lumumba Institute became the spokesman of all the new world that today is fighting in Africa for humanism, progress, the dignity of man, man freed of imperialism, freed of racial discrimination, freed from hunger and poverty. Every African patriot who passes through this school, either from the east, the north, the south or the west of Africa, takes with him part of P. G. Pinto's heart, his enthusiasm, his wisdom, his determination and courage.

And neither will our organization ever forget P. G. Pinto. He was with us at our last executive committee meeting held in Algiers in April 1964. A modest man, knowledgeable in many matters, knowledgeable on African and world problems, wise and well balanced.

Pio Gama Pinto (left) Bildad Kagia (centre) and Joseph Murumbi

The Daily Nation reports the assassination.

Many of us knew him from personal contacts either in Kenya or elsewhere in Africa, Asia or Europe. P. G. Pinto was murdered because he stood in the way of neo-colonialism, he was undoubtedly removed by those who wish to go on exploiting, misusing and oppressing Africa and the Africans. Pinto fought and fell in battle.

But he did not lose. This crude murder is merely a proof of the weakness of these reactionary circles which hired the murderers. Pinto will go on fighting. In every African patriot, in every democrat throughout the world. And our organization will also honour the memory of this great journalist, by fighting even more effectively for the materialization of the ideals of freedom, equality, democracy for which Pinto was working. We shall never forget our heroic colleague.'

Sources: AwaaZ Issue 1 2005
*   Oginga Odinga, 1967.*

POLLY (POLYCARP) FERNANDES

Polly Fernandes was a very popular sports writer with the *Nation* newspapers specialising in the game of football. He declined our invitation to write for this book.

RASHID MUGHAL

Writer

I entered journalism via the Letters to the Editor columns in the mid-1960s. Inspired by seeing my letters published without any editorial changes in various newspapers and magazines, I enrolled for a course in Freelance and Speciality Journalism through the London-based International Correspondence Schools.

The editors at *Sunday Post, East African Standard, Daily Nation* and several local and international publications popular in Nairobi in those days—including Henry Reuter's *Reporter* magazine; and *Drum,* black Africa's largest circulation monthly out of London—soon invited me to write articles and features for them.

I joined the *Nation* in April 1967 as a trainee proof-reader. Within a few months, I was promoted to head of shift. In 1969 I was appointed head of the proofreading department. As an authority concerning matters of style, I wrote and compiled the first *Nation Style Book* as a definitive bible for reporters, sub-editors and proof-readers.

Soon, the *Nation* began to experiment with electronic photo-typesetting and to phase out the hot-metal linotype. By 1970, the *Nation* with its first-generation of Lumitype phototypesetting computers—was regarded at the time as 'technologically the most advanced

newspaper in the world,' ahead of *Time, Newsweek, The Economist* and *Playboy* magazines.

My rise at the *Nation*—literally from the shop floor to the top—was quite remarkable. By dint of hard work and accepting every challenge with a positive mental attitude, I rose in quicksuccession from proof-reader to sub-editor and foreign editor on the copy desk, editing everything—including letters and editorials, local and international news, and various columns and articles written by established correspondents and writers—chopping, changing or rewriting copy to fit a given space and writing some clever headlines under deadline pressure. Those days were fun and I was keen to learn from the many expatriates, some of them former Fleet Street professionals.

I enjoyed the game of chess so I started a regular column on Fridays, and organized some international matches to popularize the game as a sport in Kenya. I appreciated movies and reviewed both Hollywood and Bollywood films. I covered theatre and drama at the Donovan Maule and National Theatre. I was a voracious reader always wanting to stay on top of things, so I took the Evelyn Wood speed reading dynamics course at company expense in order to review new books.

Given my impeccable copy editing and rewrite skills and an excellent sense of layout and design, it was little wonder that when I was offered the politically volatile position of chief sub-editor, I opted instead for the lateral, non-political position of group features editor which fell vacant around the same time. The call to Africanize rendered it difficult for the management to hire expatriates from Britain anymore. When John Eames left, I edited a few issues of the glossy *Africana* magazine for the World Wildlife Fund which was produced by

RASHID MUGHAL

quality of writing and each magazine assumed a distinct personality with bold layouts and lavish use of duotones, sepia and full colour. This in turn lured advertisers to place more colour advertising in the *Nation* than in any other publication, thanks to my strong belief that good content attracts good advertising.

I did my best at all times to cram each magazine section with well researched and well written features, articles and columns on fashion, entertainment, the music scene, social issues, book reviews, humour and much more. I wrote a great deal of the stuff myself sometimes while looking for new and talented writers. In the process I nurtured many writers and columnists who went on to become household names in Kenya. (The late Wahome Mutahi of 'Whispers' fame was one of them.) As a result, advertising revenues and newspaper sales on Wednesdays, Fridays and Sundays soared.

I was born in Nairobi in 1946, of 1894 vintage Punjabi stock! As a polyglot punjabber I was always spewing puns and so-called 'mughalisms.' This led me to write a popular humour column called 'Characters' which, Mr Rodrigues once told me, often made His Highness the Aga Khan chuckle when he read it in his Aiglemont residence in Paris.

Marketing & Publishing, a Nation Group company, in my spare time.

As features editor, I serviced the features needs of the daily and Sunday editions of the Nation Group by originating ideas for news features and general interest feature articles and commissioning established and new writers to write for the *Nation*. I was given a free hand and a substantial budget to revamp the content and design of the Wednesday, Friday, and Sunday magazine sections. There was a marked enhancement in the

One day, on a crystal-clear morning in 1981, as he strutted through the editorial department upon his return from London, managing director Stan Denman stopped by my desk to say I should come to his office. The editor-in-chief, Joe Rodrigues, and I walked together through the hallway to Stan's office. 'Cheers, gentlemen,' Stan said holding up a glass of champagne. 'The good news is that at the world exhibition of newspapers in London, the *Nation* earned a citation in the magazine section category—it was nominated as one of the best in the Commonwealth.'

Then came the day I intimated a personal wish to leave the *Nation*. This was soon after Salim Lone, founding editor of *Viva* magazine, had slipped off to the United States after being stripped of his Kenyan citizenship by Moi's government. The owner of Trend Publishers Ltd, Bhushan Vidyarthi of Colourprint Ltd, asked me to take over the running of Viva. I imposed a condition — I would chuck out all politically prejudicial stuff from *Viva*. 'It's meant to be a women's magazine so let's make Viva "The Complete Woman's Magazine", I said.'

I reckoned more men had started buying *Viva* out of curiosity to see what the women were reading. So why not start a new magazine to complement *Viva*, which would make women curious to see what the men were reading. The plan worked. *Men Only* became extremely popular from the word go. Occasionally, I was invited as a visiting lecturer by the School of Journalism at the University of Nairobi to share my insights with students.

At the height of my editorial prowess and popularity I decided to quit Trend Publishers Ltd to set up Kenya's first editorial agency to offer my services to publishers, advertising agencies and public relations companies. I edited dozens of magazines and controlled-circulation monthlies and quarterly journals for News Publishers Ltd, which Henry Reuter had sold to Joe Rodrigues and Stan Denman after their exit from the Nation, and launched several newsletters for clients including Del Monte, Shell, Barclays Bank and Panafrican Paper Mills. I also edited several other publications including *Executive* magazine for Space Publications; *East African Computer News*; Cynthia Salvadori's *Through Open Doors* for Kenway Publications; and many more.

Things took a turn one afternoon when Joe Rodrigues, barely 54, suddenly died of a heart attack in the fourth-floor offices of News Publishers in the Norwich Union building. His widow, Cyrilla, and Mr Denman decided to sell the company and quickly found an eager buyer—but there was a problem: the new owner wanted *me* to run News Publishers, so he asked Mr Denman and Mrs Rodrigues to persuade me into the bargain. When I met with the new owner, veteran businessman Horatius da Gama Rose, he made me an offer I could not refuse.

I ran the company as editor-in-chief and CEO with several editors under me for 19 months before immigrating to Canada in August 1988. Unlike most of the South Asian journalists of my time I was a Kenyan citizen. But, as a victim of the infamous coup of August 1982, something deep inside me died for Kenya. Moreover, the deteriorating political climate forced me to think about a better quality of life for my family.

During the past 25 years in Canada, I have worked as a copy-editor at *The Toronto Star*, *The Kitchener-Waterloo Record*, and as editor-in-chief of *The South Asian Profile*. For several years I taught copy editing, substantive editing and content editing courses at George Brown College in Toronto as part of their publishing programme, and I was specially hired at one time to do marketing research for the Star. I retired in December 2012 and since then work occasionally as a background actor in television serials and feature films. I live in Mississauga, a suburb of the Greater Toronto Area, and am presently working on a novel.

SALIM LONE
Writer

I had always wanted to be a teacher, probably because both my mother and father were. Once I went to the United States in 1961 as part of the airlift, I decided I wanted to teach also. But when after obtaining my Masters degree I began my PhD course at New York University in English Literature, I realized that high-level academic discourse – at least on literature - was not my cup of tea.

So I gave up my doctoral work and indeed a very generous four-year fellowship and turned to a newer love, journalism, to which I had been exposed when I worked as an intern at a small but progressive weekly New York newspaper, the [Greenwich] *Village Voice,* during the summer of 1963. But the most direct influence that led to my interest in journalism came in the late 1960s, through Philip Ochieng's columns in the *Nation*, which would see me get up early on Sunday mornings.

I later realized that both my career choices, of teacher and journalist, had a common root, which was my keen interest in trying to influence people to aspire to a better, more equitable world. So when I returned to Kenya from my US studies, I went to see Kenneth Bolton, the renowned but conservative Editor of the *East African Standard*, to see if I could be considered for the position of a sub-editor. He was friendly but not very encouraging, as my only experience in the field was the summer job at the *Village Voice* and more recently as an occasional book reviewer for the Voice of Kenya radio service. But I also thought that despite my MA in English, Mr Bolton seemed slightly amused by my desire to be an arbiter of the English language, since English was not my mother tongue.

Subsequently, after teaching English and History in 1968 and 1969 at Kangaru School in Embu and Pumwani Secondary in Nairobi, I ended up back in New York working for two years as a researcher and writer for Lester Markel, a renowned *NY Times* editor who won the Pulitzer Prize for integrating interpretative journalism as

SALIM LONE

a core basic media tool. He was now retired but writing a book for the *Times* on how media affected public opinion. I learned my journalism from my close relationship with him, and from having an office right next to the scores of journalists who worked in the *Times* third-floor newsroom. (The *Times* employed 125 journalists to cover the New York Metropolitan area alone!).

So when I returned to Kenya after that two-year US stint in late 1971, I went looking for a job as a sub-editor again, and was absolutely thrilled when I was hired on the spot by Mr Narain Singh, the Editor-in-Chief of the *Sunday Post*. The *Post* was sort of a sleepy newspaper which had its roots in British settlerdom in Nakuru and had been recently bought by a group of mid-level Asian businessmen led by Mr S M Shah of Midco and the owners of the English Press, who hailed from Nakuru also. The *Post* was then located at Reata Road (now Accra Road).

Mr Singh, a warm, open and astute man, who had been a film reviewer under the pen name of Toofaan (The Storm) for the *Nation*, was trying to make the *Sunday Post* more relevant to Kenyans. He explained that the paper was cash-strapped and could only offer a salary of 1,600 shillings a month. That was very small even by those days' standards, I had earned more even as a high school teacher four years earlier. But I was living with my parents, with my wife Pat (who also later became a journalist) and our two little children, so I happily accepted the job.

When I reported for work two days later, Mr Singh walked me to a room marked EDITOR. I asked him where the Editor was, and he said you are the Editor. I almost passed out. The mere thought of that responsibility was terrifying, and I protested vigorously, telling Mr Singh I had never worked as a journalist, or managed ANYTHING. I was also only 28, I reminded him. Anyway, Mr Singh said, 'rubbish; you are fully qualified'. And he soon gave me my first assignment, to go down the street to Victoria Furnitures and do a write up on their new product line! Two hours earlier, I had been terrified, now I was horrified. I told Mr Singh firmly I knew ABSOLUTELY NOTHING about furniture and would find some writer who did to go to the store. Again he said rubbish; you will do a fine article because the owner of the store will guide you. Fear of ignorance about the fine points of furniture aside, I also felt that this assignment was slightly below my dignity as Managing Editor – and one who had recently been published in the *New York Review of Books* and the *New Republic*. That was my introduction to the rough and tumble of Kenyan journalism as practised outside the *Standard* and the *Nation*. Little did I know what lay in store ahead.

To begin with, there was not a single reporter or editor on the staff, and there was hardly a budget to pay freelancers. But as indications of openness and independence grew in the *Post's* pages, a small pool of freelancers willing to write for very little began to congregate around the *Post's* Reata Road offices. They were mainly relative youngsters keen to get into writing as a way to express their criticism over government policies and actions, especially corruption, the discarded freedom struggle priorities, both of which meant that a wealthy elite was rapidly monopolizing wealth and land allocations, while the poor were left to their own devices. But most of these young men – there were virtually no women - lacked journalistic or even writing skills, so a big chunk of my time was spent with the more promising writers helping them develop their potential. Some of their names I can still recall: Henry Kimondo, James Kimondo, Magaga Alot, Victor Riitho, Blamuel Njururi.

Given my political and cultural inclinations, the paper soon came to be seen as one which gave voice to nationalist, socialist and internationalist stances, which were poorly represented in the media then. So the *Sunday Post* began to make some headway among disaffected constituencies, and the paper's university audience grew in particular, through the platform it provided for the views of lecturers and students.

It was easy to make such headway as our major independent media, which consisted only of the *Standard* and *Nation* newspapers - TV and radio being firmly under government control – were increasingly unable to highlight in any consistent way how the hallowed goals of the nationalist freedom struggle had been abandoned, replaced by an autocratic if not dictatorial system of ethnically-driven accumulation which was systematically transferring the nation's land and other wealth to individuals and political groups close to the President, groups which had mostly fought on the other side of the freedom struggle. Those who had sacrificed the most for freedom, including their lives and land, had been shunned or shunted into poverty and landlessness, and the Mau Mau were still a banned group a decade after independence. Some members of President Kenyatta's family also irregularly acquired land and other wealth. To complete the picture, internationally Kenya had become one of the few African countries which had openly joined the western bloc, who were fighting the Non-Aligned Movement of which we were supposed to be a part.

Little of this reality could be gleaned from the media. There were some very courageous and talented reporters and editors at both papers, who would occasionally undertake important crusades on some sensitive subjects. But the papers' leaderships on the whole were not interested in highlighting the woes or the betrayals or the repression that were turning Kenya into a police state with progressively limited freedoms. The opposition Kenya Peoples Union led by Jaramogi Oginga Odinga, the country's first Vice President, had of course been banned and many of its leaders detained.

Apart from the authorities' intimidation and threats to ensure media loyalty, further fealty was ensured through appointing papers' editors linked to the two dominant but intensely competitive camps within the government, both essentially led by members of the Kiambu elites close to President Kenyatta. One camp was led by Charles Njonjo, the powerful Attorney General who was particularly close to the President, in part because of his closeness to the British. The other camp was more loosely led by Dr Njoroge Mungai and included Mbiyu Koinange and James Gichuru.

The *Nation,* under the brilliant and courageous but simultaneously mercurial and propagandistic George Githii, was aligned with Njonjo, while the *Standard*, under the Lonrho stewardship of its young CEO Udi Gecaga, President Kenyatta's son-in-law, was generally aligned with the Mungai group. A lot was made those days of the Kiambu-Nyeri rivalry, but there were no Nyeri leaders who wielded any significant power.

Political alignments aside, the *Standard's* and *Nation's* editorial policy was influenced by their respective owners, Lonhro and the Aga Khan. Lonhro was a major multinational led by the renowned Tiny Rowlands, who publicly stated once that African presidents were so corrupt that there was not a single one of them he could not buy. Probably truer now than then! The *Nation's* Aga Khan, who was the spiritual leader of the influential Muslim Ismaili community, had founded the newspaper to support the new nationalism in 1959 and was now embarked on a major business expansion programme in Kenya. Neither of the owners would wish to jeopardise their substantial commercial interests by challenging the architecture of the emerging Kenyan state, even though it was illegally solidifying Presidential control over all aspects of national life, including resorting to assassinating potential presidential successors.

So as I struggled to build up the *Sunday Post,* it became clear that it was the only mainstream media that could, within the obvious limits, highlight anti-people trends. The *Post* enjoyed three advantages in doing this - we were small and weekly, and so could not have a major political impact. Another reason we sometimes seemed daring was that I was relatively naïve politically, and so ended up raising sensitive political issues a number of times without realizing their explosiveness. And finally, as a Kenyan Asian journalist working for a Kenyan Asian owned-paper, we were not suspected of supporting one of the groups who were jockeying for power in a post-Kenyatta order. Not until the 1974 general election at least!

Media issues apart, there seemed to be little effective thinking going on in political circles about how the determined drift towards dictatorship could be arrested – not an easy task when every centre of power, including the major western countries, were firmly behind the President's project of centralizing power in his core team and the Mt Kenya elite. Opposition leaders therefore generally limited themselves to condemning certain specific policies without directly linking them to the President or his family.

Much hope in challenging the system had been lost once the socialist Kenya People's Union party was banned and Jaramogi put under house arrest and denied the opportunity to participate in politics (for many years). While there were many potential leaders in waiting who were opposed to government policies, there were none who could step into the breach and exercise the skill and leadership needed to publicly challenge Kenyatta as Jaramogi had. Except in times of intense crisis, as when J M was killed in 1975, and ruling party MPs like Elijah Mwangale, Mark Mwithaga and Martin Shikuku emerged to boldly condemn the government in a way never seen before. That assassination posed the first real

political threat to the Kenyatta state; it had weathered Tom Mboya's assassination without serious difficulty.

The media in this period rarely took head on, except obliquely, the growing litany of national woes, which by the early 1970s included political repression of communities considered 'anti-government', and the naked appropriation of the vital natural resources of regions such as the Coast and the Maasai areas. There were also highly placed figures wantonly undertaking environmental destruction of forests for charcoal exports and the slaughter of elephants for the Far East's ivory market.

The one area where there was strong opposition to the government and the nature of the state itself was the University of Nairobi. Students and their lecturers would regularly attack the way the state was monopolizing power and entrenching corruption and inequality. But power continued to be rapidly accumulated by the emerging elite. The elite had been given the go-ahead to use all means necessary to enrich themselves as part of the plan to quickly create an influential class of the African rich who would be beholden to President Kenyatta and would defend the free enterprise system against socialist ideology, which still had many supporters in 1972. So determined was President Kenyatta in his desire to advocate this corrupt model as a tool to fight progressives that he publicly mocked those who were not interested in amassing personal wealth, captured in his iconic rebuke at a rally of his former fellow detainee

and now an important government figure, the socialist Bildad Kaggia. Kenyatta asked him to show what he had accumulated as a senior official.

Socialism, of the indigenous rather than the Marxist tinge, was still considered a potential threat as the idea of catering to the needs of the majority had grassroots support and numerous Kenyan politicians espoused it as well. Socialism's appeal was bolstered by President Mwalimu Nyerere's Ujaama policies across the border, and Ugandan President Milton Obote, as well focused on policies which would benefit the peasants and workers, building an equitable system. The competition between the two ideologies and capitalism in Kenya was fierce. Kenyans will recall the debate about our two ideologies, with Tanzania labelling us 'man eat man society' and our exceedingly clever riposte of Tanzania being a 'man eat nothing society'.

I held Mwalimu in exceedingly high regard – for his commitment to equality, which extended to his support for the liberation struggle in southern Africa despite its high cost, his lack of corruption and the pursuit of totally non-tribal politics. All these made Tanzania Africa's most peaceful and united country, but his economic policies gradually saw Tanzanians struggling for basic items like soap and toothpaste.

So in 1974 I went to Dar to try to interview Mwalimu. That did not prove possible but his PA Joan Wicken told me to meet with Foreign Minister John Malecela. I asked for an introduction, she said I did not need it. I asked for a telephone number. She said she did not have his home number handy but it was listed in the telephone directory. I was convinced this would not work, but I called, got him on the line, and an interview was fixed for the next day! Back home, my friends were dumbfounded with

a bold political perspective one rarely saw in the press. Who was this Peter Mwaura? I had never heard of him or seen his byline. Where had he been hiding? Anyway, it was a very controversial article. Peter was asserting that Israel was a racist state and that it would never return the occupied territories. Its grand plan in fact, Peter wrote, was to take over the rest of Palestine as well. I was a strong critic of Israeli policies, but I still did not agree with some of what Peter wrote, but it was a view worth airing.

I knew the article would annoy some influential people, but I had no clue that it would spark a firestorm. Kenyan officialdom was not used to a mainstream paper condemning Israel. Among those who called Mr Narain Singh Monday morning were Attorney General Charles Njonjo, to whom he was close, and the Israeli ambassador, and the Special Branch head. Mr Singh cautioned me that Israel was an extremely sensitive subject to be handled with extreme care. I subsequently discovered that one reason criticizing Israel was taboo was because it provided high level personal security for the President.

Interestingly, Mr Singh did not tell me not to publish articles critical of Israel. I thought he was already enjoying the attention and indeed political notoriety, and the new readership his newspaper was beginning to enjoy.

Another writer I discovered through a submission he sent via the post was Koigi wa Wamwere. It was an article about why there was no free education in Kenya and it laid out all the reasons – primarily focu ssing on the emerging class divisions, in which the rich were sending their children to private schools, etc. It caused another firestorm, and I got my death threat over it! We published a few articles by Koigi, who was a fiery and

ideological proponent of socialism and very outspoken about how Mau Mau freedom fighters had been betrayed and were landless while loyalists reaped the wind. He had just returned from Cornell University in the States but people whispered he had been studying in East Germany (which was not true). Koigi in 1974 ran for the Nakuru North seat held by Kihika Kimani, a Kenyatta confidante, and almost defeated him (he might in fact have won). For his troubles, he was detained right after the election, and released by President Moi soon after his accession along with all the other political prisoners.

In highlighting such articles and elements I do not mean to imply that the *Sunday Post* was a revolutionary kind of newspaper. My personal views apart, my editorial and communication orientation has always been a moderate one, in the belief that if one wants to win over people to a particular point of view, a strident advocacy will turn off the majority. In addition, it does not pay to push authorities too hard, because you could jeopardise the paper and so lose an indispensable tool for change.

Another area that caused us problems was Uganda, where Idi Amin was murdering and massacring opponents, real or perceived. We were able to regularly reveal information the other papers did not have, as I had come to know James Namakajo, a young Ugandan intelligence officer, who would send me articles signed NM. Amin had supporters in the Kenya elite, who had detested Obote's 'turn to the left', especially as that stance had strengthened Mwalimu Nyerere's hand in the ongoing struggle between capitalist and socialist ideologies that were rocking the region in the early 1970s. Indeed, one day the three newspaper editors – *Nation's* Joe Rodrigues, *Standard's* Frank Young and myself - were summoned by President Kenyatta to State House Mombasa for a meeting with President Amin, where Amin lectured us on reporting accurately about Uganda.

such openness, since even senior civil servants phones were unavailable, they being considered demi-gods because of their power and wealth, and so impossible to get hold of so easily (if at all).

Despite all this focus on internal politics, my first crisis at the *Sunday Post* came from an international issue. I was thrilled one morning to receive through the post a brilliantly written article with a mastery of language and

It was of course too good to last. With Mzee ailing, the struggle for succession grew more fierce by the day, and in such a period, repression is invariably the worst, to ensure that no surprise development can derail the plans of those planning to take over the next government. The upcoming 1974 election was seen as the last of Mzee's tenure and all sides battled to get the 'right' MPs elected. In advance of that election, I published an article which basically showed support for Dr Muthiora's candidacy against incumbent Dagoretti MP Dr Njoroge Mungai. The *Standard*, which was allied to Dr Mungai, and printed the *Sunday Post*, was very unhappy. Under pressure, our Board Chairman Felix Pinto asked me to change the paper's approach to politics, which was not acceptable to me, so I resigned.

I knew I would not be hired in a senior newspaper position, but I thought that my professional skills would enable me to be hired as a sub-editor, a post with very little policy control. But even that was not possible. Then help came out of the blue: George Githii, whom I knew well, offered me a job at the *Nation*. But when I reported for work, George took me aside and apologizing profusely, said there was a problem and he could not hire me. I understood. Two weeks later, he called to say the way was clear now! But lo and behold, the day before I was to start, George again called to say my employment had been blocked.

It was clear that I would not be hired anywhere, so I agreed then to start a women's magazine, which came to be known as *Viva*.

SAUDE GEORGE (1931- 2010)

By Anto de Souza, (fellow journalist) and
Kenneth George (son)

The late Saude George was born in Kenya in 1931 and completed his education in India. He was a well-known

SAUDE GEORGE

Sports Editor of the *Sunday Post*, a very popular Sunday newspaper in Kenya often rivalling the *Sunday Nation* with its sports and news coverage. His editorial skills were noteworthy, perhaps because he himself was a former Kenyan national player in soccer and hockey. At times he was very critical in his views often hitting out at some national associations; but in a constructive way. George represented Kenya at hockey as a goalkeeper from 1959 and went to the 1960 and 1964 Olympic Games in Rome and Tokyo respectively. He also represented Kenya in football in the sixties, playing alongside the great

Kenyan football player, Joe Kadenge. At club level, he played for the Goan Institute hockey and football teams in the sixties and seventies.

At an official level, George was also a member of the Kenya Goan Sports Association which annually organised the well-known M R d'Souza Gold Cup hockey tournament which attracted teams from East Africa and overseas. At press level, he was a member of the International Press Association and attended several meetings abroad in the seventies and eighties.

The *East African* in March 2003 described him as once 'a youth marked by a heady mix of football, union politics and agitating for independence … a journalist, sportsman and fighter against apartheid'.

Prior to his passing in 2010, Saude George wrote a book, *Kenya's Olympic Journey – A Tribute to those who made it possible*, focusing on the country's sportsmen in several international tournaments and the Olympic Games.

SHAMLAL PURI

Writer

I was born in 1951 in Kigoma, then Tanganyika, but have been closely connected with the Kenyan media. My involvement with Kenyan journalism started in the 1970s with *Drum* and *Trust* magazines as their Tanzania correspondent. DRUM and TRUST's East African editions were published by Drum Publications (EA) Ltd, based at the Mutual Building in Nairobi. The publishing centre was at 40-43 Fleet Street in London EC4. The magazine's overall publisher and owner was the late James Abe Bailey (Jim Bailey) but the East African edition was handled by Jasmer Singh Grewal, who was the Managing Director.

When Zairean rebels kidnapped four Western researchers in the Gombe National Park on Lake Tanganyika in 1975; my cover story in *Trust* magazine was an exclusive. I undertook a hazardous journey to Gombe to cover the story and photographed the three Americans and a Dutch researcher on their release by their kidnappers.

I left Tanzania in September 1975 because my family migrated to the UK. I wanted to remain in Tanzania but my plans were vetoed by my parents! I had no political problems and I did not go into exile. Working with the state-owned media all journalists were subject to self-censorship. You simply would not have been able to write in this newspaper if you were criticising the Government, the State or the President. Mwalimu Julius Nyerere was the de-facto editor of *The Daily News* and *Sunday News* and through his editors, including Benjamain William Mkapa (later Tanzania's President), the newspaper took on only those who agreed with the national policies. I got along well with Mkapa and everyone else working there. To this day, I remain in contact with the old guard and surviving colleagues still working on the *Daily News* and *Sunday News*. I must have been a well-behaved newsman with a good professional reputation that the journalists there still talk to me!

I have since 1975 lived and worked as a full-time journalist in the UK. I undertook advanced journalism training at the Westminster Press, part of the media giant Pearson, owners of the *Financial Times*. I was the Publisher and Editor of *Newslink Africa*, a pioneering news service for the continent for 25 years. I specialise in Africa affairs. In the UK I have gained a lot of experience working with the British media as a sub-editor, production editor, page designer and stone-sub-editor.

I was appointed the London Correspondent of the *Daily News* and *Sunday News* Tanzania and filed copy from the

SHAMLAL PURI

UK for a while. In the following years I started writing Akili Mingi, a humour column in *Trust*. It tackled controversial subjects with a humorous slant. I wrote the column until 1976 when *Trust* was merged into a new magazine - *True Love* and Akili Mingi ended. I was then 'reborn' as Michael Matatu.

That's Life: Michael Matatu at Large was first published in 1976 in the newly-launched East African edition of *True Love*. The humor column was a sardonic look at life through the eyes of a down and out Kenyan called

Michael Matatu. The column covered his various exploits in trying to make money. Apart from raising a chuckle, the column looked at the serious shortcomings in Kenyan society. I wrote this column under the pen-name of Michael Matatu for over 20 years.

Malimoto was a lead humour column in *Drum* East Africa. It was originally launched by the late Pius George Okoth, editor of *Drum* East Africa. I used to contribute to this column once in a while when PG Okoth could not find time to write it. In one issue *Drum* carried Okoth's 'exclusive' interview with Idi Amin. President Amin contacted *Drum* and denied that he had ever given an interview to P G Okoth. Consequently, he was sacked as the editor. Garth Bundeh succeeded him as editor and as Malimoto was a hit with *Drum* readers, he assigned me to continue writing Malimoto. From then on, I penned the column regularly. I continued to write for *Drum* and *True Love* as their UK correspondent until the titles changed hands. In 2006, Crownbird Publishers in London published my book *That's Life: Michael Matatu at Large*. In February 1977, when Edward Sokoine was appointed the third Prime Minister of Tanzania, I was granted an exclusive interview for *Drum* magazine.

I was appointed the London Correspondent of the *Kenya Times* and continued covering the East African diaspora in the UK. I also wrote a weekly column Letter from London for the *Sunday Times* for many years. I had been brought to the *Kenya Times* editorial team by the veteran Philip Ochieng, then its editor-in-chief. We had both worked on Tanzania's *Daily News* in the 1970s under the editorship of Benjamin Mkapa. Over the years I paid return visits to Kenya and got an opportunity to cover the Safari Rally. I shared this coverage with the *Kenya Times*.

New features agency launched

By NATION Reporter

NEWSLINK Africa, a pan-African features and pictures agency, has started its operations in London. It incorporates Harambee News Service which ceased business after six years on June 30.

The agency aims to provide full coverage of events in Africa for publication and broadcast worldwide each week.

Managing editor Shamlal Puri, a Tanzanian journalist, says the agency is planning to open bureaus in several capitals in Africa, apart from a history of correspondents in major African countries.

Established African journalists with solid experience in analysing events in their respective countries will also contribute to the news service.

For far too long, Western journalists have given prominence to coups, hunger, corruption and war in Africa.

"We aim to report on the positive aspects of economic and social development in Africa. We will not be afraid to tackle controversial subjects. Our independence leaves us free to say what we think and feel," says Mr. Puri.

I crossed the floor to the *Nation* from *Kenya Times* after working there as a senior journalist and advertising representative for several years. I left following the death of *Kenya Times'* joint British publisher Robert Maxwell. Starting as the official UK representative of The Nation Group in the UK, I helped build a strong presence for the paper in the UK generating advertising and subscriptions revenue not only from the UK, but also other parts of the world. I was officially brought into the *Nation* by Cyrille

Nabutola. I also wrote for the *East African* covering a wide variety of subjects.

In 1997, I met Mwalimu Nyerere, then retired President and an elder statesman, in London and he asked me what was I doing living in London. 'Come back to Tanzania. Start a newspaper. It's very different today.' He invited me to visit him in his village in Butiama and asked me to help out with the Julius Nyerere Foundation which he was actively promoting in the UK. When Mwalimu was hospitalised in London I was assigned to file regular reports to the Nation Group titles. On his death on 14 October, 1999, I filed the front page story for the *Daily Nation* from London. I produced UK-Kenya links supplements complete with editorial write-ups and ads in the *Kenya Times*. The ads were generated through my company Adlink International, an established agency with multi-million sterling pound billings. I have written various features for the *Nation* including the sale of an item of pottery by UK-based Kenyan potter Magdeline Odundo, creating a world record for the sale of such an art work. For a man who had first walked into Nation House in Tom Mboya Street in the 1970s, while a visiting journalist from Dar es salaam, I am privileged to have seen the paper grow.

My return visits to Kenya from London were largely to cover the Safari Rally which I did for many years for *Newslink Africa*. But for many years I was also part of *Kenya Times'* Safari Rally journalists/photographers team and my coverage was extensively published in that daily. I also visited Kenya from time to time to have consultations with *Drum* East Africa and in later years, with *Kenya Times*. I have also been visiting Tanzania from time to time and am still welcomed in the newsroom of the *Daily News* and the *Sunday News* as an old colleague. There are newcomers there who have heard of me and we do

end up being friends. I am planning to visit Tanzania and Kenya later this year and may travel to Uganda, time permitting.

Working as a journalist in three different countries has been interesting. I worked in Tanzania when I was aged 22. Working in Tanzania was not a problem for me though I felt frustrated that when you stumbled on stories that would have rumbled top politicians, you had to bite the bullet. Firstly, they would never see light of the day in the State-owned media and secondly, the Special Branch would take interest in you. Those were the days of arbitrary detentions and arrests under Presidential orders. Mwalimu Nyerere was ruthless with so-called economic saboteurs and had no compunctions throwing Asians into detention. I was not one of them as I was an ordinary reporter! But the lack of press freedom did worry me. The best way to survive in the Tanzania of the day was to mould yourself in such a way that you had no visits from the Special Branch. There was always an air of fear among the journalists working there because among the seasoned reporters of the day were appointees of the then ruling TANU party who were supposedly spilling the beans on 'wayward' reporters.

An interesting incident happened when I visited Dar es Salaam from London in 1998 (nearly 25 years after I had left Tanzania) and went to visit the then editor of the *Daily News*, Joseph Mapunda, a former colleague. Then I was the Publisher and managing editor of Newslink Africa, a pioneering African affairs news agency that was established and based in London. *Daily News* was a subscriber of the syndicated output from Newslink Africa. We were discussing delayed payments for Newslink Africa's invoices. I broached the subject with Mr Mapunda, who promptly asked his secretary to bring out the 'Shamlal Puri file'. In the file were ALL documents related to me, ranging from my early employment at the newspaper and Newslink Africa's documentation. There I saw filed a seriously critical but factual piece written on Tanzania by us and our correpondents at Newslink Africa. The feature, which deliberately did not have a byline, was never published but filed away in my personal file. That was the ONLY feature filed there. I could not understand the logic behind it but in all probability, I suspected it was a dossier on my 'anti-Tanzania' stance while living in London! But frankly, I was not anti-Tanzania as I loved the country. But I could not turn a blind eye to happenings in Tanzania as that would have been against my grain as a professional journalist.

The lessons of self-survival I learnt in Tanzania were also used in Kenya because in the days of Kenyatta, seasoned journalists were being picked up by the CID. In the heyday of the Moi Government, there were similar problems and there was a fallout between critical journalists and the regime. I was a visiting journalist from Tanzania and had to watch out as I was a guest journalist. I got along very well with everyone in the Kenyan media who crossed my path.

In the UK it was not easy to get journalism jobs in the 1970s because the media was a closed shop. There were very few Asian journalists in the British media, except for the London correspondents of the Indian and Pakistani newspapers who did not have to belong to the Union in order to operate here. I had no such sponsorship as the magazines I wrote for in India and in East Africa - *The Illustrated Weekly of India*, *Femina*, *Youth Times*, etc. had their own man in London in the form of the *Times of India* representative. Magazines such as *Caravan* and *Women's Era* to which I was a prolific writer did not have any budgets to have a London based reporter/writer. My option was to look for a job in the British media, which

NEW NEWS SERVICE

THE London-based Harambee African News Service will soon supply exclusive news and feature stories on Africa in Kiswahili for publications in the Swahili-speaking Africa. This was said by the agency's managing editor, Mr. Shamlal Puri, who is currently on a visit to Nairobi.

were not really open to Asians. The white skin was a passport to a job in British journalism!

I sent close to 100 applications but just kept on getting rejections. Some rejections were either racially based or were on frivolous grounds! I also then learned that I did not belong to the tribe of British journalists!! I was not a member of a Union to which British journalists belonged to. I was in a Catch-22 situation: I could only get a job if I was a member of the National Union of Journalists (NUJ) and I could only become a member of the National Union of Journalists if I was employed by a newspaper! I became a member of the union after Alan Rake, the editor of *African Development magazine* (in London) for whom I was a Tanzania correspondent

sponsored my application to the NUJ. My application was supported by letters of reference from Jasmer Singh of Drum Publications in Nairobi and the editors of *Daily News* Tanzania, saying I was a professional journalist. I was happily then a member of the NUJ.

I started working for a weekly newspaper called *India Weekly* published out of Fleet Street in London. I was the paper's assistant editor. As an NUJ member, the world was my oyster I could pick and choose any job I wanted to apply for. I moved on to various other newspapers and magazines, including the *Eastern Times* (later *World Times*) of which I was the Africa Editor and a Senior Editor. Working with the British media gave me the opportunity to get involved in critical journalism, something which was a taboo in the East Africa of my days.

Seeing there was no fun working for publishers, I launched Newslink Africa in 1982. This was a pioneering African affairs news agency and I was very keen to cover the continent as objectively as one could. This meant no-holds barred coverage of any country and any unsavoury happenings there. I was the head of a team of a few like-minded African and British journalists who formed part of my team. I also got an opportunity to broadcast on BBC World Service, Channel 4 TV, BBC Local Radio, ITV, alongside other networks. I am happy to have been among the handful of pioneering Asians journalists who entered the British media scene. In the 1970s, it was difficult to find Asian journalists on British newspapers. Today, the British media is an open shop and there are many Asian journalists working in the industry.

Having established myself at Newslink Africa, African publishers were keen to appoint me their London man as this helped them lessen their financial burden in getting a full time person in Britain. It is worth telling the story of my links with the Kenyan media. In the 1990s when British publisher Robert Maxwell teamed up with President Moi to establish *Kenya Times* and KTN, I was appointed the London Correspondent of the newly-launched *Kenya Times*. I remember visiting Maxwell's London office (which was based a few buildings from the London International Press Centre in Fleet Street where I was based) to discuss the newly-launched *Kenya Times*. The seasoned journalist Philip Ochieng was appointed by Moi as the Editor of *Kenya Times*. To me it was a welcome link-up with Ochieng who had been my colleague on the *Daily* and *Sunday News* Tanzania in the 1970's. I enjoyed working with Mr Ochieng who always encouraged me in my role in the *Kenya Times*. I also

became the paper's advertising representative, through my company Adlink International and brought the paper a big amount of advertising revenue. I gave many front-page scoops to the *Kenya Times* making my friends on the *Daily Nation* and the *Standard* feel uncomfortable on how the mouth-piece of KANU could get those stories! I felt that I had much better contacts then the established *Nation* and *Standard* London correspondents. I worked very hard to build up *Kenya Times'* image in the UK. But things began to fall apart - Robert Maxwell was dead and KANU did not have the money to sustain *Kenya Times*. The paper started going downhill. It owed money to a lot of creditors, including unpaid salaries to reporters. There was mismanagement on the paper. Ultimately, the paper folded up.

I was in dispute with *Kenya Times* over an issue and so I resigned. I crossed the floor to the *Daily Nation* as their ad representative through Adlink International. The man who welcome me was Mr Cyrille Nabutola, the then advertising manager. This partnership continues till today as we give them advertisements from Europe. I was happy to know that my hard work on the *Kenya Times* was noted by my friends on the *Daily Nation*. Former *Kenya Times* colleagues like Joseph Odindo, now the Nation Media Group's Group Editorial Director, gave me an opportunity to write for the *Daily Nation* and the *East African* from London. I am now the London Correspondent of the *Standard*, Nairobi, I am happy to have been offered the position.

SULTAN JESSA
Writer

I was born in Moshi in 1942, studied in Dar es Salaam and ventured into journalism when I joined The

SULTAN JESSA

Nationalist, the mouthpiece of the ruling Tanganyika African National Union (TANU), as a trainee reporter. I went for further studies to England and Germany. The Tanganyikan masses were fed up of oppression and the arrogance of the British rulers. The country was the first to gain independence and I attended the celebrations when the British flag was replaced by the new flag.

I spent several years working for the *Nationalist* under Ben Mkapa who went on to become Tanzania's President; and then I joined the *Tanganyika Standard*. I did

Sultan Jessa with the Order of Canada at the Governor General's residence.

numerous stories on the union between Tanganyika and Zanzibar and reported the many meetings between Presidents Julius Nyerere, Milton Obote and Jomo Kenyatta as they struggled to establish the East African Community. In the early 1960s, I joined the *Daily* and *Sunday Nation* as their chief correspondent in Tanzania and was based in Dar es Salaam. At the same time, I stringed for Agence France Presse, the United Press International, Associated Press, Reuters, Ceteka, the news agency of Czechoslovakia, and a number of other publications like *Africa*, *Drum* and the *Kenya Mirror*.

In early 1970s I was transferred to Nairobi to work for the *Nation* and covered parliament and all the major events; and started writing features. I was often invited to television stations to do interviews in Swahili. At the 24th biennial Boy Scouts World Conference in Nairobi, I spotted Prince Shah Mahmoud, third son of the deposed King Mohamed Zahir Shah of Afghanistan. The prince was shocked and surprised to learn his father had been overthrown. This was a scoop.

I reported on many events involving Idi Amin. I particularly remember Kampala in February 1972, when Amin assured everyone there will be no mass nationalization of properties; yet months later expelled all Asians from the country!

In July 1973, when serving as *Nation's* chief correspondent in Tanzania, I was selected to accompany three foreign journalists to ascertain claims made by Uganda's President Amin that thousands of Tanzanian solders had been killed near Mutukula on the Tanzania-Uganda border. I found out this was nothing but propaganda. There was no fighting or troop movements and Tanzanians were freely crossing the border without any incidents. I saw and spoke to seven uniformed Uganda soldiers who denied any reports of fighting and were in fact exchanging greetings on the border. An Indian *dukawalla* also confirmed there was no fighting in or near the border.

Those were the days of scoops! I covered the wedding in Nairobi of Dr Njoroge Mungai, Kenya's former Foreign Affairs Minister and had an exclusive interview with then one of Kenya's most powerful ministers, Dr Robert Ouko. I interviewed Bing Crosby, the famed American singer and actor who was visiting Kenya with his daughter, as well as Stan Musal, the superstar American baseball player. People in Kenya did not know much about baseball then but years later, my colleagues in Canada were amazed that I had personally met the baseball star. At the time I worked for the Nation group in Tanzania and Kenya, we had some wonderful, dedicated and talented South Asian journalists who made an immense contribution to the success the group enjoys today.

When the *Nation* was banned in Tanzania, I returned to my hometown, Arusha, to start my own newspaper, the

Northern News. I did some freelance work for the *Nation* group at the same time. When the ban was lifted, I returned to Dar and eventually moved to Nairobi to work for the *Nation* group again; before moving to Canada in the fall of 1973.

I have done well in Canada and retired in 2005 after working for three decades with newspapers here. I now live in Quebec with my wife Rosila. I received Canada's highest and most prestigious Order of Canada five years ago and have just been voted as one of Canada's top 25 immigrants for 2010.

WILFRED MACIEL (1932-1994)

Wilfred Maciel was born in Nairobi in 1932 and attended Dr Ribeiro's Goan School. He continued his education in Goa and the UK pursuing a BSc (Econ) degree and studied at the London School of Printing and Graphic Arts, doing graphic design, marketing and advertising. During a sabbatical in India he worked with the well-known advertising firm BOMAS, which later became Ogilvy and Mathers. There he extended his communication interests into journalism, and was one of the South Asian journalists who showed a keen interest in African affairs during the pre-independence days. It

WILFRED MACIEL

was he who was the major promoter of the immensely successful lecture tour of India by the late Tom Mboya before independence.

Years later, he became the first Indian journalist to interview Mzee Jomo Kenyatta after detention, at the world-famous Maralal Press Conference. His freelance exploits took him to Uganda, and to the Congo (where he was imprisoned for a short while). From the Congo Wilfred travelled to Angola where he was to witness the struggle for freedom from Portuguese rule at first hand.

His later meeting with President Julius Nyerere and Foreign Minister Oscar Kambona in Tanganyika was to result in Nyerere breaking off diplomatic relations with Portugal after hearing Wilfred's first-hand report on the situation in Angola.

Wilfred worked for a while as Marketing Manager of Hilary Ng'weno's newly-formed publishing company and briefly on the *Weekly Review*. Their paths first crossed when Wilfred, as marketing manager for East African Airways, gave Hilary his first film production assignment, making a training film for the airline's in-flight and reservations staff. 'This was before other advertising executives in Kenya, most of them non-African, would dream of giving an African a shot at anything remotely as creative as film production,' says Hilary.

Wilfred was part of the Public Relations team for the Congress newsletter, *Habari,* during the visit to Kenya in August 1985 of Pope John Paul II. Hilary says: 'Wilfred had time for fellow journalists and advertising men and women of all kinds and always a word of encouragement whenever things seems roughest for those who endeavoured to pursue the journalistic, publishing or printing career.' But his real interest was in advertising.

Broadcasting was another field Wilfred had been active in. Starting with the BBC in London and then AIR (All India Radio) in Bombay, in 1965 he joined the VOK as a news reader. Unfortunately he lost the manuscripts on which he had been working, including an intended autobiography and a nearly-completed biography of the late Jawaharlal (Joe) Rodrigues, that great Editor-in-Chief of the Nation Group of Newspapers.

Wilfred's colourful life was cut short in 1994 in a road traffic accident on the Thika road – a few yards from his chosen home – Nyumba ya Wazee. In his 1993 up-date which he wrote for private circulation he states: 'Despite all hazards and haphazards I am unremuneratively busier and happier than I have been in my whole adult life … daily I invade the Press Club in Chester House on Koinange Street …' He was a regular contributor to Bombay's 144 year-old *Examiner*, a weekly journal.

Source: Mervyn, Maciel, brother
          Ng'weno, Hilary, Weekly Review
          Tom Maliti who supplied the up-date newsletter
          AwaaZ, Issue 3 2009.

YUSUF DAWOOD KODWAVVWALA
Writer

'Surgeon's Diary' made its first appearance in the *Sunday Nation* of 25 May, 1980. Therefore in May this year [1913], it will complete 33 years of its uninterrupted run. Originally appearing every week, and now once a fortnight, the total number of columns published by May 2013 will come to 799. During this period, it seems to have become compulsive reading for the readers of the *Sunday Nation*.

It is interesting to note how the column was born. It was conceived at a meeting of the Rotary Club of Nairobi. Incidentally, much earlier in June 1968, I had given 'my job' talk to the club and had received a congratulatory letter from Malcolm MacDonald, the last Governor of Kenya and the then British Special Representative in Kenya. He was a fellow Rotarian and had enjoyed as he put it – 'It could not have been better, both as a light-hearted after luncheon oration and as a brief serious commentary on your job'.

I had sponsored a friend of mine as a member and he had recently been inducted into the Club. In due

YUSUF DAWOOD KODWAVWALA

course, it was his turn to give the traditional 'my job' talk whereby a new Rotarian introduces himself to the Club membership. In 1980, he was due to speak to our Club at the weekly Thursday lunch but he developed a surgical emergency the night before; and I was called upon to operate on him. Just before the anaesthetist pumped Pentothal into his vein, he asked me to convey his apologies to the Club President for not being able to deliver the promised speech.

Next day I was late and arrived a few minutes before the meeting was due to start. I informed the President, who happened to be John Karmally. He was well known as a professional wild life photographer, but his claim to fame was founding the Hospital Hill School in Nairobi. He pioneered it because his children could not get admission into the Whites only schools, available in Nairobi at the time. He therefore started his own multi-racial school. I told John that I had operated on the scheduled speaker the previous night and therefore he would be unable to give his talk. Naturally the President was not amused! 'Since you have landed me in the soup, you will get me out of it. You will be the speaker,' he said.

I had very little time to collect my thoughts and decided to relate two surgical experiences of mine in layman's language. One was amusing and the other quite sad. When I finished, I noticed that not only were all the Rotarians – some of them octogenarians –fully awake, but some of them were dabbing their eyes. They gave me a standing ovation.

Joe Rodrigues, Managing Editor of the Nation Group of Newspapers, a fellow Rotarian was amongst them. He came up to me and asked 'Could you put this in writing?' 'I spoke ad-lib but I will try,' I said. That evening I went to my study, put pen to paper and dispatched it to Joe. The rest – as they say – is history. I must add here that 'Surgeon's Diary' is not my only dalliance with the Nation Group. I wrote medical columns, 'Nation Doctor' from 1964 to 1973 and 'House Doc' for a few more years.

This account will not be complete if I did not mention something about the title of the column and the name of the author. When it was decided to publish the 'Diary', I had grandiose ideas about its title. 'Pearls from my ocean', 'Roses from my garden' and 'Stars in my sky' were some

of them. Alfred Araujo, the then editor of the *Sunday Nation* and features editor, Rashid Mughal brought me down to earth. The column was christened 'Surgeon's Diary' and the first episode entitled 'The Eye of a Needle', made its debut on 25 May, 1980. Surprisingly the second episode did not appear on the following Sunday, when it was due. Apparently, Michael Curtis, with whom I developed some differences on matters related to the Aga Khan Hospital, objected to me getting a weekly slot in the prestigious 'Aga Khan's' Sunday paper. Joe Rodrigues stood his ground and insisted that the column be reinstated, which it was.

As for the name of the author, I wanted some anonymity - for three reasons. One, I had published a novel in 1978,

my maiden fictional work and naturally there were some torrid love scenes in it. I was not sure if my readers would appreciate that. Now with the advent of the 'Diary', I was worried that my patients may not like their surgeon writing about them, even though their stories were camouflaged beyond recognition. So I chose a *nom de plume*. Secondly Kodwavwala, mighty difficult to write, spell and pronounce was a cross I had carried all my life and it was time I shed it. Finally, my father Dawood had worked very hard to make me a doctor and I wanted to honour him. So a new writer under the name of Yusuf K Dawood was born. In time my double life like Dr Jekyll and Mr Hyde was discovered by the public but by then it didn't seem to matter. They were addicted to the 'Surgeon's Diary' and accepted the author, following Shakespeare's famous quote, 'That which we call a rose – by any other name would smell as sweet'.

The assumed name had another fallout benefit. The writing income went into a 'Yusuf Dawood' account which, I could not draw upon. It was later converted into the Marie Rahima Dawood Foundation, a charity which gives university scholarships; bursaries for occupational courses to slum dwellers to make them financially independent; prizes to celebrate excellence by giving the best in various endeavours and donations to reputable organizations like 'Freedom for Girls' and those which sponsor meals in schools and wheelchairs for the disabled.

Five years after its inception, my readers suggested that I compile a book of the 'Surgeons Diary'. A newspaper column however popular is ephemeral - they argued. And so in 1986, the first volume was published by Longhorn Kenya, successors to Longman, under the title *Yesterday Today and Tomorrow*. This was quickly followed by *Off my Chest* in 1988. On its heels came *Behind the Mask* in

1995. *The Last Word*, the fourth volume in the series was published at the end of last year, making it a quartet.

The next natural step is a radio and TV series. The 'Diary' which constantly proves that truth is stranger than fiction has ready material for medical drama. It would be original and Kenyan and could become our export material for radio and TV stations in the English speaking world and beyond. Instead of the canned material we receive and use from all over the world, some of it dubbed, an easy way out in my view - we could produce a TV and radio series of our own. It would add a feather to the cap of innovative ability for which Kenyans are known and admired. I am sure an entrepreneur or an enterprising media station will pick up the gauntlet.

Though this book is meant to record the achievements of journalists, my role as a columnist followed the publication of my maiden novel, *No Strings Attached* by what was then known as Heinemans in 1978. Thus my creative fictional writing preceded my factual 'Diary'. Since then I have written five novels, an autobiography called *Nothing but the Truth* and four books based on the

'Surgeon's Diary' as mentioned before, making a grand total of eleven books. My twelfth, an explosive novel is complete and ready in my computer, awaiting a bold publisher with international marketing reach!

Finally, I am often asked why the 'Surgeon's Diary' is so popular and has become such a compelling read. Going by what many of my readers tell me, they buy the *Sunday Nation* only because it contains the 'Diary'. Others say that the first page they turn to in the *Sunday Nation* is my column. I think that there are a few reasons for its popularity. Firstly, they are true stories and readers can relate to them. Second, they are clinical cases, which if read at a scientific meeting would be couched in technical terms. For the purpose of the 'Diary', I just render them in layman's language so that they can be easily understood. That is why they are read by all sections of our society, from the highest intellectual to the lowest worker, young and old, men and women of diverse ethnic origins. Of course the stories are derived from the rich multicultural practice I enjoy and that makes them appealing to all. Finally, the stories follow the universal rule of good journalism. They are educational, informative and entertaining.

I was born in Bantwa, Saurashtra, India in 1928 and arrived in Nairobi in 1961. I never trained as a journalist but learnt on the job. I now live in Muthaiga and work as a surgeon at the Nairobi Hospital, and teach and examine medical students at Kenyatta National Hospital and in the Region.

Author's note: In 2014, Yusuf Dawood was awarded the Wahome Mutahi Literature Prize. Established in 2006 by the Kenya publishing industry, the prize is awarded biennially to an author who espouses the values of the great satirist, the late Wahome Mutai.

ZOEB TAYABJEE

Writer

I was born in Nairobi in 1947. My mother was from Tanganyika, my father from Surat, India. I did my schooling in the Jamhuri High School but could not go for further studies because of poverty. I started work at the age of fifteen and held two jobs simultaneously. During the day I was a telephone operator in Ahmed Bros, a well-known clothing shop on Delamere Avenue. At 5.00 p.m. I would rush to the Empire Cinema on Hardinge Street to sell popcorns to the incoming clientele.

ZOEB TAYABJEE

As soon as the doors closed and the movie began, about 6.15, I would rush to Kay's College on Latema Street to study accountancy. The lesson lasted an hour and I would then go home for dinner; we stayed on Grogan Road. At 9.00p.m. I returned to the cinema to sell more popcorn to the night show audience.

I maintained this rather gruelling routine for four years and have no doubt that it helped me in later years to rush from one cricket club to another to collect the scores and get an insight into the progress of the matches.

As a teenager I was keenly interested in sports, especially soccer. At school, every Monday my class teacher would ask for Zoeb's soccer report and he would read it out to the class. The two giants of the football world at that time were Gor Mahia and Abhaluya F C and City Stadium would be packed with their fans in every match. I could not always afford the entrance fee of 3/- but was often let in to act as ball boy.

This was my entry into journalism. When I joined English lessons in the New Era College, Kul Bhushan, the owner, encouraged me and taught me how to write a sports column. I took up cricket and joined Asgher Kassam's Furaha Travel Cricket Team. In 1978 Asgher was the cricket correspondent for the *East African Standard (EAS)* and after the game on Saturdays I would rush to the EAS offices and help Asgher to write his column. A year later when Asgher moved to the *Nation*, I replaced him. I read international sports magazines: *Sports Star* from India and *The Cricketer* from the UK; these gave me an insight into the cricket scenes in Asia and Europe.

In 1980, Asgher left the *Nation* and I took over. The *Nation* offices were more centrally located, the newspaper had a wider readership, the editing was better, I was given more

space and the sports desk was very supportive. Rashid Mughal, the features editor, was particularly helpful to me. I included table tennis and snooker but this sport died when most of its best players left the country and snooker was overtaken by pool. I covered the East and Central African championships in 1978 and 1980 and the Arlem Tournament in Goa in 1989. The former were bedevilled by communal tension and selection problems and were a great challenge.

In 1996 I created a 'destructive' character, 'Bhim Sala Bhim', who would peer into a crystal ball every few weeks and comment on general cricket matters. I vividly remember when once – only once when Bhim's predictions had gone awry - some fans wanted to floor me. But what can you do when the crystal ball develops a hair-line fracture? My journalistic association with the *Nation* was to last a quarter of a century during which time I popularised and mainstreamed cricket.

There was a time in Kenya cricket when religious and communal differences stoked the most intense passions of rivalry, mainly between the giants of the late seventies and early eighties namely Sir Ali Muslim Club, Nairobi Gymkhana, Aga Khan Sports Club and Premier Club. Coming from a religious and communal affiliation of one of the four, I had to walk a tight rope, with imagined

SPORTS STARTS HERE 4/3/87

Wives 'run out' ... of patience!

Behind every great cricketer, there's a woman. The Nawab of Pataudi had the sex symbol of the Indian screen, Sharmila Tagore, following him everywhere despite her hectic filming schedule; Imran Khan has plenty of women chasing him everywhere, while some of our local cricketing heroes have some ravishing beauties as their better 'halves. But these women are also the bitter halves.

It is rare for people like me to bump into such women, but from time to time I earn a compliment or two from some women connected with cricket. Especially when

No one could have imagined that women had anything to do with cricket, but cricket is becoming the bone of contention in many households. Two anonymous women cornered ZOEB TAYEBJEE (pictured) to offer their sharp wit and well-intentioned views on the sport. Now read on...

"Why not?" I say to myself. As I nodded agreement, I could see the devil in her eye. She had a way of implying that she was deadly serious, and I could not help but support to her views

accusations of bias hanging over my head with every report. In the circumstances I tried very hard to be unbiased and critique what was best for the game. It was hard to please everybody. Clashes with players, clubs and national cricket officials were quite common, as it is with sports writers all over the world.

On one occasion a prominent cricketer wanted to throw me in the pool and an administrator wanted to break my neck! I faced a ban from one club for my comments which the officials did not like. Players tried to pressurise me to write in their favour but I had great support from thousands of fans during that time. Some kept on pushing me to call 'a spade a spade'.

Before 1986 the ICC allowed non-nationals to be included in the national team. I felt this was unfair so I wrote to Hon. Kenneth Matiba who was then the Minister for Culture & Social Services. At a Coca Cola Sportsman of the Year Dinner in Nairobi, Matiba announced that henceforth only Kenya citizens could be selected for a national team. One result was that Tom Tikolo was given the coveted captaincy. It was around this time that Africans took up competitive cricket.

Kenya's cricket body, the KCA, held cricket together and enforced discipline; there were no strikes in its time. Today, as Roy Gachuhi of the *Nation* says, 'cricket has lost its soul, it is only a skeleton'. There are no regular cricket columns any longer in the press and audiences are scattered. In the 1970s, 80s and 90s the cricket grounds would be packed and so passionate would be the crowd that matches would have to be abandoned due to inter-club riots.

For a living I worked as a clerk and in 1987 joined Marubeni Corporation travelling widely for 20 years. In 2007 I established my own company, Topsel Trading Company Ltd. I continue to take an interest in national and international cricket.

THE REVOLUTION OF PRESS FREEDOM IN KENYA

An interview with Sudhir Vidyarthi
Courtesy: Asian Weekly, Straight Talk, May 27, 2013

Sudhir Vidyarthi takes us back in time to the 1930s, during the uprising of the freedom struggle where press was used as the authorities' mouth piece and how it has evolved from those days. Vidyarthi draws parallels between press freedom and politics, sharing along his own defining history that led to friendlier relations between Uganda and Kenya.

Your father, Girdhari Lal Vidyarthi, is known as one of the pioneers of press freedom in Kenya. Please tell us a bit about him. My father was born in Kenya, so was my mother. My grandfather came to Kenya in 1895 to work as a clerk in the railways. My father started the first vernacular newspaper in this country called, *Habari Za Dunia* in 1938, along with my grandfather. He followed that up with *Jicho* (meaning the eye), *Ramogi* and also *Muigwithania* (a Gikuyu newspaper). He started printing *Colonial Times* sometime in the 1940s. *Colonial Times* was a paper which was half in English and half in Gujarati. A lot of famous people like M S Thakur, Pranlal Seth, D K Sharda, Baldev Moolraj, Tarloknath Shankardass and Justice Chanan Singh wrote for the paper.

Some of the Africans who contributed included Mzee Jomo Kenyatta and Tom Mboya among others. In 1945 my father was charged for sedition by King George's government. He carried a series of articles titled, 'Burma Week' which highlighted discrimination of African soldiers. The articles delved into how Africans returning from Burma were dropped off at the Embakasi station

while the Whites were received amidst much pomp and flair. They were given lands and farms while the Africans would just be ignored.

This led to him getting a two year sentence with hard labour as punishment. In one of his newspapers, he carried the lines 'Up Up the National Flag, Down Down the Union Jack' again expressing views against the government and he was in prison for a couple of months. By the time he was out, the British government had cancelled all advertising in his newspaper and that killed the *Colonial Times*. In early 50s, he sold part of the shares to the Gathani family, who didn't play a huge role in running the newspaper as they were predominantly in business and not media.

What were some of the philosophies that your father lived by? Free, Frank and Fearless! That was his motto. He was a very learned man. 'Vidyarthi' is not our surname but a title that he got (similar to *Shastris* and *Pundits*) when he was studying in India. Both my father and uncle studied in a Gurukul which was a very strict institution. My uncle ended up being a *Pundit* while my father was a scholar in *Sanskrit* literature and he could speak a lot of languages.

At what point did the struggle for press freedom really take off? I think it was there from the early 40s. There were a lot of articles written by the freedom fighters and the newspaper we used to print (some regional newspapers) at our press concentrated on the fight for independence.

Let's talk about The Colonial Times. How did it operate? We had our own printing press and my father was in touch with the freedom fighters who used to contribute for the *Colonial Times*. My father gave them space in the

newspaper to express their views. The printing was not like how it is now. It was done by type-faces. M S Thakur, a Maharastrian would do the editing of the paper. My father had an interest in a company called, Fine Art Photo Engravers, which used to make zinc blocks for printing. Also, the distribution was done by us. I remember, he used to have a Volkswagen Combi in which we used to distribute the paper, then come home and help him count all the coins.

Was that the beginning of your future career in printing and media? Actually, that was never the intention. I studied at Arya Samaj and City Primary Schools. When schools were separated area-wise before independence, I moved to Highridge Primary School and eventually to the Duke of Gloucester School. I was working at Fine Art Photo Engravers with my father when we heard that the *Tanganyika Standard* (Tanzania Argus) was shifting to off-set litho printing and their setup of block-making was up for sale. So, we decided to buy it. That was my first real job. I ran Fine Arts in Dar-es-Salaam and while there, I met many important people like Benjamin Mkapa, Frene Jinwala (who was in exile from South Africa and she ended up being a Speaker of the National Assembly in SA after independence) and even Adarsh Nayar, very well-known photojournalist in Tanzania who now lives in England. Of course, Mohammed Amin was in Dar-es-Salaam then; he ran a studio.

At that time, what was happening in Kenya as far as press freedom was concerned? I think as Africans became ripe for independence, the colonialists became even more cautious and strict. There was vetting of articles and of course, we could only publish news released by the Ministry of Information and Broadcasting which had to authorise the printing. A lot of times my father printed articles that were not cleared by the Ministry and that got him into a lot of trouble. He was in prison for a total of about five years.

What were some of the restrictions or bans imposed on the press? I don't remember that but I know as a young boy, we would learn that my dad was arrested or taken to prison for printing something that did not go down well.

In what ways did the press express their resistance to the government's red tape bureaucracy? When there was a story that was banned, the editors used to leave that space blank to show to the public that there is information that the government has refused to release.

How was that received by the public? Very well! I think, the government wasn't happy that the public knew that there was information missing - that gave rise to speculation.

When did you take over the reins from your father? Actually, my brother Bhushan looked after the family as we were very young. We took over the business of printing when Fine Arts was in its doom days. My brother Anil started Colourprint Ltd on Kirinyaga Road about 43 years ago. I had to run away from Tanzania when Julius Nyerere embarked on nationalisation in Tanzania. We moved to Kenya with all our machinery overnight. We were approached by Gurdial Singh and Shafiq Arain from Uganda (Uganda Peoples Congress), and they said that they were starting 'The People' newspaper in Uganda. They needed our help in setting it up and we relocated to start Graphic Arts, Uganda. That is when my interest in newspapers started and I learnt the editing side of a newspaper. We were given an old machine by the German Social Democrat Foundation to print 'The People' on. During that time, I ran into trouble with the government and was picked up by the intelligence in Uganda because

of Obote's 'Move to the Left' pronouncement. When you make printing blocks they would face in the right direction and when the newspaper is printed, it is printed correctly on the left. When the intelligence guys saw that the blocks were facing towards the right, they ordered my guys to change the blocks to the left. The next morning, the photograph appeared of Obote pointing to the right instead of left and after two days, I was picked up by the Head of Intelligence. Luckily, Graphic Arts was in partnership with the Milton Obote Foundation, and since Obote had appointed me as the MD of Graphic Arts, I was quite close to him. I was taken to Obote and had to show him the entire printing procedure and how the blocks are done and that's when I was set free.

Go on... I stayed in Uganda for about eight years until Idi Amin took over and decided to throw out Asians. I was exempted from leaving the country because I was in the category of those who provided essential services; like teachers, doctors, et cetera. Milton Obote Foundation was taken over by Amin's government and they named it the National Trust. They carried on printing 'The People' which became a government mouth-piece for them. I was there for two years and eventually escaped from Uganda. At that time, I was not even permitted to buy a ticket to travel because of Foreign Exchange and the fact that there was no money coming in. A friend helped me get clearance for a ticket costing 900 shillings to England.

Did you ever return to Uganda? Yes, that time was known as 'Obote 2'. I had then become Obote's Campaign Manager for elections. I actually lived on the same floor at Nile Mansions which was built for the Commonwealth Prime Ministers Conference! I used to play scrabble with Obote every now and then. He was very fond of having his Rose wine in the evenings. We did his entire printing for the campaign in Kenya including his presidential

portraits. While we were printing for Obote, we had problems with the Kenyan government. One day I was escorted up by *Nation* newspaper's George Githii and taken to the Norfolk Hotel where Charles Njonjo wanted to meet me. They wanted to know who was paying for the printing I was doing for Obote. Charles Njonjo said, 'If Obote wins, we will tell him that we Kenyans helped him.' I told him, 'You mean, Sir, WHEN he wins…' When Obote won, I got a call from Charles Njonjo's secretary to schedule a meeting with Njonjo. I was asked to deliver a message to President Obote from President Moi. At that time, the ties between Kenya and Uganda were broken and he asked me to help send a message across. If you go back to archives in the *Nation,* you will see this coverage which has Githii and Henry Gathigira of *Nation* newspaper in it. When we returned, Njonjo called me in the evening and said, 'Can you give a message to President Obote to call President Moi?' I did not know the protocol and told him, 'I have Obote's personal number, why don't you call him directly?' He said, 'Young man, you don't know protocol. Moi is a senior president and he will not call Obote.' I rang Obote and asked him to call President Moi. After two days, there was the famous meeting at the border near Webuye which led to the two countries mending their fences. I was somewhat responsible for this. Later, I went to Uganda and Obote was ready to give me back by company and also another company Uganda Litho Colour Packaging which was owned by our family in partnership with Javed Shah; but I had already started a printing company here and was not sure if I wanted to stay in Uganda. We had started publishing magazines with Salim Lone. He was the editor of the Sunday Post. There was *Viva* – a magazine that men loved to read. There was also *Africa Perspectives, Fahari Ya Africa Mashriki* (Pride of East Africa) and *Men Only* – which was banned by the government and still remains banned.

What were its contents? Just women and stuff that men liked to read about. One day, Salim Lone was called by Njonjo to his office and he threw the copies of *African Perspectives* at Salim and said, 'I don't want to see those in the streets of Nairobi again.' And that was the end of that magazine. We never printed that magazine again.

Was that the effect of people in power? Oh yes! Njonjo's word was IT! But, the struggle for multi-parties had started strongly by then. We met with Kenneth Matiba who wanted to start a newspaper which was not part of the system – thus came, '*The People*' as the first opposition paper. They asked us (Colourprint) if we would like to print it and all of the brothers had the zest to do it. We printed 10,000 copies of *People* and within four weeks we were printing 40,000 copies! I named it '*The People*' because of my connection with the Ugandan publication by the same name. I showed Matiba my father's motto, 'free, frank and fearless' but he did not want to keep it free! So, it was turned into 'fair, frank and fearless.' *The People* was so popular that there were times when we used to print up to 60,000 copies. When they turned it into a daily paper, that marked the downfall of that newspaper.

Was the government okay to let you print a paper that opposed the system? Oh, there were a lot of problems! Colourprint was burnt down many times, our machines were disabled, parts of the machines were broken, et cetera. We used to be in court with the government for a long time! At one time, my brother, Anil, was charged for sedition. What is most interesting is that my father was the first man to be charged with sedition in this country and my brother was the last; exactly after 50 years! There was a cartoon in the newspapers to that effect saying, 'History repeats itself.' My father was defended by Achhroo Kapila and my brother was defended by his son, Ishan.

Did that push you out of the press/media business? No. In the late 90s, I was invited to venture into the radio business with Kiss FM. Of course, there were problems with the launch as our CEO, Patrick Quarcoo, put up huge signboards of beautiful girls with suggestive pouting lips. Moi was offended with the name – Kiss. But Kiss FM stayed on despite the opposition and from one radio station to another, we expanded to launch the *Star* newspaper after William Pike moved from *New Vision* in Uganda.

Where is the print medium headed in these times of social networking sites and blogs? I think after the last 10 years, there has been more freedom for the press. It's a change from the Moi era where we were told what to print. Of course, with blogging and social media thriving at present, it is difficult to muzzle the voice of the press.

THE RADIO JOURNALISTS

'This is 7LO...' -TRACING THE PATH OF HINDUSTANI BROADCASTING IN KENYA

by Neera Kapur-Dromson

Technical facilities were not advanced enough to enable correspondents on the battlefront to broadcast personally. Yet, the radio became a political instrument besides being an organ of information. It was a way to influence its citizens. Few of Kenya's urban Indians or Africans could afford radio sets (together with the license fee that came with each set), even fewer understood the language. The history of broadcasting to British East Africa from the war right up to decolonization in 1963 was closely connected to political networks that would sustain the various 'vernacular' language broadcasts.

From Imperial International Communications Ltd to Cable & Wireless

Radio broadcasting began in what was then Kenya Colony in 1927 to relay news. A year later, a regular English service was started for the approximately 300 settlers, each of who paid a license fee of approximately £2. In fact, Kenya was a first amongst the British colonies to have a regular broadcast service. By 1930, a charter was granted for the communications operations of the British Empire to a single private company, the Imperial International Communications Ltd. Later that function was assured by 'Cable & Wireless', well known for undersea cables worldwide. English broadcasts continued throughout the war, with short intervals of Asian and African broadcasts to keep the people informed about their relatives on the war front.

Before the war, the general policy had been to discourage radio for African subjects. Cable &Wireless (C&W), the only radio station in Kenya Colony served the needs mainly of the Europeans and a few Indian listeners. With the outbreak of the war, they had to extend their English broadcasts to Hindustani, Swahili and other regional languages to distribute propaganda about wartime development and try to exert their influence through a few soothing songs and some music.

The Hindustani Service, C&W

The Hindustani service began as a 15 minute interval during the regular English service sometime in 1944. They operated from a modest facility at Memorial Hall on Delamere Avenue. Jagdish (Chui) Ahluwalia was the first Indian announcer on this service. Music and light entertainment, mostly Indian film songs, formed the core of the relay. His role included changing discs, what one would call a 'disc jockey' – today's DJ with restricted capabilities and limited facility especially as the disc had to be changed every three minutes. Since the programme lasted only 15 minutes, this meant that he could play only 4 songs per day!

With the advent of the gramophone industry and the vinyl discs, the rich tradition of Indian music – classical, popular, and folk – was more easily available to the listeners. This was the era of a flat double sided disc with a spiral groove in the middle rotating at 81, then at 78 rpm for 3 minutes flat. Coming from a tradition of 10 to 15 minutes for each song, to shorten it to 3 minutes, was a big challenge to the musicians, if not a near revolution – not until the 33 1/3 rpm LPs and 45 rpm EPs arrived later to provide a capacity for longer songs or additional songs on the same side.

The rudimentary makeshift studio, eight feet by eight feet, was not sound proof, so any small sound was also transmitted. (I vaguely recall visiting a home-made studio made sound-proof with egg shells and their cartons years ago!) The studio was linked to the control room by a small passage. There was a small table for the announcer, on which was placed a portable gramophone with some discs. Remember the famous HMV records? 'His Master's Voice', with the dog listening to the sound of his master coming through the big horn…for those who understand Hindustani, HMV became famous as *'Asli kutta chhap'* - the real-original dog trademark!

Long before the Hindustani service was increased to 3 or 4 hours per day and they had enough funds to buy their own records, and have a library of their own, Assanands and Shankardass, the two music stores in Nairobi, willingly loaned their latest Hindustani song and music records, perhaps in exchange for promotion. Unfortunately, both the music stores are now gone. Assanands got burnt down by fire some weeks ago, Shankardass Music House closed down many years ago.

Mussa Ayub was only 20 years old when he joined the team at C&W on a part time basis, (his friend Jagdish Ahluwalia roped him in, while he himself left sometime later) soon after they had shifted to new offices on Sclaters Road (now Waiyaki Way), Kabete, next to the then Prince of Wales School (Nairobi School). Mussa and some other colleagues told me that the offices were still there, but when my husband and I went looking for them, we could not find any trace. A heavily guarded telecommunications block stood in the area indicated to me and the *askaris* guarding the place did not know what I was talking about, nor would they allow me in.

Sardar Mohamed joined the service for a brief period but he too left soon after. Mussa took over the reins, controlling and managing the department, single handed at first; all in all he would remain a radio/TV journalist for a period of at least 20 years. He started off on a part time basis. By the end of the 1940s, the Hindustani service had grown under his supervision and dedication, his programmes fast becoming affairs of some consequence. He resigned from Caltex Oil Company to become a full time radio broadcaster.

We could call him the pioneer of Hindustani Service in Kenya. Born in Kijabe, brought up in Ewaso Nyiro in Maasailand and in Kijabe, his education (and that of the children in the family) was assured by his uncle Haroon Ahmed, who actually started a boarding school for them - both in Kijabe and in Ewaso Nyiro - and who would become his Programme Manager at the Hindustani Service many years later!

This is 7L0 Nairobi…

The new style of announcing in the daily service came with the establishment of C&W. The station was broadcast on shortwave from VQ7LO (Local oscillator at which frequency it transmits). Richard Coltart headed the Programme. Few people may remember that Alain Bobbee, who was to later gain fame for his bistro, was initially a renowned broadcaster on C&W! He had actually been invited to Kenya by the British army in the early war days as a soldier, perhaps for intelligence purposes because he was a polyglot with fluency in several European languages. In any case, this grand connoisseur of Western classical music, and a musician himself, would be appointed Deputy Programme Manager at C&W. He was to say '…broadcasting, even in the comparatively modern 50s, was a brave business in which you turned your hand to everything and anything…' And they did.

Mussa Ayub confirmed this to me, 'In the beginning our roles were not clearly defined. We did all that was required to make the service run. Whether it was playing discs and perhaps a little patter, or writing and reading

any announcements, stories, reading and translating news, looking for new recruits, creating and assuring the development of new programmes, the accounts - just about anything. Yet, in all this, there was a sense of adventure and of fun.'

The media was of course controlled

News supplied by the *East African Standard* newspaper was in the beginning read in English. When a Hindustani news broadcast was permitted, it had to be translated word by word directly from the news supplied to them by this daily paper - that in its earlier days had held strongly colonial viewpoints. Later, political commentary was offered in carefully measured amounts, but remained largely polemic in content. All that went on air had to be first submitted for approval. Anything highly political was censured.

Afro-Asian Links

In 1947, India gained independence. The jewel in the crown was gone; the British Empire lost its prized possession. An independent India's All India Radio (AIR) now used their English language service to criticize the fragmenting British Empire. Their Gujerati Language programme had the largest impact in the Indian diaspora through their cultural and musical relays.

To show their solidarity and in an attempt to make a bridge between India and the East African liberation struggle, Apa Pant, the first High Commissioner of a newly independent India to Kenya, stimulated the birth and transmission of a Swahili Service in the External Division of All India Radio (AIR) to East Africa. It was at the height of the Mau Mau struggle for independence when the half hour Service commenced in 1953.

My friend from India, Veena Sharma, who holds a PhD in African studies and is a fluent speaker of Kiswahili,

headed the service from 1979 for over 20 years. On one of her visits here to the Homa Bay area in 1986, she met with a group of 'community radio' listeners who called themselves LAIRs, listeners of AIR! Through the request programme (for Bollywood songs), they connected with and sent greetings to other LAIR listeners all over. When the service was temporarily reduced after Indira Gandhi's assassination in 1984, and regular programmes replaced with mourning music, Veena tells me that the faithful Homa Bay listeners still tuned in with reactions of condolences, of solidarity (this time from their side), or other comments.

Swahilis, especially *taarab* musicians from Mombasa had been much influenced by Indian music, especially Indian film songs and their tunes, to which they applied Swahili lyrics. Sometimes they also included Indian instruments like tabla and harmonium. These became an important part of their repertoire for orchestra at weddings and concerts. Besides Indian cinema and All India Radio, the local Hindustani service was also to become an important avenue for their resources. By this time, radio sets were increasingly affordable, although the license fee of 40 shillings was still high and electricity had not yet reached remote areas of the country for full transmission.

Importance of Language

The post independence effects of India and birth of Pakistan reverberated right across the Indian Ocean to Kenya. Religious identity, allied with nationalistic affiliations, showed up in debates amongst listeners over the use of language in the Hindustani Broadcasting Service…Urdu or Hindi? An advisory committee inclusive of Mohan Singh, Mrs Ghelani and Vinay Inamdar, headed by Basheer Mauladad, was nominated. Justice Channan Singh led the formation of a lexicon/ glossary of the appropriate language mix of Urdu and

Hindi words (Hindustani) that may be used by the journalists on the service.

Kenya Broadcasting Service

In 1959, radio broadcasting was nationalized. The British Colonial Government in Kenya took over control of all broadcasting services and existing programmes from Cable & Wireless. The station became known as Kenya Broadcasting Service (KBS). More staff was recruited for the Hindustani department. D K Sharda and Dev Raj Chibber still read the news. Mussa Ayub continued to give it expansion, encouraging others to join in, among who T N Soni, Pritam Chaggar, Bikram Bhamra and Chaman Lal Chaman would reach an iconic cult status.

Air time was increased. They now operated from the newly built studios opposite the Norfolk Hotel, next to the Kenya National Theatre – strategically placed! The ultra modern broadcasting house had three studios of different colours for the different departments. Green studio for the Swahili service, blue for English service; the Asian service was housed in the red studio. It came equipped with a continuity studio, production facility and a newscasters' den, a far cry from the earlier eight feet by eight feet box room!

By the end of the 1950s, the radio had become an important source for news. Kenya Broadcasting Service's Hindustani Service recruited Arvinda Dave from All India Radio. News in Gujerati was introduced. This service enlarged its role to put itself in perspective of its environment. Anti-colonial discussions and forums gained momentum - and in all these there were few breaks for commercials.

Whether it was the doyen of Urdu literature, Ishaq Mirza Qari's 'Ankhein Meri Baqi Unka', a satirical current affairs programme, Pritam Chaggar's 'Chacha Sahib', also a satire, or Zafar Mirza's 'Qaziji', a serial dealing with topical issues through wit and humour and ably presented by the famous theatre actor, Harbajan Preet. Or, Narain Singh 'Toofan's' political commentary - his nom de plume 'toofan', an attempt to reverberate the necessary storm for a current affairs feature? Writers, journalists, poets often used a pseudonym to sign off their works by a word symbolic of their personality or work.

'Where are we in all this? Are we well informed for the coming of Kenya's independence?' Mirza Qari would ask himself and his audience. Makhan Singh, renowned activist would have had much to say on his mobilization of a strong trade union movement, while Dr Visho Sharma gave the latest updates on the Legislative Council proceedings besides reading the news in English.

The radio played its part in enlarging the Afro-Asian world. Debates on the rights of Africans and Indians continued, especially with Haroon Ahmed taking over from Sajjad Shamsi. Haroon's nationalistic spirit gave the service an increased national broadcasting image. Self-educated, he became a prolific writer-journalist and freedom fighter. Bravely challenging colonial rule, Haroon's constant demand would be for democracy and equality for all Kenyans. Being the veteran journalist/broadcaster that he was, he pressed for human rights and social ethics - these often brought him in conflict with the ruling government.

Between 1955 and until independence in 1963, the service saw its full potential come to the fore. The Hindustani service became increasingly influential and served as a springboard for local musicians, poets, dramatists who enjoyed a massively enlarged audience. Reflective of the contemporary social scene, their mostly original works – plays and short stories – were creative, often bold.

Joginder Paul wrote short stories in Urdu, Radha Krishen Shastri in chaste Hindi; Joe D'Sa presented a programme in Konkani. Even their musical compositions and lyrics had to be original. Ghazals or bhajans, shabads or folk, classical or light, in Hindustani, Gujerati, Punjabi or even in Kiswahili – the challenge that the work had to be original, enhanced their creativity. Remember Deedar Singh Pardesi's 'Salma'...or Raghbir Singh Rahi's 'Mpenzi wangu' in Kiswahili? These were hits then. I wonder if anyone sang a Hindustani song to an African tune!

Bashir Butt, Sheila Markandey, Ragi Tara Singh, Sital Singh Sitara, Mutlashi, Kali Das Gupta Raza, Pt Laxminarayan 'Gardish' Shastri, Sohan Singh Josh – the list of singers, musicians and poets was long. My father's original work of fiction 'Achoot Kanya' was broadcast. Shakoor Haroon Ahmed's original multi-layered comedy 'Dhani Ram Money' was very popular. There were special programmes for children (Phluwari) and for women (Mahila Samaj), 'Radio Doctor' for out patients or those in hospital. The late Inderjeet Dhillon (film maker Mohinder Dhillon's younger brother) had a programme for teenagers (Bhor ki Bela and Sanj ki Bela). Even the Orient Art Circle, an association of music, poetry, dance and drama (formed by Nalini Devi, the wife of India's first High Commissioner to Kenya) started a weekly programme of music and poetry on the Hindustani Service.

They interviewed visiting artists, local and those from abroad. They met with Ministers and Heads of State – all this through an on-the-job training. And sometimes, they forgot their professionalism. While doing the commentary for the famous Safari Rally during which the two Singh brothers had won, radio commentator Bikram Singh Bhamra (also a Sikh) was so overwhelmed that he lost his voice, threw away the microphone and ran towards the two brothers!

Sudesh Sharma, Darshi, Olga Ngugi, Tochi, women broadcasters made their mark. Tarlochan Gill Chaggar started as a continuity announcer on the radio and rose to the ranks of producer and initiator of television programmes like *Mambo Leo, Kipindi cha Vijana, Duniya Wiki Hii.*

Future radio broadcasters like Allaudin Qureshi, often started as young artists on *'Phulwari'*, a programme for children presented by Ram Moorti Maini (well known as *'Bhaiya Moorti'*). From the age of ten, Allaudin has continued performing, contributing, directing, presenting programmes like *Shabaab* and *Nau Bahar* on air. Even today, Allaudin's Sunday night programme of *ghazals* on East FM is highly appreciated by lovers of Urdu poetry globally.

People were so versatile then

Beside a full time job, my father painted, wrote poetry and prose, was involved in amateur theatre and wrote some radio plays. Doing many things at once was a norm. Many of them were multilingual. To speak, read and write in Urdu, Hindustani, Farsi and English was common. With a pen-name like *Gardish* that he had chosen for himself, it was no wonder that Pandit Laxminarayan Shastri *'Gardish'* was always on the move and unstoppable. He was a scholar of Sanskrit, a priest at the Hindu temple, an astrologer, a healer, a poet of Urdu - *mushaira* on stage and on air.

The *mushaira* that went live on air brought together some of the best known poets of the Urdu language of the time in Kenya. (Urdu was an important part of the curriculum at the Government Indian Boys' School, now Jamhuri School). In this *mehfil* (event), the poets were challenged to elaborate (through recitation or song) an opening line given to them on the spot. The theme could be on any subject – the weather, love, nationalism. Very often, Pt Laxminarayan Shastri's or Kalidas Gupt's brilliant use of flowery imagery and masterly use of language as they elaborated the theme extempore filled the studio's air space with *'Wah wah!'* in total admiration. Sometimes, they were asked to repeat their lines. What was important was the spontaneity, the competition that brought about the best in the language.

With the exception of a few like Dr Visho Sharma who had obtained the required training in the Bush House BBC studios in London for reading news, the majority was completely fresh to the journalistic scene; these veterans learnt the required skills on the job. Good speech, voice control, delivery, pace, pitch, necessary pauses…what seemed common was that they were all polyglot. Shifting from English to Kiswahili, Urdu, Hindi, Punjabi, Gujerati - some could even speak the Konkani of the Goans - they picked up languages as fast as the need arose. These pioneer self-made journalists created a desire for people to listen. The tonality and grace of their voice was learnt, acquired. Most importantly, language and its creative use were important.

Mussa Ayub had a full grasp of Gujerati, Punjabi and Konkani as well as Kiswahili. His *'Karsan Kaka'*, a satirical play in Gujerati on various current affairs of the day (written by Haroon Ahmed) became a household name in its heyday. But, perhaps he is best remembered for his voice. A 'natural' radio voice! He was not trained for radio broadcasting, but clearly so many years later, his voice, deep and haunting, remains with those who had the privilege of hearing it. Today, he is a legend of the industry. His name is allied to the history of the service.

When I visited him some weeks ago in his son's house, I found in him a quiet and unassuming man, but full of stories when provoked, even of some slight mischief, but most importantly of a humanity and humility so rare, almost as if he didn't realize the importance of his historical role. I was surprised to see a symbol of 'OM' hung on the otherwise bare walls. Even more surprising was the absence of a radio set. 'I don't listen to the radio anymore,' he said. 'Now it is all computerized. There is little room for innovation. It was challenging then – the production, the programming. Handling this challenge brought us big pleasure. The language had style; we paid great attention to its usage, whether it was Urdu or Hindi, Punjabi or Gujerati. Our words were selected with care. Today it is all robot-like, technical, instant release, no life, no soul….'

Towards Independence: Kenya Broadcasting Corporation

By 1960, it became evident that independence was inevitable. Having used the radio to suppress the nationalist movement, the British colonial government did not want this important mass media to be passed on to the independent government. So, Kenya Broadcasting Service became Kenya Broadcasting Corporation.

Under this service, television was introduced to Kenya in 1962. The first transmitting station was on a farmhouse in Limuru. Some of the radio journalists were transferred to the newly established television department. Amongst them was Mussa Ayub. A BBC team flew in to give them a crash course. They would be sent for further crash courses to the UK, USA and to Canada. Mussa Ayub was soon appointed Head of Productions and Transmissions Control. He was behind the scenes for programmes like 'Here and There', Press Conference, 'Face to Face', 'Time will tell', Christmas programmes or Ring Us Up. He stayed for ten years in the Television media. By 1972, the Africanization policy had become imminent; Mussa Ayub would resign without asking for his benefits.

The momentum of the new visual medium of broadcasting had come with its own excitement. The picture on the television screen had to tell its own story. With Kenya's independence round the corner, broadcasting authorities decided to have a 'rainbow coalition' of newsreaders on primetime at 9pm. Reading news was always an honour as you were assured of a serious audience who sought your word for being informed. And when the audience also became spectators, your word together with your image carried greater weight. The prestige was incomparable.

No wonder that hundreds of applications were received! Auditions were held for the different 'races'. A 'white', a 'black' and a 'brown' (all men of course) - Peter Clare, Norbert Okare and Visho Sharma - were selected to read the news. I was still very young to remember much, but can recall these very impressive and polished newsreaders with their high flown British accents on the 9 o'clock news at night.

We lived in a tiny 2-roomed maisonette in the Nairobi South 'B' area then with a Gujerati family just adjacent to our place. The lady and her two daughters would come to watch TV each evening, but when the Indian film was telecast (I can't remember for sure if it was a Wednesday evening), then a whole bunch of young children would appear as if from nowhere, half of whom were not even known to us. After a couple of weeks, it became too much and we started closing our doors, only to have them pelting stones at our windows; in the event, they broke a couple of them! Not soon afterward, even the Indian film was brusquely discontinued on TV!

Considering the passionate way of life he led, Visho Sharma was able to give the best of himself in his part-time journalistic career. His young, full and variegated life ranged from works on social, legislative, economic and colonial history, on constitution…a barrister by profession, a journalist, broadcaster and poet by passion; and a leftist by conviction. His father, Lal Chand Sharma, had been unjustly taken as a prisoner in Tsavo by the British administration during the First war. Visho Sharma was a young boy during the Second war. It was almost natural then that he grew up with a 'war psychosis' and with a strong political stance in life. Here was a barrister and economist with an incredible clarity of diction - whether in chaste Urdu or in Oxford English - he became a regular name on the radio Hindustani service and on television. His authoritative views of 'Report from Parliament' and 'Brain's Trust' are still remembered.

Voice of Kenya

Soon after independence, Kenya Broadcasting Corporation was nationalized into the Voice of Kenya through an Act of Parliament. Administration of this commercial enterprise once again came under government control. Achieng Oneko, Minister for Information, Broadcasting and Tourism, was to say, 'Broadcasting is a powerful weapon, which if misdirected can do a lot of harm. It is not primarily a profit making concern, but would be used for constructive development of the country, to popularize the policy of the government and to keep people informed.'

After his release from detention by the British Colonial Government in Kenya, freedom fighter for Kenyan independence and founder of the trade union movement in Kenya, Makhan Singh, worked as a translator, preparing news bulletins in Hindustani for the VOK Hindustani Service - at a time when it was headed by Haroon Ahmed. In her book *Unquiet: the Life and times of Makhan Singh,* Zarina Patel delves into the long and frustrating saga that Makhan Singh was made to go through after Haroon Ahmed had persuaded him to give a series of talks on the life of Jomo Kenyatta for the national and general service at the VOK – this in a post-independent Kenya.

Makhan Singh prepared and re-prepared scripts as per the requirements of various departmental heads, including James Kangwana, deputy Director of the VOK, Daniel Gatuga, Head of the National Service, Stephen Kikumu, Controller of Programmes, J Wanzala, M Kari and Harun Anzia. In the end, the talks were never relayed. *'From 25 March, 1966 to 17 April, 1967, he made 62 calls and 31 visits to the VOK, he noted each call and visit and has left a detailed account of this miserable story. His family was much disturbed and saddened by this deliberate and merciless tormenting of a great patriot and leader…'* extract from *Unquiet* (italics mine). Even his 20 minute talk in Hindustani for Kenyatta day celebrations marking the arrest of Jomo Kenyatta by the colonialists (20 October) was broadcast in an edited version, without the names of Kenyatta's fellow detainees, Fred Kubai, Karumba, Bildad Kaggia, Paul Ngei and Achieng Oneko.

The period of glory for the Hindustani Service on the Voice of Kenya was over. Air time for transmission of the Hindustani Vernacular Service on radio was reduced by the new authorities. News briefs in Hindustani on Voice of Kenya television were discontinued. Kenyatta's 'Africanization' policy was extended to all civil service departments. The 180,000 Asians (about 2% of the population at this time) became anxious. The job status of civil servants of Asian origin was in jeopardy. The radio broadcasters, producers, engineers who left, did so with heavy hearts. They had put so much of themselves, of their passion, and of their creative energies in their careers.

Even today, they look back with nostalgia to 'those days'. In 2009, these pioneer broadcasters (notably Pritam Chaggar and Chaman Lal Chaman) organized a 'Voice of Kenya Re-Union' evening in the UK (where they reside) to recount their memorabilia and listen to archival records; they also published a brochure to mark the occasion.

With the onset of television, with programmes mostly in English initially, some Kiswahili and a little Hindustani, listeners had also become viewers, but radio in general did not die out, especially with the arrival of the transistor. The radio had become more than entertainment. Coming from an oral culture, listening habits were easily formed. In fact, the radio was almost a necessity - absolutely not a luxury – an inexpensive and reliable source of information reachable to masses. Besides the electricity needed to power television sets is still not available outside the urban areas.

The radio media continues to flourish. Breakfast, lunch or dinner, the radio remains switched on in many homes especially at meal times – as if it is a part of the family. The voices of the journalists still carry our emotions. We listen to them, criticize their views, or agree with them; sometimes, we swear at them. Often, we love them. We may never see them, but their deep, throaty, or husky voices remain with us for a long time!

Today, there are over thirty licensed radio stations in Kenya, many privately owned, targeting special members or ethnic groups. East FM and Sound Asia, two private FM stations emerged about 13 years ago to cater to the mainly Hindustani listeners, not only in Kenya, but in the diaspora worldwide. I ask myself if the future of broadcasting lies in the internet.

Courtesy Old Africa magazine - This article (except for some additions) was first published in Issue No. 43 October-November 2012.

THE BROADCASTERS
MUSSA AYOOB
Writer

It all began in 1947 as fun – I accompanied a friend, Jagdish Ahluwalia, who had started part time radio presentation from the then Cable & Wireless (C&W) 'studio' situated about ten kilometres from Nairobi's town centre, near Nairobi School then Prince of Wales School, on the way to Nakuru. I not only did not know anything about radio broadcasting; growing up in Kijabe I had never even seen a radio.

At that time C&W allowed a 15-minute slot in the evening for Hindustani music. The 'studio' was used by the English Service and this was their break time. We played gramophone records which we borrowed from the Assanands and Shankar Dass music shops on Government Road and Isher Singh Magon on River Road. After playing them in the evening we would return them the next morning and borrow some more.

The broadcasting facilities were in the transmitting building of C&W. In a corner, away from the transmitters, with just a rough curtain partitioning us we played the music; sound proofing was as yet unheard of! The equipment consisted of a turntable, a conventional microphone and switches to turn them on and off. Jagdish would give the introductions while I would change the needle on the 'pick up' and play the record. In time to come we would alternate the duties. When Jagdish left the country, he recommended me for the part time job

MUSSA AYOOB

and I took over. In the early fifties the studio was shifted to a new facility still in the same compound but nearer to the company offices. The English Service was now given a larger studio with a proper broadcasting desk and an adjoining waiting room. Next to this the Hindustani Service was given a smaller studio with its own waiting room which could be used for live broadcasts. Both studios were served by a common control room.

Before the move I was offered a full time job to handle the Hindustani Service which I took up and the air time was increased to 45 minutes, still evenings only. With the help of a part timer I introduced new programmes by bringing in outside contributors such as *Phoolwari* (children's programme); *Mahila Mandal* (women's programme); original story reading; live vocal and instrumental music and *mushaira* (poetry reading). We used our small waiting room as a live programme studio. The most arduous task was the introduction of the news bulletin. Arduous because the bulletin which was supplied by the *East African Standard* newspaper group had to be collected from the English Service studio after it was read at 9.00 p.m. It then had to be translated into Hindustani while maintaining programme continuity and read towards the end of the programme.

At this time we were given funds to purchase our own records and thus build a small music library. In 1952, T N Soni was employed as an additional full time broadcaster and for the first time, commercial announcements were introduced. Our first advertisement lasting over one minute was that of Coca Cola which had just been introduced in Kenya. We were then promoted by being given a completely separate new building with a continuity studio and a proper live programme studio; our own control room, a roomy office and a built in record library.

Two more full timers were employed, Chaman Lal Chaman and Pritam Singh Chaggar, and with the introduction of morning and lunchtime programmes our broadcasting was now done on more or less professional standards. With the advent of the cumbersome but very useful tape recorder; we began to pre-record programmes and thus reduced our need for live programmes. During this time many new programmes were developed – radio dramas, outside events, interviews of personalities (politicians were out of bounds).

In the mid-fifties it was rumoured that the government was considering taking over the broadcasting station. A big, modern broadcasting station was being built in the town opposite the Norfolk Hotel and in the late fifties; the English and Hindustani Services were taken over by the government while still using the C&W premises. A senior civil servant, Sajjad Shamsi, was appointed head of the Hindustani Service – the convivial camaraderie of the radio station was replaced by strict civil service discipline and new salary scales were applied to us. The new name, by the way, was KBC – Kenya Broadcasting Service. After over a decade of broadcasting and much thought I decided to quit and try my hand at something new. I resigned and went to India. In Bombay I met a 'Barre Sahib' who took me to his estate in Hyderabad and there I decided to put up a project of dairy and poultry farming. It was doing very well but after two years, owing to family circumstances, I had to return to Kenya.

I was sourcing commercial spots for the Hindustani Service and earning a rather erratic income when I ran into my previous C&W boss, Richard Coltart who was then acting controller of programmes in the KBC. He offered me a senior producer's position in the Hindustani Service which I readily took up. The head of the Service was Haroon Ahmed, my uncle, and we were very conscious of being accused of nepotism – luckily very soon I was offered a transfer to the KBC TV Service which was scheduled to go on air in 1962.

I was given an intensive training course in all areas of television including the production of local English programmes conducted by a team of full crew from BBC Bush House, London. It included camera, design, graphics, lighting, sound and other areas. I, who had never before seen the inside of a television studio 80'x15' fully equipped with various gadgets, was now a producer/

director of local programmes. (Most of the programmes were imported on 8mm film). The pioneers of Kenya Television were four producer/directors and I was one of them. Many of the programmes we aired then are still continuing, shows such as Kenya Kitchen, Ring Us Up, Press Conference and Children's Magic Shows. Others were Face to Face, Xmas Window and Indian classical dancing. Starting 1965 an Indian movie was shown once a week. Until at least 1972, TV was aired only between 6.00 to 11.00 p.m.

I was also appointed Head of Productions. Soon after independence the BBC team was replaced by a team from the USA and the name was changed to VOK (Voice of Kenya). My controller and I were sent to the USA where we were attached to different TV stations including a four month stint in Canada. At this time a Kiswahili Service was developed and included locally produced original shows.

James Kangwana was the first African Director of Broadcasting and he took over from the Americans. Achieng Oneko was the first Minister for Information and Broadcasting and he decreed that the Hindustani Service airing time be curtailed and be amalgamated into the vernacular service. He felt that the small minority did not warrant lengthy air time forgetting that most of the revenue from advertising came from the South Asian community which played a major role in the economy. The acquisition of video recorders and an outdoor recording van made life a lot easier.

Before Africanisation could affect me I left and joined my father-in-law's car hire business. And so, a half-baked rustic from Kijabe had risen to a position of responsibility in the media world of both sound and video. I was born in Kijabe in 1926. My parents were born in Nairobi and my grandparents who were farmers in India, arrived in Kenya in 1918.

ALLAUDIN QURESHI
Writer

Though born in Kampala, Uganda in 1940, I have since lived in Kenya. My ancestral home is Lahore, now in Pakistan. My maternal great grand-father came to work for the Uganda Railway and my mother was born in Nairobi.

I have been surfing the airwaves of Asian broadcasting in Eastern Africa with love and devotion for over five decades. As a young primary school boy of ten I recited Alama Iqbal's poem in Urdu - *Lub pe aati hai tamana meri* - on VOK's *Phulwari* programme. Next was a short radio play written by me about the need for swimming pools for Asian children in schools and community centres. Children used to make use of rain water trapped at construction sites as swimming pools with disastrous results such as being electrocuted by random naked electric wires. *Shabab/Naubahar* was a weekly radio show directed to teenage listeners. It covered youth activities in the country and had discussion panels, short stories, poems, plays - all in Hindustani. It featured music loved by young people, the Beatles, Elvis Presley and Cliff Richard were included.

I rubbed shoulders with radio pioneers in this country such as Mussa Ayub, Haroon Ahmed, T N Soni, C L Chaman, Pritam Chaggar, Darshi Didi, Sajjad Shamsi and Sudesh Chetan. It was radio plays that led me to write and act in stage plays. Initially I acted in and wrote Hindi/Urdu plays but later was probably the first Asian to be accepted as an Associate Member of Nairobi City Players, a predominantly English-speaking *Mzungu*

ALLAUDIN QURESHI

group. I have worked with Jaribu Arts and Theatre Group, Donovan Maule and Phoenix players; I formed NATAK an Asian Theatre Group and authored numerous original Urdu, Hindi and Punjabi plays based on local Kenyan themes.

I am an accredited correspondent with the *Sunday Nation* where I have been writing regularly about Asian cultural activities in my column ASIAN SCENE since 1986.I was commissioned by the World Health Organization to write and present an Aids Awareness show which was aired for nearly two years. I was also involved with Commercial

Radio Advertising and won several awards for creative and quality radio advertising. I was voted the Best Local Writer for my radio play *Kya Tum Na Aao Gay*, an original script about the relationship between indigenous and immigrant Kenyans. This script was later translated into English as a stage play. Since 1995 I have been freelancing with East FM. Every Sunday night I light up a SHAMA for the PARWANAS of Asian culture, as I relay poetry, ghazals and traditional music. My presentation ANJUMAN enjoys listenership throughout the world. The main change, apart from the modern technology, is the content. From being educational and informative the stress is more on the musical side. However I am happy that the show I present is traditional both content and music wise.

I live in Nairobi with my wife Naseem who has always inspired and supported my creative ventures. We have three sons and six grandchildren.

CHAMAN LAL CHAMAN
Courtesy: Voices of Kenya Union, 30 November, 2008

Chaman Lal Chaman arrived in Kenya in 1952 from the Punjab, India. Working as an accounts clerk, he started writing short stories in Urdu for radio broadcast. In 1956, he joined Cable & Wireless as a news reader and announcer. He rose to become a producer of radio and television programmes in the Kenya Broadcasting Service; and then head of Radio Operations, in charge of programme planning for all languages including Kiswahili, English and other regional languages. He had the rare distinction of interviewing India's first Prime Minister, Pandit Jawaharlal Nehru, in Delhi to cover the Chinese aggression on India. He wrote about 500 play scripts and is a celebrated poet with four publications in Punjabi and English, and has over 35 recorded works sung by India's most famous singers.

CHAMAN LAL CHAMAN

In 1974 he resigned from the VOK and moved to the UK where he continued to work for the BBC, Sunrise Radio and others. Currently he is undergoing health problems and declined to write for this book.

DEEDAR SINGH PARDESI
Writer

I was born in Village Pattar Kalan, Punjab, India on 14 July, 1937. My father was a farmer in India who came to Kenya in 1942 in search of a better life. He was both a father and mother to me as my mother passed away when I was only two. My elder brother Lashkar Singh (writer of my popular hits *Ek Tu Howein Ek Maen Howein* and *Goriye Ni Lae Ja Dard Vandake*) followed him to Kenya in 1949 and myself in 1951.

From the age of five I was drawn to music and rendered a *Shabad* in my local village *gurdwara*. I was rewarded by one of my elders with a silver rupee which encouraged me to further my interest in singing. It is of course a God given gift but I seasoned my voice by singing the songs and ghazals of K L Saigal, Talat Mahmood and Rafi Saab. Years later Ustad Ali Akbar Khan, the great Sarod player of India, tried very hard to persuade me to go to India with him for classical training, but I was in the middle of my teacher training course and could not take the chance.

On arriving in Kenya I started presenting my items on Cable &Wireless in the children's programme *Phulwari* with Bhaiya Moorti. This programme received a tremendous reception from both children and parents and I used to have numerous letters from my fans requesting me to repeat many of my renditions. It spurred me on to take up an active role in the entertainment scene in Kenya.

When I started singing on Cable & Wireless at Kabete, the only two people who were presenting the programme were Mussa Ayub (as head) and Tarlok Soni (as his assistant) and all other broadcasters came much later. I along with other poet friends created the Kenya *Punjabi Kavi Sabha* organisation. My voice was aired across East Africa on VOK for 25 years. My popularity was such that no programme was complete without my participation. People used to wait for my rendition eagerly along with

DEEDAR SINGH PARDESI

my radio broadcasts. I became a household name across Kenya, renowned for my unique voice and soulful songs like *Salma* and *Tootte Dil*. Despite having no formal training, I was honoured by Ustad Ali Akbar Khan Sahib who was touched by my unique rendering of *Heer* and blessed me with his diamond ring and gold buttons. I had the opportunity of singing *Chaudhvi Ka Chand* in the presence of my idol, the great Rafi Sahib, who came running onto the rostrum to embrace me warmly, saying: *Kudha ne aap ko bahut achhee awaaz di hai - aap yahan ke Mohd Rafi ho.*

One of the greatest challenges in my life was when I was invited to the Bombay Film Industry in 1969 as a playback singer. Famous actress Rehka and I were launched in the film *Do Shikari* where I had my hit song *Zindagi Ae Zindagi* in the playback of Biswajeet. I was left with a daunting decision whether to stay on in Bombay or return to my permanent job in Kenya. Having near superstar status, I was strongly advised by the great lyricist Sahir Ludhianvi and music directors Chitra Gupt and Ravi to stay on in Bombay and continue as a key playback singer for Hindi Films. In fifteen days of my visit to Bombay I sang for four films and was inundated by requests for several other films. I had a charming duet with Asha Bhonsle *Mere Dil Mein Raho Arzoo Ki Tarha*. However, despite the glitter of Bombay I made the final decision to return to Kenya as the lifestyle of Bombay did not appeal to me.

Singing has remained a hobby in my life. By profession I was a qualified teacher. I taught in Kenya for seventeen years in Juja Road, Ainsworth and Highridge Primary Schools. I was offered the position of headmaster in 1975, but for the sake of my children's education I decided to move to the UK. Here I continued teaching for twenty years in a secondary school, eventually retiring as Head of the Geography Department in 1993.

In the UK, I have recorded songs with BBC TV, had live shows and performances and my songs are regularly played across the Indian radio stations. I have visited Kenya on several occasions. Recently I was taken by Sikh Channel UK to interview prominent industrialists and several of the Gurdwara committees in Nairobi, Kisumu, Nakuru, Makindu and Mombasa.

HARBHAJAN PREET
Writer

I was born in the Punjab, India, in 1929, and joined my father in Nairobi in 1947. My father, who had retired as an administrator in the Post and Telegraph's Department in India, had immigrated to Kenya a year earlier.

I first made my mark as a freelance presenter of radio plays, short stories and talks on the Kenya Broadcasting Service, then known as Cable & Wireless. Along with my friend Mohammed Bashir, I approached Ishak Mirza Qari, the doyen of Urdu literature in Nairobi, to put in a word on our behalf with the Kenyan broadcasting authority. This facilitated the route of my introduction to broadcasting in Kenya.

The programmes I presented on air on a regular basis were:

> *Aap Poochhte Hain* - an informative programme which entailed a question and answer format based on questions sent in by listeners and answers by a team of presenters that comprised Mohammed Bashir, Dilbagh Chana and Ran Swaroop Sharda.
> *Qaziji*- the most prized serial dealing with topical issues, full of wit and humour scripted by Zafar Mirza. I played the leading role and listeners often thought that Qaziji was a real life character.
> Talks – history of the East coast of Africa.
> *Sagar Kinare* - a magazine programme covering news and events in Mombasa.
> Plays and short stories scripted by Mohammed Bashir and Chaman Lal Chaman.

On Kenya Television, I did a brief stint presenting excerpts from the stage play 'Hassan' by James Elroy

HARBHAJAN PREET

Flecker with Dilbagh Chana, a monologue as Dr Faustus in Christopher Marlowe's play 'Dr Faustus' and Wajir Secondary School's Inter-Schools Drama Festival prize winning play, 'Mohammed Hassan of Griftu'.

Some of the challenges that I recall encountering during this period included travelling the long distance to the Cable & Wireless Radio Station on limited resources, the lack of pre-recording facilities and the presentation of live programmes.

I migrated to the UK in 1978, after retiring as a tutor in Mombasa's Shanzu Teachers' College. In Cardiff, Wales, where I now live I presented an Asian radio programme, *Saat Rang*, for ten years. I am the founder member of an Urdu poetry group, *Bazm-e-Adab*, which I set up well over twelve years ago. I have also co-founded a Punjabi poetry group which has been meeting regularly over the last several years. My full time employment was as director of the Race Equality Council of Cardiff, and as a tutor in Adult Education. Retired, I currently am a part time Home Office Interpreter for the UK Border Agency.

PRITAM SINGH CHAGGAR
Writer

I was born in 1933 in Panwa, a small village in the Punjab, India. I completed my studies at the Ramgarhia College and during this time witnessed the struggle for Independence and thereafter the 1947 Partition and the bloodshed of innocent people.

I migrated to Kenya to join my father in January, 1950. My first job was with the Post Office where I experienced once again the arrogance of colonial rule and could not tolerate its treatment of us. I quit my job and started my own grocery business so that I could be my own master. It was March 1955 when I met Mussa Ayoob and with my knowledge of Urdu and Persian I decided to join him at Cable & Wireless, as a broadcaster. In my mind I was happy to get a chance to try and make the Asian listeners aware of their rights as equal human beings. No broadcasting training facilities were available, so I learned the ethics and code of broadcasting on the job. We were only three full time broadcasters but with the help of freelancers we were able to deliver a variety of programmes in a 36-hour week.

With the limited resources at hand I was required to present all sort of programmes including news

translation and reading. The news was prepared and delivered to me from the *East African Standard* for translation into Hindustani. Those days, Foot and Mouth disease and Agriculture Minister Bruce MacKenzie were the lead stories. Asians and Africans were non-existent, no reference was made to their contribution in promoting the economy and employment. Through our programmes we managed to create a purposeful cultural platform with the spirit of equality.

In 1959 Kenya Broadcasting Service took charge of all types of broadcasting including the Hindustani Service together with its staff of four. I was in charge of the Hindustani News and it was not difficult to convince the News Editor to add news of Asian interest. Gradually listeners of all communities became familiar with the positive side of activities amongst each other. In addition to many other programmes a fortnightly satire play, discussing a variety of subjects focussing on the short comings of the administration, was popular - I enjoyed it the most.

The biggest challenge I faced was to break the barriers between first, second and third class citizens and treat all like one family of people of all races and communities; it was not an easy task. So, I used the broadcasting platform to reach out to my listeners making sure I remained within the confines of codes and ethics. After leaving my full time job, I continued to contribute as a free lancer and enjoyed the fulfilment of my mission.

I migrated to the UK in 1992 in search of a better education for my children. I managed to continue broadcasting even here in the UK. I worked for a number of radio stations including BBC Asian Network; and thereafter I set up small stations country-wide to raise awareness of the Asian Community to the need to have its own radio stations and to air programmes of its

PRITAM SINGH CHAGGAR

choice. Finally I established a Community Radio which is still running.

Back home in Kenya, after the establishment of East FM, I was invited along with my wife Tochi to set up Soundasia88 which we did and are proud of. My only comment is that both these stations focus largely on Bollywood and musical entertainment. In our opinion, the management and staff should pay more attention to highlighting the day to day issues facing the common man in the national arena.

SAJJAD AND DARSHI SHAMSI

By Allaudin Qureshi

The late Sajjad Shamsi was a master poet, linguist and administrator. He was born in Nairobi of illustrious ancestry – that of Shamas Tabriz who was the master of the revered 13th century Sufi saint and poet, Jalud din Rumi.

Sajjad wrote poetry in Persian, Urdu, Arabic and English as well as books on religious and cultural philosophy. He was the programme organiser/director of the Asian National Radio facility of the Kenya Broadcasting Service and a patron of Nairobi's City Arts Society.

During his time at the broadcasting studio, a host of radio cultural programmes were introduced bringing in cultural diversity and refined musical and creative taste.

His late wife, Darshi, was a regular radio presenter. Her daily request show, *Jaam e Sehat*, targetted all those of the community who were ill and confined to hospital. A weekly presentation of *Shabab* for teenagers and her flair for selecting Bollywood songs wowed her fans endlessly. She also participated in radio plays and story reading sessions.

TOCHI CHAGGAR

Writer

Kenya's first South Asian woman broadcaster

I was born in Nairobi in 1944. My parents were very simple who came to Kenya in 1927 in search of a better future. My father was a carpenter by profession.

Music was my passion from the school days. I was still studying when I started participating in group religious singing with the Voice of Kenya and took on a variety of

OBITUARY » THEY WERE GREAT SOULS WHO MADE A DELIGHTFUL DIFFERENCE TO THE LIVES OF MANY

Curtain falls on couple that ruled Asian art

Didi Darshi and Shamsi Sahib were a rare breed of artist and exceptional human beings

BY ALLAUDIN QURESHI
alllaudin_qureshi@yahoo.com

News of the passing on of one of Kenya's veteran radio and literary personalities Sajjad Shamsi and Didi Darshi was received with profound sadness by the artistic and literary fraternity.

The couple, who in yesteryears ruled Asian cultural symposiums and radio airwaves, had been living a fulfilling retirement in England.

Shamsi Sahib died earlier and his wife Darshi, unable to perceive a life without him, breathed her last on January 15.

Didi Darshi and Shamsi Sahib were a rare breed of artist and exceptional human beings.

Shamsi a master poet, linguist and an administrator par excellence was born in Nairobi into a devout Muslim family whose illustrious ancestor was none other than Shamas Tabriz, master of the famous and revered 13th century Sufi Saint and poet Jalalud din Rumi.

Sajjad wrote poetry in Urdu, Arabic, Persian and English and held various top-ranking positions in the civil service during the colonial regime in Kenya.

Before migrating to England, he was the programme organiser/director of

From left, Shamsi Sahib and Didi Darshi at their home in London. Below, the couple during their days with the Kenya Broadcasting Service.
PHOTOS / CORRESPONDENT

He was a patron of Nairobi's City Art Society.

Whilst in England, he lost his sight in a car accident but managed to write five books of Urdu poems and an anthology in English. This became possible due to the love and dedication of his wife Darshi who learnt the Urdu language and became his "eyes".

Darshi, affectionately known as Didi, was a popular radio presenter. Her daily

As a young man struggling to make his presence felt as writer, broadcaster and actor, I personally received tremendous support from both Didi and Shamsi Sahib. They were always there to offer sterling advice and encouragement during my formative days at Broadcasting House. I will remain ever grateful.

The couple is survived by Didi's daughter Neeru Ghelani of Nairobi and son Kiran who resides in England. Ken-

roles in the Drama Section. In 1963 my talent and quality voice earned me a part time job as Continuity Announcer with the Hindustani Service. A year later in 1964 due to the wind of change local staff took charge of the Voice of Kenya TV and I was selected for the job of Production Assistant. During the course of my duties I was trained by professionals from NBC (USA) and BBC (UK). I produced and assisted in programmes like Mambo Leo, Here & There, Nyimbo za Dini and It is a Small World. Later on I became a permanent member of the crew for the Outside Broadcasting Presidential Mobile Unit.

I was the only Asian female among the multinational staff facing the new challenges with extended responsibilities. The spirit of learning, delivering and working hard was a source of great satisfaction. Meeting dignitaries on a regular basis was a memorable exercise. The new era of life in a free Kenya was pleasant and enjoyable as opposed to the days when one could not travel with the whites in a bus and could not use the same loo.

After my marriage in 1970, I decided to leave the full time TV job but continued to freelance for the

TOCHI CHAGGAR

After commissioning the Station, things did not work out favourably and we decided to return to the UK. I then set up a Production House to produce advertisements for the Asian Radio Industry. In addition to that I am currently presenting a weekly show called 'Gulshan Gulshan' for a community radio, Asian Star, broadcasting from Slough near London.

VISHO SHARMA (DR)
Writer

I was born in May 1933, on what was then exotic Park Road, Nairobi (lions were cited on that strand just a year before). My father, Pandit Lalchand Sharma, a head law clerk, and later a businessman, was a legend, having escaped death during a World War I court martial. After three of his colleagues had been executed by Settlers conniving with authorities fearful of the spread of the North-American born *Ghadar* (revolution, for India's freedom) movement in East Africa, a recent arrival from rural Punjab, Lalchand's death sentence was commuted to 20 years rigorous imprisonment because the Scottish prison doctor wasn't convinced he was 18. My mother, Shanti Devi, was born in Nairobi, in 1911; she lost her mother before she was two. She was the daughter of Pandit Baisakhi Ram, co-founder of the Nairobi Arya Samaj. My father was from hardy peasant stock from the stony Shivalik Hills of the Himalayas; my maternal grandfather was from Ludhiana, Punjab. He crossed over in a dhow in 1895, as cashier on the Uganda Railway. All three forebears served as significant leaders, especially in the cause of women's rights.

While pursuing my Ph.D. at the London School of Economics, I was introduced to broadcasting by my sister, Sheila, who did a lot of moonlighting at the BBC's Hindi and Urdu services. During a brief visit, in 1954,

VISHO SHARMA (DR)

Mussa Ayoob asked me to read a Chaman Lal Chaman story in Hindi-Urdu on the Hindustani programme of Kenya's broadcasting station which had continued its Second World War handle: '7LO.' It's not hubris to say that it truly resonated with the listeners, who found it novel. To the discriminating, the diction, inflection, and enunciation were of a style at par with the best offered in Delhi, Karachi, and London.

Returning to Kenya in 1958, I worked at the Attorney-General's Chambers. I had been called to the Bar, but

Hindustani Service. In 1986, I moved to the UK for the sake of a better education for my children. Since there was no licensed Asian radio station in the UK, I started broadcasting for a pirate radio called Sina Radio. In 1989, I was instrumental in obtaining the very first Asian Radio License, 'Sunrise Radio', where I worked as a broadcaster and producer until 1992. After leaving Sunrise Radio I continued broadcasting programmes for Spectrum Radio and Star FM. In 1997, I was invited, along with my broadcaster husband Pritam Chaggar, to set up the newly licensed Sound Asia 88fm in Nairobi.

much preferred teaching to wig-and-gown declamations in Kenya's law courts. (I had won highest university honours in debating and oratory, including the V K Krishna-Menon Trophy). University of Nairobi was replete with Englishmen without Ph.D.s securing a position higher than theirs was a hurdle they didn't want me to breach. Besides teaching, broadcasting (and acting) remained my principal avocations. I taught after-hours, at the Nairobi Polytechnic as well as the Extra-Mural Department of the University - some nights travelling as far as Magadi, Machakos, and Muranga. The subjects ranged widely: Economics, law, politics. Several nights per week were spent broadcasting.

Before long, a leading columnist, Narain Singh Toofan, and another journalist gathering fame at the time, Kul Bhushan, were very kind to me; they often wrote that I was arguably the best broadcaster in Hindustani and English. Writing mostly for the *Daily Nation*, N S Toofan was a leading critic and opinion maker. One of the weighty points he made, on account of his educational background, resonated with Basheer Mauladad, chair of the body that governed the Hindustani service, Kenya Broadcasting Service and later the Voice of Kenya - as the names changed. A cantankerous issue was the use of language (picking from Hindi and Urdu words that were easily understood, or needed to be popularised for their better nuance). Toofan suggested and Mauladad ruled that all broadcasters should follow my practice of blending judiciously Hindi and Urdu. In the event, a glossary was assembled, which greatly drew from the words that I had used commonly. This gave everyone, but a handful, a great sigh of relief.

My other contribution was to raise the level of discourse. The common fare of songs and stories should not suffice, I implored. I put on 'our' Hindustani radio service a number of series based on my own research. These dealt with the history (economic and political) of the Indian contribution to East Africa's development. N S Toofan generously remarked that it was my voice that leavened even the driest subject and piqued the reluctant listener's interest. In serial after serial, including the pre-independence one on the unfolding drama of constitutional changes, the Asian contribution was highlighted by me, torching the *'dukavaalaa'* epithet and gently replacing it with the fairer metaphor of 'fundi.' As word got out, and my efforts spread to the English medium, the Attorney-General chose me to revise the whole corpus of Kenyan statute law to bring it into compliance with the independence constitution - art imitating life, or the other way round!

When TV came to Kenya, in 1962, authorities wanted a rainbow coalition to be portrayed. From a large list, they chose me to be the Asian broadcaster along with one African and one European. In the event, after broadcasting on the English radio service, and TV, I was appointed chairman of the witty-intellectual Brains Trust weekly programme on TV.

As I noted earlier, the challenges I faced had a lot to do, unfortunately, with race. Persons of my complexion (I sport a dark tan) faced discrimination both before and after independence. Ironically, it was broadcasting that finally secured for me the job I had long been denied at the University of Nairobi. The University wanted to extend its outreach via radio and TV; this time, in 1965, they simply couldn't come up with any excuse not to hire me. As fate would have it, though, there was further irony: the job at the University eventually panned into an offer, in 1967, by a US University, who wanted an expert to put on television their mass course relating to the total African and Asian experience (including the Middle East).

Journalism has a way of whittling benumbing book-knowledge into digestible script bytes. The training in BBC and Kenya broadcasting had enabled me to write the scripts and produce and direct the widely acclaimed Nonwestern World series (at Western Michigan University). All manner of awards came from it. I became a tenured, full professor in record time; won top University, State, National and International awards, including being elected Fellow of North America's Association of African Studies and Chairman of the international Research Committee on Punjab. Head of the largest WMU department, I became President of the Faculty Senate (the highest elective office). I retired at age 75, to concentrate on writing, especially on contract bridge - dovetailing two passions beside broadcasting.

Now at 80, frequent travel back to Kenya is sprinkled with trips to old hometown haunts and visits with retired broadcasters as well as with those still plying the mike. Broadcasting on 'our' service, I regret to say, is replete with piffling banter and poor enunciation of English words. But there is greater mass participation; moreover, there is sign of a new life.

PHOTO JOURNALISM

In a world where a book, a newspaper article, a leaflet or a poster are a highly subjective means of communication and expose the writer's bias as much as convey new information to the reader; photography captures the truth.

Here is a quote which says it all: 'Without image-based evidence, we might believe that smart bombs never miss or American soldiers don't commit atrocities or that sweatshops are figments of some bleeding heart's imagination. Without photojournalists, we'd also know a lot less about animal abuse, deforestation, corporate pollution, and much more. Without photographs and video to paint a more complete picture, it'd be a whole lot more difficult to inspire everyday people to embrace everyday activism. This, my friends, is the clout of the camera.'

Or so we assume. Photojournalists are expected to accurately represent what they witness. Yet any image can be doctored to create an 'improved' picture of reality. This is particularly so today with the revolutionary advances in photographic equipment. With the explosion of camera apps on our smart phones, we are all photographers, and pretty good ones at that, since the quality of Smartphone images now rivals that of digital cameras. Even photojournalists are experimenting with mobile phones because their virtual invisibility makes it easier to capture unguarded moments.

In the twentieth century, or most of it, photography was a much more challenging art. Shutter speeds, f-stops, film speeds, ISOs: Aspiring photographers had to master the mechanics of a camera before they could hope to create an arresting image. And then of course was the dark room with its enlarger, the trays and the brown bottles. 'It seemed like magic to me,' recalls one budding photographer, 'that a piece of the world could actually be preserved on a piece of paper'. Photography has always been more subjective than we realise, each picture a result of a series of decisions – where to stand, what lens to use, what to include and what to omit from the frame. Even the ultimate decision – whether to click the camera or walk away.

Before the days of the internet and even television, it was photojournalists who brought to us the visual realities of situations in faraway places. They did so often at great risk to themselves and in gruelling conditions working long hours away from home; but they made the world smaller and helped to hold leaders more accountable. Of course, as with any language, there were those who produced poetry and those who compiled shopping lists.

Paul Theroux explains: 'To be a good photographer, you need to gain admittance. You need to gain acceptance. You don't just whip out your camera and stick it in someone's face. People have to allow you to take a picture. For the kinds of pictures that Priya Ramrakha took in Africa, he had to be very close to people. You didn't see him, but he had to be in the foreground to get the picture. When you see the faces in his pictures they are always of people who are calm, who like him, who aren't noticing him. And if they do notice him, there's no animus in their face. Or, more interestingly, they don't see him at all; they're looking right past him. The great journalists find a way of not threatening the subject, and that's how you get the great picture and the great story.'

Eliot Elisofon, a renowned *LIFE* magazine photographer, defines 'the great photographer.' 'He has to have what we call a "photographic eye"... and lots of training and experience ...' In 1961, Elisofon met with Priya's family and arranged passage for him to Art Center College in Los Angeles. There Priya studied his craft and exhibited many of his African photographs at the University of California. His coverage of Martin Luther King Jr and John F Kennedy also garnered the attention of photo editors at *LIFE* magazine, already familiar with Elisofon's young protégé.

In the following pages we get a peek into some of the most iconic photographs shot by Kenya's South Asian journalists in the twentieth century, together with brief accounts of what inspired them and the challenges they faced.

THE PHOTO JOURNALISTS

ABDUL AZIM (SAYYID)

Writer

I was born in Nairobi, Kenya in 1944. After leaving school in 1961 I undertook a two year correspondence course in photo-journalism with the New York Institute of Photography. During my courses I was advised to take up press photography as I was doing very well in all the subjects from sports, portraits and general photography.

I used to do lot of sports and I remember the time the Indian cricket team came to Kenya and the Nawab of Pataudi was the captain. During the match at Nairobi Gymkhana against Kenya, the Nawab was clean bowled in the first over and I got the photograph. The *Standard* photographer missed the shot. The newspaper used my shot and from then onwards I used to get a lot of freelance assignments from it. At that time the editor-in-chief was Kenneth Bolton and the rest of the staff in the news desk were expatriates and they were very cooperative. There was one Goan photographer, Emiliano Jones, under whom I worked.

I was employed in the Kenya Police Headquarters in the finance section where I examined vouchers and prepared salaries for the police force. In May 1968 I resigned from the police as I was offered a full time job at the *East African Standard* where I worked until 1980. When Emiliano migrated to Canada, I was promoted to Chief Photographer and later to Assistant Photography Editor. All the department heads were very cooperative and I had no complaints. During this time the large sized paper changed to a tabloid and was the first to use colour pictures with the result that the sales really shot up.

ABDUL AZIM (SAYYID)

In 1980, when cameras were changing radically, I decided to train in video-graphy. I freelanced for two years with the American network CBS and travelled widely. I covered the assassination of Indira Gandhi, the Haj pilgrimage in Saudi Arabia, the Ethiopian Famine and many other global events. That was the time when Mohamed Amin, the world famous photographer, offered me a job. It was great working with Mo as he was called. I did photography and sound for him and learnt a lot. I was with Mo when he lost his arm in Ethiopia during the fighting. During that time, Mohinder Dhillon, head

of Africapix and a great friend of mine, informed me that Associated Press (AP) was looking for a photographer and recommended me to Jerry Grey, the Chief of Bureau. I joined AP in 1986 and am still with them.

During my work as a photo-journalist I have faced many challenges. It was a turbulent time with the assassinations of Tom Mboya and J M Kariuki and frequent strikes at the University of Nairobi. At that time the GSU was very aggressive towards journalists – as a *Standard* photographer I broke my leg when GSU goons beat us up during one of the University protests. But nevertheless I have enjoyed the work. While in the *Standard* newspapers I was three times named photographer of the year, and my photography was published in the World Press, also three times. In addition, I have won international photo competition awards from Guinness International and Nikon.

I was near City Hall in 1998 when the American Embassy was bombed. I had the camera and two rolls of film, the digital camera had not yet come out. I rushed there - it was terrible! There were bodies everywhere. I shot the photos and in the next thirty minutes my pictures were all over the world. In all the major newspapers! It was this series of pictures which won me the SPOT NEWS PHOTOGRAPHY and the PULITZER Awards.

In 1995, a few months before Black Hawk Down and the start of the Rwandan genocide, I was in Somalia. Myself and a lady reporter from AP were kidnapped. It was a nasty experience; the kidnappers kept threatening to shoot us. At one time I said to them, 'kill me BUT if Allah has not written for me to die I won't'. That's the time they released me but they kept the reporter and told me to arrange for a $300,000 ransom for her release. The talks went on for 24 days and I was wired by the USA troops

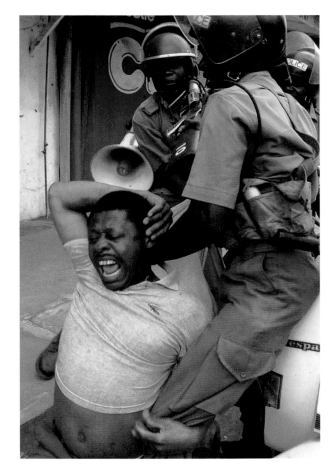

Bomb Blast at the American Embassy, 1998

who were recording the conversations. In the end she was released after the elders got involved.

On another assignment in Mogadishu we were with Pakistani troops and were caught in the cross firing. I fractured my right leg and some ribs and was evacuated to Nairobi. This was the time AP lost one photographer and Reuters two journalists when the crowd killed them as they went to cover a house which had been bombed. For AP I have covered other wars in Ethiopia, Congo and Rwanda.

I have trained many freelancers – while in the *Standard* I trained messengers as photographers since they were interested in the subject. South Asian photo-journalists have made a great contribution to making news a visual reality. Some other well-known names are those of Mohamed Amin, Priya Ramrakha, Azhar Chaudry, Mohinder Dhillon and Anil Vidyarthi. To date I have been 27 years with AP and enjoy my work.

AKHTAR HUSSEIN (1933-2008)

By Anwar Hussein (brother)

Akhtar Hussein was the eldest of five children, all born In Mwanza, Tanzania in 1933. His parents hailed from the Punjab region of Pakistan, but moved to Tanzania in 1928 when his father, Mohammed Hussein, obtained work in the British Civil Service.

Akhtar went to school in Mwanza. He took up photography as a hobby and spent his school years snapping shots of big game on the reserves of his native country. It quickly became obvious that Akhtar had a way with a camera and when he left school he was determined to pursue a career in photography. Self taught, he opened a small photography shop in Mwanza

AKHTAR HUSSEIN

called 'Photo Artists' and began taking photographs of local people and wild life. His big break came when, around 1957, he was invited to move to Nairobi to join the *Nation* as a staff photographer.

He spent several happy years at the *Nation* at a time when Kenya was going through massive changes. He covered the Mau Mau uprisings, the rise of Jomo Kenyatta, the Uhuru celebrations, the British Royal Family visiting Haile Selasssie in Ethopia and many other events throughout East Africa, resulting in his

becoming the *Nation's* chief photographer. The famous photo of Seraphino Antao, Kenya's first athletics sprint champion, racing against a cheetah was set up by Akhtar. The cheetah won! Akhtar's reputation grew and he was approached by major newspapers in England to photograph news events and features all over Africa.

The picture editors at the *Daily Mail*, one of the UK's best selling newspapers, were so impressed with Akhtar's work that they asked him to come to London, an offer that Akhtar could not refuse. About 1967, he moved there and enjoyed living and working in London. With his amiable nature he easily mixed with his peers in the British press and gained considerable experience.

But by now Akhtar had ambitions to work in the United States. He decided to take his chances to work there as a freelance photographer. He had plenty of contacts in the British press and regularly covered feature stories for most of the British national newspapers and several up-market magazines. He photographed everything - Presidents, film stars, music icons and everything else in between. He covered a number of film sets including the Bond series, getting on well with stars Sean Connery and Roger Moore.

As a freelance, he also had the freedom to travel extensively. He covered several major Royal Tours with the British Royal Family including Queen Elizabeth's historic first visit to China in 1986. He loved horses and photographed major equestrian events - his pictures illustrated many books including *Bruce Davidson, World Champion of Eventing and Eventing: The Classic Equestrian Sport.*

Akhtar continued to live and work successfully in the States, first in New York and then in Dallas, Texas. He

Journalists Akhtar Hussein, Anil Vidyarthi and others with Jomo Kenyatta

returned to England every Christmas to spend time with his brother Anwar, also a photographer, and his family at their farmhouse in rural Wiltshire. Anwar's own wife had died young and he had not married again.

In 2007, with a career of over 50 years and thousands of published photographs, Akhtar made the decision to return to England for good. He spent a happy Christmas in Wiltshire, but sadly passed away, having suffered a stroke, on January 25, 2008.

ANIL VIDYARTHI

By Shravan Vidyarthi (son)

Born in Nairobi, Kenya in 1944, Anil Vidyarthi began taking pictures in 1960 with a Box Brownie camera at the age of 16.

He acquired his first Nikon in 1962 while working in a dark room on River Road. On the recommendation of *Nation* journalist Chhotu Karadia, editor-in-chief John Bierman agreed to take in Vidyarthi. There were few photojournalists in those days, and most photographers plied their trade in Nairobi's studios. Before independence, the old *Nation* building bore the marks of colonialism. Caleb Okwera was the only black African photographer at the *Nation*, who worked alongside Vidyarthi. 'I remember we had segregated toilets in the building - the European staff had their own private latrines,' recalled Vidyarthi.

Vidyarthi's first assignment was to photograph a derailed train near Nairobi. 'We jumped on a plane to get an overhead shot. I started shooting with a camera from the *Nation*, and after two exposures the film ran out. In those days, to save film, photographers would leave behind unexposed frames in the camera so that no film was wasted. I had no idea that was the case when I started, but luckily I still got the shot!'

In 1963, Vidyarthi became a staff photographer at *The Nation* newspaper. Vidyarthi covered Kenya's independence celebrations in December 1963. Many Kenyans will remember Vidyarthi's photo of Jomo Kenyatta jumping over a stream in the Masai Mara game reserve on his way to greet American astronauts vacationing in Kenya. 'Before the astronauts came, President Kenyatta and J M Kariuki were taking a walk near a small pool of water,' Vidyarthi explained. 'Then Kenyatta jumped over it. I had three cameras around my neck and quickly, without focusing, clicked the shutter a few times. There were 30 photographers waiting, but I was the only one who got the shot. The picture was on the cover of *The Nation* the next day, and Kenyatta ordered hundreds of prints to send to leaders around the world whenever they inquired about his health.'

In 1964, Vidyarthi covered the independence celebrations in Malawi and the 1965 visit of Chinese premier Chou en Lai to Tanzania. 'In 1966, I covered the infamous Limuru conference, when Oginga Odinga was thrown out of Kenya's government. At the conference, I also ended up in front of the camera, when President Kenyatta posed for a rare picture with the press corps.'

Vidyarthi left *The Nation* in 1967 for a brief stint in the printing industry and then joined the Derby of College of Art in England to pursue a two-year degree in photography. As a student, Vidyarthi photographed stunning images of unrest in Belfast, and anti-war demonstrations in London, some of which later appeared in the British Press Photographer's Yearbook of 1970. In 1971 he moved to New York City and found casual photography work at *Life* magazine and in his spare time built a portfolio of images ranging from Harlem street life to off-Broadway productions. Later that year he traveled to England, Italy, Lebanon, Iran (for the inauguration of the Shah), and finally to India. By October of 1971, war raged between India and Pakistan, and Vidyarthi covered the conflict for various English newspapers.

ANIL VIDYARTHI

In January of 1972 Vidyarthi returned to Kenya and once again took up work in the printing industry. In the early 1980's, he returned briefly to photography and covered President Moi's state visit to India for *Viva* magazine. Today, Vidyarthi works as Managing Director of Colourprint Limited printing press. Throughout the 1990's Colourprint came under attack for printing opposition publications, and it was firebombed, then raided by the Moi government, and Vidyarthi himself was arrested and tried for sedition but later acquitted.

Today, Vidyarthi photographs Kenyan wildlife and landscapes, and publishes his pictures in calendars and diaries. His connection to *The Nation* continues, where his daughter, Smriti Vidyarthi, is a news anchor and reporter.

Jomo Kenyatta jumping over a stream in the Masai Mara game reserve on his way to greet American astronauts vacationing in Kenya

Bob Astles- Former British Army NCO who became Idi Amin's right hand man in Luzira Prison after the overthrow of Idi Amin

Robert F Kennedy inspecting a guard of honour mounted by NYS at Embakasi Airport. Behind him is Tom Mboya and Jeremiah Nyaga

L-R Njoroge Mungai, Oginga Odinga, Mbiu Koinange (behind Oginga), James Gichuru, Mzee Kenyatta, Dr Kiano (Behind Kenyatta), Tom Mboya, Bruce Mackenzie, Achieng Oneko, Ngala Mwendwa

Chou-en-Lai, Prime Minister of China, inspecting a guard of honour. On his left, President Karume of Zanzibar

ANVER VERSI

Writer

I was born in Nairobi in 1947 to Hassanali and Zainab Versi. My fore parents came from Kutch in India arriving in Zanzibar in 1890. My name is Anwarali Versi though this became shortened to 'Anver Versi' by a sub-editor when I got my first byline and I decided to stick with it for professional purposes. My father worked with the Kenya Police and we lived in Ngara in Nairobi but during the tense Mau Mau period, my mother and I moved to Mombasa.

I joined the Aga Khan primary school and remember being an avid reader. In secondary school, I discovered the pleasure of writing. Teachers said that Amin Kassam and I were the best writers in the school. We competed fiercely to produce the most exciting essays which were often read out to the class. On one occasion, a student from another class collected a couple of shillings and offered to pay me if I would let him read my latest essay. That was when I realised it was possible to earn by writing. Sadru became an outstanding sub-editor at the *Nation* before moving overseas.

I developed an interest in photography - inspired by images captured by the likes of Mohamed Amin, Azhar Chaudry and Mehmood Quraishi. Nation Newspapers had opened a bureau in Mombasa and I felt a strong urge to become part of this world of journalism. I remember seeing a young Norman Da Costa typing away in the *Nation* offices and wanted to be like him. He was to become the *Nation's* Sports editor.

I took my camera around the town, shooting whatever I found interesting or unusual. I managed to sell a lot of these photo-features to the *Nation* and the *East African*

Standard. My first full feature was a profile of the town's master perfume-maker who used traditional methods to produce a range of outstanding scents. It was published as a full-page feature in the paper but the byline was attributed to the paper's bureau chief! He apologised for the 'error' but paid me what was a small fortune at the time. This seemed a good way to earn some money.

It was while I was at the University of Nairobi that I first ran into Joe Rodrigues, then the managing editor at the *Nation*. I had taken refuge in the *Nation* offices while fleeing from paramilitary guards who had been sent to disrupt a sit-in we had staged on the university grounds. Joe sat me down and got me to write a short piece from the student perspective. It was published under a pseudo-name; and Joe said despite being a 'trouble-maker' I could write. 'Come and see me when you've finished uni,' he said.

Freelance freedom

After university, in the early 1970s, I found myself in a difficult situation – my application for Kenya citizenship had 'gone missing'. This meant that many occupations were closed to me. The only venue was teaching and free-lance journalism. I went for both – teaching full time and covering sports and anything else whenever I could. The *Nation's* sports editor, Peter Moll took a liking to me and kept giving me bigger assignments.

I was also given several subbing and editing contracts at the *Nation's* head office in Nairobi. Although Joe Rodrigues was not the Editor in Chief, he was the lord and master on the floor. His ability to run the ever expanding organisation was astonishing. He knew everything that was happening everywhere. He also insisted that I learn every aspect of producing a newspaper, from allocating daily jobs to reporters and photographers, to spending

ANVER VERSI

time with the advertising department, to reading for libel, to learning the art of sub-editing, to working in the hot-metal presses in the basement and to stone-subbing before signing off the pages.

On the staff, there were a number of journalists, editors and sub-editors who had come from the UK. The advantage they had was their technical knowledge but they lacked the feel for what was happening locally. We had some superb and very well connected local journalists but they often lacked the technical knowhow of projecting their stories most effectively. Joe was determined to close the gap through thorough and rigorous in-house training to lift the technological knowhow of the locals because he said, 'Only we can tell our stories as they should be told'.

Work permit issues forced me into freelance journalism where I had to learn how sell my work to very demanding international editors. In the process, I learnt how to identify stories, how to construct them for various publications, how to write to length and how never to miss a deadline. As editor at an early stage, I learnt how to commission, edit and rewrite virtually all copy, the importance and impact of design and illustration, how to 'package' features to their maximum effect; how to distinguish wheat from chaff in submissions and how to spot latent journalistic talent. There was very little margin for error – lack of sales meant no income for me.

I was delightfully surprised at the help and support I received from a variety of people. Mohamed Amin of *Camerapix,* Brain Tetley, Joe himself, Polly Fernandes and Alan Armstrong at the *Nation,* Mohinder Dhillon of *Africapix,* Salim Lone of *Viva* magazine and later Adrian Grimwood at the *Nation's* Mombasa office - all kept sending assignments and contacts my way. This enabled me to string for a number of overseas media outlets and to work on documentaries and special projects. Perhaps my most exciting project early on was an assignment to cover the Ali-Forman Rumble in the Jungle in 1974. This was an unbelievable experience and brought me in contact with broadcasters such as David Frost and the American writer Norman Mailer who was to write a brilliant book on the fight.

Another memorable assignment was to join a group of photographers for the first satellite launch from the San

Marco platform in Malindi and a solar eclipse captured from the Lake Turkana area. I don't recall turning down any assignment during this period – I wrote film and theatre reviews, book reviews, investigative stories, exposed some scandals but most of all continued finding fascinating stories in the day to day life of the people.

Eventually, because of my citizenship status, it became impossible to me to continue to work in Kenya and I left for the UK around 1983. I ran into several of my earlier contemporaries who had also left Kenya. They helped me get stints in some broadsheets but my first love was reporting Africa. The Africa that was being projected in the British media at this time was completely unrecognisable from the Africa I knew. I wanted to tell the other side of the story and began looking for an outlet.

This brought me into the world of the pan-African press in London. I must have been a bit of a work-aholic. I was appointed editor of *Drum* West Africa, worked for *Africa Journal* and wrote *Football in Africa,* the first history of the game for Longmans and it became a best seller in 1986. But it was when I joined IC Publications around 1985, that I felt I had finally found my niche. I was free to use all my production, editing and other journalistic experiences to raise first *New African* magazine, and later *African Business magazine,* to world class status. Today, I am proud to say that *African Business* and *African Banker,* both of which I edit, have a large circulation in over 100 countries and both are considered world class. African Business has won the annual Diageo African Business Reporting Best Media award twice (the latest in June 2013) and I won the Best Journalist award in 2005. The Boston University based APARC organisation has also been kind enough to give me an award for 'Outstanding Services to Journalism'. I also participate in African centred conferences.

In the UK, I discovered a wealth of accumulated knowledge in the media industry and why some products were successful while others struggled. I also discovered that while there was no single magic formula that led to publishing success, successful media houses understood and applied all the essential principles and did everything better than others. They knew that nine-tenths of the work that went into each issue or each programme was, like the iceberg, submerged from view.

The pan-African publishing scene, alas, was unaware of the submerged depths and believed that if they could replicate what they saw in other media, they would achieve the same success. The absence of dedicated institutions of journalism in most of Africa has meant that publishers, journalists and editors do not have firm foundations for their ventures and continue to emulate, copy and imitate the media leaders without being aware of the principles involved. This is perhaps one of the reasons why many media houses remain fragile and confused and the media as a whole has lacked the kind of power and authority it enjoys in advanced countries. But this failing was also a great opportunity for me to construct the underpinnings necessary and set the publications I worked on, on their successful trajectories.

I believe the greatest service that *African Business* has served has been to highlight African successes, without ignoring the challenges and to analyse the continent's economic development as realistically and truthfully as possible. I believe it has also served as a bridge of knowledge within Africa itself and the outside world. All along, as editor of a pan-African publication, I was determined to switch our primary contributors in various African countries from mainly Western stringers to African journalists. This has meant unearthing local talent and then nurturing it to internationally accepted standards.

I now divide my time between London and Copenhagen where my wife, Dr Assia Brandrup and my two daughters, Jamila and Yasmin, live.

ANWAR SIDI
Writer

My photojournalism life has been an extra-ordinary journey through this world which I undertook 27 years ago when my first picture was splashed in the front and sports pages of most major newspapers around the globe.

On that Thursday afternoon in 1985, while President Daniel arap Moi was flagging off cars in the 1985 Marlboro Safari in Nairobi, at the age of twenty-four I was 300 km deep in the picturesque Taita Hills armed with my Canon AV1 camera. From the horizon a Nissan 240Rs, car No 31 of Hans Schuller and Wolfgang Stiller, emerged from a tight corner sideways. The driver lost control and it rolled over several times before finally resting on its side. I kept clicking this spectacle while doctors administered first aid and the rescue military helicopter arrived and airlifted the badly injured duo back to Nairobi. I knew I had captured something special and was eager to see the images; little did I know that my world would never be the same again. With a film in hand my next task was to transport it back to Nation House in Tom Mboya Street, Nairobi. I had travelled to the Taitas in the back of a tiny Datsun pick-up. I returned that way and reached Nairobi in the evening.

The following day the picture of the heavily bandaged Schuller was splashed on page one of the *Daily Nation,* and there were more in the inside pages. International news agencies based in Nairobi, AFP (France), Reuters and Associated Press, ordered for more prints and within

hours they were published in most major newspapers in the world in different time zones. Overnight I was a celebrity. I also then became the youngest member in the Nation family and remain to date, one of the longest serving contributors alongside Dr Yusuf Dawood of Surgeon's Diary fame in the *Sunday Nation* and Gavin Bennett of Motoring.

The Schuller picture vindicated my disappointment two years earlier when a Sports Editor published the picture of Najmi Kassam, my first in the media, during the 1983 Embakasi training rally, but forgot to give me credit. When I inquired, he dismissed me with the words 'there will be a tomorrow!'

My 'tomorrow' had arrived unexpectedly in 1985. My internship was over and I could be trusted with other assignments in cricket and rugby. But I chose to remain a motorsport photojournalist and will never give up my camera until the day my Maker decrees otherwise. Overnight I was up there with the best. This gave me the impetus to perfect my profession, always looking for another world exclusive.

After the 1985 episode I took time to reflect. It had been indeed a long journey for a boy born and brought up in Chuka, Meru where there were no special or private schools - we were all equals. My father was a police officer and we did not have a privileged childhood. I attended local schools, learnt Kimeru and did all the small things little boys of the 60s and 70s did, including crafting hand-made wire cars which we raced around every Easter after watching the Safari Rally cars. My heroes then were Joginder Singh, Shekhar Mehta, Vic Preston Junior, Sandro Munari, Rauno Aaltonen, Peter Shiyukah, Parick Njiru and Jonathan Toroitich - the many local and world class drivers of that era.

ANWAR SIDI

I could not be like Joginder but became a member of the motorsport fraternity in a different way - I could admire the newspaper pictures of the Safari cars. I was humble enough to understand that exclusives do not come every day to photojournalists. They go looking for them, always trusting one's instinct and experience. This came in handy in 2001 when Michelle van Tongaren braked in time to avoid hitting a nine-year old Safari fan.

In Meru I could not get close to my childhood heroes but later I was lucky to cover their sunset years. I started

JOURNALISM FOR THE NATION

THE FACE THAT WENT AROUND THE WORLD:
This picture of a veteran international rally driver who
bit the dust of Kenya during the Safari of 1985 made the
front page of the *Daily Nation* and was filed by an
international news agency for world consumption. The
picture was taken by Nairobi freelancer Anwar Sidi
Hussein. For him, being on the spot was luck. The rest
was sheer skill. It's the perfect news picture, the type
of picture that wins awards. Technically, it has clarity.
And the composition of the picture could not be bet-
tered. It has news value, drama and great human
interest. Anwar Sidi Hussein captured it all.

BOB HITCHCOCK

218

Heia Safari? Bei der Wüsten-Rallye durch Kenia rasen die Fahrer Tag und Nacht und strapazieren sich buchstäblich bis
zum Umfallen. Im Bild der Wagen des Heilbronner Teams Siller/Schuller, das sich bei der nächtlichen Kollision mit ei-
nem Brückenpfeiler nur Prellungen zuzog.

300 Kilometer vor dem Ziel wirft den Führenden ein Motorschaden zurück:

Erwin Webers Pech ist Juha Kankkunens Glück

Frankfurter Rundschau

Wenn Sport-Manager die Fäden in den Händen halten ... (Seite 8)

9-4-85

Ein „Greenhorn" sorgte für lange Gesichter im Ziel
Der Finne Juha Kankkunen fuhr zum erstenmal bei der Safari-Rallye mit und gewann / Weber kurz vor dem Ziel gescheitert

GERMAN N/PAPER 9/4/85

9-year old Anwar Sidi in Chuka

with a fresh couple of hands who journeyed to Kenya every year for testing and competition. They were world champions like Tommi Makinen, Juha Kankunnen, late Richard Burns, Colin McRae, Carlos Sainz, Didier Auriol and Sebastian Loeb. We developed a close relationship as I continue to do so with all home grown drivers. They and the media were to label me a World Rally Championship photojournalist; a status I give little thought to as I continue to perfect my profession. I got their autographs and was consulted about possible car breaking sections by manufacturer teams. Since then, I have done work for some of the best known auto journals in the world like Auto Sport, Rally Sport, Motoring News and Rally Course; but my association with the Nation Media Group remains the longest and most constant.

I have never put money ahead of my profession. A good example is the Anwar Sidi Rally Bulletin which I distribute free to fans, drivers and sponsors before every rally as a service. I also publish a 72-page Rally Magazine Annual and Motorsport Calendar which ranks highly among fans in Kenya and across the globe.

I love motorsport dearly but of course my family comes first. Fortunately they understand my passion. Last year, according to a Synovate report, I generated press publicity worth KSh15 million for the Kenya Commercial Bank (KCB) Kenya National Rally Championship through photographic contributions to motorsport magazines, excluding my service to the daily press. My career has taken me beyond my work station of Nairobi to East Africa and beyond. I decided to become a professional World Rally Championship photojournalist, the first one in the South Asian community, when I covered the British RAC Rally and the Acropolis Rally in Greece without any assistance from anybody. At 53 I am just beginning . . .

AZHAR CHAUDHRY
Writer

I was born in Jamsher, India, in 1945. Two years later, at Independence our family moved to Pakistan. My father then joined my grandfather who had come to Kenya to work on the railways. I followed in 1956. After completing my secondary schooling, I joined the *Standard* newspaper as a Lino Operator. At the same time I trained with Masud Qureshi of the well-known family of photographers. Later I did a course on the same subject from the London School of Arts.

In 1963 I moved to the Nation as a photographer where my closest colleagues were Mike Parry, Akthar Hussein, Kul Bhushan, Cyprian Fernandes and Sultan Jessa. My seniors were Mike Chester, the news editor, and Joe Rodrigues, the editor. I started as a junior photographer under Akhtar Hussein. When he left I took over as Chief Photographer and later Picture Editor. I was then working with Chandu Vasani, Yahya Mohammed and two other photographers.

AZHAR CHAUDHRY

I was a keen rifle shooter and used to practice together with the principal of Utalii College. He admired my cooking and got me interested in a cookery course at the College. The result was that I left the *Nation* in 1980 and moved into the restaurant business. Of course I continued to dabble in photography and worked for a while with Mohammed Amin.

While at the *Nation* I travelled widely all over the world with former president Moi and the Aga Khan and his former model wife the Begum. In Kenya, among many

Three heads of states of East Africa together in a historical moment

others, I remember covering Charlie Chaplin, John Wayne and Robert Mitchum. Indian actors Dilip Kumar, Sunil Dutt, Raj Kumar and singer Lata Mangeshkar were other notable personalities who appeared in my lens. I accompanied Prince Charles and Princess Anne who visited Kenya in their youth and Sean Connery on a trip to the Maasai Mara.

In 1966 I covered Tom Mboya's funeral and that was quite a challenge as in Kisumu there was a lot of rioting and gunfire and I got beaten up. In April 1968 I was standing

under a tree covering the Safari Rally. The dust from the cars whizzing by must have disturbed the beehive above me and I was badly stung by a vicious swarm of bees.

As a photographer I met two really flashy characters – Saudi arms dealer Adnan Kashoggi and Playboy chief Hugh Heffner. Kashoggi flitted around the world in his 'personal flying carpet', a green and white Boeing 727 equipped with everything from gold-plated bathroom fittings to special wardrobes for his Arab robes and French Cifonelli suits – at the time, the most expensive in the world. Hefner, had the most chutzpah, arriving in Kenya in 1970 on a jet-black DC-9 jet plane with a revolving bed (covered in a crush of animal furs), accompanied by Bunnies in leatherette minis, each with their own quarters.

In 1988 I translocated to South Africa in search of a better life. I established Daawat restaurant in Cape Town, have a restaurant at present in Jo'burgh and am considering relocating to Dubai. For a Muslim restaurateur in a western context, it's a conundrum since many people enjoy wine or beer with their curries.

CHANDU VASANI
Writer

I was born in 1939 in Thika, Kenya. My father came to Kenya in 1904 from Jetpur in Gujarat, India. My mother was born in Kisumu. I completed my primary schooling in Thika and secondary in Jamhuri High School, Nairobi. My father owned a timber and hardware shop in Thika. In it he had allocated space for a dark room where he did some simple photography and I used to assist him with the processing of the films. In those days we had 2 cameras: a Box Brownie which took a 620 film and a Baby Brownie with a 127 film.

My first job was with Kenya Canners, I then joined the Standard Bank of South Africa as a clerk/cashier. I had been there eight years when one day the European Bank Manager addressed me with a racist remark – I walked out. I then joined an outfit run by the film-maker Sharad Patel but found that the photography section was virtually dormant. My brother, Shashi, at that time was doing photography with the *Nation* and was able to secure a 3-month probationary contract for me with Achieng Oneko's Ministry of Information, Broadcasting and Tourism.

S K Gajree, a professional South Asian photographer headed the department and the printing was done by two South Asians and an African. It was 1964 and I covered the Republic Day celebrations. I now had my feet on the first rung of the ladder to recognition. 1965-66, I joined the *Tanganyika Standard* as Chief Photographer and covered Chou-en-Lai, Gamal Abdul Nasser, Che Guevara and other international leaders who visited Tanzania.

My brother, Shashi, passed away in 1967 and I returned to Nairobi and took his place in the *Nation*, working alongside Azhar Chaudhry and Njuguna. 1967-8 was the build-up to the Asian Exodus precipitated by Kenya's Africanisation programme and Britain's betrayal of her overseas British citizens. I went to the Embakasi airport and was shocked to find hundreds of my fellow compatriots with their luggage waiting patiently to board planes headed to the UK. So distressing was the sight that I just clicked my camera once and then left. The picture was of a Punjabi woman sitting forlornly on her suitcase and clutching her passport.

The Nation's advertising department was run largely by South Asians and the bulk of the advertising support came from Asian owned business enterprises. I wondered what the future would hold for them – and myself.

Shashi Vasani meets President Jomo Kenyatta

Air Force Christmas card

British Asians protesting outside
British High Commission, Nairobi,
1960s

Sean Connery in Muthaiga Golf Club, March 1973

President Jomo Kenyatta with traditional dancers at State House reception on
Jamhuri Day

Mayor Margaret Kenyatta greets
Indira Gandhi at Nairobi Airport

Desai Memorial Hall, Nairobi - 1967

CHANDU VASANI

At the *Nation* we were a well-coordinated team and were allocated different assignments. Once I was to accompany Kul Bhushan to Mfangano Street only to find the *Nation* car was not available as it was taking a European lady shopping. I was feeling under the weather and requested that it also drop us to our destination. My boss, the news editor Mike Chester, insisted that we should walk. So I walked out!

I then took to freelancing. In the 1970 Agricultural Show in Nairobi, I got a scoop photographing President Jomo

Kenyatta as he stepped out of the BAT stand accompanied by B M Gecaga. I had managed to persuade his security detail to let me stand in front of the President's Land rover and click my camera. The *Nation* had allowed me to continue using their Press Pass provided I gave them the scoops. And Mr Gecaga was so impressed he opened up new possibilities for me.

In 1973 I married Madhukanta Patel, headmistress of Shushi Bal Gruh Day Nursery, and got increasingly involved in the school administration. In the nineties when photography became digitised I finally put away my cameras. The school closed down in 2006 and we are now retired in Nairobi.

EMILIANO JONES
Writer

I was born in Kenya in 1939 and educated at the Dr Ribeiro Goan School in Parklands. My parents emigrated from Goa which was then a Portuguese colony in British India.

I attended a one-year course at the Germain School of Photography in Manhattan, New York, but this did not include photojournalism. Back in Kenya, getting a job in the *East African Standard* during the colonial era was like asking for a trip to the moon. The editorial board comprised of reporters and photojournalists all of whom were hired from the UK.

I did try asking for a job with the *Standard* the usual way making an application – this was ignored. At first I thought because I lacked the experience. However, I was confident that I could handle an editorial assignment. I was naïve to think that at that time that I would qualify for a job. Little did I realise the editorial floor of the

newspaper was for *whites only* written in invisible ink. Asians were employed in the type setting rooms and other places where the newspaper was printed with an English man in charge.

So I started taking sports pictures of the British playing rugby and soccer on a Saturday, but only if I did not see the staff photographer doing the same. One Saturday I took a picture at a rugby match, had it printed and handed it to the *Standard* sports editor. His name was John Downes. He looked at me seriously and said, 'Did you really take these pictures?' as if to say he could not believe it. I said yes but I could not write the caption because I did not know the players. He said not to worry, he would take care of it. From then on Downes gave me assignments on weekends when their photographers were unavailable.

I did not have to process the film, just hand it to him. But this also gave me access to the darkroom when their darkroom technician was not available and I willingly did the official photographer's pictures too. I did not realise it then but I had nudged my foot into the door of the editorial room AND of course, the drumbeats of *Uhuru* could be heard in the distant horizon.

The managing staff of the *East African Standard* consisted of Kenneth Bolton, the Director and Editor and Eric Marsden, the editor. The other reporters were Peter MacDonald, Murray Ritchie, Martin Revis, Penny More, and John Ansel. The photographers were John Perry, Vic Tomasyn and Peter Heathcote. One day I met for the first time, John Perry, the chief photographer of the newspaper. He asked me if I would like to work for the paper. I couldn't believe it! I said, 'Yes.' He then asked when I could start. I replied, 'Now!' I was offered the job full time in March 1966. I am still in touch with John

Drought in Masailand

Ostrich nesting

EMILIANO JONES

Perry who is in England. John was and is a gentleman from the day I met him.

All eyes were on me to see how I was performing. I had to prove that I could handle the assignments and be good if not better. Overall the reporters with whom I went on assignments were good and cooperative and we eventually became friends. Although I got on fine with them; socialising was out of the question. After work I couldn't say, 'Hey Bill let's go for a beer.' The atmosphere was as the English would say, 'It's simply not done old chap.'

Like everything in Kenya during the British administration the white folks got paid more the than Asians for the same job. My case at the *Standard* was no exception. The other photographers earned more than me. It was better than working as a Bwana Karani in an insurance company which I did before I landed at the newspaper.

One racial incident really rattled me - it was when I was sent to do a picture story on the Nairobi Dam. This was around 1967, post independence! There was a yachting club that was exclusively for whites and a swimming pool was being constructed and the paper needed a photograph. When I approached the manager, he refused to believe that I was a photographer from the *Standard* and asked me to leave the premises. He wouldn't even agree to phone the editor to check out my credentials. I left and informed the assignment editor, Eric Bayles, of the incident. Later I returned to the club; but with a reporter and completed the job and the matter was taken up with the yachting club.

During my tenure with the paper, my picture story *Drought in Masailand* was accepted and published in the *World Press Photo Competition (1967)*. And later on, the *British Press Pictures of the Year Competition* accepted a picture - a story of *Ostriches Nesting*.

This blissful period with the newspaper came to an end due to the Africanisation policy. To continue working in Kenya without citizenship meant one needed a work permit. The English reporters and photographers left and Africans were trained as reporters who I must say did a fine job of reporting. An African photographer by the name of Jared Oyombera was on the staff with me and I was asked to help him. I told him to let me know if he needed help. He, however, said he knew everything about photography because he had a studio in Kisumu. It was a sensitive issue and I let it rest at that.

By the way, there was another Asian photographer employed later by the name of A K Azim. He was an excellent photographer and was still there when I left. When Africanisation came in the editor, Kenneth Bolton, did get me a work permit for one year. He said he couldn't assure me of a renewal. In any case, I had already made up my mind to leave as most of the reporters had left or were leaving.

My wife and I left Nairobi on 14 August, 1970 for Canada. I did not join the Asian exodus to England. Whenever I passed through London the weather put me off! I was too used to the Kenya sunshine. In Canada I couldn't get a job in the newspaper field so I opted to work in the advertising field with a company that required photographers with my experience. I enjoyed the work although I would have preferred to continue in journalism. I did do picture stories in my spare time that I sold to newspapers and magazines. I am now retired.

KULWANT (KANTI) SANDHU
Writer

I was born in 1943 in Eldoret, Kenya and attended the Duke of Gloucester School in Nairobi. I then went to the Yadavindra Public School in Patiala, India, to complete my 'A' Levels. I got into photography in 1967 when I had come back from England on a three week holiday. My uncle, Mohinder Dhillon, who was on a protracted photographic assignment in Aden, called and asked me to just look after his business till his return. I learnt photography and cinematography by just following Mohinder on assignments.

I spent five years with Africapix from 1967 through middle of 1972. Around July 1967, Dr Hans German, a German TV producer, who Mohinder Dhillon knew, had come to town. He wanted to hire a crew to go for a one day shoot to the Congo and film the mercenaries who had taken over the town of Bukavu. So I, along with another Africapix staff member, Satwant Matharoo, went with the German producer. I was the audio technician. We flew in a private chartered aircraft to Kigali in Rwanda and then crossed the border to Bukavu on foot, carrying our heavy equipment.

We were going in for just the day but ended up spending 4 or 5 nights. It was, in many ways, a hair-raising experience, especially for me as this was my very first assignment. The leader of the mercenaries called 'Black Jack' gave us permission to film anything except himself. There was sporadic firing along with mortar attacks aimed at the white mercenaries that we were with. One night there was a lot of firing going on. We were getting nervous as it got closer and louder. At one stage we went under the beds we were sleeping on hoping that any stray bullets would be above floor level. Next morning, we were informed that they had been shooting stray dogs because of the fear of rabies.

KULWANT (KANTI) SANDHU

By the way, when we went into Bukavu, we did not have any change of clothes as we were supposed to get out the same day. The town is very pretty and is often referred to as the Geneva of Africa. But there was no electricity or water as the Congolese Government had cut the supplies of these commodities. So we had to brush our teeth with beer or soda water or any Pop and there was no change of clothes for five days. The food was great, steaks and plenty of beer, all free. The mercenaries had some sort of power generator to work some of the appliances and a few gas cylinders. They had ransacked the homes of the residents who had fled, and taken cans of food and meat from their fridges.

Next day we were taken on a tour of the town, there were decaying corpses lying everywhere and evidence of looting, cars littered everywhere, both new and old, and broken shop fronts. There was much to film and record. After a few months the mercenaries in Bukavu were overrun by the Congolese army with help from some other nations. Some of the mercenaries were captured as they were fleeing. A few of them got captured in Burundi.

(I must here thank Satwant Matharoo for reminding me of some of the details.)

On another occasion one of the American Broadcast Networks called in the middle of the night (in those days communication was done either on the phone or via telegrams) asking us to cover a previously extinct volcano that they thought was billowing smoke, etc. The volcano was just south of the border in Tanzania. The network suggested we hire a plane and go get coverage of whatever was spewing out of the volcano – we did that;

but there was no sign of any volcanic activity. We called the network and reported the same. They then insisted that we go by road. So four of us (Mohamed Rashid also of Africapix, Anil Vidyarthi of *Daily Nation*, Sean Hawkins and I) set out in the office VW. The road after Namanga towards the mountain was just a small narrow dirt track. We had one puncture before we got to the base of the mountain. Again, there was no sign of any kind of volcanic activity. On our way back we had, I believe, another two punctures. We then decided to leave the car, gather our equipment and started walking.

Soon the sun went down and being in a sandy environment, it started getting cold. We felt the cold even just sitting on the track. At one stage we heard loud rustling in the forest. Our unanimous decision was to move out quickly as we suspected the presence of a herd of elephants. We walked for hours and finally as the morning light started getting brighter, we saw at a distance what we thought was a dust storm. Gradually we realized that it was a lorry. Somehow they saw us and gave us a ride to the only hotel at the Namanga border from where we made a radio call to the Africapix office. In the final analysis – we spent a lot of time and money but to no avail.

I have been in the States since middle of 1973 and retired three years ago from Western Michigan University after working in their Media Services area for 37 years. I worked as a photographer, film cameraman and eventually as producer director in video production. In 1983 I won the Silver Award from the prestigious International Film & Television Festival of New York for my camera work on a documentary project.

KRISHAN SHARMA
Writer

I became a photographer at the very young age of 18. My interest in photography started whilst I was still at school in Mombasa. A book store on Salim Road in Mombasa influenced my desire to be a photographer. I used to visit the store and browse through glossy photographic books. I was so enamoured by works of photographers like Karsh of Ottawa and his studies of the famous that I think I romanticized the profession. I had a choice: to follow into my elder brother's footsteps and study law or be a photographer; obviously I chose the latter. This profession has given me a unique opportunity to see the world and study mankind through my lens.

I moved to Nairobi merely two years after becoming a photographer as I had an opportunity to learn colour processing with Maxim Ruston who started the first colour processing lab in East Africa. My desire to be my own boss led me to start my own business as 'Fantasia Photographers' where I specialized in portraits and became a social society photographer.

Photographing British society at various hotels and all-white clubs gave me an interesting insight into the decadent British society of Kenya. This was around 1958. However, I wanted to be more than just another photographer and thus I headed for London, England in the spring of 1959. I worked for a while at a photographic studio in Oxford Street and studied photo journalism. My work was influenced by a famous photo journalist at the *Observer* newspaper in London. I spent three years living with the Petos. Michael Petos had done work with the Welsh miners, the Royal Ballet, and was doing a book on Margo Fontaine the prima ballerina, and photo essays in Russia. I remember spending endless hours with him in the darkroom studying how he created photographs in

KRISHAN SHARMA

the lab. He taught me composition and how to look for a story in a photograph.

I worked in Fleet Street as a free-lance photojournalist. In 1963 I was asked by the *Sunday Times* of London if I would go to Kenya to cover the independence of Kenya and travel with Malcolm MacDonald; he was going to oversee the independence of Kenya. This was my opportunity to travel, photograph and observe the upcoming leaders of Kenya. I travelled with Jomo Kenyatta, Tom Mboya, Kibaki and many others. These were indeed exciting days. I had the opportunity to be at the first African Heads conference in Addis Ababa hosted by Emperor Haile Selassie. This has been my first and only glimpse of African Royalty.

But all wasn't rosy. These were dangerous times for photojournalists. I lost two friends in the Congo around 1964. The newly independent countries in Africa were all of a sudden governed by politicians who had no idea of the rules of engagement with the press and could react in a most undesirable and unpredictable manner, with impunity if I might add. I almost never made it out of Zanzibar after the revolution.

I had no desire of dying young! However, to give up my profession I had to find another that would give me a livelihood. This is when I became an insurance agent and moved to Canada. I retired in my late 50s so that I could learn to smell the roses. Now my time is spent observing, learning and accepting life on its terms. Although my home is Toronto, Canada where I live with my wife Carol, I have a home by the sea on Margarita Island in Venezuela. This is my winter retreat and I have used this base in South America to travel around this part of the world. In a way my life on the island has brought me back to my childhood days on the African coast! A small world!

MOHAMED AMIN (1943-1996)
By Salim Amin (son)

The turmoil of Africa's emergence into the 20th century has long been the focus of the critical eye of the Western World. From exploration to exploitation; from fear and famine to fame and fortune; from war-torn horror to wildlife wonder; it has all been exposed to the relentless gaze of the international press.

No one has caught its pain and passion more incisively than Mohamed Amin, photographer and frontline cameraman extraordinaire. He was the most famous photo-journalist in the world, making the news as often as he covered it. 'Mo' trained his unwavering lens on every aspect of African life, never shying from the tragedy, never failing to exult in the success.

He was born into an Africa at the high noon of colonial decline, and by his early teens was already documenting events which were soon to dominate world news. He witnessed and recorded the alternating currents of his beloved continent and beyond, projecting those images across the world, sometimes shocking, sometimes delighting millions of television viewers and newspaper readers. Through the gaze of his camera lens, he showed the world what some were afraid to see and what most people wished they could ignore.

His coverage of the 1984 Ethiopian famine proved so compelling that it inspired a collective global conscience and became the catalyst for the greatest-ever act of giving. Unquestionably, it also saved the lives of millions of men, women and children. He served as both the inspiration and as a catalyst for Band Aid, USA for Africa and Live Aid.

Born in Nairobi, Kenya on 28 August, 1943, the second son of a poor railway worker, Mo was soon faced with racism, an inevitable product of colonialism. He never forgot those underdog years and fought against prejudice the rest of his life. He rose to become one of the world's most renowned photographer, cameraman, TV producer/director, author and publisher.

From the time he acquired his first camera, a second-hand Box Brownie, Mo's future was determined. He never

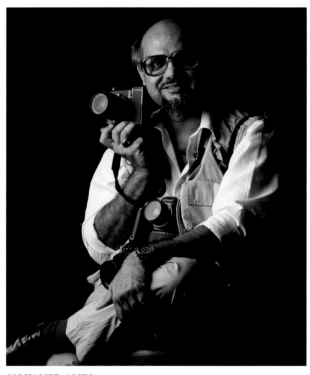

MOHAMED AMIN

received any formal training as a photo-journalist. Self-taught he quickly learned photographic and darkroom skills and was already applying them to commercial use when he went to secondary school in the then Tanganyika. Before he was 20 he was a recognized force as a freelancer in Dar es Salaam and his work appeared in all the Fleet Street national newspapers.

Mo's career can be traced as that of a Photo-journalist 1958-61 and as a TV cameraman and photographer, 1961-62.He founded Camerapix in 1963. In a career spanning

Korem Ethopia1984

Elmolo boy with crocodile 1980

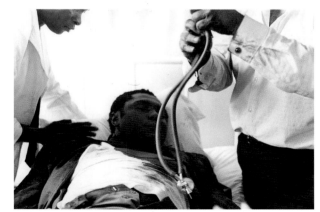

Tom Mboya assasination 5 July 1969

Idi Amin ordered white residents to kneel before him and swear an oath of allegiance 1978

President Idi Amin 1977

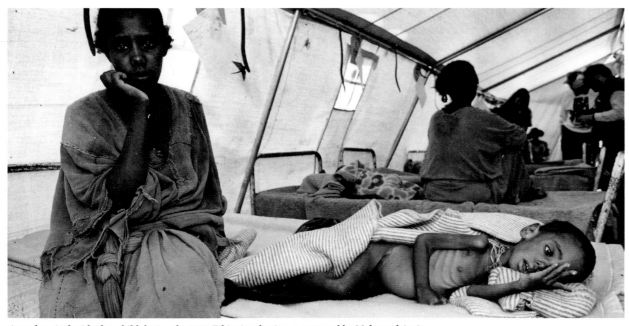

A mother sits besides her child during the 1984 Ethiopian famine as captured by Mohamed Amin

more than 30 years, 'Mo' was our eyes on the frontline in every situation and his honest unwavering approach to photojournalism earned him the unconditional respect of both friends and enemies alike. Mo covered every major event in Africa and beyond, braving 28 days of torture, surviving bombs and bullets, even the loss of his left arm in an ammunition dump explosion, to emerge as the most decorated news cameraman of all time.

Mo's remarkable life was cut tragically short in November 1996 when hijackers took over an Ethiopian airliner forcing it to crash land in the Indian Ocean killing 123 passengers and crew. Mo died on his feet still negotiating with the terrorists. By any standards, Mo's life was truly

extraordinary; action-packed, full of pain and passion and inseparable from the troubled chronicle of emergent Africa.

MOHAMED SHAFI
Writer

I was born in Nairobi, Kenya, in 1951 and attended Park Road primary school and City High school. I did my A Levels in 1970. I first became interested in photography at the age of eight. In 1968 while I was still in school my cousin Mo Amin used to take me along, with him as a soundman.

My first experience wasn't very pleasant. After pretending I could process film I managed to ruin one and Mo sacked me. But three weeks later he took me back. He then gave me some proper training and I never looked back. I progressed to working as a still photographer, covering events in Kenya for international news agencies such as Reuters and AP, also for magazines including *Newsweek*. I vividly remember my first camera, bought by my father. It was a Pentax costing twelve hundred Kenya shillings. It was this camera I used on my first assignments while also training as a darkroom assistant and stills photographer. I also learnt how to be in charge of sound while on location with Mo shooting for television.

My mentor, Mo Amin, gave me some good advice on photography. The first day I worked for him he warned me not to become too big-headed about taking photographs. 'Anyone can take a photograph,' Mo told me. 'What makes a good news photographer is the speed with which he can deliver the picture to the news desk.'

Soon my photographs were being used around the world. Although the training was perfect, Camerapix would not pay me a salary and I had to be supported financially by my father. In 1970 I was filming in Pakistan when I became the target for a mob assault. Despite a bleeding nose and head I managed to protect my camera and rushed to the local newspaper to sell my pictures. Once I had learned the photographic news skills I moved on from Nairobi to England, but there life was not easy. In 1973 I moved to Newcastle and worked at a weaving factory in Gateshead, doing twelve-hour night shifts five nights a week and then on to the Plessey telecommunications factory at Beeston.

On my father's death I had to return to Kenya to carry on his construction business. In August 1982 the coup

MOHAMED SHAFI

in Kenya saw us lose all our belongings as well as being personally attacked. The scale of looting was so incredible that if the looters had had another day, I think they would have completely dismantled our building brick by brick. In the brief hours the local people had to themselves during the attempted coup, they managed to clear out almost every Asian shop in the city centre and many of the Asian houses. I was back to square one, my cars and lorries had bullet holes in their engines.

As I was jobless I started work once again in 1983 with Mo Amin's Camerapix. However he promised to train

me as a television cameraman, and pay me a salary of Kshs 2000 per month, about US$50. On my way to film around Mt Kenya I discovered that the country was facing a major drought. I raced back to Nairobi and told the BBC correspondent, Mike Wooldridge. On seeing my pictures he agreed the situation was serious. We drove out to film his piece and then send the material to London. The next day it made the lead news story and was picked up by hundreds of foreign newspapers. When Mo saw the BBC News in London he was shocked and called Visnews to ask who had covered the story. He could not believe it was me.

That story was my big break. From that moment, Mike Wooldridge used me as his cameraman on all assignments outside Kenya. My confidence grew and my work improved. It was a period of great excitement and I hardly noticed I was working fifteen hours a day, seven days a week. Although many of the scenes I filmed were painful I felt I had to be there, that I was the right person to show the world the problems facing Africa. All the time I wanted my work to help the people I was filming. I was more interested in covering hard news. Mo Amin's advice was: 'No story is worth getting killed for. You can never be absolutely sure about a situation but you can cut down the risk by doing the right planning.'

I have a great passion for my work but for my children it was a difficult situation. I have been an absentee father always working.

MOHINDER DHILLON
Writer

I was born in British India approximately in 1931 in a remote village of Babar Pur where births were not registered in those days. In 1947, my father working for the Railways came to fetch the family to join him

in Kenya. I was 16 years old. In India the medium of teaching was Urdu and my English was non-existent with the result that I did not sit for the Senior Cambridge exam in those days. But I remember very well the camera advertisement: 'Buy Kodak Box Brownie and shoot your mother-in-law.'

My father had bought me a very simple Box Brownie for 14 shillings and I started taking pictures and processing them in a natural darkroom at the end of a kitchen without windows. I improvised processing in soap dishes, using an ordinary light bulb wrapped round with yellow paper - the yellow glow emitted a safe light to look at the images develop on film and then place them on small sized photographic paper for prints.

At this juncture the first Indian hockey team captained by the legendary Dhian Chand visited Kenya; and I never stopped clicking my simple camera selling prints for 50 cents each. I tried to become a professional photographer but the Indian photographers were portrait photographers in the studio and were reluctant to teach me as they regarded me as future competition.

The whites were downright racist but a Jewish lady, Mrs Edith Halle running Halle studio, gave me the opportunity. Halle studio had a contract with the *East African Standard* to supply them news photos of daily events. My photographer-boss, Peter Howlett, treated me so badly that my stammer became worse and I could not get the words out without physical jerks. He would then say, 'go and have your jerks outside'.

But the social editor Lesley Clay sent a circular to all the editorial departments recommending me. Without any formal training I developed an eye for composition and a gift to recognise what makes a good picture. One day

Karamoja Famine Victim - Uganda –
Lucky to receive uncooked corn

Young Somali boy carrying a lethal weapon

Idi Amin with benefactor colonel Gaddafi in Kampala

The picture that tells a story of hunger
and desperation

Desertification, sand dunes and
Kamana River

Sikhs in the war

Misery of a child with mother on the border of Somalia, Ethiopia and Sudan

MOHINDER DHILLON

I took a dramatic picture of rows of Mau Mau suspects being screened and in the middle a frightened child under a sisal string bed with drops of light highlighting the boy's predicament. Soon I started to market my picture overseas and I was launched as a News photographer. The *Standard* hired a staff photographer, John Perry from London and we got along well - the Brits from England were different from the colonial ones!

When Miss Halle fell ill, I bought the Studio paying in instalments. I trained my late wife, Ambi, to take passport pictures and one day her luck changed when a British Army purchasing officer came in to have his I/D and passport pictures taken. He liked the pictures and made a verbal contract to send all the British Army personnel for their pictures. They came in lorry loads crowding the 2nd floor of old historical Nairobi House with queues over-flowing onto the steps.

Our bread and butter were guaranteed and that left me free to concentrate on news pictures. A picture I took appeared on the front page of the *Daily Nation's* very first edition. In 1960, George Pipal of United Press International (UPI) came to Kenya to recruit a 16mm cameraman for TV. He left me a 6-page instructions booklet and I was launched as a TV cameraman. In 1961, I was joined by Fleet Street journalist Ivor Davis who had come to work for the *East African Standard*. Together we formed Africapix which became the biggest private News photo and TV agency in Africa catering for international demands. Our company was flying high and I was quite proud of my own achievements especially as I came into this profession to earn a living, but which later became a passion. But there were risks … in 1964 I was almost executed at Stanleyville airport in the Congo!

I was lucky to link up with professional journalists like Mike Buerk of BBC TV and David Smith of ITN News, London. Buerk, on his maiden assignment with me to cover the Ethiopian Famine, made a short appeal on behalf of UK charities and raised US$15 million. This assignment to film the appeal was a real challenge both for Mike and me. The military regime did not want to show us the real famine. In Uganda, when I went to cover Obote's return to power I ended up photographing a terrible famine in the Karamoja district and got help from all over the world. The secret of success of a story is to get there, quickly shoot and dispatch the pictures to raise the awareness of the world at large.

A sensitive film maker always ends up getting emotionally involved and becomes a dedicated reformist concerned about the problems. There is a lot of anguish and frustration in filming children dying like flies. The world media was interested in the story of famine which became the title of a documentary *African Calvary*. The late Mohamed Amin and I pooled our footages to produce this documentary.

Then one fine day in 1967 I managed to travel to Aden in South Yemen to cover disturbances between the British and Yemenis where there was a general strike and the airport was closed. This event launched me as a much sought after combat film maker and I ended up covering major global wars and rebellions in Vietnam, Afghanistan, Indo/Pakistan, Arab/Israel, Congo, Biafra, etc. I shot an award winning film in Vietnam entitled *Vietnam-after the Fire* narrated by black cabaret singer Earth Kitt.

A few times I was in situations where there was a real danger that prisoners were being tortured for the benefit of television or still cameras. I then made the difficult decision to stop shooting; I had no doubts about my decision to walk out on what would have been world scoops in Bangladesh and in Aden. Had I stayed and continued photographing, the torturing would have intensified and I know that lingering thoughts would have disturbed me for the rest of my life. In some quarters I was regarded as an idiot for leaving, in others as a high-minded hero.

During my work in Kenya I have trained dozens of technicians. At one time my company 'Factual Films,' with a Kenyan partner, employed about 50 people. We took the entertainment via mobile cinemas to villages throughout the country, FREE. We covered our expenses

An elephant in the Amboseli

Mama Ngina Kenyatta, Mwai Kibaki and Daniel Arap Moi in days gone by

Kenyan Army Mutiny at Lanet Camp

Kenyatta after Lancaster House Conference with Tom Mboya and Achieng Oneko

Pamela Mboya grieving

showing advertising films selling brands suitable for the rural market. Some of the trainees became big names. One was John Adewa, the other was the late photo-journalist Mohamed Amin whom we spotted in Dar-es-Salaam. We appointed him our stringer and later trained him to shoot 16mm film for TV and 35mm for Cinema Newsreels when we represented Pathe News and Movietone news. And at one time I worked round the clock to have him released from a Zanzibar prison.

No one had seen pictures of Jomo Kenyatta, Kenya's future president, in detention. The British had blocked all roads leading to him. Through a clever ruse I was able to obtain the very first pictures of imprisoned Jomo. Late Professor Wangari Maathai always said I helped her lay the foundation stone for the Green Belt Movement (GBM). I had taken my Scandinavian media friends to her modest house in Nairobi South C and the film I took of that meeting, when aired internationally, attracted a number of donors who enabled the GBM to set up branches countrywide. I also filmed *Birth of Athletics* - a world famous and very moving Kenyan film starring founders like Sir Derek Erskine. And finally, I am the film maker who shot the historical trilogy *White Man's Country, Black Man's Land* which is now preserved in our national archives and shown at national occasions.

MOHINDER SINGH MARJARA (1944-1966)

Mohinder Singh Marjara, a British citizen, was born on 20 February, 1944 in Nairobi, Kenya. He was the son of Late Mr Atma Singh Marjara and Mrs Dhan Kaur Marjara. He was the last born in a family of five brothers and two sisters.

He completed his primary education at City Primary School, Nairobi, and the secondary education at the

Lost newsmen: Hopes fading

JENS ALBREKTSEN   JOSEPH NGERE   MOHINDER SINGH MARJARA

THE   two   Nairobi   news   from Mr. Senn.   He had tele-   about whom nothing has been

Mrs. Dhan Kaur Marjara,
P.O. Box 2555,
Nairobi.

31st March, 1966.

His Excellency, President of the Republic
of Kenya, Mzee Jomo Kenyatta.

Sir,

I shall be deeply grateful if you would use your good offices to help me secure information from the Governments of Uganda, the Sudan and the Congo (Leopoldville), the fate of my son Mohinder Singh Marjara, aged 21, a press photographer, who has been missing from the Sudan, Congo (Leopoldville), Uganda border area since he left Juba, Sudan, on 13th January, 1965.

Numerous inquiries directed at the Kenya, Congolese and British Governments have so far failed to furnish any information, either way, about my son's whereabouts and I therefore appeal to you to authorize an inquiry and seek any further information whatever about him and his two colleagues.

The only information to reach here has been conflicting reports of the party having been arrested and/or murdered by the rebels (Nationalists). Mohinder was travelling in a brick red V.W. saloon car, Reg. No. KGK 918, in company with one Jens Albrektsen (24) a Dane, another photographer, and one Joseph Ngere (35), a Kikuyu from Kenya who was employed as a driver by Africapix Picture Agency.

I shall be pleased to furnish any further particulars you may desire. Appreciating, Sir, that you have very important matter of State with which to deal and please forgive me for taking up your valuable time.

I have the honour to be,
Sir,
Your most obedient servant,

(Mrs. Dhan Kaur Marjara)

Technical High School, Nairobi. He was a very bright student and excellent athlete. He won numerous awards in athletics; and was a very good singer.

After finishing High School in 1963, he joined Africapix, a news agency, as a press photographer. On 10 January, 1965 Mohinder (21) left Nairobi on a news assignment for Africapix, in the company of his colleague also a press photographer, Jens Abrektsen (24) a Dane, and a Kenyan driver, Joseph Ngere (35), in a brick red Volkswagen saloon car, Registration Number KGK 918.

It is believed they headed to Sudan via Gulu, Uganda, and were last seen in the southern Sudanese town of Juba heading towards the border town of Arua on the Congolese/Sudanese border.

According to unconfirmed reports all three of them were either arrested or executed by the Congolese rebels but no trace of them has ever been found.

Efforts to institute an enquiry into the disappearance of three of them by Kenya, Sudan, Congo, Uganda and British Governments were not successful. In Kenya, letters written by Dhan Kaur Majara, a distraught mother, and Mohinder Dhillon, his employer, to President Jomo Kenyatta seems to have fallen on deaf ears. There is no record of any response. The Danish Embassy in Nairobi said 'they were informed and ….. had no further comment to make'.

And that seems to have been the end of this truly tragic story.

PRIYA RAMRAKHA (1935-1968)

Priya Ramrakha was born in Nairobi in 1935 and raised at his family's home on 2nd Avenue, Parklands. His grandfather, Shamdass Bootamal Horra, born in Punjab in northern India, had travelled in 1896 and found employment in Kenya as a stationmaster on the Uganda Railway. His family prospered, and Priya's father worked in Nairobi as a consular official.

For Priya photography had begun as a hobby, taking pictures with a Kodak box camera and making prints after school in the evenings. When he was about twelve years old he told his father he wanted to buy a Rolleiflex, which at the time cost about 1,200 shillings. And he waited until his father could buy it on installments.

Photography quickly grew into a passion for Priya. As a teenager he drove to Laari in the Rift Valley to photograph a massacre of Kikuyu loyalists killed by Mau Mau freedom fighters. Later that year he traveled to Kapenguria to cover the trial of Kenya's future president, Jomo Kenyatta, charged with masterminding the Mau Mau rebellion.

These first photographs were published in *The Colonial Times*, an anti-British newspaper established by Priya's uncle, Girdhari Lal Vidyarthi. Priya befriended African leaders, rebel soldiers, and everyday people alike. He was trusted and respected, and he possessed the imagination, inventiveness, and perseverance to earn the access that would allow him to capture his subjects in striking detail.

Priya's photographs suggest that he saw his pictures from great distance, and then moved carefully into close proximity with his subject while meticulously gauging composition and exposure to create a seamless image. His picture of a youthful Daniel Arap Moi holding a spear is a striking example. Shot for the Colonial Times in daylight, just outside their old printing press on Nairobi's Reata Road, Priya used a wide-angle lens positioned

diagonally below the then future president. The result is an inspiring portrait of a young freedom fighter, looming large in the frame, eyes fixed, and hands poised on the spear.

In Nairobi in 1959, Priya met Eliot Elisofon, a renowned *LIFE* magazine photographer who epitomized the young Ramrakha's desire to create detailed portrayals of Africa through his photography. Africa had always been presented in the West as a primitive land inhabited by uncivilized people, and Elisofon began a series of photographic expeditions to redefine such limited perspectives of the continent. Impressed by Priya's zeal, Elisofon took him on as an apprentice and critiqued his work regularly.

By 1963 Priya returned to Africa to cover the pomp of Kenya's independence. He became a stringer for both *Time* and *LIFE*, travelling across Africa to document the festivities of decolonization. Priya relished the opportunity to work at home, and he travelled widely throughout the continent – to Zambia where he formed a close friendship with Kenneth Kaunda and photographed intimate family portraits of the Zambian premier, and to Ethiopia where he documented Haille Selassie during Queen Elizabeth's royal tour in that country.

Priya was unflappably devoted to getting a story, carefully negotiating the racial politics of the era. 'Priya certainly stuck out because he was Indian,' explained John de St Jorre, a former colleague and reporter for *The Observer* newspaper. 'But it didn't faze him. We were in Salisbury, Rhodesia, in 1964 and planned to cover a press conference at the Rhodesian Front ball hosted by Ian Smith, the leader of what had become white-led Rhodesia under Smith's Unilateral Declaration of Independence

PRIYA RAMRAKHA

from the British. We knew there would be a problem getting past security because "Priya Ramrakha" doesn't really sound like a very promising name to an exclusively white regime. So when we applied for press accreditation he decided to make himself Irish. I think we called him P O'Rourke. Or P O'Rarker!'

'He was the only person of color there apart from the waiters, and the heavies at the door immediately took him aside. But he was very cool about it. He simply pointed to his accreditation and took it all in his stride.

Biafran War child soldiers

Time and *LIFE*. Carlson's death was documented heavily in the world press, and Priya had the exclusive story.

On the front line

'I remember developing his films at Sapra Studio in Nairobi,' said his friend, Satwant Singh. 'We were under orders that if Priya was coming to town we should be on 24-hour standby to open the lab. He sometimes called me at three or four in the morning from the airport and I always woke up, got the keys to the lab, and processed his film. He would sleep on the floor or in a chair and then head straight to the airport again the next day.'

Energetic, creative, always in motion and thoroughly professional; Priya documented political uncertainty across Africa, including the Congo, Somalia, Zanzibar, and Nigeria. 'One of the greatest advantages that Priya had over other journalists was that he knew where to go in Africa,' explained Jonathan Randal, a former reporter for *The Washington Post* and *The New York Times*. 'He was a very Westernized journalist, but Kenya was his country and Africa was his continent. He had the antennae out in all those directions.'

Yet with every new assignment, Priya seemed to move closer to danger. Veteran cameraman Mohinder Dhillon recalls Priya's narrow escape in the Congo in 1965, 'Priya and George Clay, a reporter with *NBC*, were walking along a road into Stanleyville. Snipers opened fire and George was shot in the head. Priya was unharmed.' In Aden, a year later, Priya and a fellow photographer found themselves at gun point, threatened by an angry mob, and forced to talk their way out of possible execution.

Priya took risks, but it was always with the belief that there was a good story to find. 'He was not looking to

A youthful Daniel arap Moi holding a spear

Priya got his pictures, we covered the festivities and Smith's speech, drank some of rebel Rhodesia's sanctions-busting champagne, and had a good laugh about it all when we got back to the hotel.'

In December of 1964, Priya's photographs of Dr Paul Carlson, an American missionary executed by rebels in the Belgian Congo, appeared on the front pages of both

die young and have a good looking corpse. Far from it! He had a lot to look forward to,' says Randal. Priya had many ambitions, and one of them, to be a frontline photographer for *LIFE* magazine, had already been fulfilled. But he had also invested himself deeply in Kenya. He bought a house, and had plans to open his own photography studio, and his colleagues encouraged him to put together a collection of his best African photographs for publication.

The final assignment

Perhaps his most powerful pictures depict the human faces behind the Biafran War – child soldiers in military uniform standing to attention, their small, bright white shoes in perfect symmetry, or his picture of stern faced female recruits in training, holding wooden rifles to their shoulders and marching in unison. In one of Priya's most haunting photographs, a wounded Nigerian soldier stares directly into the camera, hands clasped together in prayer while he is borne away on a stretcher.

Nowhere was Priya's burning desire to use his photographic talents more poignantly expressed than in his coverage of the Biafran civil war in Nigeria. 'Priya charted Biafra's tragic course — from the exultant independence declared by Ibo tribesmen to the stark horror of their starving children caught in the savagery of civil war,' wrote *LIFE* publisher James R Shepley. He returned again and again to Biafra and, like many photojournalists covering human suffering, he was 'emotionally torn to pieces' by what he saw. Yet week after week he shot pictures of the tragedy and always asked, agonized, 'Why can't the world understand?'

In October 1968, Priya rushed back to Biafra. He wanted to make one more trip to the front line, hoping to capture what many believed to be the first movements towards peace in the region. For days, Priya and his close friend, *CBS* correspondent Morley Safer, camped at Lagos airport before they finally hitched a ride to the Biafran battle zone on a decrepit DC-4. Near the town of Owerri, Priya set out on foot with a convoy of Nigerian Federal Troops. Along with Safer and a group of four journalists, he went looking for pictures.

On that humid morning, the convoy of soldiers and journalists came under a surprise ambush from Biafran rebels. Under a hail of gunfire, Priya had been hit in the arm and back. Safer crawled on the ground, dragging Priya's body to safety, but he died just before they reached an aid station. Two days later, Priya's elder brother, Ved Ramrakha, and his cousin, Anil Vidyarthi, travelled to Nigeria and brought Priya's body back to Nairobi.

Though Priya was only 33 years old when he died, he lived a life too passionate and rich for it to be remembered simply for its brevity. Morley Safer remembered Priya as one of very few photographers who possessed, 'the eye, the instinct, and the quickness of action to capture the moment.' Priya's work is testament to his dedication as both African photojournalist and historian of his time. Unquestionably, he had the talent and humility to allow his photographs to speak for him, and his pictures capture the vision of a remarkable man who expressed his quiet sensitivity, and his love for Africa, from behind the camera lens.

Source: AwaaZ, Issue 2 2005.

RASHID DIWAN
Writer

I was born in 1949 in Nairobi, Kenya. My parents came from British India, now Sialkot in Pakistan, during the 1930s. I went to Park Road Primary School and then to G N Secondary School both in Nairobi, but I did not complete my secondary education. I was inspired by cameramen like Akhtar Hussain and Mohinder Dhillon and ended up as a dark room assistant at Halle Studios. It belonged to Mohinder and was my stepping stone to the world of photo journalism.

Mohinder could not escape my deep enthusiasm for photography and took a lot of interest in training me in

RASHID DIWAN

still photography and cine coverage for TV news which was my passion. I remember one day Mohinder just gave me a cine camera and told me: 'today you are shooting for ITN'. I had a lot of competition from other cameramen but I kept on struggling and with the help of Mohinder's wife, Ambi, I was sent on various assignments and I quickly gained considerable experience. Still struggling against favoured cameramen, I got frustrated and with Mohinder's blessings joined Mohamed Amin who had recently been deported from Tanzania and was looking

for assistants. I jumped at the opportunity and worked for him as an 'all-rounder'. I enjoyed working tremendously for both Africapix and Camerapix.

One of the experiences that comes to mind is when I was working for Amin and we were covering the East African Safari and were getting some fantastic pictures. While waiting for the cars at one point we were brutally attacked by thousands of bees which stung us mercilessly. Azhar Chaudhry was with us and as he had a prosthetic leg he could not run and fell. We tried to help him but the bees were all over us and Azhar could not get up . . . we had no choice but to run leaving our jackets on him so that he was protected, and look for help. Luckily some farmers came by in a car and we went back and collected Azhar who was foaming from his mouth. One of the farmers took us to his house and gave each of us an anti venom injection and later drove us back to Nairobi. The next day we had our faces and hands swollen with the stings!

Another time, when I was still working for Amin, we went to Kigali in Rwanda to film the mercenaries and we got exclusive footage in the camp where only we were allowed in. We spent three weeks with the Maasai making a documentary on their lives, got arrested in Busia filming Kenyans being expelled from Uganda, filmed game cropping in Tanzania, Tom Mboya's funeral, etc.

Kenya was by then ruthlessly 'Africanising'; my father had a butchery and the landlord wanted to take over the shop but my father resisted whereupon he was deported from Kenya to the UK. Naturally we left with him. I was offered a job by the BBC in Scotland but this meant me moving away from my family. I declined and ended up in our family business. Later I started my own wholesale business selling fashion accessories, screen printing and

embroidery. After 35 years in this business I handed it over to my employees and walked away into the life of retirement which I am enjoying.

My passion for photography is still ablaze but more as a hobby than a profession. I personally feel that this interest in photography has stimulated my imagination and creativity which, to date, has been a great asset to me.

SATWANT MATHAROO
Writer

My parents came to Kenya from the Punjab, India, my father and his brother were in the building trade. BISHEN SINGH ROAD was named after my father's brother. The locality of this road was in front of our family house in Pangani/Park Road area, very near to Forest Road.

I was born in Nairobi in1942. My education was at the City Primary School and later at the Eastleigh Secondary School. Apart from schooling, my childhood memories are of playing cricket and hockey, I was a member of the 21st Nairobi Scout troop. Manjeet Dhillon, Mohinder Dhillon's brother, was a Queen Scout and head prefect at Eastleigh Secondary School.

After leaving school in 1958, I joined Halle Studio owned by Mohinder Dhillon, Nairobi, where I learned photography, that included black and white developing and printing. In 1959 I moved to Dar-es-salaam and was the first Indian to be employed as a staff photographer in the editorial section of the *Tanganyika Standard* Newspaper. At the *Standard,* I photographed all kinds of news events, sports, visiting dignitaries, the proclamation of Tanganyika's self-rule and finally independence in 1961. I also photographed the funeral of the Sultan of Zanzibar and Belgian refugees arriving into Dar-es-

Agricultural Show Kenya, 1962

A wheel flying off from a car crash at the Nakuru Race circuit
narrowly missing an official

Kenyatta 1963 at pre-election rally in Eldoret

Princess Anne with a cub at the Nairobi National Park's Animal
Orphanage during her visit to Kenya in 1971

SATWANT MATHAROO

salaam after fleeing from the Congo. My mentor was my older brother Mohinder Singh Matharoo who was the chief photographer for the Tanganyika Government.

In 1962 I moved back to Kenya and joined Africapix, a picture news agency representing ITN, BBC, Pathenews, Associated Press, United Press international, CBC & CBS. At Africapix I photographed and filmed many hard news stories including the bloody Zanzibar revolution; the Kenya Army mutiny at Lanet; plane crashes; ferryboat accidents; mercenaries in Bukavu (Congo)

and Somali 'shifta' attacks. I photographed the Born Free lions, Elsa and Boy; a spear making tribe in Tot-Tambach region; Maasai drawing blood from cows; released Mau Mau freedom fighters; bomb disposal exercises; a rain forest fire on Mt. Kilimanjaro; flamingoes dying on Lake Magadi; the plight of white farmers selling out and the Asian Exodus; Tom Mboya's funeral and Kenya's Olympic Gold Medal winners.

From 1959 to 1971, I photographed the East African Safari Rally including the famous win by the 'Flying Sikh' brothers Joginder Singh and Jaswant Singh in Volvo PV544.

Like many international photojournalists, I too have been subjected to personal violence, notably once in Uganda. As I entered Mulago Hospital where President Obote was hospitalised after the failed attempt to assassinate him, five plain clothed security bodyguards beat me with rifle butts and kicks. I too was hospitalised at the same hospital and the camera equipment was trashed to pieces.

In 1972, I moved to the UK. Although a news photographer at heart, but with growing family I changed direction and found myself working in a couple of highly successful commercial and industrial photographic firms. I also ran a Video Cine wedding and photographic business. I am a former member of the British Institute of Professional Photography. At the 1990 Photokina in Cologne, Germany, I was awarded a fast film loading certificate on a Hasselblad Camera film magazine.

1996 saw us move to Vancouver, Canada. Here I started my own wedding and commercial photography business and teamed up with local photo studios on a part-time basis. I have also been a former member of the Professional Photographers Association of British

Columbia. Am semi-retired now but the photography passion is still in my blood, be it a rainbow, ice fields or the 100-year old Sikh marathon runner Fauja Singh, whose picture running here in Surrey, Vancouver was supplied to a Kenyan publication through my colleague Mohinder Dhillon.

SHASHI VASANI (1934-1967)
By Chandu Vasani (brother)

SHASHI VASANI

Shashi Vasani was born in Thika in 1934 where he did his schooling and assisted in his father's photography and dark room. He opened studios in Mwanza and Machakos before turning his attention to news pictures. The Aga Khan's East African Newspapers (Nation Series) Ltd launched *Taifa* in April, 1959 and Shashi joined John Keen, W W Awori and others on the staff. A year later he moved over to the newly born *Daily Nation* and rose to become its Chief Photographer – a post he held until his sudden death from a cardiac arrest in 1967 at the age of 33.

SELECTION OF CAMERAS USED IN PRE-INDEPENDENT KENYA

Credit :Satwant Chana HSC, Director,
Africolour Labs Ltd., Nairobi

ADMIRA 16A ELECTRIC

EXAKTA MODEL CAMERA, GERMANY

GANDOLFI

Gandolfi is a British small craftsman-type operation who have made large format cameras in the traditional style using wood and brass for many years. Recently they have begun making more modern versions, still large format but using newer materials and techniques, although the traditional cameras are still made as well. They are one of the oldest camera makers still in existence. Gandolfi was founded by Louis Gandolfi in 1885, the last brother, Arthur, died in 1993.

(Photo courtesy Chandu Vasani)

HASSLEBLAD

LEICA

The name Leica is a combination of the first three letters of Ernst Leitz surname and the first two from the word camera; lei-ca. It was originally built in 1913 by HYPERLINK "https://en.wikipedia.org/wiki/Oskar_Barnack"Oskar Barnack who conceived the Leica as a small camera that produced a small negative. It transports the film horizontally and was refined to include a large viewfinder with several framelines and had a functional combination of circular dials and square windows.

PENTACON SIX MM FILM CAMERA

The Pentacon Six were cameras made in the former East German Democratic Republic from the late 1950s to 1990. A professional camera with many accessories and lenses, the bayonet mount and the design of the camera were copied inside and outside the Warsaw Pact countries.

PENTAX

The name 'Pentax' was originally a registered trademark of the East German VEB Zeiss Ikon but, as all Germans patents were annulled with the country's defeat, the name 'Pentax' was taken by the Asahi Optical company in 1957. Since then the company has been primarily known for its photographic products, distributed under the name 'Asahi Pentax'. The company was renamed Pentax Corporation in 2002.

THE NEW AUTOMATIC PENTAX K2DMD.

The fascination of motor drive.
At two shots a second, your film consumption (and costs) can be fantastic . . . but the action you'll be capturing will be even more fantastic. A left jab, a steal at second, a photo finish . . . the potential is enormous. The integral intervalometer lets you shoot at two frames per second, one frame per second, one frame every two seconds — or you can shoot single frames. You can set an exposure counter that will let you preprogram to shoot a set number of frames, and there's a remote control terminal that will allow remote triggering or a time-lapse timer. Potential . . . and more potential.

ROLLEIFLEX mm
German made film camera

Rolleiflex is the name of a long-running and diverse line of high-end cameras originally made in Germany in 1929. These medium format twin lens reflex (TLR) cameras were notable for their exceptional build quality, compact size, modest weight, superior optics, durable, simple, reliable mechanics and bright viewfinders. They were popular and widely imitated.

OTHER CAMERAS

KONICA

CANON

NIKON

OLYMPUS

MINOLTA

GAGGING THE MESSENGER
Security Risks and Threats to Kenyan Journalists

I would rather have a completely free press with all the dangers involved in the wrong use of that freedom than a suppressed or regulated press - Pandit Jawaharlal Nehru

A survey released on 3 May, 2013, World Press Freedom Day, shattered the generally held view of journalism as a glamorous and alluring profession. Peter Mwaura, writing in the *Saturday Nation* of the following day stated that, 'almost to a man, Kenyan journalists face security risks and threats'. His article makes chilling reading, he writes:

'The survey documents case studies of journalists who have been attacked and harassed by state authorities and political goons. It states that over 90 per cent of journalists have been threatened at least once in their career, more than half (53.9 per cent) been threatened at least twice and almost 20 per cent more than five times.

"That over half of the respondents reported receiving threats more than once … confirms that journalists are increasingly working in a hostile environment in Kenya. Threats to the media have a chilling effect not only on the physical safety, but more importantly, on freedom of expression," says the survey titled "Safety and protection of Kenya journalists: Is it common sense or common cents?"

The survey, which covered all of the country's 47 counties, is the first of its kind in Kenya. It was funded by the Hivos Regional Office of East Africa and supervised by the Media Council of Kenya.
The findings are based on the responses of the 282 journalists out of the 307 interviewed, representing a 91.9 per cent response rate. Over 40 per cent said that the threats came from politicians while another 34 per cent indicated the threats came from organised groups. Eight per cent said they faced threats from business people, while three said they were threatened by religious groups.

Threats from politicians and political goons are the biggest threats to journalists, especially during elections. Other high risk assignments are related to corruption, land and issues relating to local leaders. Most of the threats come in the form of threatening telephone calls, threatening messages, trailing by unknown people and actual bodily harm. The survey also states that some journalists – and this is the first time it is being said publicly – have disappeared.

The findings are bold, and perhaps surprising. They are also critical of media owners and journalism training institutions. Forty-eight per cent of the respondents failed to report threats on account of no action was taken in the past despite reporting, while 23 per cent felt their employer or editor was the source of the threat.

Another interesting finding is that only 3.2 per cent of the journalists said they knew the laws on freedom of expression and only 2.5 per cent knew about the Code of Conduct for the Practice of Journalism in Kenya and the Media Act.

The lead researcher, John Gachie, a media consultant and trainer, has delivered a document that increases our knowledge and awareness of a problem that many thought was only applicable to such countries as Somalia, Cameroon, Gambia, Guinea-Bissau and Syria.'

The 2013 figures for journalists world-wide who have been persecuted in the line of duty were computed by *Reporters Without Borders* as follows:
- 71 journalists killed
- 826 journalists arrested
- 2160 journalists threatened or physically attacked
- 87 journalists kidnapped
- 77 journalists who fled their country
- 6 media assistants killed
- 39 netizens and citizen-journalists killed
- 127 bloggers and netizens arrested

These disturbing and very distressful revelations were made in 2013 but this does not mean that the dangers facing journalists are recent in origin; though no doubt they have got steadily worse in the fifty years of our so-called independence.

The first journalist to be charged with sedition in Kenya
From the very brief writings of the South Asian journalists (and in one case even of a typesetter) I have learnt of actual deportation and 'silent' pressures which forced journalists into exile and printing presses to be raided.

The very first journalist in Kenya's history to be jailed and fined for sedition was G L Vidyarthi. Haroon Ahmed and Natwarlal Amlani followed suit. They were the victims of colonial displeasure for exposing, to a national and international public, some of the injustices and machinations of British rule in Kenya. The practice of slapping on hefty fines on some flimsy excuse and so forcing a newspaper to close down was a common tactic of the government then.

In April of 1945 Vidyarthi was convicted for sedition on two separate occasions. His first sentence earned him a one hundred pound fine. G L had published an article which exposed the injustice where wounded African soldiers returned penniless to Kenya; whereas their white counterparts were rewarded with land and property throughout the country.

The second sedition charge was earned after the *Colonial Times*, on 22 December, 1945, published a letter written by a W L Sohan in which he asserted that the British treatment of Indians in India was comparable to the atrocities against the inmates of the German and Polish concentration camps. Another charge was made against an article published on 28 July in the Gujarati section in which 'the British were admonished for expropriating African lands for their own use'.

The Resident Magistrate, R A Campbell, ordered four months' rigorous imprisonment for Vidyarthi and Sohan in the first case. On the second, he imposed a fine of 1000 pounds or three months' hard labour on Vidyarthi, and a fine of 200 pounds or one month's hard labour on Vanshi Dar, the proprietor. After his release, Sohan travelled to India but, in April 1947, was denied a re-entry permit. In spite of spirited attempts by the Indian community to facilitate his return, Sohan was never allowed back into Kenya.

Around 1946, the owner and editor of *Mumenyereri*, Henry Muoria, and the Indian proprietor of the printing workshop that published his paper, H G Patel, appeared in a Nairobi court to defend themselves against a charge of sedition.

In January 1947, 15,000 African workers went on strike in Mombasa. The *Daily Chronicle* carried a leaked government document claiming that the police had instructions to fire on the workers. Haroon Ahmed, the editor, was arrested and charged with making an alarmist statement and sentenced to six months imprisonment

with hard labour. The publisher, Natwarlal Amlani, went to prison for three months also with hard labour. They had been given the information by Gurwand Sheth, a civil servant, but Haroon refused to divulge his source in court.

The E A Indian National Congress raises the alarm

In its 19th session held in Mombasa on 20, 21 and 22 August, 1948, under the presidentship of D D Puri, the following resolution was tabled: 'The session also expresses alarm at the growing number of prosecutions against the Indian and African press and considers this as a direct challenge to the freedom of the press.' It was proposed by R P Joshi, seconded by P N Mehta and supported by Joseph Kathiki.

In the 20th session held in Eldoret on 5, 6 and 7 August, 1950, the resolution stated: 'This 20th Session of the East African Indian National Congress views with grave alarm the recent legislation providing for drastic penalties by way of confiscation of printing machinery, etc., of newspapers and feels that such legislation endangers the freedom of the Press. It further feels that this legislation giving wide powers to the Courts is unwarranted and should be repealed.

In order to maintain good relations with the Press, this Congress considers that the Government should set up a Press Advisory Committee to advise Government on matters affecting the freedom of the Press generally with members thereon drawn from journalists of all sections of the Press. It further calls upon the Indian Members of the Legislative Council in co-operation with the members of other races to make representation to Government with a view to such action.' The resolution was moved by M V Dave, seconded by Baldev Moolraj and passed unanimously.

In 1952, the *Daily Chronicle* was sold after the Colonial Government had charged it with about 50 cases of libel and European firms had withdrawn their advertisements in the paper.

Michael I Fernandes wrote an interesting column for the *Daily Chronicle* under a nom-de-plume. In the early 1950s when the *Chronicle* came under a more conservative ownership, he was appointed as editor. In the Government's view, however, the paper was still too extreme and Fernandes was declared *persona non grata* and had to leave the country. Nelson Nunes, a one-time journalist with the *Citizen* newspaper, states that 'Michael moved to Tanganyika and had to keep his border crossing into Kenya secret from the Kenyan authorities'.

When the *Daily Chronicle* was bought out by more conservative forces in 1952, its intrepid editor, **DK Sharda**, started his own paper, the *Tribune*. Sixteen months later the colonial authorities revoked the license for his press. He then continued to cyclostyle the *Tribune* on a small multigraph machine but further restrictions were placed on him. D K then immigrated to India, it is not clear whether he was deported or it was a case of disheartenment.

Post-independence, it was our neighbouring country Uganda which deported a journalist – of course no reason was given. **Billy Chibber** was posted in Kampala, working as a foreign correspondent for the Kenyan *Daily Nation* newspaper and *The Hindustan Times* and reported on policy and events in post-independence Uganda. In 1966 he was served with a deportation order which deemed him to be an 'undesirable immigrant' and given 24 hours to leave the country. On account of holding a British passport, he was ordered to return to Britain despite being a permanent resident of Nairobi.

But the British Secretary of State demanded to know the reason why he was being deported before allowing him entry onto their shores. George Githii, Editor of the *Daily Nation*, appealed to President Jomo Kenyatta who stepped in to 'save' the situation - he took Chibber in and thereby breached an East African agreement whereby a person deported from one country could not enter any of the two other territories. Did he take such a grave action in order to 'help' Chibber? Unlikely. More probable was a desire to extricate his friend, President Obote, from a sticky jam. Back in Nairobi and at the *Nation*, Chibber was kept 'incognito' writing inconsequential pieces which required no byline.

In 1966 **Pranlal Sheth**, Jaramogi Odinga's right hand man, together with several other South Asians was deported. Pranlal was a Kenya citizen yet he was put on a plane to India. In President Jomo Kenyatta's own words, 'because he was the brains behind KPU (Kenya Peoples Union). In the following year **Ghulam Mohiyuddin Paracha**, a typesetter working with Vidyarthi's Colourprint press in Nairobi was deported to Pakistan and had his citizenship revoked in 1967. Again no reason was given. Could it have been because the Vidyarthis printed Odinga's KPU leaflets, campaign materials, etc.? Soon Odinga himself was to be detained and the KPU banned. Paracha had previously served with Pio Gama Pinto at the Pan African press.

Unfortunately, some might argue that post-independent Kenya has treated the issue of press freedom in a reactionary fashion that is not remarkably different to experiences under colonial rule. G L's sons and their printing press have suffered post-independence under similar circumstances that had afflicted the Colonial Printing Works. In March of 1988 *Beyond* magazine, a Christian publication, was banned and thousands of copies were found and destroyed.

The Vidyarthi brothers have continued the tradition of their father in being 'Frank, Free and Fearless'. During Moi's dictatorship their press, **Colourprint,** printed Salim Lone's *Viva* magazine, Pius Nyamora's *Society,* Njehu Gatabaki's *Finance,* Bedan Mbugua's *Beyond* and other writings critical of the regime. And they have paid the price with several police raids to vandalise their presses and confiscate the publications.

In January of 1994 the press was raided at night by two hundred armed policemen who confiscated 15,000 copies of an opposition publication. In April of 1995 the printing press was once again raided, copies of *Finance* magazine confiscated, and several machines were disabled. **Anil Vidyarthi**, Girdhari Lal's second born son was tried for sedition in a case that lasted two years at the High Court of Kenya. He was acquitted after the sedition law was repealed from the Constitution and Kenyans looked towards a future free from the laws of censorship. It proved to be a false dawn, however. In 1996 Colourprint was the victim of an arson attack when almost the entire press was fire-bombed. The mysterious circumstances of the matter were investigated but to this day information surrounding the motives and perpetrators of the crime remains inconclusive. Ironically, G L Vidyarthi was the first journalist in Kenya to be arrested on a charge of sedition and his son, Anil, was the last.

'**Jawaharlal Joel Joachim Rodrigues** was a journo's journo,' writes Cyprian Fernandes. Hilary Ng'weno, the *Nation's* first African editor-in-chief says Joe is Kenya's finest editor to date. He describes him as, 'the quintessential newspaperman. An accomplished reporter, a skilled sub-editor, a dab hand at design, he had been the Nation's backbone as managing editor . . . he was the man who made the paper happen'. Philip Ochieng calls him 'the backbone of the *Nation'*. Yet he was ordered to resign by Sir Eboo Pirbhai, the Aga Khan's

representative in East Africa, and he was warned that he was in personal danger. Of course no reason was given. Was it Africanisation, or had he been too tolerant of Israel and so unsettled the Aga Khan's Islamic bias? Or was he just a victim of the running battles between the government and the media? In 1981 he, together with Joe Kadhi, Pius Nyamora and others, spent a week in police cells for having described an unsigned letter from the KANU headquarters as 'anonymous'.

Pio Gama Pinto, the patriotic journalist, editor of *PanAfrica* and several other papers, was assassinated. Pranlal Sheth, one-time journalist was deported and **Chander Mehra** of the *Nation* was declared a prohibited immigrant, perhaps he says, 'for telling the truth'. **Karim Hudani,** also of the *Nation* was constantly harassed and received threats over his support of Jaramogi Odinga and the Arab League vis a vis Israel, and his criticism of the Africanisation programme. In 1979 he applied for, and was granted, political asylum in the UK after he had been arrested and charged with sedition, only to have the charges dropped.

The case of **Salim Lone** is probably the most infamous of all. He had already been rejected by the *Sunday Post* and the *Nation* for his independent political line and his pro-Palestine stand. He was editor of *Viva* magazine in 1982 when, just two months before the coup, he was tipped off that the CID were on his trail. He went into exile but in 1986 was persuaded by Hon. Elijah Mwangale, Kenya's Minister for Foreign Affairs, to return to his home country which needed his exceptional talents. Salim returned only to be arrested again, thrown into the Nyayo torture chambers, have his Kenya passport revoked and be forced into exile back to the USA. He returned after Kenya's Second Liberation in 2002 and took up a low key political role becoming in time, Raila Odinga's right-hand man. Following the 2013 General Elections, he and his wife Pat left suddenly, virtually overnight, seemingly never to return.

Cyprian Fernandes, the *Nation's* intrepid investigator and contact with the politicians of the time, had to flee the country when his wife was informed that 'there is a bullet with his name on it'. He had first-hand experience of the 'gagging' phenomenon and this is what he has to say:

'Death threats to journalists and other prominent people were fairly common place in Nairobi, Kenya during the late 1960s until my departure in 1974. It was also pretty common to be picked up by the dreaded Special Branch for interrogation and/or deportation. As a political journalist in Kenya, you had to walk the political tightrope with the precision of a brain surgeon. You lived with fear of deportation every day to the point it became second skin and you thought nothing of it. To survive one placed his or her faith in the truth, as we had been told on the masthead of the *Daily Nation*: The Truth Shall Make You Free. Problem was publication of the truth more often than not resulted in the worst of fates. The truth, in fact, made a prisoner of you, rather than set you free. Also, there were not too many editors who were brave enough to publish. If one fell through the cracks, watch out. For example, if you exposed the President, Jomo Kenyatta and his Kikuyu cronies, for exploiting a loop hole in the Constitution and freely sharing out Crown Land, at the least you would be deported (providing the British High Commission or your representative diplomatic was aware). If you were a Kenyan, the chances are that you would be dead.

The assassinations of Tom Mboya, Pio Gama Pinto, J M Kariuki and Robert Ouko are tangent reminders.

So a death threat is not to be taken lightly anywhere in Africa, or anywhere else in the world for that matter. The holocaust and atrocities of the ilk virtually in every corner of the world loom large in the mind.

In the absence of a story of that magnitude, I cannot recall any journalists being killed, but plenty being deported, for indiscretions of revealing the truth or being associated with digging up the truth such as the Mau Mau oathing ceremonies post-independence or "seen" to be supporting the Luo opposition leader Jaramogi Oginga Odinga. There were rare moments when ministers were exposed for graft and corruption, but these were indeed rare.

On the other hand, as far as the world knew, thanks to friendly nations with interests such as Britain and the US, Kenya was cited as a great example of an emerging African country. It was to a large extent at peace with itself, even though in the broadest of terms, a single party administration is no substitute for democracy. However, multiracialism of sorts was on view, tourists thronged in their thousands as did billions in foreign aid. To the outside world, mainly by the tourist telegraph, Kenya was idyllic.

The reality was quite different; I could not get my best stories published. Forget publish; I could not even talk about them to my fellow journalists or other people. The late Boaz Omori, Editor, *Daily Nation*, was for me the gentlest of souls you could ever meet. He had been promoted over the head of the most professional Joe Rodrigues. Boaz got the job because he was a black Kenyan and he was unlikely to cause any waves. For that matter, neither was Rodrigues (a brown skinned Kenyan), but Rodrigues would be un-bending on principle. On one occasion, after I had handed in a story, Boaz looked

at me, with that unique super large smile lighting his face, and asked: Are you trying to get us both killed?'

Robert G Gregory, in his book *Quest for Equality* writes: 'Because of their anti-European stance, the Asian newspapers, like those everywhere in a relatively free economy, could not endure for long merely on the basis of sales. Survival was hazardous not only for financial reasons, but also because of government intervention. All the editors and printers who were interested in reform encountered stiff opposition and repression from a colonial administration that was intolerant of criticism. Perhaps it is true, as the historian Felice Carter has stated, that the Kenya government, when considered in a colonial context or in the world scene, permitted a remarkable freedom to the press. The number of editors and printers, Asian and African, however, who in Kenya or elsewhere in East Africa were deported, fined or imprisoned, who lost their licences or were ordered to stop publication, or whose presses were shut down is considerable. The South Asian journalists were repressed despite the fact that none of them expressly condoned or advocated violence. Strongly influenced by Gandhi, they called at most for non-violent civil disobedience.'

Most recently, new legislation has emerged that once again raises questions regarding the freedom of the press in Kenya. Even after the dictatorship ended, freedom of expression has remained a thorny issue for the government.

Victor Bwire, Deputy CEO and Programmes Manager of the Media Council of Kenya, wrote in 2013: 'A new study has revealed that the working environment for journalists and media workers in Kenya is increasingly becoming hostile with 91 percent of journalists working for local media houses indicating having faced security threats in the course of their work. Among the reasons cited as major challenges facing journalists in Kenya is lack of or inadequate facilitation for journalists while in the course of duty, poor pay and wanting working conditions, working under managers who were not trained journalists, and, in some extreme cases, taking instructions from unethical editors.'

Sources: *The Media Observer, April-June, 2013*
Seidenberg, Dana, 1983
Gregory, Robert G, 1993
Saturday Nation, 4 May, 2013
Patel, Zarina, 2006
The Golden Years
The Murumbi Trust, 2015

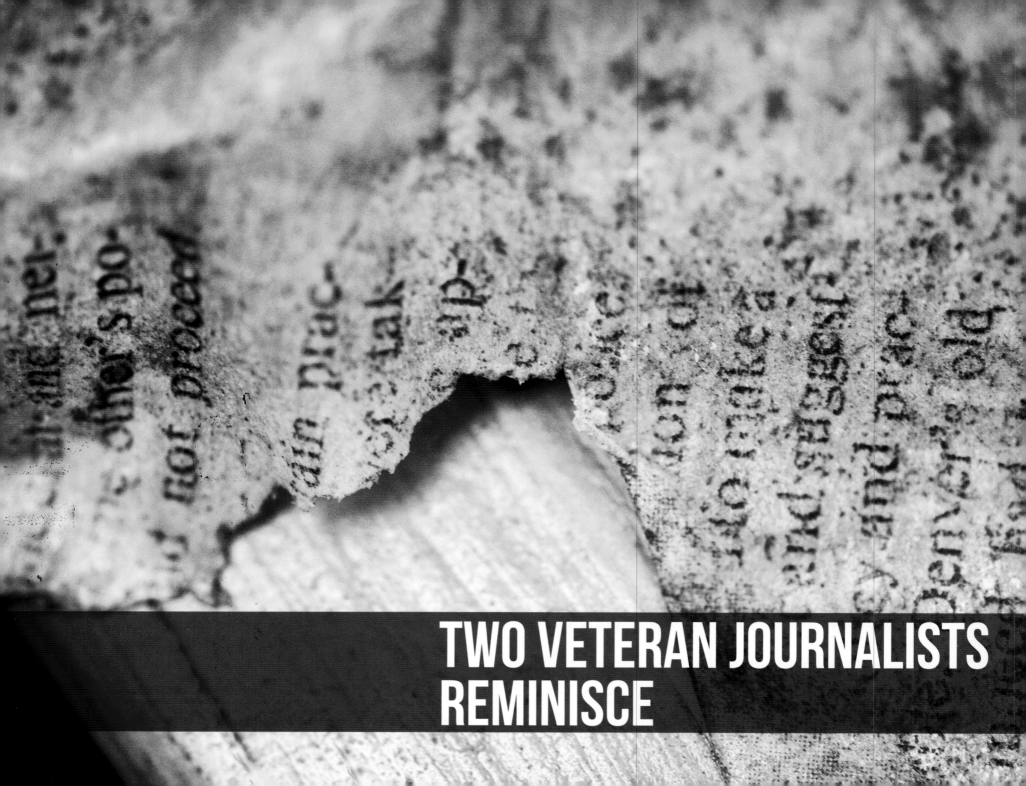

TWO VETERAN JOURNALISTS REMINISCE

HILARY BONIFACE NG'WENO

Hilary Ng'weno, born in 1938 in Nairobi, attended Harvard University in the USA where he graduated with a degree in nuclear physics, but made his career in journalism. In 1962, he joined the *Daily Nation* as a reporter, ninety per cent of the staff was Britons, the rest were South Asians. Africans were all in the Kiswahili language *Taifa*, the Nation Group's first newspaper. Earning a ridiculous salary even as a trainee; Hilary left after nine months and joined Esso in PR.

1964 was the year of the coup in Zanzibar and the rebellion in the newly independent Tanzanian and Ugandan armies; the *Nation* and *East African Standard* newspapers were subsequently banned in Tanzania. Hilary received a call from Michael Curtis, the founding CEO of the Nation Group, inviting him to join the Nation as editor-in-chief and take over from John Bierman, the founding editor.

'I was not trained for the job,' says Hilary, 'but clearly they were looking for a fall guy if anything was to happen to their newspaper.' He took the job, as the first African editor-in-chief of the *Daily Nation*, provided he was in full control of what went on. He was assured of this by the Aga Khan whom he met personally in Paris; the only condition was that the paper should not publish anything against any religion.

At the age of 25, Hilary concentrated on writing the editorials making no changes in the content, busy learning the ropes. After eight months he 'wanted to make an impact, not just be used'. But immediately this led to tensions and after eighteen months on the job, Hilary quit. 'My employers were my trainers ..... my tension should have been with the politicians, not my employers', he states.

'Whites had been taken hostage in the Congo and Kenyatta had been asked to mediate,' Hilary explains. 'He starts and the next thing is the USA and Belgians fly in and rescue the hostages. Kenyatta is furious – obviously they just used him to make their own plans and were not serious. The rescue is world news but Achieng Oneko, Kenya's Minister of Information, instructs Hilary not to run the story. Curtis is MD and says the same. The *Standard* too has decided not to run the story. 'I refused to comply . . . I asked the Government to give its reaction and published the story on the front page,' says Hilary. 'I realized then that I was completely on my own and that I was working for an organization that was much bigger than the paper . . . one that was not protecting journalism. There was no support for my views or concerns . . . I was there only as a token image.' Hilary could not stand the racist and patronizing attitude. 'I was an African in an African country but things had to be done their way,' he protested.

He decided to do things on his own and became a columnist for the *Newsweek* and *Guardian* and after eight years, started his own. In 1973, together with artist Terry Hirst and Oscar Festus, he founded *Joe*, a comic magazine that focussed on humorous political satire and circulated in many parts of Africa until the late seventies when its publication ceased. In 1975, Hilary founded *The Weekly Review*, a journal of political news, commentary and analysis followed in 1977 by The *Nairobi Times*, a Sunday newspaper that later became a daily. Because the advertising community was still controlled by foreigners, it tended to favour the foreign owned publications like the *Nation* and *Standard*. Advertisers were also not too keen to deal with publications that were likely to stir the wrath of the government with inflammatory political reports.

HILARY BONIFACE NG'WENO

Nevertheless, *The Weekly Review* went on to dominate the weekly news scene for 24 years until May 17, 1999, becoming one of Africa's best news magazines. Due to diminishing revenue from advertising sales, Hilary, sold *The Nairobi Times* in 1983 to KANU, Kenya's then ruling party. The paper was renamed *The Kenya Times*, but its popularity suffered as it was seen to be the mouthpiece of an oppressive dictatorship. *The Kenya Times* wound up in July 2010.

Hilary diversified his media empire which included other periodicals such as *The Financial Review, The Industrial Review* and *Rainbow*, a monthly children's magazine. His publishing company, Stellascope, was acquired by KANU when the latter purchased *The Nairobi Times*. Hilary then moved on to television broadcasting and penned two works of fiction. He is currently the Managing Director of Kenya History & Biographies Co. Ltd. His 14 half-hour documentary based on the political course of Kenya from pre-1963 to 2007 is a masterpiece of historical chronology.

The motivation for his present work seems to arise from his concern that 'present day journos are young and are very unaware, not even interested in, past history. Makhan Singh, Fitz with his connection to Kenyatta, mean nothing to them. It is not a conspiracy on the part of the Nation Group but rather the individuals . . . we need to remind them. I wanted to make documentaries about the journalists so I asked for the information but there was no interest'.

Journalism has to do with ideas impacting on society and Hilary highlights the importance of photo journalists, especially in today's non-reading culture. 'I can immediately tell this is a government photo because of its poor quality. Today's technology where the camera corrects itself is easier but then Mohamed Amin, Mohinder Dhillon and others had to make their own corrections. They had to go by looking. The world picked out their pictures because of the quality. Amin, because of his interest in the news, its versatility. Pre and early post independence there were no African photojournos or media persons because of colonial restraints - it is Asians such as the Vidyarthis who publicized the fight for freedom.'

While recognizing that the present media has to deal with a much more complex situation, Hilary decried the low level of reporting. 'A simple rule of journalism is that the first or second para should tell the reader the whole story, the rest is elaboration. Often the latest news item gets reported with no reference to the earlier story.

In interviews no research is done with the result that simplistic, half-baked questions are asked instead of incisive questions counter posed with corrections and reminders . . . In the old days the main concern was government but today the main concern is industry, and advertisers rule. Commercial/financial/industrial power is greater than political power and the shareholders have to be pleased. And the values in journalism are totally different. The journalist of today is interested in music, in comedy - not the makers of a nation. Good editors and journos get recruited in large companies for PR where they get better pay. We don't have conglomerates where the paper can run at a loss'.

Hilary Ng'weno has served in many national and international organisations and in 1968, was awarded the John D Rockefeller III Award for his work in journalism as well as his involvement in nature conservation.

Source: Hilary Ng'weno, interviewed by Zarina Patel, 27 November 2012.

JOE KADHI

Joe Kadhi qualified from the International Press Institute as a journalist in 1962. The IPI was based in Nairobi's Royal Technical College which was initially built for the South Asian community, and is now the University of Nairobi. The founder and director was Sir Tom Hopkinson who, after the Institute closed in 1968, went on to start the school in Cardiff, UK with Frank Barton. Until then the British had held the view that journalism was an in-born talent and required no training, the USA on the other hand had developed schools of journalism in the eighteenth century. The school in the University of Wales has trained many well-known Kenyan journalists.

Independence was dawning and the nationalist movement needed to come out with a publication to mobilize the people and bring them together, KANU was more progressive than KADU – but the leaders had no time to write and had no experience of publishing. South Asians played a very important role in liberating Kenya, especially in the field of journalism. Margaret Kenyatta, under the care of Ambu and Lila Patel, was working as a book binder – during the Mau Mau Emergency days when Ambu Patel ran a small press in Mathare Valley for the publications of the Land and Freedom Army. In 1960, Pio Gama Pinto, who had worked on the *Daily Chronicle* and the *Colonial Times* prior to his detention, together with Jaramogi Odinga and James Gichuru, founded the KANU newspaper, *Sauti ya KANU*.

In 1962, following his first diploma, Joe Kadhi needed to do an internship and so he joined Tom Mboya's newspaper, *Mfanyakazi*, a bilingual mouthpiece of the Kenya Federation of Labour. Pinto found him there and said, 'You are working for a British stooge, an American spy, come and join the nationalists'. Kadhi did. He was employed by Pinto in the PanAfrican press and, at the age of 22, Kadhi became editor of *Sauti ya Kanu*. His colleagues were Henry Gathagira, Harun Muturi, Achieng Oneko and others.

Kadhi who joined the *Daily Nation* particularly mentions Kul Bhushan as a 'superb business writer . . . the Aga

Khan was very dissatisfied with the business pages until Kul took over. It was very unfortunate that the Nation's 50th anniversary supplement did not mention Kul, or for that matter Cyprian Fernandes or Alfred Araujo.' He rates Joe Rodrigues as 'the best editor-in-chief ever . . . he trained Africans, sent them to the University of Nairobi, USA and UK as full time members of staff with full salary. None of the white editors had ever tried this'.

Regarding Joe's abrupt and unexpected dismissal from the *Nation*, Kadhi points partly to envy – was he getting too close to the Aga Khan for the comfort of the Group chairman, Albert Ekirapa, an African! But Kadhi feels personally responsible for the dismissal as it was closely connected to his visit to the Middle East, including Israel, a visit that Joe had sanctioned. Kadhi had met with Anwar Sadat and Abba Eban, he admired the former as 'the only Arab leader who recognized Israel for the sake of peace'. But Naim Kadar, the Arab League Ambassador, wrote a long letter stating that Joe Rodrigues had sent Joe Kadhi on a mission to write against Muslims. Earlier, through Michael Curtis, the Aga Khan had decreed that all pro-Israel news had to be toned down. Kadhi was then not only the Assistant Group Managing Editor of the *Daily Nation* but was also very close to Charles Njonjo, so Joe Rodrigues became the sacrificial lamb. When leaving Rodrigues told Kadhi: 'I am going because of you but keep it up for the sake of freedom of expression.'

In 1990, Kadhi himself became a victim of 'higher powers'. In the July Saba Saba demonstrations the police had shot 13 Africans dead and the story was splashed world-wide. Then president Moi called Kadhi, as Managing Editor, to stop the story. Kadhi contacted Philip Ochieng at the *Kenya Times* who said: 'His Excellency has told me to call you re the same.' Ali Hafidh of the *Standard* too had side-lined the story.

Kadhi could not bring himself to tell the reporters to stop writing. 'They had been on the streets dodging blows and bullets, they had torn clothes and broken cameras, and they were enthusiastically writing the story. How could I tell them to stop?' he agonised. So he not only accepted the story, but splashed it on several pages with dramatic photographs and instructed the circulation manager to increase the print run. In his own words: 'That is how the *Nation* lost a Managing Editor and the University of Nairobi got a lecturer.' Kadhi was retired in September 1991.

Kadhi joined the University of Nairobi's School of Journalism as a lecturer and at present holds the same position in the United States International University and is a member of the Media Council. His main concern is the upliftment of the standards of journalism in Kenya. He emphasises the difference between 'professionalization', the legal aspect, and 'professionalism', the ethics of journalism and has co-authored, with Michael Kunczik, the book *Ethics in Journalism: A reader on their perception in the Third World.* He reminds us that only recently a 160-year old newspaper, the *News of the World,* was closed down on the issue of 'ethics'.

Kenya's Media Council is a statutory body and there is an underlying fear of government control or interference. 'This does not have to be so,' Kadhi maintains, and cites the example of India where the government finances the media council and yet the press is free. Many books are being written by scholars in India on professionalism – how you write a story, the ethics of it, the nuts & bolts of writing a story. 'Indians are perfecting the art of ethical principles which include participatory journalism in which subterfuge plays a big part,' he says. He has special praise for Tehelka.com, an Indian organisation known for its investigative journalism and exposure of

JOE KADHI

corruption. It maintains that subterfuge, that is getting a story in a clandestine manner, is not unethical as long as the end aim is to expose corruption, and the British have accepted this argument. The Americans have the oldest code of ethics, it was laid down by the American Society of Newspaper Editors (ASNE) in 1922 and states, among other clauses, that 'freedom of expression is not a gift, but a basic human right'.

Freedom of expression is useless without freedom of information and government is the biggest custodian of information. According to Kadhi, India has one of the best freedom of information acts in the world. 'People have a right to know if it is affecting their lives,' he claims. 'Section 79 of the old Constitution of Kenya made exceptions to freedom of expression, but in the new 2010 Constitution, articles 33, 34, 35 have freedom of expression and article 35 has freedom of information entrenched.'

Speaking to African journalists, Kadhi urged them to penetrate all arms of government and ensure that those in leadership positions were competent and honest. Where corruption and nepotism were found, they should be exposed. He encouraged them to participate in the formulation of laws that concern the Press. He said through negotiation, editors could lobby for security of tenure to cushion them against interference by media owners. The editors, he said, could then be bold enough to reject stories dictated by media owners.

Sources: Joe Kadhi, interviewed by Zarina Patel, 22 April 2013
Loughran, Gerard, 2010.

IN THE ERA OF NEO-LIBERALISM

Extracts from 'Statistics in the Media – Learning from Practice' by Karim Hirji

There is no such thing, at this date of the world's history, as an independent press. You know it and I know it. There is not one of you who dares to write your honest opinions, and if you did, you know beforehand that it would never appear in print. I am paid weekly for keeping my honest opinions out of the paper I am connected with. Others of you are paid similar salaries for similar things, and any of you who would be so foolish as to write honest opinions would be out on the streets looking for another job.

If I allowed my honest opinions to appear in one issue of my paper, before twenty-four hours my occupation would be gone. The business of the journalist is to destroy the truth; to lie outright; to pervert; to vilify; to fawn at the feet of mammon, and to sell the country for his daily bread. You know it and I know it and what folly is this toasting an independent press. We are the tools and vassals of the rich men behind the scenes. We are the jumping jacks, they pull the strings and we dance. Our talents, our possibilities and our lives are all the property of other men. We are intellectual prostitutes.

Shocking, almost scandalous, words especially when you consider that they were delivered as a toast before the prestigious New York Press Club. The speaker was none other than John Swinton, the former Chief of Staff at the *NEW YORK TIMES*. Swinton was called 'The Dean of His Profession' by other newsmen who admired him greatly; and he made this candid confession way back in 1953.

Sadly, this statement is as true today as it was then. India's first Prime Minister, Pandit Jawaharlal Nehru, once famously said: 'I would rather have a completely free press with all the dangers involved in the wrong use of that freedom than a suppressed or regulated press'. Yet, it was the same Nehru who introduced the first amendment to India's constitution to curtail press freedom. The issue of press censorship is deep rooted and ingrained in the governance system of the so-called 'democratic' structures.

Karim Hirji in his book *Statistics in the Media – Learning from Practice* out rightly declares that 'Pure objectivity is a myth'. He writes: 'Media are not socially neutral. They are confined by existent social and economic relationships. These relationships embody control over resources, wealth, power, and social institutions. They determine key decisions taken in society. They affect what social groups derive from health, education, leisure, police protection, tax policy and other societal services or functions. The operation and contents of the mass media by and large reflect and reinforce those relationships.

But societal relationships change, mostly slowly, at times rapidly. Some forces pull in one direction, other forces push in another direction. Contradictions driving the changes are expressed in the media. Openly or not, consciously or not, directly or otherwise, media take sides. Most defend the *status quo*, protect the rich and powerful, and mask reality. A few uphold the interests of ordinary people, consistently engender humanistic change, and function as venues of public enlightenment. And some flicker in between, here one moment, there the next, but frequently on the power side of the social divide.

The issue of the quality media reports is not merely a technical matter. It is also linked with the opposed tendencies – guardian of public interests or promoter of special interests – observed in the media. Alignment of one or the other impinges on the technical quality of the media. The relevance, type, transparency, selectivity and accuracy of statistics on major domains of society found in the media are also affected.'

A few pages later he states: 'In almost all the nations of the world, the bulk of the mass media, public and private, are wedded to the capitalist system and its basic ideological tenets. This influences the issues they focus on, how they are covered, and the issues that are sidelined or neglected. The structure of the existent economic system, at the national and international levels is taken as an eternal fact of life. No alternative exists. You can question the workings of the system, point out the rivalries, disagree on short term measures, occasionally castigate one group of capitalists like the bankers, or criticize the capitalists from China. But you do not question the foundation of capitalism, or the basic tenets of the neo-liberal economic theory.

Competition, investments, entrepreneurship, economic liberalization, privatisation, free trade, market economy, intellectual property, private-public partnership, donor funds: these are the buzz words for economic progress. Nationalization, state control, integrated economic planning, price and rent control, equality and fair distribution of income, living wage, workers management, cooperative and state farms, control of currency flows and repatriation of profits, self-reliance to confront economic domination, free health care and education, guaranteed employment, food self-sufficiency, intermediate technology, tackling unequal exchange and dependency – these are considered outmoded ideas that block economic progress.

Systemic bias appears in usage of words like socialism and communism. Thus, we read that the problems of education or agriculture in Tanzania have their roots in the previous policy of socialism. If you say that, you have said it all. No more questions are asked. But why does the ordinary person in Tanzania face exactly the same set of problems as the ordinary person in Malawi despite the curious fact that Julius Kambarage Nyerere was an avowed socialist and Hastings Kamuzu Banda, a rabid anti-communist? That mystery is not explored under this shallow scheme of explaining local and global affairs and trends.

African academics and the media need to break away from economic illusions fostered by "the donors". They should cease their total reliance on mainstream economics. This is a pseudo-science that brands suffering imposed on millions as economic reform. Ejecting people from work, cutting old age pensions, and depriving health care to children is called austerity. Tens of thousands of empty houses together with expanding homeless numbers on the street is just the way the market works. It masquerades as a science but serves bankers, bureaucrats and billionaires. It provides but little for the common people, especially in Africa. For the African economies it serves to perpetuate high unemployment, rural impoverishment, food insecurity, structural dependency, high level corruption, and exploitation by multinational corporations. In current parlance those who promote the dominant world-view are objective journalists. Their systemic biases are not biases, since every media professional abides by those views. These biases are internalized. The holders are not even aware of the historically and factually prejudicial nature of what they espouse.

The minority of journalists that query the dominant view, promote alternative perspectives, are branded politically-motivated persons. What they write is ignored or criticized in minute detail. Their views are declared as historically outmoded.'

Hirji's advice to journalists is: 'A journalist with integrity must be frank and open about her fundamental leanings. She needs to articulate them in a rational manner, and provide moral and factual justifications for them. To hide behind the facile mask of objectivity, or an apolitical approach is to deceive herself and the public. But at the same time, she must have respect for the truth as an uncompromisable tenet in every particular task that is undertaken.

The anti-people, anti-humanistic forms of systemic bias need to be exposed and avoided. On the other hand, pro-people, humanistic forms of systemic bias need to be fostered. At the same time, the latter must be tempered with rigorous control of methodological bias. Sound ethics and respect for the truth must march hand in hand if humanity is to survive and prosper on this planet'.

Source: Hirji Karim F, 2012.

FIRST THINGS FIRST

A Journalist's Perspective on Media Policy
By Tom Maliti

First published in ***Exploring Kenya's Media Policy: 1963 - 2013,*** Working Paper Series 1, Copyright 2015 by Media Policy Research Centre. Reprinted with permission.

Key policy highlights

The broadcasting sector is where government control has been the most overt. Since 1963, successive governments have taken the same approach to the broadcasting sector. The first step is exclusion. The second step is limited expansion, with restrictions, whether legal or not. The third and final step is complete opening up. In tandem with each of these stages of liberalisation of the broadcasting sector have been changes in the political environment.

During the close to three decades Voice of Kenya was the sole broadcaster in the country, Kenya became and remained a one-party state. When the first privately owned television and radio stations were licensed to broadcast, there was increased public agitation for opening up the political space that led to Kenya returning to multiparty politics. The government only completely opened up the broadcasting sector, issuing frequencies for broadcast outside Nairobi and so on, once KANU was voted out of power in 2002.

Introduction

External factors have contributed in a significant way to how the media works in Kenya. Government control and intimidation have been the biggest external factor to date that has been at the back of the minds of journalists and

owners as the media evolved over the past five decades. This has been followed closely by changes in the political environment. As agitation by clerics, political leaders, lawyers, and other groups for opening up Kenya's political space grew, the government's control and intimidation of the media has eased.

The broadcasting sector is where government control has been the most overt. For close to three decades after independence Kenya had only one broadcaster, the Voice of Kenya (VOK). At independence VOK was under the department of information. Voice of Kenya consisted of one television, two radio stations that broadcast in English and Swahili, and radio broadcasts limited to a few hours each day in other languages such as Hindi, Kikuyu, Kikamba, and Maa.

The first government of independent Kenya inherited Voice of Kenya from the outgoing British colonial government. At the time it was named the Kenya Broadcasting Services. Its journalists were primarily white men and women, many of whom retained their British citizenship at independence and so their employment status changed from citizen to expatriate.

As part of the transition from a colonial government broadcasting service to one under an independent Kenya government, a journalist from the British Broadcasting Corporation, Patrick Jubb, was brought in to lead the organisation.[1] Also, as part of the transition, Kenya Broadcasting Services recruited African staff. Some of the staff came from the world of print media such as the newspapers *East African Standard* and *Nation*.[2]

---

1. Matheson, A. (1992). *States of Emergency: Reporting Africa for Half a Century. Media Matters.*
2. Khamisi, J. (2014). *Dash before Dusk.Kenway Publications.* p.77.

Complete State Control: 1963-1989

The recollections of two journalists who worked at the Kenya Broadcasting Services and then Voice of Kenya in the early years point to the government having not developed a policy to guide the station. The only policy initiative focused on Africanising the newsroom. It seems anything else that could be interpreted as policy developed on a need basis or depended on which high-ranking policy-maker was more powerful. And the journalists responded accordingly. It is clear that at independence there was no discussion of whether the state-owned broadcaster would be public service-oriented. It is also clear that, by default, Voice of Kenya served the interests of the government of the day or powerful factions within it.

Joe Khamisi, who joined the staff of Voice of Kenya in 1965, recalls that the station's orientation to serving the interests of the government of the day developed as a result of who was consulted when newly independent Kenya wanted to shape its public broadcaster. Khamisi was part of the first group of journalists who joined VOK when the government decided to Africanise the newsroom. Before taking up his new assignment at VOK, Khamisi was working for the *Nation*, which was later renamed *Daily Nation*. VOK's news editor at the time Khamisi joined was Alastair Matheson, who renounced his British citizenship at independence and became a Kenyan citizen.

In his 2014 memoir, *Dash before Dusk*, Khamisi recalls,

> Before KNA (Kenya News Agency), VOK's associate in the Ministry of Information, was established in 1963, Kenya reached out to the Ghana News Agency (GNA) for technical

and policy advice. The West African country had been independent since 1957, and GNA had had plenty of time to perfect the art of skewing news in favour of President Kwame Nkrumah. That was the line KNA chose to take, and since VOK depended on KNA for news, there was no way it could have deviated from the official line in news coverage.[3]

According to Matheson, the transition to a broadcasting service dependent on the Kenya News Agency was not smooth. In his memoir, *States of Emergency: Reporting Africa for Half a Century*, Matheson writes that in the lead-up to independence the Kenya Broadcasting Service relied on the British Broadcasting Corporation for foreign news. At the time, KBS aired BBC news several times a day, at the same it was being broadcast from London. Matheson said that Information and Broadcasting Minister, Achieng' Oneko, introduced 'drastic changes' after independence and required the state-owned broadcaster to cease using the BBC relay.

'I did not object to the change, only that not enough time had been given and we were expected to produce a foreign news bulletin several times a day—from what sources?' wrote Matheson. 'But that didn't bother Oneko, so we had to do what we could. Until other arrangements were made, we just taped the BBC newscast and used that material for our next bulletin,' Matheson continues.[4]

Once the Kenya News Agency was established, the government signed a contract with the Reuters News Agency to supply it with foreign news. This did not end

matters, according to Matheson. The Soviet Union also arranged to supply KNA with foreign news from the Tass News Agency in Moscow. 'But the snag was that the Kenya Government had already signed a contract with Reuters News Agency in London for its service. Oneko therefore had to tell the Russians that while Kenya would welcome the Tass service it would not be able to pay for it. The (Soviet Union's) Ambassador had no option but to give it free,' writes Matheson. 'It was a case of the left hand not knowing what the right hand was doing.'[5]

Matheson said once that was settled then Oneko 'was breathing down our necks' demanding the Kenya Broadcasting Service use as much of Tass news as possible. 'We told him that with the best will in the world we were finding it difficult to use much from Tass—not because we were dye-in-the-wool anti-Communists but because the news was not only stale, it was really lacking in interest to Africans,' Matheson writes. He writes the news they received from Tass included articles about tractor production in Stalingrad and wheat output in Ukraine.[6]

'Even when the first Soviet "sputnik" rocket was launched, the news reached us first from Reuters in a brief urgent "bulletin". It was not until the following day that Tass sent the story, which began, "Our glorious heroes of the Soviet Union yesterday soared up into space,"' writes Matheson.[7]

According to Matheson, it was not just the Kenyan government that determined editorial policy at the state-owned broadcaster. Oneko would remind them of an Organisation of African Unity (the precursor of

today's African Union) resolution that member states should not print or broadcast anything derogatory of one of its heads of state. "Just at that time there had been harsh criticism of Ghana's Kwame Nkrumah by the International Commission of Jurists, and we were ordered not to use that story, as it went against the OAU resolution," Matheson said.[8]

The government also sent a list of 'epithets' to the newsroom that were to be used to denigrate the South African government and Ian Smith's government that had unilaterally declared independence for South Rhodesia (present day Zimbabwe). 'One day I nearly split my sides laughing when I heard on the English channel of the Voice of Kenya radio, our news reader saying: "In Salisbury [present day Harare] today racist rebel Ian Smith declared, My racist minority government will not tolerate."'[9]

'Although it went against all my teachings about impartiality in news reporting, I and other Whites in the newsroom slavishly tried to follow Oneko's orders but I personally had no quarrel with changing the words for Mau Mau fighters from the colonial "terrorists" to "freedom fighters", explains Matheson.[10]

In Khamisi's opinion, the Voice of Kenya lost its credibility completely with its coverage of two major milestones in the country's history: the 1966 conference of the ruling Kenya African National Union and the war against bandits and incursions by Somalia. The war with Somalia and bandits in the north-eastern part of Kenya was later referred to as the shifta wars, the term shifta being considered derogatory by some.

3. Khamisi, *Dash before Dusk*, p.87.
4. Matheson, *States of Emergency*, p. 73.

5. Matheson, *States of Emergency*, p. 73.
6. Matheson, *States of Emergency*, p. 74.
7. Matheson, *States of Emergency*, p. 74.

8. Matheson, *States of Emergency*, p. 74.
9. Matheson, *States of Emergency*, p. 74.
10. Matheson, *States of Emergency*, p. 74.

He described the March 1966 KANU delegates conference as the first big test for VOK as a public broadcaster.[11] KANU's leader, then President Jomo Kenyatta, had called the delegates conference to cut the powers then Vice President Jaramogi Oginga Odinga enjoyed as vice president of the ruling party.

'It became obvious to us that the Permanent Secretary in the Ministry of Information and Broadcasting, Peter Gachathi, a Kikuyu like Kenyatta, and not the Director of Broadcasting, James Kangwana, a Mijikenda, was calling the shots on all major broadcasting decisions,' Khamisi writes in *Dash before Dusk*. 'Hence the issue was not so much about VOK's independence, integrity or objectivity, but defending Kenyatta's political interests at all costs.'[12]

'Gachathi, who spent most of his evening hours at his bar in Kilimani, was a very powerful official and was part of a Kikuyu clique that was closest to Kenyatta. He was a product of Alliance High School as were many of the early top government officials such as Duncan Ndegwa and Geoffrey K Kariithi.'[13]

At the delegates conference, which is also commonly referred to as the Limuru conference, the single post of national vice president was split into eight posts, each vice presidency representing the eight province of the country at that time.

'At VOK we were under strict instructions to support KANU's position and demonise Oginga Odinga and his group as enemies of the nation. I was one of the shift news editors at the time and stories filed by the Presidential Press Unit about the events at Limuru were openly biased

but we were under instructions to carry them without change. As a result, the Odinga group was thoroughly humiliated in the eyes of Kenyans,' Khamisi writes.[14]

After the March 1966 KANU delegates' conference, Odinga and his supporters ditched KANU and formed the Kenya People's Union (KPU). The government banned KPU in 1969 turning Kenya into a one-party state. Multi-party politics only returned 22 years later.

The second milestone in Kenya's history that Khamisi claims marked the complete loss of VOK's credibility was the 1960s cross-border theft of cattle in north-eastern Kenya that occurred at the same time as Somalia was advocating for the formation of a greater Somalia. The campaign for a greater Somalia aimed at uniting all regions with a Somali population in the Horn of Africa region into one country. This meant getting the Somali people of north-eastern Kenya, the Ogaden region of Ethiopia, then French Somaliland to join Somalia. Somalia itself was an amalgamation of British Somaliland and Italian Somaliland. To date, some in Somalia still advocate for a greater Somalia.

Khamisi writes that the Kenyan military began trying to prevent the cattle raids that started in 1963. The raids were conducted by Somalis on either side of the Kenya-Somalia border. Despite their efforts, the Kenyan military suffered losses and was also losing the war. In July 1966, the then Defence Permanent Secretary, Dawson Mlamba, admitted that the army and police were incurring 'mounting' casualties and wanted the Ministry of Information and Broadcasting to lead a propaganda effort against the Somali militia. 'Mlamba sent out instructions to our Ministry that all war reports had to be cleared by his office. The government was concerned that reports filtering from the war front showing Kenya on

the defensive could dim morale in the armed forces and anger Kenyans. Hence, Gachathi felt the responsibility of war reporting and any censoring should be left to his ministry.'[15]

As the two permanent secretaries were involved in a spat over turf, Somalia was conducting its own propaganda effort. 'Seeing that Kenya could be fiddling with the facts, Mogadishu upped its propaganda war by beaming Somali and Kiswahili broadcasts into Kenya and jamming Kenya transmissions. Kenya was in no position to match that propaganda assault. VOK's editorials, which were supposed to articulate the government's hard-line position and rally masses, were seamless and dense in content,' Khamisi writes.[16]

'Apart from losing the war in the field, we were also losing the propaganda war. Director Kangwana, a former broadcaster himself, had virtually ceded control of VOK to higher authorities who manipulated it for all reasons other than nurturing it as (a) reliable conveyer of fair and accurate news,' he continued a few paragraphs later.[17]

The war ended when Zambia's then President Kenneth Kaunda mediated between Kenya and Somalia and got Kenyatta and Somali Prime Minister, Muhammad Haji Ibrahim Egal, to sign a ceasefire agreement in 1967. 'To me, the shifta war and the events of Limuru helped to spur the state's stranglehold on the public broadcaster that continued for decades thereafter,' Khamisi concludes.[18]

---

15. Khamisi, Dash before Dusk, p.87-88.
16. Khamisi, Dash before Dusk, p.89.
17. Khamisi, Dash before Dusk, p.89.

18. Khamisi, Dash before Dusk, p.89.

---

11. Khamisi, Dash before Dusk, p.87.
12. Khamisi, Dash before Dusk, p.87.
13. Khamisi, Dash before Dusk, p.87.

---

14. Khamisi, Dash before Dusk, p.87-88.

Opening Up Television: 1989

It is upon this foundation that Voice of Kenya grew and remained the sole broadcaster in the country for close to three decades. During the same period, the ownership and diversity of the print media expanded. Voice of Kenya remaining the sole broadcaster into the 1990s was not a legal question. Article 79 of the constitution at the time guaranteed as a fundamental right the freedom of expression. The government, however, interpreted this freedom in the narrowest sense possible. This was a policy that carried through from the first president to the second president. So the issue of opening up the broadcasting sector was more about government control than anything else.

By its actions, the government showed that it did not want to open up the ownership of broadcasting licenses and frequencies because then it would lose control of a key part of the media. To listen to radio or watch television you do not need much schooling unlike if you wanted to read a newspaper. With the advent of the pocket radio, you did not need to be at home to listen to the radio. And the pocket radio did not need electricity; it worked on batteries. Once the batteries' power was exhausted, placing them in the sun for some time was enough to recharge them. It is this power over the information most of the country received that the government sought to control for close to three decades. In line with that thinking, cynical journalists have been known to quip that freedom of the press is only for those who own the press.

Since 1963, successive governments have taken the same approach to the broadcasting sector. The first step is exclusion. The second step is limited expansion, with restrictions, whether legal or not. The third and final step is complete opening up. In tandem with each of these stages of liberalisation of the broadcasting sector have been changes in the political environment.

During the close to three decades that Voice of Kenya was the sole broadcaster, Kenya became and remained a one-party state. When the first privately owned television and radio stations were licensed to broadcast, there was increased public agitation for opening up the political space that led to Kenya returning to multiparty politics. The government only completely opened up the broadcasting sector, issuing frequencies for broadcast outside Nairobi and so on, once KANU was voted out of power in 2002.

In 1989, the government took the second step to opening up the broadcasting sector, but only for television. A privately owned media company was licensed to broadcast but only in Nairobi. The company was politically connected. The government issued the licence and a Nairobi-only frequency to the Kenya Times Media Trust. The company was a joint venture between the British media company, the Daily Mirror Group, and KANU. Kenya Times Media Trust also owned *The Kenya Times* and *Sunday Times* newspaper.

The government gave the Kenya Times Media Trust a television broadcast licence despite more established media houses applying for such licences much earlier. The government simply ignored the application by the Nation Media Group, which began publishing its first newspaper in 1959. It also ignored a similar request from Stellagraphics Limited owned by Hillary Ng'weno, who had been publishing *The Weekly Review* since 1975. A few years after founding *The Weekly Review*, Ng'weno began publishing the *Nairobi Times*, a daily newspaper, which he later sold to Kenya Times Media Trust in 1983. Ng'weno's application was ignored despite the fact that he was already supplying the Voice of Kenya with programs that ranged from soap operas, to entertainment shows, to a televised version of the popular 'Je, Hii Ni Ugwana' social commentary by Leonard Mambo Mbotela.

In retrospect it is not that the government feared the Nation Media Group or Hillary Ng'weno would cause upheaval in Kenyan society. It is just that it would be easier to control a television station partly owned by the ruling KANU party than one owned and managed by a more independent entity.

In 1996, Hillary Ng'weno's Stellagraphics was awarded a licence and in 1998, the Nation Media Group was given its television licence.[19] Like the Kenya Times Media Trust, they initially got frequencies to broadcast in Nairobi alone.

Opening Up Radio: 1996

It was not until 1996 that the first privately owned radio station got its licence to broadcast. And as happened with the first privately owned television station, the station was only given a frequency to broadcast in Nairobi alone. The licence was awarded to 98.4 Capital FM. Again, the script of awarding a politically connected company the license to broadcast that applied in the case of television was also used for radio. The London-based multinational Lonrho owned 98.4 Capital FM. The chairman of its East Africa operations was Mark Too, who was close to then President Daniel arap Moi.[20] Too also doubled as chairman of 98.4 Capital FM. The station's managing director was Linda Holt, who was once married to Bob Holt, a one-time chief executive of the Kenya Times Media Trust.

19. Wanyeki, L M (ed.). (2000). *Up In The Air?: The State of Broadcasting in Eastern Africa. Panos Eastern Africa.p.41.*
20. Wanyeki, L M (ed.), *Up In The Air.* p.40.

When 98.4 Capital FM began its broadcasts, it changed radio programming forever in Kenya. It introduced a format of breaking daytime broadcasting into three-hour segments. Before then, Voice of Kenya, which was later renamed Kenya Broadcasting Corporation, did not broadcast in segments. The format at the state-owned radio stations for non-news programming was between half an hour and an hour. The only time that format was broken was when the state-owned broadcaster aired programmes targeted at schools.

For the first two years it was on air, 98.4 Capital FM only broadcast music programming sprinkled with quizzes and presenters sharing entertainment gossip. The presenters played mostly American chart music and privileged rock. The assumption at the time was 98.4 Capital FM was focussed on generating advertising revenues with its emphasis on entertainment, and not news which would involve significant investment but lower returns.

Information and Broadcasting Minister, Joseph Nyagah, said as much in an interview with *eXpression* today published in June 1998 in which he sought to explain that the broadcasting licences issued to privately-owned radio stations did not bar them from airing news programming.[21] 'Music attracts a bigger audience which advertisers like,' Nyagah told *eXpression* today, a journal on the media and human rights that was published by the Media Institute.[22] Portions of Nyagah's interview were reprinted in *EXECUTIVE* magazine of August 1998.

In an interview published two months later in the business monthly *EXECUTIVE* magazine, Holt acknowledged that 98.4 Capital FM's licence did not impose any restrictions. She, however, said that together

with the licence, 98.4 Capital FM did receive a letter from the Information and Broadcasting Minister in which he told them they could not broadcast news. Holt told *EXECUTIVE* magazine that she wrote to the minister in 1997 to seek permission to broadcast news, to which the minister replied, 'yes because we had proved our professionalism.'[23]

Holt did not question the legality of the minister's letter. It also does not seem that any journalists who worked at the station were involved in the discussion about whether it was necessary to comply with a clearly illegal letter.

The station eventually began airing general and business news in May 1998. Holt said this happened because BBC began an FM relay broadcast of its programming in February that year and Capital did not want to lose listeners. Coincidentally, at the time, BBC's FM relay in Nairobi was transmitted by Capital.[24]

To date 98.4 Capital FM continues to broadcast news but it has changed ownership. The programming format it introduced in 1996 is followed by most FM stations in the country, irrespective of what language they broadcast in or whether their programmes include call-in shows on current affairs or other issues.

Once Moi served his final term in office and KANU was voted out of office in 2002, the government liberalised the broadcasting sector even more. The government allocated out-of-Nairobi frequencies to the established media houses, enabling them to reach a wider audience. The government put the squeeze on those individuals who had been given broadcasting licences and allocated frequencies but had not used them. These individuals

were required to either use their licences and frequencies or forfeit them.

Towards an independent Media Council of Kenya
When looking at the divisions of the media world in terms of broadcast and print, it is clear that the broadcasting sector has been the subject of heavy government control. This is not to say that the print media has operated without hindrance. Just like in the Voice of Kenya newsroom, newspaper and magazine editors have received phone calls from cabinet ministers, senior civil servants, and others who have thought a news story is likely to be unfavourable. The aim of those calls has been to stop publication of the story or to change its emphasis.

Not only have the phone calls been made but editors and reporters have been jailed, sometimes for a day, sometimes longer. And, on occasion, a publication has been banned. With political opponents of the government being detained or force into exile in the 1970s and 1980s, the message was clear to the rest of society: conform or else! This and the pressures in the newsrooms saw journalists self-censor during that period.

When multiparty politics was restored in 1991, allowing the formation of opposition parties and giving space to those opposed to the government to speak more freely, print media also became more critical of government. This and the slowly-slowly opening up of the broadcasting sector prompted the government to form a task force on media laws in December 1993. Ostensibly, the aim was to shape the regulatory environment to take into account the new realities of a more open and diverse media. The task force presented its report to the Attorney General in late 1994. Nothing more was heard of the task force or its report until news leaked at the end of 1995 that the Attorney General was planning on tabling two bills.[25]

21. *EXECUTIVE magazine. August 1998. p.53.*
22. *Ibid*

23. *Ibid*
24. *Ibid*

25. *Wanyeki, L.M. (ed.), Up In The Air. p.48.*

The bills aimed at creating two regulatory organisations, one for media companies and the other for individual journalists. The proposed regulatory organisations were to be led by boards appointed solely by the government without any reference to anyone. The media, human rights organisations and others strongly opposed the bills. The Attorney General eventually shelved the bills. A year later the Attorney General re-established the task force and it was reported to have recommends similar to the earlier discredited bills. The report was not made public and the Attorney General did not prepare any new bills[26].

That was not the last attempt by the government to control an increasingly assertive media. In 2000, it emerged that the government had proposed amendments to the Books and Newspapers Act to, among other provisions, require publishers to submit to the Registrar two copies of each edition of newspapers or books before distributing them to the public. Another proposed amendment was to fine any vendor selling a publication whose copies had not been submitted to the Registrar. The fine was set at one million shillings.

Journalists, media managers, and owners saw this as an attempt to legalise censorship, something that had never been done before. Previous cases of censorship involved calls to newsrooms or other forms of intimidating journalists. Such actions were aimed at specific stories. In some cases, security agents had seized from newsstands and vendors copies of editions of newsmagazine considered sensitive. These seizures were sporadic. The proposed changes had the potential of legalising regular seizures of publications deemed undesirable.

It was widely believed at the time that the law targeted a section of the print media euphemistically referred to as alternative media.[27] These were eight-page to 16-page weekly papers printed on coloured paper (blue, green or pink), of roughly A-5 size, with politicians and politics as their main subjects. Some of them like *Kenya Confidential*, published by Blamuel Ngunjiri, aimed at reporting political developments and details about politicians that mainstream media ignored or feared to touch. Politicians financed some of them and used the publications to attack their rivals. The politicians usually remained in the background. The remainder of the weekly papers were simply vehicles of extortion.

A common characteristic of these publications was that they did not have an office, providing only a post office box address at the back of the paper for any communication with the publisher or editor. It was generally assumed this is why the proposed amendment targeted vendors because they were easier to locate.

In response to this new attempt to control the media, journalists got together and set up a media industry steering committee. This committee worked on a framework for self-regulation to address concerns about media standards and practice that seemed to be the reason behind the proposed amendments to the Books and Newspapers Act. The committee's goal was to have the framework ready before the National Assembly returned for its last session of the year, which was set to begin in October that year. The thinking was that with such a framework agreed to by the media industry, members of parliament could be lobbied to vote against the proposed amendments to the Books and Newspaper Act or simply drop them.

The committee met several times in 2000. Professor Robert Pinker, who at the time was a member of Britain's Press Complaints Commission, shared his views at one of the meetings. Pinker said that the British media had been in a similar place some years earlier when the government threatened to legislate controls. Pinker said the media realised it was important to put aside rivalries and develop some form of self-regulation before the government stepped in. Pinker encouraged the media industry steering committee to continue with its plan for self-regulation and conclude it as soon as possible because the instinct of politicians across the world was to legislate controls over the media.

The committee also held a major meeting in Mombasa where the framework of a media-backed but independent Media Council of Kenya was agreed on and a draft code of conduct was developed. Present at the Mombasa meeting were editorial representatives of most media houses, journalism lecturers and freedom of expression advocates. Among them were Wangethi Mwangi, Editorial Director of the Nation Media Group; Mitch Odero, Managing Editor, *East African Standard*; Makau Niko, News Editor, Nation FM; and Isaiah Kabira, News Editor, KTN. Also present was Dr Lewis Odhiambo, Deputy Director of the School of Journalism at the University of Nairobi. Dr Smokin Wanjala was also present in his capacity as Executive Director of Clarion, a rights advocacy group. Rosemary Okello-Orlale, Executive Director of the African Women and Child Feature Service, was the coordinator of the media industry steering committee. Part of the committee's work was funded by the Friedrich Ebert Foundation.

Eventually, the committee launched a Media Council chaired by Ambassador Bethwell Kiplagat, who, at the time, was running the Africa Peace Forum. Among the members of the council was, Muthoni Wanyeki, who at

---

26. Wanyeki, L M (ed.), *Up In The Air.* p.49.

27. *This account about the proposed amendments and the work of the media industry steering committee are based on my recollection of events. At the time I was editor of eXpression today and sat on the committee representing the Media Institute.*

the time was the Executive Director of Femnet, a Pan-African network of women's organisations based in Nairobi. After the unveiling of the council, it did not meet for a long time. The proposed amendments to the Books and Newspapers Act, however, were never passed.

The 2000 attempt at self-regulation later on influenced the legislation that formed the autonomous government-funded Media Council of Kenya. The formation of this council did not mark the end of tensions between the government and the media. That is bound to continue because of the media's role in shedding light on public affairs and the government's instinct towards keeping matters away from public scrutiny.

OVERVIEW of the MEDIA in INDEPENDENT KENYA
By Dr George Nyabuga

The media has grown tremendously since independence. While state and political clampdown and intolerance blots Kenya's postcolonial media's historical, it has experienced a resurgence marked by a proliferation of not only traditional media (mostly radio and television, and to some extent print – newspapers and magazines) but also *new* media characterised by the growth of online media (majorly Internet based publications).

Current media developments and freedoms are partly the fruits of a hard-fought for Constitution promulgated in 2010 after many years of blood, sweat and tears. Prior to that promulgation on 27 August, 2010, and perhaps going back almost twenty years to the fall of the Berlin Wall and its domino effect on the collapse of autocracy and dictatorship, Kenya's media experienced from time to time episodes of serious state clampdown. Although the right to information and the freedom of the media has always been enshrined in the constitution, these liberties have always been *granted* reluctantly especially during the single-party era of 1980s. The stranglehold of the media, sources of information and channels of communication by the ruling establishments was premised on the very fact that information was emancipatory and that the media, whether traditional channels of communication like radio, newspapers and television, or even the folk media like rural theatre, were perceived to be a 'threat' to the political status quo of pre-1991 because of their influence on the political process in the country.

This chapter examines Kenya's media during the postcolonial period. The arguments advanced in this chapter are divided broadly into three sections. First, the chapter looks at the media from independence to 1991 when the political space was dominated and somewhat strangled by political intolerance and Kenya African National Union (KANU) party dictatorship. It bases the arguments on the idea that the fall of the Berlin Wall marked a turning point in Kenya's media landscape as indeed the political space. This is based on the notion that Kenya's second president Daniel arap Moi, despite pressure from western nations, successfully fended off the heat and, in fact, intensified the suppression for fear that the media was a key factor in the change agenda.

Secondly, the chapter examines the media post-1991. It looks at this through the lens of the liberalisation of the media engendered by the founding of the first *independent media* platform (the Kenya Television Network owned by people close to the government). The founding of KTN was a watershed in Kenya's media history, an epochal moment marking the relaxation of state stranglehold on media space.

Thirdly, this chapter looks at Kenya's media after 2010. The year 2010 marked a major turning point for Kenya due largely to the promulgation of the *new* constitution which ushered in a new era of increased media and civil liberties.

Containment policy
At independence, the media was conscripted into Kenya's development agenda. Given the idea that mass communication was necessary in the articulation of state policy, and could be used as a public sphere, it was charged with the responsibility of playing a critical role in the eradication of ignorance, disease and underdevelopment.

As per early communication and media scholars, for example, the media continued to be seen as the magic bullet, a potent force for development, a 'mass educator', a vital tool for modernisation and development because of their great influence on the 'masses', public opinion and behaviour.[1] This may have been repudiated by recent arguments holding that the media merely reinforce pre-existing beliefs and opinions[2] but at the time the media was a critical resource that had to be used as part of state mechanism to communicate state messages, contribute to policy discussions and resolutions, set government and political class agenda and be part of national social engineering.[3] Thus starting with the immediate post-colonial era, Jomo Kenyatta's government applied a 'containment' policy, seeking to consolidate its hold on the media, and largely considered the Voice of Kenya (currently Kenya Broadcasting Corporation) a government mouthpiece. Even the *East African Standard* and the *Nation* did not escape state tentacles however. In effect, the media became 'unwilling' partners in the country's social, economic and political development agenda. Accordingly, media interests were considered subordinate to the interests of the collective.[4] Samuel Kiiru sees this era as one in which the media was expected to promote Kenyatta's development ideology based on the *harambee* philosophy.[5] Accordingly, the media was expected to communicate the government agenda, and support policies aimed at national development. This thus became part of Kenyatta's plan to centralise or consolidate power as media space was seen as a public sphere through which the citizenry could agitate for change.

By becoming an agent of state, media freedom consequently suffered. Critical political commentary became suppressed. The coverage of *oppositional* political activities was seriously curtailed. In short, free political discourse became a casualty in this arrangement.

The arguments above gave rise to political and government decisions to limit and strangle media space. Mainstream media, particularly radio, due its wide reach in Kenya, was to remain in the hands of the Kenya African National Union (KANU) party and its apologists or opportunists who used this to maintain their parasitic relationship with those in power. Licences for alternative or 'independent' radio and television broadcast stations remained locked away in the cabinets of the ministers for information and communication and government bureaucrats who took direct orders either from the president or his appointees. It was not until the 1990 that the first licence for a private television station was granted to the Kenya Television Network. Its then owner, Jared Kangwana, was close to the Moi government and its broadcasts were perceived to be 'conformist' even at their most critical.

Nonetheless, although the colonisation and control of the media of communication intensified under Moi, Kenya's founding president, Jomo Kenyatta, had years earlier especially in the 1970s, but starting immediately after independence, secured control of the media partly as a way of stifling free political discourse. To Kenyatta, Moi and those close to the centres of power, the media was meant to advance the interests of the government and the central authority. To effect this objective, controlling and regulating media operations were crucial and paramount.

To quote Fred Siebert:

> Authoritarian governments gave equally definitive answers to the problem of controlling and regulating the newer electronic media of mass communication, radio and television broadcasting. Two factors dictated state policy on these media. First, the general principals of authoritarianism provided a solid basis for regulation. Radio and television, like the older media, must further the interests of government and must help advance the cultural and political objectives of the central authority. The second factor was the nature of the media as electronic communication. All types of broadcasting required the use of electromagnetic waves, of which the supply was limited. These channels were the property of the state; consequently their use was subject to state control.[6]

Siebert's description fits Kenya's position especially in the years before 1990. The presidents and the ruling party KANU intent on controlling radio and television and to some extent newspaper content and operations effectively managed to colonise the public sphere by securing the control of the system of political communication within the Kenyan society. This monopolisation of the media was of course detrimental to participatory politics as it starved the Kenyan populace of the critical information, the vital oxygen necessary for effective participatory political process in any modern polity or state.

Before further discussion of the media in post-colonial Kenya, it may be imperative to have a glimpse into the then political environment.

Setting the foundation for intolerance

Despite adopting a Westminster constitutional model providing for political pluralism at independence on 12 December, 1963, multipartyism effectively lasted only a year. After numerous defections to KANU, and unable to secure development funds for their constituents, the only opposition party at the time, the Kenya African Democratic Union (KADU), 'voluntarily' disbanded making Kenya a *de facto* single-party state. In a construction of what Alex Thomson calls 'consensus' politics[7], the decimation of the adversarial multipartyism political systems was considered necessary as newly independent African countries attempted to stave off the 'divisive and perilous' competition to 'save' the fragile African states.

Like in many African and other newly independent states, this was considered a necessary condition for social, economic and political development. For example, Julius Nyerere, Tanzania's founding president called political pluralism a 'luxury that we in Africa cannot afford … we have little time and there is too much to do to allow ourselves such an idle pastime'[8]

Like other African states, Kenya had by 1966 effectively outlawed (although not in the statute books) multiparty politics. The disbandment of KADU gave Kenyatta the opportunity to consolidate and personalise power, effectively laying the foundation for autocracy ostensibly because adversarial politics characteristic of multipartyism was undesirable and unjustifiable at this infant stage.[9]

After the proscription of Oginga Odinga's Kenya People's Union and detention of the party's leadership, Kenya was until 1982 a *de facto* single-party state. In 1982, following a failed military coup, Moi changed the constitution to make Kenya a *de jure* one-party state and embarked on charting the country's political trajectory based on '*Nyayo* Philosophy', a doctrine advocating love, peace and unity. However, Moi's era was to turn detrimental to participatory politics and democracy in Kenya as he sought to consolidate power by stifling opposition and persecuting critics, including journalists and media practitioners.

The executive's centralisation of power effectively emasculated other branches of government as well as mechanisms for maintaining checks and balances particularly the legislature and the judiciary but also including the media.

As a *de jure* one party state between 1982 until 1991, the media and other channels of communication in Kenya were seen as tools to be used by the ruling party to enhance 'development and unity'. Indeed Moi's Nyayo Philosophy of peace, love and unity[10]was perceived by those close to the centre of power as the vital sinews holding the country together in a sea-of-chaos, a reference to the regional turmoil pervading neighbouring countries like Somalia, Sudan, Ethiopia and to a *lesser extent* Uganda in the immediate neighbourhood and farther afield in states like the Democratic Republic of Congo. To Moi and his somewhat highly sycophantic political disciples, the media was a vital political tool through which he would communicate his policies, expound and elucidate his philosophy to the *masses*. He thus perceived 'free' or 'oppositional' media organisations as potential cause of social or societal breakdown. He and those close to him often accused the 'independent recalcitrant' media houses and journalists of misrepresentations, falsehoods, irresponsibility and being agents of 'foreign masters'.

Kenya post-1991
The collapse of Berlin Wall and attendant developments around the world set in motion widespread change in Kenya. Aside from the political changes marked majorly by the reintroduction of multipartyism in 1991 (occasioned by the 1991 repeal of Section 2A of the Constitution), the year birthed major developments.

Apart from the Kenya Broadcasting Corporation, the successor of the Voice of Kenya, which operated a

national radio and television station and other local language radio stations across the country, and the Kenya News Agency, the Ministry of Information-run news agency, the other 'independent' media organisation, specifically the Aga Khan-owned Nation Media Group and *The Standard* owned until 1992 by the British Lonhro Group, were hardly free or independent. Just like any other authoritarian regime, Moi was hardly criticised by the local media. In most cases he had a hand or indirect control of their operations. As head of state, he appointed the management of state-run KBC. The *Nation* and *Standard's* owners relied on 'his goodwill' for their operations. Besides, their commercial interests far outweighed the social, 'watchdog', sentinel responsibility and guard against abuse of power and other political malpractice. Thus the media were seen as either complicit or fearful of criticising Moi and his government's excesses as evidenced by their skewed or uncritical reportage or commentary of events taking place especially at the height of the president's power in the 1980s. Even though there was criticism of his government, few media were bold enough to heap blame directly on him for the mismanagement of the political process.

The events leading to the reintroduction of multi-party politics in the country and wider political participation meant the 'release' of political communication channels from the grips of the powerful political elite or those engaged in the exercise of disseminating party propaganda and political information. This was an essential step for effective change even though there was continued control or manipulation of the media of mass communication either directly or indirectly through harassment, intimidation or undercapitalisation of media by cutting off critical advertising and commercial support for 'oppositional' media organisations. In some instances, extreme measures like the arrest and detention of recalcitrant journalists and the crippling of printing presses were employed. In April 1993 for example, the police dismantled the Fotoform printing press for allegedly publishing a seditious document in what was seen as a direct assault on press freedom and freedom of expression and the reluctance of those in government to tolerate criticism.[11] Evidently, the real reason was the publication of information unfavourable to the political establishment in publications like *The People* newspaper and *Finance* magazine owned by opposition politicians Kenneth Matiba and Njehu Gatabaki respectively. Matiba and Gatabaki, as proponents of political change through either the media or their party channels, became victim of Kenya's 'controlled' judiciary and suffered numerous incarcerations for their ideological positions and opposition to KANU government and the mediation of political communication through their media organisations.

Given that the media were for many years under state (and ruling party KANU) control, 1991 did not really mark the end of state or political clampdown and domination. KANU and its apologists still jealously guarded local media against encroachment from recalcitrant political actors, opposition politicians, parties and organisations seeking liberalisation as a precursor to political pluralism. The state-owned Kenya Broadcasting Corporation continued to be dominated by KANU and President Moi and little was heard of the opposition. In fact, Moi and KANU were accorded 80 percent positive or favourable coverage while the opposition received mainly negative reportage.[12] 1992 was the worst year for the opposition in terms of coverage on state media. While '99 percent of KANU's activities were covered positively and only 1 percent negatively by KBC radio and TV news ... only 4 percent of opposition activities were covered positively'.[13] This disparity was the basis for the opposition ire which

constantly complained of media bias and consequently unfavourable political environment. This complaint was upheld by the Commonwealth Observer Group which confirmed that most media in Kenya and particularly KBC 'devoted its news coverage to chronicling the comings and goings of the President [Moi], his Ministers and various government functionaries'.[14]

The contention over the right to access the media of mass communication and the use thereof was one of the main agenda in the 1997 Inter-Parties Parliamentary Group (IPPG) meeting comprising both opposition and ruling party KANU Members of Parliament (MPs). Recognising the need for change, the parties agreed to reform Kenya Broadcasting Corporation Act, chapter 221 of 1990, to liberalise the media and chart a new democratic course by making the Kenyan political process more open and transparent. Prior to 1997, available programmes broadcast by the stations were highly biased towards KANU and the ruling elite and political communication was starved of *balanced* and *impartial* information. The IPPG thus agreed that media coverage, especially in the state owned Kenya Broadcasting Corporation would accord the parties and politicians equal and favourable coverage as a means of accessing and influencing the electorate.

Paradoxically, this was not to become the norm in Mwai Kibaki's regime regardless of promises that political parties would be accorded fair and equal reportage especially in state-controlled and public-funded media. Although Kibaki's *laissez-faire* approach extended to media management, the night of 2/3 March 2006 would mark a low in his government intolerance of media freedoms. On that night, government security apparatus raided *The Standard* newspaper and its television subsidiary, the

Kenya Television Network, in what Security Minister, John Michuki, said was aimed at protecting the state against threats from recalcitrant journalists and media organisations. In that attack, reported widely all over the world, on the Internet, and traditional media; the government confiscated and set ablaze thousands of copies of the newspaper, dismantled the press and beat up staff. The thugs who later turned out to be security officers switched off the television station for 24 hours.

The media post-2010

As indicated above, August 2010 marked a turning point in Kenya's postcolonial history. For once, media freedom is guaranteed in the constitution. The Constitution of Kenya 2010 specifically provides for Freedom of Expression (Article 33) and Right of Access to Information (Article 35) as well as Freedom of the Media (Article 35). Such constitutional guarantees have been hailed as being critical to the development and wellbeing of the media.

However, recent developments point to a resurgence of state intolerance of media freedom, and are considered the genesis of the enactment of unfriendly legislations. The Kenya Information and Communication (Amendment) Act and the Media Council Act both enacted in 2013 are seen as part of state and political efforts to effectively silence critical reporting.

The Kenya Information Communication (Amendment) Act creates a Communication and Multimedia Appeals Tribunal, which falls under the state-controlled Communication Authority of Kenya. The Tribunal will have power to impose hefty fines on media houses and journalists, recommend de-registration of journalists and make any order on freedom of expression. The Media Council Act establishes the Media Council of Kenya in order to promote and safeguard media freedoms in the country and establishes the Media Council's Complaints Commission. The new legislations enable government-controlled regulatory board to fine journalists up to 500,000 Kenyan shillings and media companies up to 20 million shillings if found guilty of flouting a government sanctioned code of conduct.

While the government and its apologists see the laws as critical in the protection of media freedom and accountability particularly in an ethnically-divided country, opponents see them as offending constitutional guarantees provided by Articles 33 and 35 and as part of wider plans to forestall media freedoms in Kenya.

'We have witnessed a slide back in Kenya, now we fear for the domino effect in the region,' said Amadou Mahtar Ba, chief executive officer of the African Media Initiative, a Nairobi-based pan-African. 'We had expected bolder actions toward improved governance, transparency and accountability, all impossible to realize without a strong media in a friendly regulatory environment.'

Such feelings are widespread especially among journalists, media practitioners, owners, civil society organisations and others who see rising state and political intolerance as extreme retrogression in media freedoms and civil liberties and perhaps a slide back to the dark days of the 1970s and 1980s.

Conclusion
As the arguments above hold, Kenya has and continues to experience varying media fortunes due largely to political developments. Granted, past political and state intolerance were the bane of greater media suffering. The Moi presidency was particularly repressive. After the 1982 coup, suppression of media intensified due to Moi's belief that the media was part of the change agenda

propagated by organisations and individuals seen as anti-Moi government.

The collapse of the Berlin wall birthed gales that swept through the world and marked the beginning of the dismantlement of the KANU and Moi dictatorship. The reintroduction of multipartyism in 1991 and attendant expansion of the political space were epochal in the history of Kenya's media. However, it was not until much later that the country started to genuinely enjoy media freedoms as the removal of Section 2A of the then Constitution to reintroduce multipartyism hardly guaranteed media or indeed civil liberties.

Yet, while the country now 'enjoys' greater media freedoms as a consequence of a new constitution promulgated in August 2010, there are fears that the liberties are under threat from intolerant political actors including government and recalcitrant politicians, due to their enactment of legislation seen as eroding the freedoms guaranteed by the Constitution of Kenya 2010.

Notes

1. See for example Schramm, Wilbur. *Mass Media and National Development: The Role of Information in the Developing Countries.* Stanford, California: Stanford University Press, 1964.

2. McQuail, Denis. *Mass Communication Theory.* 4th edition. London: Sage, 2000.

3. See for example McNair, Brian. *An Introduction to Political Communication.* London: Routledge, 1989.

4. McNair, Brian. *The Sociology of Journalism.* London: Edward Arnold, 1998.

5. See Kiiru, Samuel. 'The Bittersweet Relationship between the Media and the State' in Nyabuga, George and Kiai, Wambui (eds.) (2011) *The Media in Kenya: Evolution, Effects and Challenges.* Nairobi: University of Nairobi and Ford Foundation, pp. 39-54. Harambee literally means pulling together and was popularized by Kenyatta as a concept of pulling the country together to build a new nation.

6. Siebert, Fred. 'The Authoritarian Theory of the Press' in Siebert, Fred, Peterson, Theodore and Schramm, Wilbur. *Four Theories of the Press.* Illinois: University of Illinois Press, 1969, p. 35.

7. Thomson, Alex. *An Introduction to African Politics.* 2nd ed. London: Routledge, 2004, p. 111.

8. Nyerere, Julius. *Freedom and Socialism: Uhuru na Ujamaa.* Oxford: Oxford University Press, 1968, p. 48.

9. See, for example, Odhiambo-Mbai, Crispin. 'The Rise and Fall of the Autocratic State in Kenya' in Oyugi, Walter, Wanyande, Peter and Odhiambo-Mbai, Crispin (eds.) *The Politics of Transition in Kenya: From KANU to NARC.* Nairobi: Heinrich Boll Foundation, 2003, pp. 51-95.

10. Moi has immortalised his philosophy in arap Moi, Daniel. *Kenya African Nationalism: Nyayo Philosophy and Principles.* London and Basingstoke: Macmillan, 1986.

11. See for example U.S. Department of State. *Kenya Human Rights Practices, 1993.* January 31, 1994. [online] Washington, D.C.: U.S. Department of State, 1994. Available at: http://dosfan.lib.uic.edu/

ERC/democracy/1993_hrp_report/93hrp_report_
africa/Kenya.html. [Accessed 20 June 2014].

12. Kibara, Gichira. 'The Challenges to and Efficacy of
Election Monitoring' in Oyugi, Walter, Wanyande,
Peter and Odhiambo-Mbai, Crispin (eds.) *The
Politics of Transition in Kenya: From KANU to
NARC*. Nairobi: Heinrich Boll Foundation, 2003,
pp. 280-302.

13. Institute for Education in Democracy (IED),
Catholic Justice and Peace Commission (CJPC) and
National Council of Churches of Kenya (NCCK)
*Report on the 1997 General Elections In Kenya 29-30
December*. Nairobi: IED, CJPC and NCCK, 1998.

14. Commonwealth Observer Group. *The Presidential,
Parliamentary and Civic Elections in Kenya,
29 December 1992*. London: Commonwealth
Secretariat, 1993, p. 27.

AUTHOR'S NOTES

The writing of the story of South Asian Journalism in Kenya would not have been possible without the in-put of the concerned journalists themselves. I was determined that the book should record their stories as related by themselves rather than my personal interpretations. This was a challenging task as very few of the journalists were still resident in Kenya; almost all were spread out over the globe and no centralized address list or information existed. And of course several were deceased.

Kul Bhushan, now resident in Delhi, not only urged me to write this history but also gave me some initial contacts. After that it was one journalist putting me in touch with another; it was a journey of discovery and much camaraderie. I would like to mention in particular the assistance I received from Anil Vidyarthi, Norman da Costa, Shamlal Puri and Anver Versi. In all, I was able to locate 38 journalists almost all of whom penned for me their brief bios and attached photographs. For the 29 journalists no longer with us, family members or colleagues stepped into the breach; where such contacts were not available I searched the archives and 'drew a picture'. In the process I made friendships and learnt a lot – my deepest gratitude and appreciation go to the journalists who have made this book possible. To complete the record I have noted the names of the journalists who declined to present their bios.

To start me off on this project a group of well wishers provided financial support. My thanks go to the Rattansi Educational Trust, the Chandaria and Premchand Foundations, the Khimasia Foundation and to Rasik Kantaria. As the writing progressed, Maurice Makaloo and Rosemary Okello of Ford Foundation agreed to fund the publication of the book. I am truly indebted to the Ford Foundation for its consistent support, both financial and moral, in my writing career.

The journalists have been the main source of information and other colleagues have helped to expand the subject. Kul Bhushan and Dr Nyabuga wrote a chapter each; Samia Nasar, Neera Kapur-Dromson, Ali Zaidi, Warris Vianni, Karim Hirji and Sudhir Vidyarthi have allowed me to include extracts from their writings/interviews. In-depth conversations with Hilary Ng'weno and Joe Kadhi gave me valuable insights into the post-independence world of journalism. David Easterbrook of Northwestern University, USA sent me relevant documents.

When the script was written it needed to be 'read'. Dr George Gona of the University of Nairobi and Dr Diana Lee-Smith, MAAK (A) graciously offered to do so and made very pertinent comments and suggestions. Zahid Rajan, my partner, then undertook to publish the book and the product is evidence of the painstaking attention it has received. Our son Raahat kept us going with his occasional 'What! Not finished yet?'

For clarification: To avoid duplication, I have not credited my own writings, the bios of the journalists and other contributors bear the names of the authors. The journalists have been listed alphabetically except in the colonial period where they are placed together with the newspaper they worked for, or were involved in.

CONTRIBUTORS

George Morara Nyabuga is a Senior Lecturer in the School of Journalism and Mass Communication, University of Nairobi. Prior to joining the University he was the Managing Editor in charge of the Weekend Editions, and Media Convergence at the Standard Group. Nyabuga taught Journalism, and Cultural and Media Studies at the University of Worcester in the UK, 2005-2008. He also taught International Media and Communication, and Comparative Politics at Coventry University, UK. He is the author of, among other works, *Click on Democracy: Uses and Effects of the Internet on Kenyan Politics* (2009) and co-edited with Wambui Kiai the *Media in Kenya: Evolutions, Effects and Challenges* (2011). Nyabuga's research interests include the sociology of journalism, and new media, journalism and media theory and comparative media systems. He holds a PhD in Media, Politics and History from Coventry University.

Warris Vianni is an independent scholar. He read law at the London School of Economics and at Cambridge and writes on Kenyan affairs.

Kul Bhushan: After freelancing and passing an IPI advanced journalism course, Kul Bhushan joined *The Nation* as a Senior Reporter and Education Editor in 1967. Promoted to a Sub Editor in 1972 and appointed its first Business Editor in 1973, he moved to *The Standard* in 1980 as the Economics Editor. In 1982, he was invited to the World Bank/IMF/IFC headquarters in Washington to interview its directors and its then President, Tom Clausen. He was honoured with the Business Journalist of the Year Award by the Kenyan President Moi in 1986. He resigned in 1988 to concentrate on his publishing business and media consultancy. He also worked as a correspondent for PTI, UNI, AIR, IANS, AFP, and WSJ among others for over 15 years. The author of 31 books, he is known for his *Kenya Factbook*, he edited and published 16 editions from 1972 to 2000 in Nairobi. In 2005 and 2006, he authored *How to Deal with VAT* and *Working with VAT* by Pearson in New Delhi. From 1997 to 2006, he worked for United National Industrial Development Organisation (UNIDO) as editor and media consultant at its headquarters in Vienna, Austria, and later in New Delhi where he now lives and works.

Neera Kapur Dromsom is a fourth generation Kenyan of Indian origin, born and brought up in Nairobi. Her great grandparents arrived into the then British colony of Kenya in the late 1800s from British ruled India. After a year of University in Canada, Neera studied Indian classical dance. She started contributing articles, particularly on culture, for the Kenyan daily, the *Nation*. Stories told by her grandparents, especially her mother about early life in Kenya, as also tales from Hindu and Punjabi folklore, together with the various Indian dialects she heard, helped shape her thinking. Neera comes from a family of dramatists. Her father and paternal grandfather were actors on stage in Nairobi; her father also wrote and performed radio plays and poetry in Urdu and Farsi. Quite naturally, she joined the Kenyan Asian theatre group NATAK in its various capacities, from co-directing to acting on stage to more writing. Marriage to a French diplomat took her to various parts of the world including North Africa, France, India, further enriching her Universe. While based in India, Neera started her first book, *From Jhelum to Tana,* a biographical memoir, published in 2007 by Penguin (India). She continues to write on socio-cultural subjects for various journals, as also for *Old Africa*, published in Kenya.

Ali Zaidi, born in Delhi in 1954, worked as a lecturer in Economics at Delhi University, as an advertising copywriter and at Mainstream Journal of Contemporary Affairs. He first came to Kenya in 1985 to work as a schoolteacher in Kitale and Nairobi before returning to Delhi in 1986, where he worked at Apollo Book Publishers. He came back to Kenya in 1989 and joined Executive Magazine as sub-editor, becoming editor in 1992. In 1998, he joined *The EastAfrican* weekly newspaper as senior editor. Currently, he is consulting editor at the same publication. He is married to the sculptor Irene Wanjiru.

Tom Maliti is currently a trial monitor with the International Justice Monitor, a web portal that publishes reports on cases at the International Criminal Court. In the past he has been editor of *eXpression* today and *EXECUTIVE* magazine. Between 2001 and 2011 he was a correspondent for The Associated Press in its East Africa Bureau. Maliti began his career in 1992 as a features reporter for *The Frontier Post*, an English language daily newspaper in Pakistan.

BIBLIOGRAPHY

AwaaZ magazines.

Aiyar, Sana. *Indians in Kenya - The Politics of Diaspora*. Harvard University Press, 2015: USA & UK.

Brennan, James R, POLITICS AND BUSINESS IN THE INDIAN NEWSPAPERS OF COLONIAL TANGANYIKA, *Africa: Journal of the International Africa*. Institute 81.1 (2011): 42-67.

Cole, Peter and Harcup, Tony, *Newspaper Journalism*, Sage Publications Ltd, 2010: London.

Dharsi, Hussein, Zanzibar's *Samachar,* http://journals.cambridge.org https://husseindharsi.wordpress.com/tag/zanzibar-samachar/

Durrani, Shiraz, *Never be Silent – Publishing and Imperialism in Kenya 1884-1963*, Vita Books, 2006: London.

East African Standard newspapers.

eXpression Today, October 2012.

Frederiksen, Bodil Folke (2011). Print, Newspapers and Audiences in Colonial Kenya: African and Indian Improvement, Protest And Connections. Africa, 81, pp 155-172 doi:10.1017/S0001972010000082.

Greenwood, Anna & Topiwala, Harshad, *Indian Doctors in Kenya, 1895-1940,* Palgrave Macmillan, 2015:UK.

Gregory, Robert G, *Quest for Equality – Asian Politics in East Africa in 1900-1967,* Orient Longman Limited, 1993: New Delhi.

Gregory, Robert G, *India and East Africa –A History of Race Relations within the British Empire 1890-1939,* Oxford University Press, 1971: London.

Hirji, Karim, *Statistics in the Media – Learning from Practice,* Media Council of Tanzania, 2012: Dar es Salaam.

Jeffrey, Robin, *India's Newspaper Revolution*, St Martin's Press, 2000: New York.

Kamath, M V, *Professional Journalism*, Vikas Publishing House, 1980: New Delhi.

King, Kenneth and Salim, Ahmed, Ed., *Kenya Historical Biographies*, Nairobi Historical Studies 2, East African Publishing House, 1971: Nairobi.

Kovach, Bill and Rosenstiel, Tom, *The Elements of Journalism*, Crown Publishers, 2007 : New York.

Loughran, Gerard, *Birth of a Nation – The Story of a Newspaper in Kenya*, I B Tauris & Co Ltd, 2010: London.

Marx, Karl and Engels, Frederick, *The German Ideology* 1845, Lawrence & Wishart, 1965: London.

Nasar, Saima, The Indian Voice: Connecting Self-Representation and Identity Formulation in Diaspora, *History in Africa*, Volume 40 (2013), pp 99-124.

Nation Media Group, *The Golden Years*, Nation Media Group, 2010: Nairobi.

Nyabuga, George and Kiai, Wambui, Ed., *The Media in Kenya –Evolution, Effects and Challenges,* School of Journalism and Mass Communications, 2010: Nairobi.

Ochieng, Philip, *I Accuse the Press – An Insider's View of the Media and Politics in Africa,* Initiative Publishers, 1992: Nairobi.

Odinga, Oginga, *Not Yet Uhuru*, East African Publishers Ltd, 1967: Nairobi.

Ogot, Bethwell A, The Untold Story, Ed: E S Atieno Odhiambo and John Lonsdale, *Mau Mau & Nationhood: Arms, Authority and Narration*, 2003: UK.

Okungu, Jerry, *Dreams Gone Wrong*, Unpublished Autobiography.

Opinion newspapers, Parivaar Communications, Wembley, UK.